MR EXPLORER DOUGLAS

Mr Explorer Douglas

John Pascoe's New Zealand Classic
revised by

GRAHAM LANGTON

CANTERBURY UNIVERSITY PRESS

First published in 2000 by
CANTERBURY UNIVERSITY PRESS
University of Canterbury
Private Bag 4800
Christchurch
NEW ZEALAND

mail@cup.canterbury.ac.nz
www.cup.canterbury.ac.nz

ISBN 0-908812-95-7

Designed and typeset at Canterbury University Press
Printed by Rainbow Print, Christchurch

Cover: Colour photograph by Mike Bradstock

Portait of Charlie Douglas
ATL F-56776

Frontispiece: *Mr Explorer Douglas*
ATL F-56777

To friends of Charlie Douglas

CONTENTS

PREFACE

For almost fifty years from 1867 the Scottish-born Charlie Douglas lived on the West Coast of New Zealand's South Island. During that time his primary activity was exploration, in hazardous conditions and often for little or no pay. He found no significant passes, minerals or other valuable resources, but for his perseverance, his overcoming of obstacles, his durability over forty years of work, and his discovery and recording of difficult country, Charlie Douglas ranks as one of the great explorers of New Zealand.

Douglas explored because he was curious about all aspects of his adopted home region. A loner by choice, though he made friends up and down the Coast, Douglas observed the world of later nineteenth century Westland with an acute and sometimes caustic eye. He developed his own home-spun philosophies, as well as theories of geology and conservation. Through his reports, letters and maps he revealed much of the detailed topography and ecology of South Westland at a time when this could only be discovered by personal observation.

John Pascoe was a mountaineer, writer, photographer and archivist who was inspired by the story of Charlie Douglas. Many of Pascoe's own mountain expeditions were influenced by Douglas's work, and Pascoe often delighted his companions with stories of Douglas.

Pascoe did a great service to New Zealand history in rediscovering and preserving as much as possible of the writings and sketches of Charlie Douglas, and in making a large proportion of that material available to the public in 1957. *Mr Explorer Douglas* was reprinted in the same year and in 1969, but it was soon out of print and much sought after as the story of Charlie Douglas continued to fascinate.

It is the story of a man with strengths, faults and foibles. In his explorations and surveying Douglas displayed to a considerable degree the determined qualities of Pakeha pioneering in New Zealand. His explorations were useful because they were recorded and contributed to discovery of the natural world and the process of settlement. Not only is this the story of Charlie Douglas, but it is also an account of the evolution of South Westland in the second half of the nineteenth century, when human endeavour was essential to survival and progress.

This new edition is a full revision of Pascoe's original work. It follows his writing and patterns, and uses the words of Douglas himself as much as possible, with all their eccentricities of spelling, punctuation and expression. Some of the original has been smoothed out or re-ordered to make it more suited to readers of a different period. Errors, where noted, have been corrected. New information has been added where appropriate and most people mentioned by Douglas have been identified. Many of Pascoe's original sources have been consulted in the process.

As with Pascoe's original *Mr Explorer Douglas*, about a third of this new edition is devoted to the life of Charlie Douglas, and some two-thirds to his writings. An appreciation and evaluation of Douglas, in all facets of his personality and work, has been provided near the end.

The support and encouragement of Dorothy Pascoe and members of her family have been very important in the creation of this new edition. Dorothy Fletcher of Hokitika and Tom Ward of Eastbourne clarified the story of the original Tom Ward's death. Phil Barton of Wellington alerted me to the existence of the Harris letters. Craig Potton kindly made available a number of his colour images. The assistance of many who work in the Alexander Turnbull Library is much appreciated, and thanks are due to other libraries and archives that responded quickly to requests. Sandra Parkkali created the map and the logo. Richard King has been a most efficient and yet tolerant editor. My family supported me in many different ways, especially with finance and computing skills – this book could not have been produced without them. Thanks are also due to everyone who offered encouragement by showing enthusiasm for this story of the life and work of Charlie Douglas.

Graham Langton
January 2000

The Life of
Charlie Douglas

INTRODUCTION

A. P. Harper, involved in New Zealand mountaineering from 1890 until his death in 1955, was Charlie Douglas's exploring companion for two summers, 1893–95.

Harper was observant and recorded more about Douglas than anyone else. He took many of the existing photographs of Douglas and the pair kept in touch for years after their explorations together ended. Harper was also the first to indicate the scope and value of Douglas's work in Westland to the world outside the Survey Department.

John Pascoe learned much about Douglas from Harper, who, at the age of eighty-nine and only three months before his death in May 1955, wrote a Foreword to the original Mr Explorer Douglas. *It makes a fine introduction to many aspects of the life and personality of Charlie Douglas.*

In 1893 I had come back from London, after a very difficult business trip, and wanted a complete holiday. I wrote to G. J. Roberts, Hokitika Survey Office, to ask if he could let me join one of his field parties for three months. He replied that the Government was anxious to find a pass free of snow and ice, in the summer, for a mule track to the Hermitage. He offered me the opportunity to join Douglas in this work, an offer which I gladly accepted. I swagged over Arthur's Pass from Christchurch and was introduced to Douglas the morning after my arrival in Hokitika. He was a spare 'lightweight' man of fifty-three, about five feet ten inches in height and, from the wrinkles round his eyes, a man with a keen sense of humour and most friendly disposition. One took to him at once.

It is remarkable that a man like Douglas could have done so much valuable exploration and sent in such outstanding reports for seventeen years before anyone, outside official circles, realized his very existence. I think this was largely due to G. J. Roberts's official viewpoint, which was 'the Service knows, the public don't matter'! Yet it is only right to record that very few people today realize the immense debt owed to Roberts for his own work in the Southern Alps. He was a very high grade surveyor and the fixation and altitudes of the peaks was to him literally a labour of love; office hours and field difficulties of the mid 'seventies' and 'eighties' were of no account but he was fanatically opposed to publicity.

The first real publicity of Douglas's work was when my *Pioneer Work in the Alps of New Zealand* came out in 1896. The *Alpine Journal* (London) commented:

'The hero of Mr. Harper's book – strange to say – is not himself, but rather Mr. Douglas, a veteran explorer to whose labours, extending over many seasons, his younger comrade does full and generous justice.'* But such was his modesty that I felt it necessary to express a wish that 'he will forgive me for dragging him before the public from his remote corner of Westland; and hope he will look upon my action in so doing as evidence of the great admiration I have for his past work'. Douglas never actually referred to what I'd written about him, but I know he was quite pleased.

Roberts had a curious tendency to keep certain semi-official reports as private for himself. This peculiar habit undoubtedly prevented much of Douglas's work from being known, except to a few. I think the special status held by Douglas and, later by me, as 'explorers' was partly responsible, for we were not under the Chief Surveyor of Westland (Mr. Barron) nor under the Surveyor-General. Both these officers said it was a special job for Parliament, when we asked for any concession; in one case I had to go to Mr. Seddon for a decision, no doubt a very convenient way to dodge inconvenient requests!

However, in spite of his dislike for publicity, Douglas took steps to prevent anyone else getting credit in later years for what he had done. Reference to his letter to me of 5th October 1896 shows this clearly. He certainly anticipates the possibility of 'some fraud' getting hold of his map and notes and getting away with 'any credit that is to be got out of them'.

Now after sixty years, his own notes are being used, but his fears of possible credit being taken by the author have not been realized, for Douglas is the central figure, and his work is credited to him alone. The publication of the mass of information, so painstakingly gathered by John Pascoe and his helpers, ensured that personal reminiscences were used from Colin Macfarlane, Jim Gunn and others who had worked with him in the field. There were also contemporary documents and letters to Mueller and Roberts. Pascoe was eager for me to add my own memories of the man himself who was so interesting. I was his mate for two years, under very hard conditions, and saw much of him after I'd taken up other work. There can be very few men alive today who knew him as intimately as I did. Pascoe has dealt with the biographical facts and his work in the field; my part, in this foreword, is to try, as well as I can, to let others see my old friend Charlie as I saw him.

Naturally the value of his work and his outstanding skill as a bushman and naturalist were known to some leading scientists such as Dr. Cockayne and a few others. I had amusing evidence of this on one occasion. I was stuck up at

---

* Quotations such as this have been corrected from the original sources. Harper relied on his memory.

the old pub on the east bank of the Otira by bad weather; there were several others also waiting for the river to go down. After a day or two the rain slackened off and I was going out to see if I could find a possible ford. Someone asked me where I was going; I said, 'To see if I can find a ford, as I must get away.' An oldish man reading a book said, 'Cheap bar-room talk.' I asked the barman who he was. He said, 'Mr. Alexander McKay the geologist.' I went over to him and asked if he was referring to me. He said, 'Yes; cheap bar-room talk, find a ford!' I said, 'Mr. McKay, have you ever heard of Charlie Douglas?' He said, 'Yes, I know about him.' I replied, 'Well, I was his mate for two years.' He stood up and held out his hand: 'Sir, I apologize!'

The expression 'a lovable man' used to be heard more often than it is now. Such men in my long experience are in a minority, but Charlie Douglas was one of them. He had his faults, but who hasn't? One readily forgave them for he was always considerate of others, generous to a fault, utterly unselfish, and if he ever criticized a man it was justified. I have never talked of his 'major vice' but it has been mentioned in this book, namely periodic short bouts of drinking – but I will say this, that annoying as it was by causing loss of time in fine weather, he never gave offence, was never quarrelsome or used bad language. His 'vice' was exercised quietly and none of his friends ever held this against him as a habit which made him in any way objectionable. I think, in his quiet way, he was the most popular man south of Ross. He was known to everyone as 'Charlie'.

When I first met him there was no evidence of an old bushman patronizing a 'new chum'. He gave me a natural courteous welcome with a very merry twinkle in his eye – which later on he confessed was due to 'the girl things' I had been wearing, and he had 'wondered what he had got hold of'. I was wearing knickerbockers, having swagged over from Christchurch! Always humorous, very considerate of his mate, Charlie never used bad language or enjoyed tough stories.

Before we started work, Charlie made it a condition that all accounts for stores would be in his name. He knew the storekeepers, some of them combining a store and a pub, in South Westland, and was anxious to prevent a newcomer being exploited. This consideration was typical of the man. When one of these storekeeper-publicans threatened to sue me for goods supplied, after I had left for other work, Douglas, who had been paid my share, intervened. This explains passages in his letter of 25th April 1895.

This reminds me of another promise he insisted upon, with which I so cordially agreed that we made it mutual – namely that if either of us were killed in the mountains, we were not to make it known where the body was; it was agreed that it should be left and not hauled out for burial in civilization.

Douglas said he'd seen too many corpses carried out to Ross, in a rude coffin, by well meaning friends, who got drunk at every stopping place and frequently used the box to play cards upon. He said, 'I think most of us who love the mountains, would prefer to be quietly buried there than be hauled out over the bad country.'

Living as we did, in a small 'batwing' tent or under large boulder shelters, we had much time on our hands in wet weather. This gave me a chance to know Douglas well as we talked of many things. We read a lot and had our three games of cribbage on most nights. Our score board was marked out on the cover of my field books – which I still keep as a relic.

Douglas must have been a very active man in his early days, his work proves this, but after seventeen years on the Coast [actually twenty-six], the excuse 'there's plenty of time' gradually took hold of him. He called this the 'demon of tomorrow', which resulted in loss of much valuable time, on some occasions, by not taking advantage of good weather.

I have written about Douglas so often during the last fifty years that there must be some repetition in this foreword, but one or two things recorded by Pascoe reminded me of others not uninteresting. The mention of Charlie's love of his pipe recalls that once he showed me how to make a pipe in the bush. Take 1½ inches of the bark stem of the nei nei tree which is just below the pineapple top of the tree and hollow out a bowl and fill it with wet salt for three or four days. This hardens the wood. Then get the leg bone of some bird for the stem. I still have such a pipe which I made when I broke my own.

Charlie always admitted that he hated, almost to the point of fear, two things: taipos (wetas), which he spells 'typos', and those dark brown bush creeks the bottom of which is hard to see. He couldn't swim, and always said 'not being able to swim saved my life many a time'. He really funked tackling some of those dark brown streams. Another mention he made was of having eaten two giant kiwis, and he would have eaten the great dodo if he could have found one. In that case he told me how he was crossing a large swamp, jumping from nigger-head to nigger-head. He sprained his ankle, and had to crawl for days. In these swamps one finds clumps of what we called 'black scrub', which indicated a dry island. On one of these he found two giant kiwis – nesting. He ate them and the egg, and was in no doubt at all that he had saved his life. In his account of the birds in Westland he just touches on the story and reckons that his critics would have done the same or they would not have lived to report the kiwis.

When out for months with a friend one is apt to discuss all sorts of things, especially with such a well-informed man as Douglas. One day I was telling him of our College Chapel at Oxford and I said, 'It is curious that we have never talked about our beliefs or churches?' Charlie said, 'Ay-he, now I'll just tell you the story of my being bushed.'

He was exploring some river and was prospecting ahead of his camp for the best route when the weather suddenly changed in the afternoon and a bad storm came up. He turned back at once to get his camp in order. Just about dark he realized he was 'bushed' and couldn't recognize any object. So at dark he sheltered behind a big tree, kept a fire going with much trouble and, as he said, he smoked and swore all night 'for allowing himself to be bushed'. I must say that the idea of Charlie being really lost in the bush was hard to believe. However, at the first streak of dawn he realized where he was and in eight hundred yards or so he came to his camp. A huge tree had fallen across his tent and a large broken limb had gone into the ground in the middle of his bedding. He said, 'I took off my hat, and apologized for swearing.'

Douglas was very caustic about the 'fixings' I had brought over for tackling the glaciers. The ice-axe soon proved its value to him, but he was obstinate about goggles. The result was a bad dose of snow blindness after a long day on the Franz Josef. I got much quiet amusement over the way he looked after his pair of goggles after that experience. They came next to his pipe!

Some of his humorous sayings may be repeated. 'The barometer doesn't affect the weather much on the Coast' was his answer to my asking if the glass was rising. 'The hot spring near the Fox smelled badly enough to cure any-thing,' and 'Do it now, it will save an oath later.'

Like all men leading a rough and lonely life, Douglas was very shy about meeting strangers in social life. In 1907 I took my wife and two children to Lake Kaniere for the Christmas holiday. Dr. Teichelmann had lent us his hut on the eastern side of the lake and it happened that Charlie was camping nearby to avoid Christmas in Hokitika. He wouldn't consent to meeting my wife, as he said he'd been away in the wilds too long to speak to a lady, but I was sure once the 'ice was broken' that my dear old friend would not only give us great pleas-ure but would enjoy the meeting himself. He and I would go out eeling at night, returning about midnight, but I couldn't persuade him to come to the hut for a cup of cocoa.

One night my wife met us when we landed, and after he had been intro-duced, she insisted on his coming back with us. He was very silent and shy, retiring as soon as he'd had his cocoa. The next night, however, he came up with me without demur, and stayed until the early hours chatting quite freely. He was there lighting our fire early next morning and practically lived with us until we left. He never seemed tired of talking to my wife of all sorts of things and obviously enjoyed every minute. When we left for Hokitika by rowing across the lake, Charlie came down to see us off. He bent over my wife's hand like an old courtier and said, 'Mistress Harper, you will never know what a treat it has been to me to talk as I have to you.' He remained standing on the beach with his hat off until we were out of sight. That was the last time I saw him. After he had had a stroke, Dr. Teichelmann told me not to go and see him as it was not known whether he would recognize me. If he did, it would be painful to him not to be able to talk to me.

When I sent my manuscript of *Pioneer Work* in 1896 to my friend Sir Scott Keltie, the secretary of the Royal Geographical Society of which I was a Fellow, with a power of attorney to arrange publication, I asked him to place the work of Charlie Douglas before the council in hopes that the society would recognize its value in some way. He was awarded the Gill Memorial Prize as recorded in this book. No one deserved it more, for Douglas's exploration, in my opinion, was outstanding.

He was one of the greatest friends of my long life. I am proud that his position in New Zealand exploration will always stand at the highest level.

A. P. Harper

ONE

Origins and Family

Charles Edward Douglas was born in Edinburgh on 1 July 1840 and his birth entered at the General Registry Office. On 10 September he was baptised by the Reverend David Runciman, Minister of the Parish of Newington within the Parish of St Cuthbert's. Newington is not far from the centre of Edinburgh.

When Charles was born his father, James Douglas, was fifty-one years old, and his mother Martha, née Brook, was forty. Charles was their sixth and last child, the youngest of four boys and two girls. A little is known of the heritage of each parent, enough to show that Charles was born into a fairly well-to-do and established family.

James Douglas, born in 1789, worked at the Commercial Bank of Scotland from 1812 and was appointed accountant there in 1823. His father, also James, had from 1771 served a thirteen-year apprenticeship to become a goldsmith, first with Robert Clark, and then with Archibald Ochiltree, both in Edinburgh. The elder James's father, Archibald, had been born, perhaps in 1706, at Darnock, Dumfries, and had died in 1776. In August 1772 James, the goldsmith apprentice, married Elizabeth Houston, resident in Chapel Street, where her father was a stabler. James worked as a goldsmith, silversmith and jeweller in both Edinburgh and Dundee, acquiring the freedom of the latter town in 1794. He died in 1810, and his wife in 1833.

Martha Brook must have married James Douglas in 1820 or 1821, by which time he was well established in his profession and soon to be appointed accountant. Martha was born in 1800 to Elizabeth, née Bruce, and her husband, Mr Brook. Nothing is known of him, but Elizabeth's ancestry was of some note. Her father, Adam Bruce, was probably a Writer to the Signet (a lawyer) in Edinburgh, and thus part of the cultural élite. Adam married Margaret, née Fettes, who also came from an established family. She was the youngest child of a marriage in 1749 between Margaret, the daughter of James Rae, an Edinburgh surgeon, and William Fettes, an Edinburgh merchant. The eldest son of this marriage, Margaret Fettes's brother, died in 1836 aged eighty-six as Sir William Fettes, a baronet of wealth made as a merchant.

The children in the family of James and Martha Douglas spanned almost a

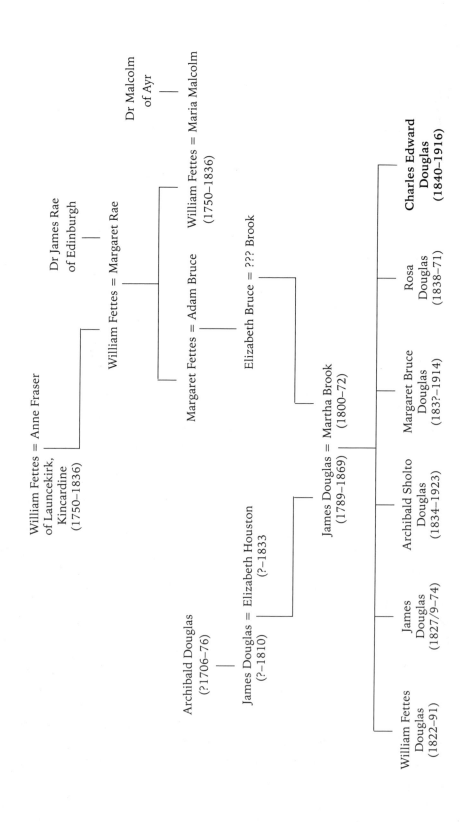

generation, for the oldest, William Fettes Douglas, had been born in 1822 and so was about eighteen when Charles was born. At that date, 1840, one sister, Rosa, was two, and Margaret some unknown years older. The other brothers, Archibald Sholto and James, were six and eleven or more years old.

One significant family trait appeared in the father James. As well as the routine of banking, he had creative urges to sustain him, for he was an enthusiastic amateur painter. But little is known of the other family members, even after childhood. The Douglas parents, James and Martha, died in 1869 and 1872 respectively. Rosa died in 1871, and Margaret remained a spinster until her death in 1914. James, the brother, became a timber merchant in Dutch Guiana (now Surinam), married a slave, Anna Dasiana, there, had three children who were emancipated, and died in 1874. Sholto became a banker and died in 1913. The eldest brother, Fettes, became the best known. Like other family members, he began in the Commercial Bank of Scotland, but after ten years left to become a professional artist. He exhibited his first picture in 1845 and nine years later was elected to the Royal Scottish Academy. His skill was in painting detailed still life and he enjoyed travelling in Italy and collecting coins and missals. He was elected president of the Academy in 1882, but his period in office was marred by disputes and difficulties. Fettes died in 1891.

It is a pity that more is not known of the home life of this family with children of such disparate ages. One wonders what affections, or lack of them, what bonds and conflicts founded traits in the character of Charles. These are research riddles that face any biographer, and in this case they must remain unanswered. An understanding of some of the early life and perceptions of the young Charles is completely unobtainable.

Apart from the record of his birth and baptism, the story of Charles Douglas cannot begin before his time at the Royal High School of Edinburgh. Even here there is little detail of his education. Charles was definitely at the High School from mid-1850 to mid-1853, and possibly longer. In 1848 the school had a roll of 463, and in the mid-century the sons of well-off Scottish families passed through its classes. As a source of culture the influence of the school was profound.

Already some of the masters had passed into literary and other history. Allan Masterton and Willie Nicol drank whisky with Robert Burns in 1789. Burns wrote, 'O Willie brewed a peck o' maut, And Rob and Allan cam to see,' and Masterton set the words to music. Perhaps Charlie Douglas sang in the Okarito Hotel the chorus: 'We are na fou, we're nae that fou, But just a drappie in our e'e.'

Opposite: *The Douglas and Fettes families.*

For his first year at the school Charles Douglas had as master Dr W. M. Gunn, a noted biblical and classical authority. William Steven's *History of the High School of Edinburgh* (1849) includes an excellent account of the scholar's day and week written by Dr Gunn himself. From this we know that Classics was then compulsory, and that Douglas would have had at least one year of Greek, and more of Latin. Of a school week of thirty-two hours, twelve were spent on Classics, ten on English (which included Religion and Elementary Science), five on Writing, and five on Arithmetic. In summer, by holding the Arithmetic class at an early hour in the morning, there was an additional hour a day for Classics. Greek was begun in the third year, with four hours a week.

After Gunn died in October 1851, Douglas was for two years under Dr A. H. Bryce. Douglas does not appear in the list of the Rector's class of 1854, but the extent of his classical knowledge, evident later in life, suggests he may have continued at the school. If he did leave in 1853, he would have been only thirteen years old. Douglas joined the ranks of the 'Former Pupils', which included literary men such as Sir Walter Scott and George Borrow. Judges, doctors and administrators abounded, among them Lord Dalhousie, Viceroy of India. Alexander Graham Bell, the inventor of the telephone, was another notable former pupil.

What Douglas did for the next few years is quite unknown. Some South Westland people thought that he was partially trained as a medical man, but there is nothing to corroborate this, and it is unlikely at the age he then was. One of the difficulties in studying Douglas's youth is that his own surviving papers have very few references to his origins. It was not that he was impersonal in his diaries and reports. On the contrary, he was often delightfully discursive in reminiscence and personal opinion. But he confined most of his references to South Westland and did not reflect nostalgically on Scotland. Expatriate he may have been, but he did not sigh for his homeland.

At sixteen he began work at the Commercial Bank of Scotland in Edinburgh, where his father and three brothers worked or had worked. A small manuscript book in the head office gave these details for Charles Douglas: 'Entered the service of the Commercial Bank of Scotland 3rd February 1857 as an apprentice in the accountant's office. Left bank in September 1862 for New Zealand.' The reasons for his leaving the bank at twenty-two are unknown. It is also not clear whether the decision to emigrate was his or his parents'; whether he went under a temporary cloud or as a man of enterprise.

It was nothing novel for the youngest son of a well-to-do Scottish or English family to put aside failure or lack of interest in a career at home by seeking the glorious uncertainty of an existence in a new land. There were also strong links between Edinburgh's Royal High School and the colonisation of the

Otago Province in New Zealand, which may have been responsible for Douglas's choice of destination. Former pupils included Captain William Cargill, the first Superintendent of Otago, John McGlashan, secretary of the Otago Association, and William Murison, an early owner and editor of the *Otago Daily Times*. Another ex-pupil was James (later Sir James)Hector, at the school 1845–49. A surgeon and geologist, Hector was the explorer who in 1858 found a key pass in the Rockies, later used by the Canadian Pacific Railway. He arrived in Otago eight months before Douglas and was soon exploring and geologising. Their paths later crossed in South Westland.

In the Otago settlement, Douglas would be sure of companions of a similar background. It is clear that the Douglas and Fettes descendants had abilities and position. Otago needed new blood and vigorous youth. The future of Charles Douglas and many others lay in their own hands once they reached the shores of the South Island of New Zealand.

TWO

Otago in the Early 1860s

On the evidence of Charles Douglas himself, he arrived in Port Chalmers on 27 December 1862.[1] This could only have been on the *Pladda*, of 982 tons, which came from Glasgow with over 190 assisted female immigrants. The passenger list has not survived.

Colin Macfarlane, his friend of the Cascade country, remembered that Douglas went inland in 1863 to a sheep run, and that his employer's name was 'Falloo'.[2] This was probably W. G. Filleul, who had several runs in North Otago.[3] His station diaries do not exist, and it has not been possible to verify that Douglas was employed at Papakaio or other Filleul runs. A fascinating account of the experiences of some of Filleul's cadets was given by E. S. Elwell, who had been brought out to New Zealand by Filleul in 1857. However, in his book *The Boy-Colonists* (1878) Elwell does not mention Douglas.

W. H. Scotter's history of North Otago pastoralists noted that when the 'boy-colonist' was on the Filleul station, 'there were at least eight men including three cadets',[4] but Douglas himself gives no clues about what he first did, except a tenuous one about eeling that suggests he spent some time in the Otago countryside:

> In Otago it used to be a standing joke to send a new chum out at night with a torch and spear to catch eels in the wet grass. He was told the eels came out of the water and travelled from one bog hole or lagoon to another. When he came back without any he was laughed at. Those who sent that new chum out were just as green as he was, eels do travell through the wet grass on a foggy sultry night from one lagoon to another, and, in a quaking bog, work their way under the turf.[5]

Whatever the delights of being a cadet on a sheep run with a pernickety boss, they must have palled on Douglas, who left to join the Central Otago gold rushes. William Wilson thought that Douglas was at Gabriels Gully in 1863, but this field had opened in 1861 and it is more likely he prospected at the Shotover River, near Lake Wakatipu. Douglas referred to both the river and the lake in his manuscripts.[6]

In fact the rush to the Shotover had begun not long before Douglas set foot on Otago soil, and the runholder W. G. Rees had, for a time, supplied hungry miners, some of them his shearers, with flour and mutton. The stimulus of gold brought many diggers to Lake Wakatipu, and by 1863 Queenstown was no longer a camp on a sheep run but a noisy town of grog shanties, merchants, and streams of miners. In its first seven months 191,825 ounces of gold were sent to Dunedin.

As the first finds became exhausted, men pushed further into the ranges, and suffered snowstorms, floods and meagre living to seek their fortunes. Tales of the period are vivid with the caprices of luck and mischance, but there is an undercurrent of forthright courage and often comradeship of a high order. Physical energy was spent willingly to overcome obstacles in isolated and dangerous gorges, and in cross-country journeys of great difficulty. The roar of floods was never far away.

Otago was a testing ground of pioneers. Many gold seekers turned to the land or to some sort of trade after the height of the rush. Unknown arrivals such as Douglas would learn in that rugged country how to look after themselves, to use their ingenuity at improvising and their sinews to survive natural hazards. What the young Scot did not know about hill and mountain country he would quickly have discovered in the wilds of north-west Otago. Soon he was to change this land of sun and wide spaces for an environment of a different character. Sometime after the mid-1860s Douglas went to the West Coast, and stayed there till his death.

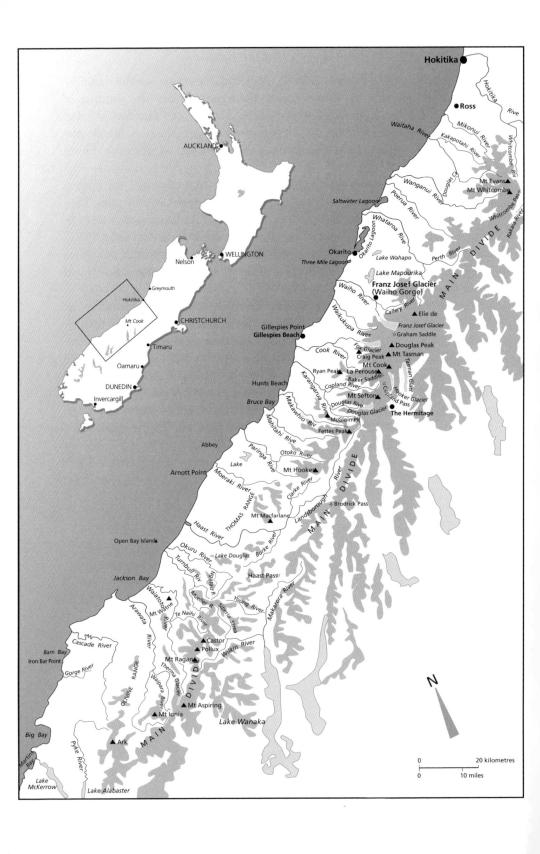

THREE

South Westland in the 1860s

Charlie Douglas scarcely appreciated the value of his work as an explorer in South Westland. In the 'Soliloquy Letter' he wrote, '. . . it is my only regret that I came to a small country like New Zealand', and added, 'I ought to have gone to a continent where there was unlimited scope for exploring & roaming about, but alass I didn't find out my mistake till too late.' These sentiments expressed by Douglas show that exploration was for him a passion, something he had to do, and not merely a hobby or occupation.

It is true that Stuart, Burke, Wills and others were making names for themselves on the continent of Australia, and that in the early 1860s Dr Livingstone was exploring Lake Nyasa in the heart of Africa – feats that would seem to Douglas to be so much more considerable than his own. Yet by then New Zealand no longer needed 'broad brush' explorers, covering vast distances. The general outline of the country was known to Pakeha. The requirement was for detailed exploratory work, and in that way Douglas was to enrich the story of South Westland.

To understand the difficulties and the accomplishments of Douglas's explorations, it is important to realise what kind of country he faced in its primeval state for nearly forty years, until the infirmities of age left him incapable of working in such terrain. South Westland in the 1860s was a land of contrasts – rainforest and flooded rivers, sudden and ferocious gorges, unexpected and pleasant grass flats, tumbled blue ice and upheaved rock moraines, and a rugged, nearly harbourless coast. The swift rivers were unbridged, and some coastal headlands were untraversable even at low and calm tide. Above these rose great mountains whose summits had never been climbed.

The weather lent a similar diversity. Clear frosty winter days, of such hazeless splendour that the Southern Alps looked as though they were greeting the rollers from the Tasman Sea, were in dramatic contrast to the onrush of the nor'west storms, which pelted sleet on the high country and rain on the low. All would be blanketed with invisibility when the tumult of rain and wind gave the forest its renewal. Then the floods carved from the banks of the rivers sacrifices of giant trees as though to emphasise the whims of nature.

If Westland lacked the spacious land of the Canterbury Plains on the other side of the mountains, it had the vastness of the Tasman Sea as horizon for its sunsets and birthplace of its storms. If it lacked the grace of cultivated farm lands, it promised the enticement of hidden minerals. Its graces were the blossoms of the rata, the fronds of ferns, and the songs of birds as yet unsavaged by animals or people. Mountains and forest, rivers and gorges: these were the features of a harsh but fascinating wilderness.

Of human striving and human occupation there was little recorded and much to come. Westland had never sustained a large Maori population. But the isolated and scanty settlements of the mid-nineteenth-century Poutini Ngai Tahu were no real indication of the rich and varied West Coast heritage of the Maori, largely unknown to the Europeans who followed. South Westland features in the stories of Maui as already inhabited. Polynesian colonists reached the West Coast and in time became the Waitaha. They were merged with or supplanted by visitors and conquerors from the North Island, first Ngati Mahaki, Ngati Kopiha, Ngati Wairangi, Patea and other small groups, then Ngati Mamoe in about the fifteenth century. Finally came the Ngai Tahu conquest in the eighteenth and early nineteenth centuries.[1]

There was thus a lengthy and varied tribal history on the West Coast, with long peaceful periods when the major preoccupation was exploiting the food supplies, and other times of fierce and bloody war, sometimes fueled by the desire for pounamu, or greenstone, which had been discovered by about 1400. Ngai Tahu had little time to enjoy their dominance, for after the advent of the Pakeha in New Zealand, Maori violence towards Maori intensified. In the 1820s Te Niho of Ngati Rarua attacked and conquered the West Coast. He was an ally of Te Rauparaha of Ngati Toa from the North Island, who was similarly occupied in the east. However, Te Niho and his followers came to peaceful co-existence with Poutini Maori, and either intermarried or, like their leader, moved further north.[2]

Remoteness and lack of obvious resources to exploit meant that European exploration of South Westland was slow and haphazard for many years. The first Europeans to meet Maori near Jacksons Bay may have been sealers and whalers who called there for water. When Thomas Brunner injured his ankle on 19 November 1847 at Tititira Head, a few miles south-west of Bruce Bay, he had reached his farthest south on 'The Great Journey'. After some days' rest he turned north to rejoin his Maori companions and make the long trek back to Nelson.[3] His report suggested that there was nothing on the West Coast worth further exploration, let alone settlement.

Ten years later James Mackay saw the Coast in a more favourable light after a trip from Nelson to Mawhera Pa on the Grey River. Other Pakeha visitors followed in 1857, including Leonard Harper, then aged twenty. He and his companion Locke were guided by two Maori, Terapuhi and Werita Tainui, across what became Harper Pass, though theirs was not the first crossing of the pass by Pakeha.[4] From the mouth of the Taramakau River, near which he found traces of gold, Harper visited Mawhera, then followed Brunner's footsteps south and further, past Jacksons Bay, before returning to Canterbury. Others followed in 1858–59, including John Rochfort, a surveyor for the Nelson Provincial Government.[5] Official interest was again being shown in the West Coast.

From 1848 various attempts had been made by the Crown to purchase Westland, but there was doubt and debate about the sale rights of northern Maori who had briefly conquered the area in the 1820s but had not settled. Poutini Ngai Tahu also protested their possession, particularly in 1849 and 1857. After protracted negotiations in 1859, and travelling the length of Westland several times, James Mackay finally obtained a Deed of Conveyance on 21 May 1860, whereby Poutini Ngai Tahu sold their land to the Crown. They were under some pressure because gold had by then been found in the Buller, and Pakeha were beginning to look for it elsewhere on the West Coast. However, the Maori drove a hard bargain, securing the sum of £300 and more reserves than Mackay had wanted to allow, for the 'full and final sale conveyance and surrender' of their land. Mackay agreed that 'The whole of the river bed of the Arahura belongs to the Natives, to its source', so that they retained possession of the pounamu, but this was omitted from the official deed.[6]

The possibility of a goldfield on the West Coast stimulated a Pakeha search for passes through the mountains and the beginning of formal surveying. In 1863 Henry Whitcombe and Jakob Lauper crossed the Whitcombe Pass, a more difficult route than most others used by Maori. Samuel Butler, searching for sheep country, and John Baker, a young surveyor, had ascended the pass two years earlier, and it was to be the setting for an early chapter in Butler's novel *Erewhon*. Whitcombe was drowned in the Taramakau, and Lauper returned over Harper Pass in such poor condition that he was scarcely recognised by his friends. In November 1863 Robert Bain began a shore survey between the Waiatoto River and Martins Bay, a task made difficult by sandflies, mosquitoes and blowflies, as well as frequent rain, storms and heavy seas. The difficulties of ships staying on the West Coast – one was wrecked and whaleboats were rendered unseaworthy – brought the survey to an end in February 1864. The unlucky Bain walked back to Otago via the Hollyford, following a route opened up for Pakeha by James Hector and others.[7] Bain's work was continued by John Rochfort with Maori assistance in the south, and by Arthur Dobson in the north.

The year 1864 was a memorable one for Westland. In March, Dobson crossed Arthur's Pass from the Waimakariri to the Otira. Over a period of months the prospectors Barrington, Farrell and Simonin explored north-west Otago and South Westland in an epic trip from Queenstown to Lake Alabaster, thence to the Gorge and Cascade Rivers. They returned to Otago in winter by a cruelly direct route where the difficulties of gorges, scrub and glacier were exacerbated by frostbite and hunger. In numerous misadventures they risked death, and a spell in hospital lay at the end of their tangled trails across the ranges.[8]

Then gold was discovered in payable quantities. Earlier discoveries had been made, such as that by Lauper on the ill-fated Whitcombe Pass expedition, but the first reports of real consequence came in April and May 1864 from Albert Hunt and William Smart. After information from Maori, they separately found gold in the upper Hohonu River, a tributary of the Taramakau. Others were also involved and there were many claimants for the reward of £1,000 originally offered by the Canterbury Provincial Government. This had actually been withdrawn in August 1861, by which time it was clear gold existed – it just had to be found in quantity. Hunt eventually received £200. One of the other problems for the claimants was that the discovery was made in what the *Lyttelton Times* called 'the remotest corner of the province' and 'the best place for locating a central convict settlement'.[9]

It was the discovery of gold that brought Westland into prominence, in 1864–65, when Douglas was presumably still fossicking in Otago. Finds south of Hokitika were reported by roving diggers, whose dishes washed gold from river valleys. Two and a half thousand ounces were shipped to Nelson in 1864, and the rush was on. The rest of New Zealand, and even Australia, was excited by the prize of Westland, which yielded 52,000 ounces for the first five months of 1865. The population increased rapidly. Soon Hokitika was a town boasting dozens of hotels and grog-shops, and the Hokitika River bar was littered with wrecks. Settlers from Canterbury and further afield flocked to the West Coast by sea or, heavily burdened, on foot over Harper Pass.

Following soon after the early miners, Julius Haast made a geological survey of Westland in 1865. Two years before he had crossed the Haast Pass from Otago into South Westland, a route pioneered by Maori, discovered for Pakeha by the surveyor John H. Baker and the prospector Charles Cameron, and publicised by Haast. It was natural that many diggers left the depleted goldfields and severe climate of inland Otago and crossed the Main Divide. Haast estimated that eight thousand miners made this journey. Many of those who travelled to the West Coast were, inevitably, unsuited to the rigours of the new life they had chosen. Some returned, disillusioned, hungry and ragged, but the tough and the fortunate survived.

Pakeha exploration and settlement of Westland had barely begun at this time, and the prospectors contributed much to both, searching through rugged mountain country for gold and establishing settlements. They reached the La Perouse and Balfour Glaciers in 1866. Legend also has it that three men, Harry the Whale, German Harry and Tony the Greek, crossed Antonio's Saddle, now Whales Saddle, from the Cook River to the Copland River in the same year. There were few witnesses to these daring trips, which even today are seldom achieved. The witnesses? There were weka, kea and tributary waterfalls. Giant peaks looked down upon them, with only the occasional roar of an avalanche to show their surprise at human enterprise. 'The results of the explorations,' wrote Douglas, 'were a lonely grave here & there a few wasted lives, and a few ozs of Gold which cost £10 per oz. to get.'[10]

These pioneers deserve praise. For uncertain reward and in the face of dangers that became routine, they made the first trips through gorges and over ranges. Sadly, they left no journals to enrich our frontier literature and drew no maps for the future use of men like Douglas. Their knowledge perished with them. They exist in a limbo of tradition in a land that is popularly supposed to be without tradition. Douglas himself was explicit about the virtues of the lone pioneer.

> When the Prospector didn't consider it necessary to his own comfort to carry two pairs of blankets & Mattress & Umbrella, the Southern parts of Westland were overhauled by bands of men who in the hunt after Gold feared neither death nor the Devil. They didn't in those days sit down & whine to the Government for Tracks, they didn't wait for Subsidized Ferrys or Charity Steamers, but they boldly penetrated Forest & Mountain, crossed rivers & scrambled round Bluffs, reckless of tomorrow, so long as today furnished them with a roast Maorie Hen or a Billy of Mussells & a pannican of Skilly.[11]

In the years to come, Douglas himself followed most of the rivers to their sources. But where the unknown prospectors handed on no records but the oral tradition, if they survived to tell it, Douglas wrote notes and field books, sketched maps and scenes that in many instances gave valuable information to the Survey Department. Indeed, it has been more than just his employers who benefited, since Douglas's observations and knowledge are for all New Zealanders, part of the Pakeha discovery of the country then, and a continuing revelation to generations since.

The difficulties of coastal travel were perhaps as irksome as those of the interior. Douglas noted that 'people might be stuck for days or even weeks at a bluff'. Of Black Sam's Point at Paringa Bluff he wrote:

> Sometimes but very rarely this point can be rounded, by doing a smart piece of running, but it is hardly worth the risk. In the early days some of the Diggers gave this point, the ominus name of run-or-be-damned – there

is a fine cave under the cliff but as might be expected people have not time to admire it.

In the same 'Swamps' manuscript he also explained a benefit of discovery:

> In the early days, had prospectors & explorers only known that by keeping inland, comparatively low-lying land would be found almost the whole extent of Westland, what an amount of heartbraking waiting for tides or good weather might have been saved, but in those days people naturally thought if the sea coast is so high and rocky, what must inland be.

Even with packhorses, the difficulties on the coastal route were considerable, as Douglas shows in this description of rounding a bluff near Okarito.

> It used to be a study watching a long line of loaded pack horses with perhaps only one man driving. Going round a bluff in heavy weather, the loads were usually from 250 to three hundred pounds of a very mixed character. The horses up to the work could watch the seas far better than most men. A good packer never swore, or threw stones at his horse, but let them take their own time, the animals would all stop and watch a sea coming in, then make a run for it. If by chance they got caught, they had a way of proping themselves face or back to the waves, and holding their own, then as the sea receded off they went at a trot.

Summarising this coastal travel, Douglas explained the skills demanded of men in the 1860s:

> If, as I say, anyone wishes to get an idea of former travelling, then let him start from Bold Head along the beaches to Okarito, he will now find them in the same state as in the early days, no stores, no pubs, no ferries. He can learn how to make rafts, ford rivers, pitch tents or rig up a lean-too with flax or gei-gei [kiekie]. He will find himself keeping a keen eye for derelict fish cast up on the beach, will take an interest in mussel banks he never felt before, and will often have to chase a Weka before he gets his supper.[12]

If these were some of the incidents of travel in this land of coastal obstacles, swift rivers, hidden ravines and dense bush, what then of the settlements where men congregated to make money or to spend it? An acute observer such as Douglas could be pungent in describing them, while also showing his whimsical sense of humour.

> An ordinary digging township in Westland & other parts of the World for that matter, may begin with a few tents, or spring into existence like booths at a fair. According as the gold holds out, they go through three eras of progress, which may best be described as follows.
>
> First the calico, sardine tin, and broken bottle era. Second the weather board, and sheet iron period. Third the borough. Some never get beyond the first, a few reach the second, and still fewer the third.

Number one period has only calico for covering the stores and such like, may have walls of slabs or tree ferns. The diggers live entirely in tents, every business place is a shanty, or a store of some kind, dance houses & other places of amusement are generally attached to them. The store keeps everything from a needle to an anchor, flour, tea, sugar, whiskey, everything that money can buy, the devil take the price.

The Shanty Keeper is a cross between the store & the pub, he calls himself a storekeeper, but a few tins of sardines, and a side of bacon is about all he possesses in that line. He depends on whiskey and card playing, and sometimes calls his place an Accomodation house or restaurant. A fourteen by eighteen is about the extent of his accomodation. When bed time comes, he sleeps under the counter. The boarders are supposed to be too far gone to know whether they are lying on the ground inside or the ground outside. Chaos is the best definition of the order in which tents & shanties stand in regard to each other, and sardine tins and broken bottles singly or in heaps are the main features of the place.

In the second period, weatherboard, and iron distinguish the Archetectures, window glass appears, and the bottles are now only to be seen stacked around the Pubs, and some attempt at regularity can be seen in the streets.

The third period has brick chimneys, foot paths, a town hall, Mayor &c, and houses with gardens are to be seen everywhere. The inhabitants go to church, or chapel, and drink their stimulants at home out of a keg, or a barrell so bottles are not to be seen in the landscape as in earlier days.

Even if these extracts go beyond the 1860s, their substance is correct. In his manuscript 'Islets, Towns and Glaciers', Douglas also explained the ephemeral nature of the diggers' towns. Weld Town, for example, he noted as

another paper town situated on the beach in Bruce Bay bight. Its existance lasted about a week when, the historical Hunt's rush took place, and it collapsed as suddenly as it rose. It never even got as far as the dance house, and skittle alley era, although for a couple of nights it could boast of a population of two or three thousand souls.

A more famous place was Gillespies, described by Douglas some years after its heyday as

never even a paper township, but entirely a digging one, and has supported a fluctuating population for many years. It passed the calico era, and almost attained to the dignity of the weatherboard but not quite. It now contains a few diggers huts, a store & school house, with of course the usual pub, but its life cannot last long as the beach is nearly worked out. It has however lasted longer than any of the diggers Townships of Southern Westland, and contains a chapel – still standing – a building none of the others ever possessed.

Douglas also gave an account of the 'Five Mile', south of Okarito. It was

> one of the most flourishing places on the Coast for several years, and when at the height of its prosperity had a double, sometimes a treble line of stores and shanties extending nearly the whole length of the beach. There were Stores, Pubs, Shanties, Dance houses and other places of even less repute, but never a church or a schoolhouse. Like Gillespies it never was a surveyed township, but it passed the calico era, and nearly arrived at the weatherboard. But like other famous places its glory has departed. One or two diggers huts are now all that is left of the once famous Five Mile.[13]

Finally, consider Okarito, a township that exists to this day, in the form of holiday homes as much as permanent residences. It was there that Douglas began his life in South Westland. He wrote:

> This town is situated at the mouth of the river, and is strictly speaking a seaport town, depending for its existance on the diggings; as they declined so did Okarito, and now it has only two pubs, a store, gaol & a monthly magistrate. The few cityzens spend their time shouting for each other, and talking about the good old times never to return; how it still exists is a mystery even to themselves. But in the early sixties Okarito was a flourishing place, sections changed hands at high prices, and it sprung into the weatherboard era all at once. In those days it was entirely a public house town with a resident Warden, and staff of Police to maintain order, a Survey and Custom house, harbour master, and a remarkably rowdy class of inhabitants and visitors. It made a desperate effort to reach the borough stage but ignomenously failed. A town council was elected who at once started to tax the cityzens, but as they had no power to do so, no one was fool enough to pay, so as there were no funds even for Councillors beer it was judged best to retire.
>
> The crushing blow to Okarito was the closing of the banks, removing the Warden, and closing it as a port of entery, so it fell to its present position as a port of call for the subsidised steamer that supplies the Southern Settlers with stores. Gold mining in South Westland may be said to be almost extinct, and nothing but stock raising in the back country, and an occasional splashing of roadmans cheques keeps Okarito from vanishing altogether, and it is a pity, as its situation for a small town is good.[14]

Westland and its people emerge from Douglas's written images as a primitive society in a primeval land, where the grog-shop was as familiar as the rain, and life was rough and vigorous.

Of the routine of work and social life in a new township such as Okarito, we can piece together fragments of the period. A man would not be tempted to lie in bed for long, as Douglas explains in what he wrote about early rising:

> 'Go to the Ant thou Sluggard' says King Soloman, or somebody, but the Sandfly is far superior to the Ant: he goes for you. At the first streak of

day he proceeds to business; with a fiendish skill he soon discovers a hole
or weak spot in the blankets, in he goes followed by all his relations, and
up you must get.[15]

Once up, the stock breakfast would be porridge, bacon, bread, and tea. The
price of packing supplies of food was such in 1865 that Haast recorded some
diggers used 'not less than £3 worth a week of bread, bacon and tea'.

The men would be clothed in rough moleskin trousers, open-necked shirts,
wide-brimmed hats, stout leather boots, and burdened with swags comprising
a roll of blankets, short axe, pick and tin dish. Although desirable as a staple
basis for the main meal of the day, meat was highly priced. In Hokitika one
market report in 1865 gave the stock prices: 'One lot of fat steers averaged £38
per head, while choice beasts brought to £59; wethers realized 30s. to 80s.'[16]
The digger living in the bush could thrive on birds, as will be evident from
many of Douglas's notes. Eels could be gaffed from the Okarito Lagoon. There
were also freshwater crabs, about which Douglas wrote:

> There was a character in Okarito who used to eat them. He pounded up
> shells and all and seasoned them with pepper and vinegar and he said they
> were splendid. Perhaps they were nobody sampled them. He died after-
> wards in the asylum. Whether the crabs were the cause of lunacy, I leave to
> those who study cause and effect.[17]

Frostfish and flounder would have varied the diet, but fish do not seem to have
been a common food in the early days. As related, there was no lack of strong
drink, for those with the money to indulge their thirsts. Tobacco was popular,
as much perhaps for keeping the sandflies at bay as for its solace. At the time it
cost twelve shillings a pound.

Although mails were irregular and slow, Westland had some communica-
tions with the outside world. Initially, sea transport from Melbourne was important. The first mail from Christchurch across Arthur's Pass to Hokitika ran on
4 July 1865, with relays of packhorses between coaches. Five days was allowed
as contract time. By March 1866 the whole transalpine road was open for passenger and mail traffic. Many of the diggers were well-read and educated men,
but however fluently they could swear in Greek, there was a shortage of books
and newspapers. Amusements, as such, were the inevitable gambling and grog.
Hokitika had its 'Casino de Venise' replete with dancing girls. Those who wanted
to sleep after a hard day's work were plagued by mosquitoes, about which
Douglas also wrote.

So much for the background of life as it was when Charlie Douglas arrived
in Westland. The route by which he travelled from Otago could have been by
the Haast Pass or Hollyford; it might have been from Christchurch over Arthur's
Pass, or to Hokitika by sea. There is no evidence for either the route or the

exact date, although A. P. Harper thought it likely that he used the Hollyford trail. James Cowan, in *Tales of the Maori Bush* (1934), claimed that Douglas 'landed on Hokitika beach in the frenzied rush days of 1865', but that is unlikely. Douglas himself wrote in his 'Soliloquy Letter': 'I started first in the Okarito District', but 'started' could have two meanings, referring either to arrival on the West Coast or to exploring. In the first part of the 'Okarito' manuscript he reminisced:

> In 1867 I first went to Okarito, and as my work took me on the Lagoon all the time, I ought to know something about the place as it then was . . . When on the Lagoon in the early days I remember swimming a number of bullocks across the top end of the Lagoon.

Elsewhere Douglas makes it clear he began his explorations in 1868. This reference to stock driving, so needed at the height of the gold rush, suggests that Douglas arrived in Westland in 1867, though it could have been a year or more earlier.

There is doubt that Douglas ever took gold seriously, and William Wilson wrote that Douglas took odd jobs instead of mining for gold. But in the second part of the 'Okarito' manuscript Douglas wrote:

> When in Okarito in the early days two of us sunk a shaft at the east corner of the Lagoon not far from Andrews channell. We got down about sixteen feet and struck an ancient beach lead. The black sand was about three inches thick, and would have payed had it been nearer the surface; and not so wet. While at dinner, the shaft caved in and we took that as a broad hint to leave and so cleared out.

Whether Douglas was just hired for this work as an odd-job man or as a working partner in a mining enterprise is surmise. Harper was sure that Douglas made some money by packing flour and stores at two shillings a pound. Helped by a dog he took over 100 lb each trip to remote prospecting camps. According to Harper, Douglas stated that the men who supplied the diggers with stores made the greater profits. However, Harper also noted that Douglas worked on 'several diggings south of Ross',[18] which adds credence to the possibility that he spent some time looking for gold. Years later, in the 'Geology' manuscript, Douglas wrote: 'I much prefer hunting for mines than floating them. Money is of little use to me,' and the course of his subsequent explorations suggests it was the search rather than the finding that appealed to him.

Early in his time on the West Coast, Douglas seems to have been transitory. We know from the 'Copland' manuscript that he was in the lower Copland valley in 1867. So, the same year he probably arrived in Okarito and was odd-job man, part-time miner and packer, an experience in the mountains must have helped determine the pattern of a life in which his purpose was to roam.

It may be that Douglas did not need full-time paid employment, for it is possible that he received an allowance from his family in Scotland. They were reasonably well off and would have wanted him to get established in the new country. He was not a 'remittance man' in the sinister sense of that phrase, which to a respectable colonial society denoted a wastrel got rid of by relations, or an exported black sheep. It is clear from his 'Soliloquy Letter' that Douglas sailed to Otago to make good in the literal sense of the word. An allowance from home would have supplemented the money that he earned at odd jobs and packing. That he punctuated his roaming with bouts of drinking was not remarkable in Westland, where they were the reward for months of hardship. His experience in bush, river and coastal travel toughened him for his subsequent life of exploration and rapidly made him adept in the skills of bushcraft and mountaineering.

To the temptation of drink was added the insistence with which the storekeeper of the period offered it to the bushman or digger returned from the wilds. Harper wrote: 'To reach the store you generally went through the bar, and of course had to have a round of drinks. Then one or two "on the house," so that by the time you'd reached the store, your ideas had become inflated, and also a bit hazy.'[19] Douglas was 'never in a hurry to pay whiskey accounts made with a three pointed pencil', but he knew his drinking was 'a big vice . . . I know mine doesn't pay either mentally or materially'.[20] He was honest with himself and did not let his drinking affect other people.

It must have been at Okarito that Douglas first met Gerhard Mueller, a young Danish-German immigrant who had arrived in New Zealand in 1858. Four years later Mueller qualified as a surveyor in Invercargill, and in September 1865 he was engaged on contract to survey Maori reserves on the West Coast. From 1 May 1866 Mueller was officially an assistant surveyor in the government service and, when he had finished the Native Reserve work, took charge of the Southern District of Westland. His daughter, Mildred Mueller, who edited her father's early letters,[21] outlined the friendship of the two men, Charlie Douglas (C.D.) and Gerhard Mueller (G.M.):

> The association of C.D. and G.M. was of simple growth. C.D., not liking sheep, left them and went to the goldfields. G.M. was appointed District Surveyor of South West Coast of Canterbury, with head-quarters at Okarito. From 1866 [probably 1867-8], until transferred to Hokitika in 1871 as Chief Surveyor of Westland, they were drawn together by similarity of interests, & became friends. When not working spasmodically, Douglas spent time prospecting and exploring, and in the crowded mining town, each soon became aware of the interests of the other, and C.D. brought his geological & other specimens and the story of his movements to an appreciative listener. G.M., who had already collected both flora and fauna for

others, was only too glad to be shown Douglas' harvest and to hear details of the country they had been found in. Gold apparently, did not loom large in the mind of either man.

After a short time, Douglas tried farming, but soon returned to Okarito. He would not consider tying himself in any way, nor would he accept anything in the way of remuneration for what he brought. This naturally placed G.M. in a position he disliked, but the friendship grew, and when G.M. went to Hokitika, they compromised. Not being a surveyor, D. was provided with a Prismatic compass [according to Colin Macfarlane] and anything he needed for traverse work . . . but even this help was limited by what he would accept, and he thus acquired an 'unofficial official' standing, which could not but be of benefit to the Department. This has caused uninformed criticism. After all, achievement is barren if not used or shared, and here was someone on hand with whom D. could share his, whilst G.M., having found a man after his own heart, could not be expected to do anything else than utilize what was of value to his work. To him it was not only simple common sense, but his plain duty, and D, knowing that aspect of the situation, still gave ungrudgingly, as to a friend.

After this arrangement was made, he, to a certain extent, could choose his own field of operation, but circumstances laid the whole unexplored area of South Westland before the two men, and it is therefore likely he would be more than willing to agree to the locality which was chosen for exploration. The yearly highlight of G.M.'s work was when, having received Douglas' report, he went South, and the two (accompanied by 'Big Steve', a powerful and genial Maori [probably Kere Tutoko]), like schoolboys, travelled over the areas reported on.[22]

By the late 1860s, then, Charlie Douglas, the bushman, was leading Gerhard Mueller, the surveyor, on a series of expeditions. Douglas had begun his part-time, semi-official exploring, which was to continue for some twenty years.

FOUR

Half-time Exploring, 1868–88

'It is now thirty-five years since I started this exploration business,' wrote Douglas in his 1903 'Soliloquy Letter': 'for the last fifteen years I have been at it regularly. Before that I was generally about half my time only.' This suggests Douglas began his half-time exploring in 1868. Records to document the work of Douglas for the next twenty years are scanty and what is known comes from diverse sources. Evidence in his own writings is the most useful of all, and is supplemented by other contemporary material or observers. But it is tantalising that more records do not exist. Here was this energetic young Scot, acclimatised to his new life, but not taking up regular work. In his exploratory pioneering he was also building up experience for future adventure, yet we do not quite know how or why his dedication to exploring came about, or indeed all he went on to do.

There is good documentation of one early trip, undertaken in 1868 with Julius Haast, the Canterbury Provincial Geologist. Haast was already prominent in the scientific life of New Zealand, and in a paper published the previous year he had described the Harper, Arthur's, Browning, Whitcombe and Haast Passes.[1] From the biography of Haast by his son[2] comes an account of the journey that began with Haast's landing at Okarito on 5 March 1868. He took with him Douglas, the prospector William Docherty and two packhorses. They made their headquarters at Bruce Bay. Next, in an open dinghy, they reached Paringa, and on 13 March headed further south, to land near Abbey Rocks. Then they ran swiftly down the coast in a rough sea under north-west conditions, and found a beach near Arnotts Point, where high surf confined them to shore for nine days. On 22 March they returned to Bruce Bay, and six days later to Okarito. Haast apparently called Douglas 'the classical bunker' because of his knowledge of the classics, which suggests he had not wasted his educational opportunities in Scotland.

Douglas must have gained from Haast some knowledge of geology, for his geological notes follow the classifications and terminology of Haast. However, he felt more irritation than respect for Haast, and a vignette from the expedition, related by G. J. Roberts many years later, shows Douglas's attitude.

39

I could sundry tales unfold of that jolly old pic-nicer's rambles. Douglas was with him once. 'Man, I became very weary of the jaunt, the doctor always got a chap to carry him over the rivers, so when my turn came, I just stumbled and dowsed him and – and he never would trust me again.'[3]

It irked Douglas, always generous to his companions, that Haast stole credit from his predecessors, and this is shown in Douglas's comments on the discovery of Haast Pass.

There has been considerable argument as to who was the first whiteman who came over the pass. From all I can understand a man named Cameron came through from the Wanaka and reached the Landsbro [Landsborough] flats and on going back he met Dr. Haast either at the Wanaka or in Queenstown ready to start over with his party, and no doubt the Doctor got information from Cameron, but as is usual with explorers he makes no mention of him in his book.

Cameron like allmost all prospectors left no record of his journay except traditions of public house blowing. So to Dr. Haast who did leave an account of his journay & roughly laid off the country, all credit must be due. Here I would give a little advice to Scientific explorers, espicially to the German brand of the species, and that is make some slight acknowledgement that you do get information from the inhabitants who live about the country. If such were done you would get far more information and often of a valuable nature, information you could never acquire for yourselves.[4]

Support for Douglas's opinion was given in a letter from G. M. Hassing.

I happened to be residing at Makarora, Lake Wanaka, in 1861, and though I had not ascended the pass, I knew of its existence as an old Maori track to the West Coast. Early in January 1863 Mr Charles Cameron came to me while I had the ferry at Albertown, Upper Clutha, and intimated that he intended to explore the route to the West Coast by way of the Wanaka and Makarora. I crossed him and his horse 'Tommy' and two young lads, his nephews, over the Clutha on his journey up the lake. In about three weeks' time Mr Cameron returned, and informed me that he had crossed the saddle and ascended a mountain west of it, where he had built a cairn, and had a good view of the upper part of the river flowing towards the West Coast. He was quite satisfied that he had discovered an easy practical route to the West Coast, and as he was not well provided with food, he returned by the way he came. He received no reward of any kind, nor did he even get credit for his discovery which was subsequently claimed and awarded to Dr. J. Haast who named the pass and river in commemoration of himself.[5]

In 1881 the surveyor Thomas N. Brodrick found Cameron's powder flask of January 1863 at the top of a mountain west of the pass.[6] There is no doubt that Haast made the first complete transalpine crossing to the West Coast by a

Pakeha, but he should not have denied Cameron the honour of having been the first to have crossed the Main Divide by this route, which was well known to Maori. Unknown to all of them, the surveyor John H. Baker had reached the saddle itself in April 1861. He was looking for sheep country and so was not interested in the bush country he could see over the pass.[7]

Another angle on the Douglas–Haast relationship was given in Douglas's report on Lake Paringa in his 'Passes' manuscript: 'Dr. Haast . . . crossed the lake in 1866 and called it after Sir J. Hall, but the name did not take outside of his book. The Diggers and the Maories insisted on calling it Paringa, a name too easy to spell and pronounce ever to be taken off.' That 'Paringa' is easier to spell and say than 'Hall' can be disputed, but it is likely that Haast had little influence among either the miners or the Maori of the district.

Returning to the year 1868, when the County of Westland was established, the only other record of Douglas's activity is his reference to the Fox Glacier in the 'Cook River' manuscript.

> I have visited it several times since 1868, but in those ancient days I did not pay much attention to glaciers . . . in 68 the belt of scrub at the termi-nal was much larger, and was close up to the drift covered ice. I know it was larger because I hunted a Cow out of the scrub & it took some time to find it. Now, that belt is not a chain wide but the ice against it holds the same position as in 68.

This extract is intriguing because it shows that Douglas was one of the early visitors to the Fox terminal, that he was not at that stage very interested in glaciers, and that he was a stockman at the time.

The following year, 1869, Douglas was roaming between Lake Wahapo and the Paringa and Moeraki Rivers, where he noted a coal seam and other mineral deposits.[8] Little is known of the specifics of Douglas's subsequent activities until 1873 when, under contract to the Provincial Council, he made a five-foot-wide track from Bruce Bay to Haast, a distance of some fifty miles. Working with him were Julius Matthies and McGloin, one of several men by that name who settled on the West Coast, and perhaps the one whose name was placed on a fine peak above the Karangarua River.[9]

This was a crucial period for Douglas. He was paid for the track work in land, and this seems to be connected to the fact that early in 1874 he turned farmer and then ferryman as well. On 25 February the Westland Provincial Council received a 'petition from Messrs Ward and Douglas, cattle dealers, residing on the Paringa River, setting forth that they were willing to buy seven hundred (700) acres of land on the Paringa River at ten shillings per acre'. The following month the petition was granted for the amount of land at the price stated.[10] If Douglas had to make any actual payment, it is likely it came from the estate of his father, who had died in 1869. The terms of the deed of settlement, as well as the slowness of the law and of the mails from Scotland to New Zealand, probably meant Douglas did not receive his full inheritance until after the death of his mother in 1872.

Douglas's partner, Tom Ward, had come from England to Dunedin in 1858 and, like Douglas, probably worked on Otago sheep stations. The pair may have met in Otago after Douglas arrived. On 21 November 1866 Ward married Jane Falconer, a Scotswoman, at Arrowtown, at a time when Douglas was in that part of central Otago. Ward was in the goldfields of both Otago and the West Coast, possibly as a storekeeper rather than a prospector. In the late 1860s he was at Charleston, and in the years before he became Douglas's partner he was storekeeper at Hunts Beach, a few miles south of the Karangarua River mouth, where beach mining was practised.

Douglas seems to have concentrated on farming for no more than a year, but his intentions may have been more long term. Later in 1874 Ward and Douglas were granted protection under the Goldfields Act 1866 for a ferry over the Paringa River. The conditions were that the ferry was to be worked by boat in return for a subsidy of £50 per annum, and that the ferryman had to erect a wire bridge over the right-hand branch of the Paringa to specifications to be prepared by the Provincial Engineer, the government to find the wire and deliver it to Paringa.[11]

More significantly, there is evidence of the hard work they were putting into their property. On 26 November James Bonar, the Westland Superintendent, and Gerhard Mueller were put ashore at Paringa and camped with Ward and Douglas. The next day they looked at the site for the wire bridge and then went another two miles up the river. The visitors noted in passing 'some 300 sheep, feeding chiefly on native herbiage, and looking very well'. Then they came to 'a snug little homestead, consisting of a dwelling-house, carpenter's shop, store for provisions, fowl house, stock-yard, and two sheep yards, and a pleasant piece of garden'. The pioneering pair also had 'about twelve acres cleared and sown with English grass, which was coming up promisingly'. Douglas seemed to the visitors to be putting down roots and was commended for 'taking a great interest in acclimatization and desiring to exchange the native birds and plants of his surroundings for novelties from other parts'.[12]

Yet Douglas would not be tied to cattle, sheep and ferry. From 1875 he was again based in a 'dwelling house' at Okarito, though he probably maintained a connection with the Wards and the Paringa run for some years, and was noted on the electoral roll of 1878–80 as living at Paringa. Later attempts were made by Mueller and others to persuade Douglas to persevere with a secure and profitable career, but in 1875 he had in fact finally severed his ties to a settled occupation. Clearly he preferred to roam. His heart was in the ranges and his future with the reports and maps that one day would be part of the history of Westland.

Tom and Jane Ward continued with the Paringa run, and the last three of their children were born there. However, the run hardly provided an adequate living. Ward continued as storekeeper at Hunts Beach for a year or two and later took up a roading contract, on which he lost money. Then, on 5 August 1881, while on his way to a court sitting in Hokitika to defend a charge of non-payment for a bull, Ward was drowned in the surf at the mouth of the Omoeroa River. His horse must have stumbled crossing the wash-out of the lagoon and his body was found ten days later about sixty miles north near the Arahura River. Jane Ward sold the Paringa property in 1882 and moved with her seven young children to Hokitika, where she ran a nursing home to support them all. Douglas maintained some contact with her, and many years later Jane was to provide him with accommodation and care.[13]

Another significant occurrence for Douglas in 1874 was his first meeting with G. J. (George John) Roberts, who was to become another life-long friend of consistent loyalty. Born in Wellington in 1848, Roberts had been a geodetic surveyor in India for a time before he came to the West Coast and joined Mueller's staff in Hokitika.[14] His enthusiasm for the triangulation of Westland was built on his technical attainments and unbounded physical energy.

It was in the Westland Survey, working with and for people like Roberts and Mueller, that Douglas proved his worth. The odd jobs could be done by any men, and their efforts could be washed out by the next storm or overgrown by the virile forest plants and trees that contested with humans for the living space in Westland. But to map a mountain province – that would take brains and guts and stamina.

When the system of provincial government ended in 1876, the Westland Survey in Hokitika came under the head office in Wellington of the newly established Survey Department, which had James Turnbull Thomson as Surveyor-General. The *Appendices to the Journals of the House of Representatives* (*AJHR*) are the most useful source for reports of survey progress in Westland. Although these parliamentary papers tampered alike with the accuracy and idiom of narratives and reports by people in the field such as Douglas, at least they gave their own official summaries with some precision, and acknowledged where credit was due.

Triangulation and survey methods here become relevant. In 1875 the 'State of the Surveys' for Westland[15] looked back to 1863 and 1864 when 'rough coast traverses, mostly made by contract and with a compass only, were carried out from Grey River to Big Bay: they were merely reconnaissance surveys . . .

On the discovery of gold in 1865, settlement took place at Hokitika and Greymouth.' These shore surveys were the ones begun by Bain and continued by Rochfort and Arthur Dobson. It was pointed out in 1875 that this '*quasi-triangulation*' was not satisfactory.

In 1877 the *AJHR* gave a concise account of the Westland Survey.[16] 'There are three separate districts in Westland . . . the centre of one being Hokitika, of another Okarita, and of the third, Jackson's Bay.' It should be noted that Douglas was only partly concerned with the first, and then not until much later in his life. His earlier work was intimately linked with both the Okarito and Jacksons Bay districts. The report also printed a good tribute to Mueller: 'The present system of survey, whose introduction is due to Mr. Mueller, is a sound and practical one, the plans and records based on it being reliable; with the limit of error possible in such a rough country, where surveying is little better than underground "driving".' The 1877 account noted:

> Mr. Roberts is to extend the standard bearings through the Hokitika circuit. He has for three months, under the direction of Mr. Mueller, been engaged in selecting and preparing stations. Several of these are so high and difficult of access, that it could not be expected that the settlement surveyors would willingly resort to them for connection . . . The Westland provincial district, on account of its dense forest and numerous rapid rivers, is the most difficult country in the colony to make survey progress.

The necessary trig work would be very rough, hampered by forests, endangered by floods and involving mountaineering above the bushline, with attendant hardships and perils. (Most of the sight-lines needed for surveying were obscured by the bush, which explains the need to get above it.) It also needed qualities of determination and perseverance in the men who undertook it. Charlie Douglas, under the supervision of Mueller and Roberts, was one of them. In addition to his own explorations, he selected and prepared trig sites for the qualified surveyors. At about this time, Roberts must have polished up the lessons given to Douglas by Mueller in the use of compass and surveyor's chain, so that he could work independently. From 1878 Douglas received pay from the Survey when he made his expeditions, so he gained meagre reward for his toils and it is possible he was able to forgo any allowance received from Scotland.

In 1877 Douglas was exploring at the head of the Paringa and presumably finding it more interesting than running cattle on its lower flats. He also revisited the Paringa in the following year and found a crossing by way of the Douglas Spur to the Clarke River, a significant exploratory trip.[17] In that period he was also up the Turnbull headwaters behind Okuru. Roberts was busy further north.

In Westland Mr. G. J. Roberts, under the very great difficulties of a bush country and a wet climate, which laid him up for a time, extended bearings on from Koiterangi . . . Simultaneously, under the direction of Mr. Mueller, he observed the triangles of a major-triangulation which binds together with indisputable accuracy all the survey points north from Hokitika to Ahaura.[18]

Douglas was based at Jacksons Bay, where Duncan Macfarlane was Superintendent of the Special Settlement and Resident Magistrate. To him Douglas brought specimens, carefully labelled, which were sent to Mueller in Hokitika along with field books, plans and sketches. Douglas very seldom visited Hokitika at this stage of his life, and there was plenty to do in the south.

SURVEYING

Charlie Douglas was not a trained surveyor and the survey methods he used in the mountains were fairly simple, based mainly on compass work. Sometimes he had an aneroid barometer to record heights and pressure, but this instrument was fragile. A surveyor's chain was also used but was too heavy to carry far. Douglas was usually noting detail and his records and estimates of the landscape – relationships, distances, heights, flora and geology – fitted into a much wider scheme.

Early surveying on the West Coast was coastal. Efforts were also made to specify detail in gold-mining areas, but none of that work was reliable. After John Turnbull Thomson became Surveyor-General on 1 May 1876, he implemented more rigorous survey methods, based on primary stations whose latitude and longitude had been carefully determined. G. J. Roberts used such points to fix by theodolite the heights and positions of many of the notable features of the West Coast landscape, including major peaks. Within this known framework, men such as Douglas carried out minor triangulation, whereby bearings were taken, in a valley or district, from specified points (not always official trig stations) to the visible landmarks. A network of bearings was recorded that cross-checked each other and ensured reasonable accuracy, and the group of surveyed features could then be fitted into the wider survey.

All observations were noted down in a field book for later interpretation and application. Sketches and maps were also used to record features and their relationships. The field book was a legal document and its preservation was paramount to a surveyor, who often recorded the same information in other ways as well, such as diary or plan, to ensure its survival.

Roberts continued to make good progress, and in 1879 Mueller reported: 'The triangulation (major and minor) as far as completed, now has placed that part of Westland in such a condition that a surveyor, unless incompetent or absolutely careless, cannot possibly get into trouble with his surveys.'[19] Douglas, with his reconnaissance work by compass, was the spearhead of the attack by theodolite on the unmapped southern areas. Not only were conditions difficult, but the weather was often poor. In 1879 it was noted: 'The reconnaissance survey between Jackson's River and Dart River, contemplated in 1877, was fortunately not taken in hand last year. The long continuance of rainy weather would no doubt have made it a very difficult and costly work.'

Roberts' fieldwork involved both mountaineering, at a time when that sport was virtually unknown in New Zealand, and carrying a heavy swag, when that was a means to a worthy end and not a holiday relaxation. His rigorous expeditions to link the triangulation of Westland and Canterbury finally strained his heart and kept him to a draughtsman's table and office desk for the rest of his career. The official version in 1881 of his last major fieldwork was explicit and generous enough, though rather cold and formal.

> In Westland, Mr. G. J. Roberts, who for the last three years has been engaged in a trigonometrical and topographical survey of that district, recently completed the observation of a Ray-trace, or chain of triangles, across the dividing range, connecting the triangulations of Westland and Canterbury. This was very arduous work, conducted, as it necessarily was, for a considerable distance over glaciers and snow-fields, with trigonometrical stations 5,000, 6,000, and 7,000 feet in height . . . In 1880 the triangles were advanced as far as practicable from the Westland side, and this year they were extended on a connection with the triangulation of Canterbury Plains . . . Such results are not obtained by chance; they are the outcome of the devoted labours of two most able surveyors.[20]

Roberts' own account, in a letter written some years later on 23 August 1893, is much more graphic.

> In 1880 it was resolved by the Sr. General that the E & W triangulations should be tacked together somewhere about the Rakaia, and I, being deemed the most fool-hardy of the chain-gang, had the honour (?) of doing the work. It was a badly devised expedition; in the first place, we started too late in the year, and in the second we were far too saving of the public purse. First, we went up the Wanganui River to explore that basin and finding it practically impossible to get over into the Rangitata, we finally selected the Rakaia connection. We were so late in the season we could not tackle the high tops, but had to dodge a ray-trace across the depression abreast the Ramsay Glacier [Strachan Pass].
> Next the Canterbury C. S. [Chief Surveyor] couldn't spare a suitable man to meet me in the Upper Rakaia, so taking Dan (my Foreman) with

me, we hurried off for that district, leaving my other men to erect trigs in the Wanganui country.

Roberts and Dan Strachan went from the Wanganui back to Hokitika, crossed Arthur's Pass, and tramped from Lake Lyndon near Porters Pass to the sheep stations in the Rakaia. Roberts' letter continued:

> Our first work being the erection of beacons on the Arrowsmith. We hadn't the best of weather, but after the jungle of the West Coast, found the country very quick . . . getting jammed by precipices we worked around to the west and eventually got up to where I have marked a beacon as about 600 feet below N summit . . . we had to cross the river – the old horse did his best and we managed it, but with very little to spare. We had a very snug camp, but got some awful weather and so we just sat and smoked day after day, the rain & fog driving without a spell.

They retreated to Mount Algidus station for food, then returned up the Rakaia.

> The weather was still bad and we almost finished our food before we got a fine enough day to try the Butler Range, for I had to pick up my Westland points from that ridge. Away we went and had no trouble getting up, but were only just in time, for a south easter was coming up, smothering us with a fog & sleet, a perfect blizzard – wasn't it cold? Ugh! Little Jack, our Cook, staunch and true, albeit soft, had never faced such weather before, so next morning he was puffed and blistered . . . Eventually the skin duly peeled off and he was in a woeful plight. We snared a few wekas and rubbed him with the oil, but he got real bad . . . Of course Dan and I had a pair of lovely noses but apart from the inconvenience of not being able to wash them we did right enough.

The weather continued bad and the river was in flood. Another retreat to Mount Algidus gained them more food and blessed tobacco. Back at the camp there was

> Still no show of crossing that roaring river – and the weather got even worse than before – only one days work to do and no chance of doing it. We put ourselves on short allowance, called up and snared every weka we could hear and stoned every blue duck about. Down went the flour until we had only one scone a day between us.

They finally erected their cairn and made their sights after traversing the terminal faces of the glaciers at the head of the Rakaia River. Roberts was sick because he allayed his hunger with totara berries and he also had a bad slip on the Lyell ice. The modest account finished with:

> It was *our trade* to swag heavy loads, to climb, to ford &c. &c. and we simply did it, after a fashion. I know that we did some perilous work but we never climbed a high peak or did anything else to brag about.

In fact Roberts had achieved a considerable feat of enterprise in his linking of the triangulations on both sides of the Southern Alps. He and his parties had reached peaks of 7,000 feet over permanent snowfields, exposed to bad weather and without alpine equipment or windproof clothing, showing their enthusiasm and determination for a difficult and hazardous job. With such experience behind him, it was to be expected that Roberts would give sympathy and encouragement to Douglas, who was also working in difficult terrain.

In 1880 Douglas spent May to December in the Haast country. His companions were either Mueller or 'Tommy' (probably Tommy Law, an American miner), but sometimes he worked alone. The entries in Field Book 492[21] mention rain, birds and topographical details. The following year was much the same. A notable entry in the next field book was on 4 December 1881: 'The ducks are sociable, coming close up to me quacking, winking, & wagging their tails and perfectly happy. The Eels are large, fat and intelligent, coming out on the logs to get a sunbath – I suppose – but with a prophetic instinct they eyed me with a Demoniac glare.' The following day it was: 'Boots broke down. Went to the Paringa for another and some sugar. Came back again to my camp tired & footsore after dark.' These notes were made during his exploration of the Blue River and already it was evident that Douglas was whimsical about the habits of the denizens of the country where he camped.

Field Book 493 of 1881 also included the stories of 'The Billy of Gold' and 'King Penguin', both creations of Douglas as rare for their literary form as for their inclusion. Although Douglas may have regarded them merely as idle amusements, and the relevant pages of the field book are crossed out, they show his sense of fun at this period of his life. (See Appendix 1.)

On 1 July 1882, his birthday, Douglas wrote in Field Book 491: '42 years old must commence and grow young again. Heavy rain all day.' During that year he made many beach traverses between the Waiatoto and Barn Bay. These included his first recorded trip to the Cascade River. He also reached a point thirteen miles up the Waiatoto River.

Field Book 496 recorded that in 1883 Douglas and Mueller went through the Cascade and Gorge country. Douglas also explored up the Okuru, where he found the Actor and 'Maorie' Passes to the Young and Blue tributaries of the Makarora River.

At this stage it is worth repeating a reminiscence by Frank Howe, formerly a settler at Okuru. He gave an account[22] of a trip in the Okuru–Turnbull area with Douglas, Mueller and one other man, who was so objectionable and unhelpful that Howe would not mention his name. Howe told something of the difficulties the early explorers and surveyors operated under. There is no reason to doubt the authenticity of the story, but Howe's account cannot be fully documented from contemporary papers and it may refer either to 1883 or to a major Okuru–Burke–Haast trip made by Douglas and Mueller in 1890. Howe reckoned by the age he was on the trip that it was 1883.

> Betsy Jane, Mr. Douglas's dog, had a couple of pups, and we had to destroy them, as Betsy was our bird catcher – a valuable member of our party. But she was very reluctant to come after that, and for about three days she was on a flax lead, in case she went back.

Although Douglas had more than one dog named Betsey Jane, the best known was active in the early 1890s, which suggests a later date for the trip. If it was in 1883, the dog may have been Topsey, though it is not clear when Douglas first acquired her. According to Howe's story, he, Douglas, Mueller and 'another man' left part of their loads and went up to the head of the Turnbull River:

> It was terrific country and not a bird to be got, and that of course made for a shortage of provisions and during the first three days we lost part of a swag (mine) and it contained the compass & other necessary things. By the end of a week of this, we had hoped to come out near the Landsborough – but up and down we went, keeping high though the weather wasn't good, and during the second week we did some big ascents and descents–on one occasion down and up three thousand feet to cross a rocky chasm, making only a mile that day.
>
> This went on into the third week, and by this time we were all feeling the strain, for food got very scarce – even Betsy couldn't find anything – and the chasm and rope work and exposure tried us severely, and now we did not know quite where we really were – we couldn't pick up landmarks in such rough country and misty weather.
>
> One night, as we sat round the fire, Betsy was lying on one side of Mr. Mueller, and I was on the other. Mr. M. pointed to her and said 'I'm afraid we will have to –' and I knew what he meant. Of course Mr. Douglas couldn't kill her, so I said I'd do it, and I stretched across and put my hand under her. But she was skin and bone, poor Betsy, and to use her would not help much, and we didn't want to do it, so nothing more was said.
>
> Next day we heard a kakapo scream away across a steep snow slope, and away Betsy and I went – And – *we got it!* Douglas cut it up into four exact bits, and cooked it, but it did not go far! and Betsy eat the rest.
>
> And now, one day, when we were struggling along (for the three weeks had all been spent in high country and had told on us all) suddenly someone said 'Listen!' We listened, straining our ears – yes – away in the distance a dog was barking and cattle being driven – we could hear the sounds very faintly. Mr. Mueller and I hurried across a valley and up a ridge – we heard it again. Climbing for a clearer view, we got sight of a river – far down. Mr. M. got out his glasses, and took a long and careful look through them. 'It's the *Haast!!*' he said at last. And there away down the East bank of a River (we were above on the west) were the specks of cattle being driven along a river flat.

Back the two of us went to the others, and I went down alone against Mr. M.'s wishes, to follow the cattle down to their camp and try to get some provisions. Mr. Mueller, though not saying one word in complaint, had been pushing himself for several days – he now wasn't used to the hardships, as in his earlier days, and was a bit older than any of us. I had noticed that for some days he had had to steady himself by holding on to the grass, or anything within reach, but never a word.

The anonymous man refused to accompany Howe, so, annoyed, he went off alone, since Mueller did not want Douglas to go. After six hours Howe reached the camp in the Haast of a Mr Guthrie Stewart of Wanaka, who had driven his cattle through the Haast Pass from Otago. 'I was so starved and weak,' said Howe, 'he would not let me feed myself, but he sat beside me, cut the food up and fed me . . . When I said at last I *must* go, he gave me a big sugar bag full of meat and all sorts of stores.' Howe borrowed a horse to take the provisions near to the camp where Mueller met him with a billy of hot tea. Later they went to Wanaka for a few days' rest. Mueller continued on to Queenstown, where his friends scarcely recognised him, he was so thin. Presumably the others returned to South Westland.

This memory of a trip with Douglas and Mueller gives a vivid description of the hard life in the field. Howe also praised Douglas as a man and an explorer. 'He was kind and humorous in camp, never unreasonable or selfish, a great companion . . . he seemed to know everything – and there was precious little he missed . . . There's no one – *no* one, mind – that could touch him as an explorer.'

Contemporary documents are just as valuable and revealing. In 1884 Douglas travelled with Mueller and Roberts on the reconnaissance survey for a road line from Jacksons Bay to Martins Bay. The survey party of five men in two boats had a rough trip from Jacksons in January and had to run for shelter before landing to follow the road line and to carry food to the camp at the Cascade River. On this trip Mueller wrote charming letters, illustrated with lively pen sketches, for the delight of his young children. His daughter, Mildred, was the recipient of a letter, written on 10 February 1884, a page of which is reproduced opposite. Further on, the letter to 'little Millie' gave further explanation:

Artie can explain for you the last picture. Ask him to show you which is Papa leaning over a high rock; and Mr. Roberts trying to jump over a big boulder and one of the men with more sense than Mr. Roberts sitting on a big boulder; and stupid Charley Douglas stumbling over a boulder and losing his pipe – a good thing it did not get broken; perhaps it got cracked, but you cannot see that; and Colin Macfarlane who feels so warm that he has to take his hat off; and Charley Robinson behind, taking it quite easy and enjoying his smoke while pegging slowly along. Ask him also to shew

ATL MS Papers 0448-09

A page from Gerhard Mueller's letter to his daughter, Millie, 10 February 1884. Mueller drew a rough sketch of the coastline from Jacksons Bay to the Cascade River and showed the party's route. He wrote:

Now you ask Freddy to explain for you this Map and to shew you Mr Roberts Boat and the way it went from Jacksons Bay to Homminy Cove and the Road (as dotted) he had to walk along and where he had to take his trousers off and ford the Stafford River and the Seal Rocks where he met papa and his men. From there the whole lot carrying big swags like that to the Provision Tent . . .

Later in the same letter Mueller also described the party members whom he had sketched:

. . . Papa leaning over a high rock; and Mr Roberts trying to jump over a big boulder and one of the men [Tac Cuttance] with more sense than Mr Roberts sitting on a big boulder; and stupid Charley Douglas stumbling over a boulder and losing his pipe – a good thing it did not get broken, perhaps it got cracked, but you cannot see that; and Colin Macfarlane who feels so warm that he has to take his hat off, and Charley Robinson behind, taking it quite easy and enjoying his smoke while pegging slowly along.

you the Provision Tent and the keg the butter is in and the square box with the jam inside; that's the box dear Millie would like best and if dear Millie were here now, papa would let her have any jam she likes best. From the Provision Tent we had to climb over a high hill and walk to the Camp and here we have been ever since, having had a number of wet days and the work only half done.

Next month it was Freddy Mueller's turn to get a letter from his father. Extracts from this give interesting details of eel-fishing and of the construction of a 'futta' (a corruption of the Maori word whata, a storehouse), where provisions were stored against the wiles of bush rats.

I started for the South with Charley Douglas, Charley Robinson, Tac Cuttance and a retriever dog called Topsy. After six hours travelling we reached the Cascade River and crossed in Douglas's Canoe. That afternoon I went exploring a Branch of that River and as we had only flour and no meat we kept a sharp lookout for Eels. Douglas had a large hook with the barb filed off, which he had fastened to the end of a long stick. This arrangement is called a 'gaff' and with it the Eels are caught. When an Eel is hooked with it he immediately twists around the stick and often it happens that they escape from the pole . . . Well we saw a hummer of an Eel and fastened on and got him safely into the Canoe and tomahawked him. The 2nd one we spied was nearly four foot long and Douglas was frightened to gaff him – however we thought we risk it, more especially as we had an outrigger at the one side of the Canoe. Well he hooked him and the fellow gave a horrible pull, nearly sending Douglas headlong into the River on the outrigger side. He naturally leant to the other side to safe himself, which brought the outrigger 3 ft out of the water and the Canoe half filled. To save us from getting swamped I put my full weight on the outrigger and over we went with such force as to take in a barrel or two of water on the other side. However Douglas stuck to his game and after much heaving and struggling landed the fellow in the Canoe.

A still larger eel they gaffed by the tail, and the catch of three eels weighed about seventy pounds.

That big Eel was splendid eating – we took the backbone out, salted him, rolled him up for a night to let the salt get properly through the meat and then hung him over the smoke for two days and so he lasted us for a week.

The usual fare was either salted or tinned meat. Eels and birds gave exploring parties a welcome change of diet, and smoked eels were often preferred to smoked sea fish. Mueller went on to describe the 'futta':

a place where provisions are kept . . .1st it must not be exposed to the storms; 2nd it must be watertight and 3rd it must be rat proof . . . The posts you notice must be notched about a foot from their tops and around the thin neck of these posts, strips of tin, from kerosene tins or coffee tins are nailed, so as to prevent the rats from climbing up – the tin is too slippery for them.

It is from such clear accounts that the domestic routine and incidents of travel of these early survey parties come to reality. What is trivial at the time becomes background for history as the years pass. One can admire Mueller for his faithful descriptions written for an appreciative family, and be thankful for the illumination of detail they provide.

It was probably in November 1883 that Douglas, almost certainly alone, began a momentous journey up the Arawata River to its head, through gorges and wild scenery of the type that was such an important backdrop to his life. The variation of narrow gorges and wide river flats was both spectacular and characteristic of Westland travel. It is possible that on the Arawata journey Douglas came close to the Olivine Ice Plateau above the Andy Glacier. In a later report he noted: 'I was on the crown of the ridge in the early eighties but went no further, being alone at the time and having no alpine appliances whatever.'[23] His surmise that the Barrier branch of the Pyke River to the west was the Dart was perhaps due rather to insufficient view than to confused topography.

However, Douglas's recollection[24] that he was on top of Mt Ionia in early 1884 is probably a year out. There was a trip up the Haast and Okuru Rivers with Roberts in 1884,[25] but the Arawata traverse with the ascent of Ionia is recorded in Mueller's report of 1885.[26] Douglas is not likely to have climbed Ionia twice without some comment from him or Mueller, whose own enthusiasm for the ascent is implicit in his report.[27]

The Arawata expedition of Douglas and Mueller left Jacksons Bay on 28 January 1885 and returned there on 23 February. The party 'rough-traversed' the Arawata valley to Williamson Flat, which is one of the most glorious places in the Southern Alps. Hemmed in by gorges, this flat of a thousand acres is dominated by glaciated peaks such as Ionia and Destiny, fringed by stately forest, and guarded by a turbulent river. The grass of the flats is lush, and erratic rocks from the glacier age give shelter in storms. A visit to this place inspires reverence for its beauty,[28] and it holds pride of place as a corner of Westland that for serenity is unrivalled.

The 1885 party reached the Andy Glacier at the head of the Williamson valley and later went up the Waipara River as far as the Bonar Glacier, but the highlight was the ascent of Mt Ionia, a fine peak from any angle. Although only 7,380 feet, its shapely cone rises 6,000 feet above the upper Arawata in graceful symmetry. Mueller wrote:

I have never seen anything to approach in awe-inspiring effect the view from Mount Ionia . . . It took me two days and a half hard climbing to get to the top of Ionia. The rope had to be used again and again, both in ascending and at descending, and for well nigh half a mile steps had to be cut into the frozen snow to get footing.

These steps would have been cut by Douglas, whom the *AJHR* report does not actually mention. Ice axes were then unknown in Westland, and Harper believed Douglas cut the steps with a billhook or slasher. A miner's pick would have been the only other tool suitable, but there is no evidence that Douglas carried one. According to Mueller, 'the trouble and exertion were well repaid'.

This ascent was enterprising by any standards. Although all significant peaks in the European Alps had been climbed by 1885, the Rev. William. S. Green had made his almost successful attempt on Mt Cook, with Ulrich Kaufmann and Emil Boss, only in 1882. Other mountain climbing in New Zealand was also recent. Ascents of Mt Ruapehu in the central North Island had been made using some alpine techniques in 1879 by Beetham and Maxwell, and in 1881 by the Russell brothers and William and Ethel Birch. In 1883 Hochstetter Dome had been climbed by Dr Robert von Lendenfeld and his wife, Anna, with a local porter, H. Dew. But the complete ascent of Ionia was a landmark in New Zealand alpine history: the first local ascent of a significant peak in the more mountainous South Island, and one moreover that had required considerable preparatory exploration. Douglas and Mueller had become accustomed to the untamed wilderness, and in climbing a fine peak gained a good viewpoint for the survey. They were also among the first New Zealanders to experience the joy of mountaineering far above the bushline.

Mueller's report also commented on a glacier up the Williamson valley below Jagged Ridge, which 'is quite a curiosity in its way, inasmuch as there is no connection whatever between it and the snow or ice on the range above'. This same 'Shelf Glacier' was described by Douglas as 'a singular mass of ice . . . This glacier has no neve but is supplied by the winter snow which drift over the range.'[29] Exploratory trips after the Second World War, led by Ian Whitehead, Colin Todd and Stan Conway[30] found that both Mueller and Douglas were mistaken and that this glacier, renamed the Tornado, had a névé like others, but separated from its trunk.

In April and May 1885 Douglas was on a 'seven weeks starve' up the Okuru, having previously traversed the Turnbull. In July Mueller became Commissioner of Crown Lands for Westland, and in December Douglas helped the Macfarlane family take up their run in the Cascade River. A letter by Duncan Macfarlane, published in a Welsh newspaper, *The Chronicle*, on 10 April 1886, referred to 'my friend Douglas's caricature of the situation, entitled *Tree'd by a Flood in the Cascade Valley*'. This told how a flood forced the party to camp on a staging until the waters receded. It also mentioned that in this new kingdom of 32,000 acres where sheep and cattle were liberated for the first time, a new homestead was left in charge of Douglas. But Douglas had already rejected the life of a runholder at the Paringa, and though he helped his friends at the Cascade for a time, his wish was still to wander and explore.

In May 1886 he knocked around at the head of the Cascade, Hope and Gorge Rivers. This trip along the Northern Olivines was recounted by his companion G. T. Murray, later of the Mines Department, to Frank Simmons on 14 August 1935.[31] The substance of the reminiscence is important because it throws light and shade on the character of Douglas, by then forty-six years old, and a fully experienced bushman and explorer.

> Reputed gold finds in the Jacksons Bay, Big Bay and Martins Bay district induced the Govt to send some 300 miners by the *Hinemoa*. Murray went with them to construct a bridle track to Martins Bay for supplies and communications. He had some 8 men and was advised to see Charlie Douglas at the settlement . . . C.E.D. was with two friends . . . and recovering from a spree. Murray describes him as about 5' 10" and slight to the point of skinny-ness – Eyes steely grey and hair always worn very long (down to the shoulders) and ever unkempt. He steadfastly refused to permit anyone to cut it. His camping equipment then, as ever, was a batwing tent, one blanket sewn into a bag, tea, oatmeal . . . Topsy also. He was never loquacious, was extremely modest and spoke his few words in a slow, quiet voice – often very dry in his remarks as many stories show . . . Their first and only trip alone was along the top of the Olivine Range, to the Cascade Saddle, down the Pyke and back to the Coast and the Gorge R. On the construction work Douglas acted as scout and G. T. Murray says that he always merely followed Charlie's line with his levels. M. describes him as a wonderful bushman, with a great eye for country. C.E.D. often mentioned his college – to which he was very attached, but never his people. He was fond of solitude – even the quiet camp of the gang of 6 men irritated him and he would never stick it more than about three days with the gang. When at the main camp he never shared a tent. Once he set out on a short trip to an observation point and was gone so long that the party became alarmed and set out to look for him. He was found sitting on a stump musing and was most annoyed at the suggestion that he might be thought lost.

The links with the Macfarlane family were by now strongly forged and the friendship with Douglas secure. Their house at the Cascade was well stocked with books, and for him to spend time in this cultural oasis in a pioneer desert must have been both a solace and a reward after months of hardship in the ranges. Duncan Macfarlane was also deeply interested in Westland minerals, and Douglas added to his collection with specimens such as asbestos from the Red Hill country.

Another significant event in 1886 was the beginning of the survey career of William Wilson, who proved a staunch friend of Douglas in later years, and whose efforts to gather and preserve his papers continued those of Roberts. Men such as Douglas, Mueller, Roberts and the Macfarlanes were a small but select group. Their common struggle as pioneers on a mountain frontier gave them a bond of experience and friendship.

Anxiety about Douglas when he was away exploring was routine with his friends. Mildred Mueller recalled:

> One of the main things I can remember in childhood, was the anxiety occasioned when Douglas failed to return to the Coast when it was reasonable to expect him. His whereabouts were known only in a general way, and with any knowledge of the possibilities in even one square mile of that country, one can appreciate how disturbing the delay could be. Mr. Roberts would prowl around the Gov. offices on the chance of seeing some new arrival from the South, and would come several times an evening to report some item of southern news to Gerhard Mueller, and the sense of relief when news did come was obvious even to us children.

When families in South Westland grew anxious about the return of Douglas from an expedition, the first question to be asked was 'How much tobacco did he take?' From the answer they reckoned his probable date of return.[32]

In 1887 Mueller made another memorable expedition in the summer months of January and February. His account of the 'Reconnaissance Survey of the Clarke and Landsborough Country, Westland' mentioned Douglas, who had 'accompanied me on many of my former explorations'. Mueller's report[33] included three sketches by Douglas as well as a fine map. There is also an interesting account of Douglas's ability as a mountaineer.

> I gladly accepted – though I admit, with a certain amount of fear and trembling – the offer of Charles Douglas, an experienced and able bushman and cool-headed climber . . . to be let down by the rope and clear away the dangerous projecting stones, cross the razorback of over a mile in length, and see whether it was practicable at the other end to get off on to the grass lands again. He did this, reported favourably and then men, swags, and dogs were lowered by the rope.

This difficult spot was at 'Break-Neck Point', where the Clarke and Landsborough slips met near Solution Point. Mueller explained the method of surveying as

> rough-traversed – i.e., bearings taken with prismatic compass, and distances stepped or estimated, as the formation of ground would admit. Most of the points at which observations were taken are held by shots to mountain-peaks fixed by triangulation some years ago by Mr. Roberts.

Mueller also referred to the great difficulties of fording the Landsborough, 'a boiling, turbulent mountain-torrent'. Various natural features were named, including Mt Fettes, a tribute by Douglas to the most distinguished member of his mother's family, Sir William Fettes, and perhaps also to his eldest brother.

The prominence given to Mueller's account, Appendix No. 2 to the Report on the Surveys of New Zealand, was well deserved. Even many years later the map could be useful to people traversing that region, and the sketches by Douglas of bush and mountain scenery in the Landsborough and of the Douglas Glacier lend an unusual flavour. This must have been the first time sketches by Douglas had been printed.

Later in 1887, and also in 1888, Douglas visited the Balfour Glacier under New Zealand's highest Main Divide peak, Mt Tasman (11,475 feet). Unrecorded gold prospectors had probably visited the glacier earlier, but the trip by Douglas was the first by a map-maker.[34] In January 1888 he was on the Fox Glacier, but 'as I had neither Aneroid level or chain I didn't fix any point either on or off the glacier'.[35] His field book for that period gave traverses of the Waikupakupa, Clearwater, Stoney Creek, Lake Mueller and part of the Copland and Karangarua from the Forks to the sea, with a return visit to the Balfour Glacier.[36]

With the end of 1888 came the last of his 'half-time exploring'. For the next fifteen years he was fully employed by the Survey Department and could indulge his passion for new country undeterred by side issues except the limitations imposed by failing health and his periodic bouts of drinking.

By now Charlie Douglas was a fully equipped explorer. He was used to the wiles of the bush, the rivers and the gorges. He had a good understanding of the landscape and sufficient alpine knowledge to cross glaciers and snowfields. He was practised in the correct use of whatever survey instruments the department gave him for his journeys.

On the eastern side of the South Island mountain climbing was beginning as a recreation in a small way. Following Green's attempt on Mt Cook, several young New Zealanders were beginning to focus on the high peaks: George Mannering and Marmaduke Dixon from Canterbury, Malcolm Ross from Dunedin, and Harry Birley at the head of Lake Wakatipu. In 1890 they were to be joined by Arthur P. Harper, son of Leonard, after whom Harper Pass was named. The younger Harper began climbing in Switzerland in 1887, and in 1888, the year that Douglas was fossicking around the Balfour Glacier, Harper was again in Switzerland, writing to his mother, 'I'm simply mad on climbing.'[37] Yet not many years were to pass before Harper would find his greatest mountaineering interests lay not on the summits but in discovery of the mountain world in similar fashion to Douglas, while Douglas himself would be grateful for Harper's sound apprenticeship in the crafts of snow and ice.

On the western side of the Southern Alps recreational climbing was years away. In 1889, when Douglas began full-time exploring and related work, much of Westland was still uncharted land for explorer and climber alike, the realm of people like Douglas. The skylines were virgin, the maps scanty and glaciers unnamed, with passes above them uncrossed and unrecorded. In this land of rainforest, scrub and gorge the difficulties of terrain and climate were significant. Yet what a field this was for enterprise, and here Douglas was to continue his energetic career.

FIVE

Exploring Regularly, 1889–1903

In the period of his full-time employment by the Survey Department, Charlie Douglas was not, of course, always out in the mountains. In 1889 he was nearing fifty years of age and was probably beginning to appreciate periods spent in more permanent shelter, working on maps or writing up notes and reports. However, he was consistently active in the field, exploring and surveying wherever the department wanted. A number of his trips occurred in winter, when rivers were lower and weather was sometimes more settled, but the cold could be extreme. Within a few years the exigencies of rough exploring took their toll on Douglas.

Exploring regularly began in 1889, a year that is almost a blank in records of work by Douglas, though he was probably north of the Haast. A report to the government for the year 1889–90[1] made direct mention of him:

> The greatest explorer of the southern portion of Westland is Mr. Charles Douglass, who has been prospecting all through the Southern Alps during the last twenty years, and has not so far been able to find anything that would give immediate returns . . . there is no one who has a greater knowledge of [the southern portion of Westland] than Mr. Douglass.

Two things stand out here: the misspelling of his name, and the official emphasis on prospecting. There is almost an expectation that Douglas will find something valuable to be exploited. This report did, however, demonstrate some of his other skills in publishing his sketch map of 'Coal Formation Arnott Range', a geological map of the Cook River district, and a cross-section from Gillespies Point to Mt Cook.

The prospecting Douglas was doing always included the more valuable work of mapping. He was in the Cascade valley in February 1890 when he wrote to Mueller and referred to their forthcoming trip up the Okuru. His field book for April (592) gave aneroid readings up the Okuru and traverses up the Okuru, Burke and Haast, and on 8 July Douglas sent Mueller maps of the Burke and Turnbull Rivers. Three days earlier he had written to Roberts expressing his continuing passion for unknown country.

This Trip if I don't brake my neck will be a glorious one. No human being has even dreamt of going into the country round Alba, Castor & Pollux & Aspiring. I find my Brains getting stagnant having no new country to visit, but the map of the East Side of the Range Mr. Mueller brought with him, & a few glimpses I have got of the country showed me that here was a place unknow, with plenty of room for unknow Alpine Lakes Waterfalls & Glaciers.

This comment sets the scene for one of his most significant trips, the Waiatoto exploration, more fully recorded in Douglas's own words elsewhere in this book (pages 104–44) – a story of effort and perseverance that could only be sustained by the personal satisfaction Douglas continued to gain from 'overhauling this awfull country', as he wrote to Roberts. But there were few dividends in terms of material benefits, and Douglas himself was hard up. He asked Mueller for rulers, pencils, compass and pen, 'if there is any money left'. And to Roberts he wrote: 'If Mr. Mueller gives me the Job to put up the Enamelled Plates on the Haast Track that I suppose will be £5 or thereabouts which will pay my Tucker on the Trip.' Anxiety about money was to become routine with Douglas, despite philosophic observations to the contrary.

Gerhard Mueller, perhaps Douglas's closest associate, left Hokitika in April 1891 to continue his career with the Survey Department in Auckland. Mildred Mueller remembered in 1954 that 'one of his chief regrets was leaving D. There is no doubt he held him in affectionate regard, (and as a moral responsibility).' Douglas was now over fifty, and he did depend on his few long-term friends, so Mueller's concern was justified. Mildred also noted: 'In our childish lives, C.D. was not only known to loom large in G.M's life, but to us he was an important and marvellous man, and (significant pointer to the behaviour of our elders) so far as we heard in our own home was without fault.'

The Waiatoto expedition took from January to May of 1891. It is one of the best documented of all Douglas's explorations, perhaps equalled in this respect only by that in the Copland the following year. It was also the most exacting, and the most characteristic of the trials and joys that Westland could offer. In the Waiatoto, Douglas found fulfilment as a solitary man. In his struggle for survival against the perils of snowfall, flood and precipice he drew on all his inner reserves. His diaries of the period reveal all the humanities, the whimsicalities and the careful observations of which his nature was capable. His dry humour, his brooding and his discursive notes were never more pungently expressed.

The Waiatoto is a long valley, flats and gorges alternating, flanked by giant mountains from which fall avalanches, and washed by a river flowing from broken glaciers. Even today it is seldom traversed. The distances are too discouraging and the obstacles too exhausting to tempt all save the most resolute of mountain travellers. It was a valley worthy of a man of mettle and courage.

Douglas began his Waiatoto journey in late January by paddling and towing a canoe, ironically christened *The Surveyor-General*, up the river. In February he started the laborious work of back-packing – carrying a load, dumping it at a cache, and then returning for a further load. He records that in this labour he begins to feel that his 'Nerve & Grip are not what they once were'. His dog Betsey Jane was his company and his diary his confidant. Birds provided additional food. Clouds of sandflies by day and mosquitoes by night gave him a topic for dissertation as well as cause for irritation. Inevitable rain gave him time to think about the worth of his life and work. In the middle of February he returned to Okuru for more stores, and then he could write in his 'Waiatoto' manuscript: '. . . am now ready to tackle the Mountains at any time'.

As Douglas progressed up the river, sketching as well as writing occupied his spare time. Although lacking the artistic ability of his brother Sir William Fettes Douglas, who died that very year, his flair for topography gave his sketches accuracy and his rough wash drawing added piquancy. And they gave occasion for an amusing story of kea as art critics. Partway up the river, at Drake Flats, he was joined by another dog, Poker, belonging to local runholders the Egglings.[2]

On 27 February Douglas made the ascent in his stockinged feet of the smooth rock slabs on the western outlier of Mt Ragan, 'the grandest piece of climbing I ever did'. This was an attempt to determine the relationship of the Waiatoto with the Wilkin and Matukituki Rivers on the eastern side of the Southern Alps, but on his summit (6780 feet), now called Stocking Peak, Douglas could see very little.[3]

The weather cleared unexpectedly on 2 March and Douglas set off for the head of the valley, which was further away than he expected. He reached the Therma Glacier after 'one of the roughest days travelling I have had for years', with the two dogs 'in a delipidated condition'. The glacier he found 'magnificent' and the whole situation impressive. He returned to his camp, where storms and dangerous fords delayed his journey further down the river. Then it was back to the coast, where he recorded some of the fascinating and more printable yarns told by the ferryman at the mouth of the Waiatoto.

In April Douglas headed back up the valley again, though he had to make a run down to the river mouth to get an axe sharpened. May began with floods and heavy snowfall. More returns to the mouth, and by the middle of the month he had two good swags to carry up the Te Naihi (Axius) River, a major tributary of the Waiatoto, which he hoped would lead to an easy Main Divide pass to the Wilkin valley in Otago.

Further floods gave Douglas time to write verse and to discourse on the evils of barren nomenclature on mountain maps, and on the origins of man-kind. Then came a saga of fog, storm and snow endured in the search for a new pass: '. . . you can call it the Scroggins if you like'. Two versions of this energetic day are given, with conflicting dates – natural enough for a man to whom time was no object. The second account specified the 'day of Adventure' as 25 May. However, the bad weather conditions left continuing uncertainty about whether the pass he had seen actually led to the Wilkin. Since he did not see the lake under Mt Alba that leads to a pass of 6,000 feet and the Newland Stream of the Wilkin, it is likely Douglas was looking down from a saddle of 5,300 feet into another branch of the upper Te Naihi that circled round to come between Doug-las and the other Wilkin tributaries.[4] With winter fast approaching, Douglas headed downriver again, having done as much as he could in difficult circum-stances to explore the long and complex river system of the Waiatoto. He left a most human record of his endeavour, which ranks as one of the great feats of New Zealand exploration.

Another scene of Douglas's activity in 1891 was the lower Waitaha, but the month is unknown. Brief diary entries from August cover much that shows the energetic nature of his life. They included a 'Prospecting trip to Barn Bay & the Fork River' south of the Cascade with John Lindsay, a blacksmith at Jacksons Bay. Squalls of rain, heavy seas and heavy swagging filled the days. Fossicking up the Hope River gave no gold. In September food ran low: 'Must go away tomorrow . . . for Tucker, either fish or Birds, reduced now to dry bread and Mussels.' Later they used a penguin as bait for fish and crayfish. By the end of September the two prospectors had found only a few colours of gold. Like the efforts of Douglas to cook fish in a Maori oven, this trip was 'not exactly a success'.[5]

In the middle of November Douglas recorded in the same field book a 'Diary of Survey – Cascade and Barn Bay Road'. The entries are laconic, varying from 'Taking things easy' to 'Rain all day', and more actively, from 'Cutting Line all day, still good ground' to 'Chained pegged and took the bearings up to 2½ miles'. This work continued to 19 December. From 9 January 1892 Doug-las and his companions made further progress with the survey, until on 4 Feb-ruary Douglas could write, '. . . got swag home and work now finished'.

On 17 February Douglas was at the Waiatoto Lagoon, writing a frank letter to Roberts. He reported that he had nearly finished the sketch map of the Cas-cade, but the outline of activity in that area, found in the undated Field Book 498, must relate to earlier work, possibly more than one trip. It reads: 'Up Cascade, Red Hill, Mt. Delta and Theta, Gorge River, Sea beaches, Big Bay, Durwards Falls Trav upper Cascade from Cascade to gorge over saddle trav Gorge R to Browns refuge up Gorge to Forks'. The postscript in the letter to

Roberts – 'could you not send me down the £3 in notes in a letter. It is so long since I have had money in my pockets I am curious to try how it feels' – confirms both the chronic emptiness of his purse and that he had long since ceased to receive any allowance from his relatives in Scotland.

Between 22 February and 8 March 1892 Douglas was cutting a track up the Haast, but on 11 March the diary heading 'Journal of Trip on Reconnaissance Survey over Southern Alps' foretold the Copland exploration, an important chapter in Douglas history, covered more fully later through his own writings (see pages 148–63). The first crossing of the Copland Pass, or near to it, was subsequently to be made by the English climber Edward FitzGerald and his guide Mattias Zurbriggen on 24 February 1895, but this feat and the recording of it ignored both the substantial discovery achieved by Douglas and the assistance FitzGerald received from the work of surveyors. This whole controversy is discussed in Appendix 2.

The discovery by Pakeha and crossing of other passes over the Main Divide of the Southern Alps, such as Harper, Arthur's, the Whitcombe and Haast, have already been referred to. Other routes had also been proved by 1895: Browning Pass from the Wilberforce to the Arahura, and Sealy Pass from the Godley Glacier to the Perth River. The Milford Track over Mackinnon Pass, discovered in 1888, was also being opened up, but that was much further south. As the Waiatoto exploration showed, Douglas was keen to find other routes across the Divide. Indeed, he was instructed to do so. The government particularly wanted a tourist route direct from the Hermitage, near Mt Cook, to the West Coast, instead of the long slow journey by coach back to Christchurch and over Arthur's Pass to Greymouth and Hokitika. Douglas was to contribute, it was hoped, to the development of the tourist trade, as well as to the completion of the Westland Survey.

When Douglas wrote to Roberts on 17 February 1892, one of the important topics was the reconnaissance survey from the Copland River to the Hermitage. Douglas promised that if the Survey Department did not send him on this job he would sneak over the Wilkin Pass and on the quiet have a look at the Hooker Glacier approach, which FitzGerald later used. Douglas asked for both a tracing of the area and for silence about his intentions.

Douglas did the bulk of the exploration on the Westland side between March and May 1892, in company with Harry Cuttance of Okuru.[6] The diary for 11 March told of heavy rain when he 'sate down to groan for a day or two', and the bad weather and floods meant they did not reach Andrew Scott's homestead in the Karangarua valley, off which the Copland branches, until 27 March. In April they started traversing the Copland gorge, but track cutting and back-packing in the rough country knocked Douglas's boots to pieces, so they went back to

Scott's. On their return up the river they met the first frost of the season, and a view of the Sierra Range showed it to be 'wilder than the Wakatipu Remark-ables'. By the end of the month they were up to Tekano Creek, near what became known as Douglas Rock Bivy, and worrying that snowstorms of winter could block them.

Douglas decided that neither the head of the valley nor Baker Saddle up the Strauchon branch offered possibility of a track, and that the £50 the work had cost the government was spent on an impracticable route. It must be empha-sised that Douglas had not been asked to find a route over a high pass for alpine climbers. His instructions were to discover 'a pass available for Mule traffic to the Hermitage'. That this was altered in the official report to 'a pass available for a road across the main range to the Hermitage' does not alter the fact that Douglas was looking for a 'tourist route', not a mountaineers' pass. As usual, rain delayed the retreat downriver, and they did not reach habitation till 6 May.

The diary and report on the Copland is an honest record of the difficulties of the survey. Today the Copland Pass track is a good trip for guided tourists or mountain trampers, with the Westland gorges the least of the worries. The account by Douglas reminds us that there was once tangled going and almost impenetrable bush. What a difference a well-formed and graded track makes to a mountaineer with a load! Subsequently, in 1896 or later, Douglas, with Alf Dale and Bob Ward, young son of his former partner Tom, blazed a track up the Copland. His companions discovered the hot springs at Welcome Flat. When Douglas sent word of this to Roberts, he was asked to provide a bottle full of the spring water, with temperature readings. Roberts sent a full whisky bottle but no instructions about what to do with its contents.[7]

It is interesting to look forward to 23 August 1893 and quote Roberts writ-ing to A. P. Harper about routes over the Main Divide, some eighteen months before FitzGerald and Zurbriggen made their crossing.

> Douglas went up the Copland last season and explored its headwaters, the result being a considerable alteration in our maps of that district. My in-structions to him were not to tackle Baker's Saddle unless a mule-track were practicable. This latter he found out of the question, so he stopt right under the Saddle. He pronounced the trip as one of the most arduous he ever attempted . . . However we know all about the place now and his blazed line will be most useful to any trans-insular nomad.

After a visit to Gillespies Beach, Cuttance returned to the south and Douglas went up the Karangarua alone to opposite the Twain (now Douglas) River. But on 18 May 'the first real illness of my life' intervened. Douglas vomited blood, the dog howled, and robins were ready with leaves to bury him, he thought.

But he kept going and by the end of the month he was back at Scott's with yet another chapter of forest and flood, gorge and swagging behind him.

The demands of this rough life on the physique of a man nearly fifty-two years old were excessive and were beginning to leave their mark. Douglas still had some twenty-four years of life ahead of him, of which more than ten would be spent actively in the mountains, but his days of youthful daring and joyous energy were well past. It is not too fanciful to suggest that from the end of the Copland expedition dates an increasing cynicism, perhaps linked to his increasing ill-health. Fortunately Douglas was soon to gain the company of the vigorous Harper and then other young men such as the Gunn brothers who would help him to further good work, and stick to him in spite of his increasing trouble with rheumatism and other illness.

Yet the year 1892 was not to close without further strenuous trips. Douglas's 'Whitcombe River' manuscript, dated 25 August, shows that he spent the winter months in that wilderness. Such a place was cold and often sunless, but there was always plenty of good firewood, and the rivers were lower in that season. Much of this report is filled with technicalities of topography or geology. Extracts with observations of bird life and other interesting discursions give the flavour of the narrative without its descriptive details.

Douglas also explored the Mikonui and the Kakapotahi (Gordon) valleys in September, and the Waitaha to its head in October.[8] This is rough country, as subsequent explorers have found. Narrow canyons and wilful cataracts must have tested the patience of Douglas severely, and he would have been glad to get back to Hokitika in November for a change.

The next record of survey work comes from April 1893, when Douglas was between Kowhitirangi (Koiterangi) and Kokatahi, in what became farming country behind Hokitika. From May to September he made a traverse of the Kokatahi River to its headwaters.[9] This is also a heavily gorged valley. It is worth noting that the Kokatahi represents the farthest north of Douglas's fieldwork, if we except minor trips in the Otira watershed some years later.

In August there was a suggestion in Roberts' letter to Harper of Douglas going up the Poerua valley as its first explorer, but in fact it was not to be thoroughly pioneered till 1952, thanks to the defences of its gorges. The same letter, earlier quoted in several connections, has other valuable detail, including some insight into Douglas. To introduce Harper to the older explorer, Roberts wrote:

> You must know that my friend isn't a neutral sort of human, not he – he is a good lover and also a good hater. Well, years ago, Douglas went pottering away inland and before sending me the map of his work, wrote, begging to be allowed to christen a mountain with its radiating streams &c, of

course, I said yes–the sketch below gives a *small* portion of the result.

Well, to his annoyance, I *had* to alter the phrasing a bit and he had to revenge himself in some other fashion.

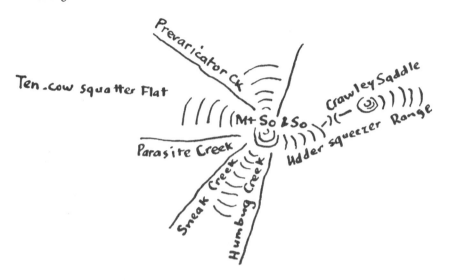

After Arthur P. Harper's return to New Zealand in 1889 he took part in pioneering mountaineering expeditions from the glaciers on the eastern side of the Southern Alps near Mt Cook. His experiences were well recorded in subsequent books.[10] In 1891 he joined with George Mannering and Malcolm Ross to form the New Zealand Alpine Club. Harper had trained as a lawyer and would have expected to enter the firm in which his father and uncle were partners. However, difficulties arose over the business practices of his father, who left New Zealand suddenly in July 1891, and Harper, as the eldest son, had to work hard to sort out the family's affairs. This included a trip to England in 1892, and by August 1893 he desperately needed a change of scene and activity. Harper accepted work with the Westland Survey at eight shillings a day, the same as Douglas. This was about the average wage of an unskilled labourer at the time.

Roberts wisely paired Harper with Douglas. They made a good combination, the active twenty-eight-year-old mountaineer and the veteran explorer. On 6 October 1893 Douglas and Harper left Hokitika, mapped Lake Ianthe, and in a dug-out canoe made an exciting trip down the Wanganui River. Then began their stirring efforts on the Franz Josef Glacier. On 26 November Roberts wrote to Harper that he was working up the next map: 'I hope you & Douglas will shine as exploring stars of the 1st magnitude.' He also reported that Douglas had written, 'Harper is a grand hand among ice.' By the end of December they had indulged in ice acrobatics and had made camps on both sides of the glacier.

Tough scrub and broken gullies gave them as much trouble as the crevassed ice. At one stage Douglas went back to Mapourika for more stores, where illness detained him for three weeks.

While Harper was to do important exploration in the Karangarua in 1894, the year for Douglas was to be a bitter one with ill-health abounding. In January rain and floods delayed Harper's surveying around Lake Mapourika. Arthur Woodham, a gold prospector, joined Harper and Douglas to help with the swagging. Some years later he was to fulfil his friendship by helping to care for Douglas in Hokitika. In February the three of them endured a severe storm in a camp above the precipices on the spur of Moltke, west of the Franz Josef Glacier, and in the middle of the night the tent fly was blown away. Harper wrote:

> Cold as I was, with my almost naked body, I almost smiled at Douglas's wild appearance. seen at intervals in the uncertain light, when we came near one another, his solitary garment fluttering in the wind, and every moment a hasty remark would be heard as he slipped with his bare legs on the wet grass . . . We then donned our wet garments, having wrung them out, and rolled in our wetter blankets, lay waiting for dawn. Poor old Douglas was chilled to the bone, and I really feared he would be unable to face the storm and journey down at daybreak.

Boiling cocoa warmed Douglas up, and after noon they forced a descent in gale and fog to the welcome shelter of the bush. Two days later in clear weather they finished their observations, but Douglas 'had another attack of his influenza'.[11]

On 12 February Roberts wrote urging Harper to put his best work into the report with Douglas on the Franz Josef Glacier, and finished with: 'Depend on me obtaining, for you & Douglas, the fullest credit for your work.' Nearly two weeks later he wrote with a hurry-up exhortation about the Franz Josef maps and reports, and referred to the instructions for Cook River work. On 11 March Roberts allowed a rather despairing note to intrude, not realising perhaps that Douglas had really been ill: '. . . poor old Douglas is done for: he is no more like my old companion than I am physically. So we must just potter along as best we can. I have backed him in all I know but in future he must steer his own craft.' He also referred to Douglas being on the spree at Okarito Forks.

A week later Roberts acknowledged the Franz Josef plan and report, and explained he had sent Douglas a duplicate of the map. Then followed a remarkably clear instruction about the method and importance of reconnaissance survey work, which gives, as nothing else can, the key to the value of Douglas and Harper as explorers and puts them in historical perspective.

> You and Douglas will please go over the map, *bit by bit*, and *cram* on to it, *rough* as you like, but *plainly*, such information about the various local

features, in the shape of timber, grass &c. &c . . . I don't care how much you crumple or soil the maps sent so long as you furnish on them the information asked for. I think I have been sufficiently plain in my notes about one important item – viz. – the fixing on the plans or writing in the reports, positions and heights *by guess* and even those not estimated on the spot but *now* set down *from memory*. Now to a man like you of legal training and therefore precise ways as to what is fact &c., this method may seem almost absurd, but, in reality it is merely the extreme of all possible methods, at all events of almost all possible.

When Cook sailed along the Coast, he fixed Cook, Tasman &c. *fairly well* and *sketched* in the main chain [in fact Stokes did this in 1851] – next our first surveyors here took a bearing or two and they *charted* in the features *a little more exact*. Then I came along and *fixed for all time* the heights and positions of all the notable peaks both on the main and lateral Ranges and from sketches with bearings mapped the intervening ridges &c. a little more exact. And *now* you go up a valley, the salient features of which are fixed and you elaborate the minor points &c. Still you havent been able to go to every creek, cliff, &c., hence you, in turn, *must sketch* in what you have been unable to measure and your *'estimated positions'* are the *best up to date* and will remain so, until a more refined survey is made in the future. And when such survey is made, no one can cavil at your work, it was Reconnaissance work simply.

Roberts seems to have been worried that Harper would be discouraged by the defections of Douglas. He wrote: '. . . don't pitch up your present work . . . I know full well the annoyances you have suffered, but I do think that, in the future, Douglas will do better', and he made other similar comments about the problems posed by Douglas's poor health.

In fact Douglas and Harper had, on 18 March, begun their memorable Cook River trip. Using the route previously explored by Douglas in the 1880s, they crossed the Craig Peak spur to the Balfour Glacier, which they traversed up to the cliffs under Mt Tasman. Harper and Betsey Jane had exciting races with fog to get bearings; mostly the fog won.[12] They returned to the Cook River valley near the end of the month.

While Douglas finished his report in April, Harper visited the Fox Glacier. He had the bad luck to twist his ankle but persevered with a trip to the Chancellor Ridge, from which he descended to the Victoria Glacier. On returning to his bush camp he found it burnt out. Later Douglas and Betsey Jane joined him to finish mapping the Fox. In May they went up the Cook River itself, where the rough going and huge boulders occupied their time and their thoughts. Harper described one cave camp as

a low-roofed cavity under a huge boulder, in which sat two ragged men on a log in front of a large fire, and a hungry-looking dog close by. The men would be of doubtful nationality, having long, unkempt hair and beards, and with skins as brown as a penny. In all probability their clothes would be hanging at the side of the fire drying, and they would be sitting, with their blankets wrapped round them, smoking their pipes and possibly playing a game of cribbage with a pocket-book marked out as a board; or perhaps both would be reading – one lying down on the dry scrub, which served as bedding, and the other sitting up. Periodically the dog would get up, and, stretching herself, would put on a piteous blind-man's-dog look in hopes of coaxing a little something to eat, but without success.[13]

By the time they reached the La Perouse Glacier at the head of the river, winter snow covered the scrub. Short of rations, they returned to William Wilson's camp at the Cook River settlement, where his cook, Bill Boyd, gave them a grand feed. For this they named a glacier after him. On 8 April Roberts had written to Harper telling him that the map and reports were what he had wanted and that the topographical map of the Franz Josef was finished. He asked Harper to 'pile on the agony' about the difficulties of the work in future reports, as the public liked that sort of thing. 'If you were to go up Cook and then sit down and simply say you'd been there, I'm hanged if they would subsidize you to go up Tasman.' He also referred to the lethargy of Douglas.

> Oh! yes, down south, they have all drifted into Maori habits 'plenty more days to-mollow' &c., and Charles in his old age has somewhat caught the infection. In the sheet of aneroid readings he sent, there is rarely an early record. In my own time many a hill we went up candle in hand reaching the grass at day-light and came down again in the dark. But a few years of this will cook any man.

Roberts promised to try and get Harper and also Douglas another shilling a day. Finally he congratulated the pair on the accuracy of their map: '. . . for compass work over such country it is simply extraordinary'.

Nearly two weeks later Roberts wrote to Harper that 'Douglas point blankly refused "to pile on the agony" and so this report on F. J. Glr will lack the "interesting" personal narrative of the Copland River'. With the Cook River job done, Harper tramped north to Hokitika and, after six weeks' office work, wintered in Christchurch.

Douglas stayed on in the Cook River district. He went up the Fox Glacier with Wilson's survey party, and it may have been on this occasion that he found 'a little below the terminal, on the southern bank, a fine hot spring', which he reported as smelling 'bad enough to cure anything'.[14]

On 10 July Douglas wrote an appreciative letter to Harper (see pages 172–74). The references to Harper's photographs are particularly interesting, showing that Douglas was intrigued by the images. There are pointed remarks about the alpine climber Tom Fyfe, who a few months later led the first ascent of Mt Cook, and about the differences between climbing peaks and surveying. There is a sad note about Betsey Jane, 'now gathered to her fathers, when on Ryans peak I sent her back to camp as there was some rock climbing to do & have never seen her since. She must have tried to follow me & gone down a crevasse or over a precipice peace to her ashes.' Douglas must indeed have mourned the loss of another faithful companion of many adventurous expeditions.

In September 1894 Harper returned to the Franz Josef Glacier, hoping that spring conditions would bridge the crevasses and enable him to get material for a supplementary report. His companion was an unenthusiastic novice who refused to climb to Graham Saddle. On their return to civilisation Harper found instructions to explore the Karangarua with Douglas, and learnt at Gillespies Beach that he was at Scott's farm.

The object of the expedition was the same as Douglas had followed in the Copland two years before: the need to find a pass to the Hermitage 'free of snow and ice for three months in the year' over which a tourist track could be made. The Franz Josef and Cook River surveys had proved that no such pass existed in those regions. In the event of the Karangarua connecting with the Landsborough and so to Brodrick Pass and Lake Ohau, Douglas and Harper were to report on that route.

They left Scott's home on 1 October 1894, and made their base further up the valley with batwing tent and 'futtah' (whata). Betsey Jane's successor was Eggs, who proved unsuitable for the bush work. In wet weather they swagged past the 'Poison Camp', where Douglas had been so ill in May 1892. Unfortunately this time Douglas was, by 17 October, attacked by rheumatism and was forced to return to Scott's.

A new mate joined Harper, but he was not interested in the hard work and eleven days later he left for the delights of Gillespies Beach. After enduring some floods and lonely travelling in the Twain Gorge, Harper was joined by Ruera Te Naihi, also known as 'Bill the Maori'. Douglas made a plucky effort and rejoined Harper on 29 November, though 'not yet really fit for work'. As usual rain fell incessantly, until on 6 December the weather cleared. By 18 December Harper had reconnoitred a route to the Landsborough, but Douglas was again incapacitated by rheumatism and for the final time had to return to Scott's.

Harper and Ruera Te Naihi made a significant exploratory trip. They went up the Karangarua, completing the survey of that river, then over Karangarua Saddle into the Landsborough, which they followed down to its junction with the Haast. There they met a track party who satisfied their hunger. On the way back up the Landsborough Harper ascended Brodrick Pass, which he found unsuitable for a tourist route. Then the pair returned to the head of the Karanga-rua, before reaching the head of the Twain River via the McKerrow Glacier and Douglas Pass. Although short of food, Harper explored the upper part of the Twain River (later renamed the Douglas). Then he and Te Naihi returned to the upper Karangarua and descended that river to reach Scott's on 7 February after a marathon nineteen weeks in the ranges.[15]

Douglas was 'very little better, and only able to walk a few yards', so Harper completed his map and prepared to go up the Copland to find a route over the Main Divide to the Hermitage. Before he could do so, FitzGerald and Zurbriggen arrived, confirming that a crossing was possible, though in their lack of bush experience they had made heavy weather of the Copland valley. Harper took them up onto Chancellor Ridge and then, via the Victoria, Fritz and Franz Josef Glaciers, they made the first crossing of Graham Saddle on 4 March 1895 and descended to the Hermitage. Harper returned alone to Westland over the actual Copland Pass to complete more survey work.[16]

The 1895 Survey Report[17] referred to the illness of Douglas and paid him a long and well-deserved tribute (see page 293). By this date he was called 'Mr Explorer Douglas' by the Survey Department, just recognition of his lifetime work.

Between December 1894 and April 1895 Douglas stayed with the Scott family at the Karangarua. He was annoyed at a rumour that Scott had 'kept' him, when in reality he paid £1 a week board for the full period.[18] Douglas was too proud to be a sponger. By the end of April he was at Bruce Bay. From the Haast on 10 May he wrote again to Harper with a lively account of photograph-ing Maori at Makawhio Pa at Jacobs River, and referred to the completion of the Cook River report. Inherently honest, he refused to write about the Karangarua for Roberts, because all the work was Harper's.

In July Douglas was installed at the Waiatoto, where there was a severe winter, as in the rest of the Southern Alps. Douglas reported that the frost froze the eels in the shallow lagoons. In September he tried to get to the head of the Waiatoto after his rheumatism was better, but, he wrote to Harper, the terrific snowfall blocked him.[19]

The Annual Survey Report 1896 printed the description by Douglas of the Cook River, noted the work of Wilson and Douglas on the Fox Glacier, and pointed some scorn at the claims by FitzGerald to have discovered the Copland route. On 13 September Roberts wrote to Harper about the reactions of Doug-las to FitzGerald: 'What a fraud that chap FitzGerald has turned out . . . Old Charlie has enjoyed reading Fitz-gerald's romancing. The old boy always kept telling me that Fitz would throw you over, just to make use of you.'

Roberts also explained that Douglas had spent the winter of 1896 in

Hokitika, working up his geological notes for south of the Cook River, which gave substance to a large-scale geological map. Much of his paper on the Fox Glacier was turned down by the Surveyor-General as being too controversial because it did not fit accepted thinking about glaciers.[20] Roberts hinted that this paper and others should be sent 'Home to Prof. Quilan who will be able to give it due publicity and also to criticise it to some advantage', but if this was done the fate of the material has never been recorded.

Earlier, in March and April 1896, Douglas worked up the Whitcombe valley with Alf Dale and Bill Fleming. He made fine sketches of Mt Evans and the party traversed the tributary valleys of the Price and Cropp Rivers.[21] Douglas also crossed the Whitcombe Pass to the upper Rakaia, and traversed from the trig station near Duncans Hut to the terminal face of the Lyell Glacier.[22] What a contrast the wide bed of the Rakaia River would have been after the confines of the Whitcombe bush. Indeed, if we except his trip to the Bealey with G. J. Roberts and his wife in 1897, this was the only time Douglas crossed the Main Divide to Canterbury. There is nothing to show that Douglas and his companions went down to the nearest sheep station, at Manuka Point, though it was merely a day's march if the river was low. By now Westland was deep in his blood and the bush spelt security – Douglas continued to be reserved and shy with strangers.

William Wilson and Douglas went south by steamer from Hokitika in August 1896. With Ruera Te Naihi, Douglas did some intensive prospecting up the Paringa, the scene of his earliest exploring in the late 1860s and early 1870s with Tommy Law. The following month he found his rheumatics troubled him less after an occasional ducking. On 5 October Douglas wrote to Harper, who by then was practising law in Thames, about his work with Wilson on the Fox Glacier. In the letter he also expressed a low opinion of some of the local inhabitants and ended with a caustic reference to FitzGerald as 'the real discoverer of N. Zealand not Tasman as so long supposed'. Roberts was the recipient of another letter written nearly two weeks later, in which Douglas gave further details of prospecting and asked to be remembered to the Macfarlanes.

Although some letters from Roberts to Harper have survived in good condition, only a copy exists of one from Roberts to Douglas, on 7 November 1896. It is partly illegible, owing to the acid of the copying ink having eaten away the paper. What remains shows that Roberts had instructed Douglas to locate reefs in the Paringa near Mount Argentum and to observe close secrecy. Roberts was, perhaps, suffering from gold fever, a state of mind endemic to many of the inhabitants of Westland.

In 1897 the official Survey Report notes that Douglas was again working on the Whitcombe valley track, which seems to have been his stand-by employment over several years. Roberts also kept Harper in touch with Douglas, writing on 12 April that 'Douglas is grading a road up the Hokitika River and I don't expect him down for several months yet'. He also mentioned his hope that he could get Douglas 'the Gold Medal of the R. G. Society'.

In fact the *Journal of the Royal Geographical Society* of May 1897 recorded the award of 'the Gill Memorial to Mr. C. E. Douglas for his persistent explorations during twenty-one years of the difficult region of forests and gorges on the western slopes of the New Zealand Alps'. Harper's advocacy had been instrumental in this award, which was well deserved by Douglas and was the only real public acknowledgement of his feats over so many years.

The same journal in December gave a summary of the speech made by Sir Clements Markham about the award, to which Walter Kennaway, secretary to the Agent-General for New Zealand in London, replied. Kennaway had himself mustered sheep in the Canterbury ranges and was a brother of Laurence Kennaway, who in his book *Crusts* (1874) had described his own explorations. In his 'Soliloquy Letter' Douglas included a wry note about the award:

> I never shone in a Home telegram but once, and it was a tolerable speciemen. Here it is, as far as I recollect. The Tzar of Russia has a slight attack of influenza. Mr. Charles Douglas has been awarded the Peak prize for explorations in the Southern Alps. Huggings the Derby murderer has been hanged. Price of Consols 3% . . .

But the prize that Douglas had gained was of some significance:

> The Gill Memorial . . . was founded in 1886 by Miss Gill, sister of the eminent traveller Captain W. J. Gill who lost his life during the Egyptian campaign of 1882 and was applied by the Council of the Royal Geographical Society 'in encouragement of geographical exploration' . . . awarded annually.[23]

Roberts, like Harper continuing to be supportive of Douglas, revealed more about Douglas's reaction when he wrote to Harper on 28 July 1897:

> it was quite evident that [Douglas] fully appreciated the Gill Prize. I suggested to him that as the R.G.S. gave him the option of L.S.D. or its equivalent, that he should get a piece of plate duly inscribed . . . to forward it to his brother in Scotland . . . But old Charlie had other views: so he wrote asking the Secretary to forward a fixed-focus ¼ plate Camera with film, spools &c. We concocted a letter of thanks and told the great man what sort of fixin' was required.

However, when the camera arrived it was too complex for Douglas to manage, so he gave it away and persevered with the one Harper had given him. A letter from Roberts to Harper on 14 October commented: 'he won't part with your old camera. I could almost fancy that he considers it his "luck" or feitch, perhaps the old pagan worships it on the quiet.'

In his July letter Roberts also gave a lively account of a trip with his wife and Douglas to the Bealey, on the Waimakariri River near Arthur's Pass.

> Charlie bobbed about with Mrs. Roberts whilst I took a series of bearings to fix certain features on the Divide. Cockayne, the Botanist, heard we were there and he came up for a chat. He didn't know that Charlie was with us, so his delight was great at meeting him and they talked botany all one night & well through the next day, the consequences being that Cockayne and Douglas purpose putting in a month this year down on the Cascade Plateau.
>
> Mrs Roberts had never been on ice before, so we went down and Charlie towed her about to her huge delight and as a memento took the Triumvirate on the ice.

Unfortunately, the Cascade trip never came off and the opportunity for Douglas to help Cockayne was lost. Douglas's seclusion on the West Coast meant he was unable to mix with many people who were interested in examining the natural world, and this limited his contribution to the work of others and perhaps also his own learning, though he read whatever he could.

Roberts' letter to Harper of 14 October 1897, like others, also revealed much about the likeable character of Roberts the man. He was primarily a mountain man and nostalgic for his energetic past. He continued to show his interest in the mountains when he was physically unable to indulge in alpine or bush travel.

> I lie awake o' nights and roam for hours along the old peaks and revel in latitudes unknown to the common herd and in the lamp-light, when alone, I run my magnifier over the photos and gloat thereon . . . Don't I hunger for the snows? Wouldn't I give 20 years for a sound heart? Don't I sneak around my wife's little rockery, when no one is near, and stroke her mountain veronicas &c. and get full up of snivelling self-pity and then coming to myself say damn with a big D. Haven't I refused promotion 5 times and coaxed the S.Gl to leave me here? Don't I put up with this miserable hole full of greatest beggary and under-bred would be's – and isn't my wife loving enough to stop also? All for what? All for the sight of the old giants in the east and south and a sniff of mountain air. And am I not just a blind old fool to write all the above.

Roberts continued with news of Douglas: 'He is now down at the Fox terminal erecting a Tourist Hut and fooling about in a C.E.D. style.' Roberts also explained that his wife and a Greymouth lady climber, possibly Jane Thomson, were heading for the Franz Josef: 'Most probably when Douglas gets up to the Waiho these two camerista will pop in at his Bat-wing for afternoon tea and confiscate him for a few weeks.'

In spite of his disabilities Douglas was still active in 1898, building another glacier shelter hut and track-making in the region of the glaciers. His companion was Alf Dale, who recalled an incident when he and Douglas were double-banking on their packhorse across the Three Mile Creek near Gillespies Beach. Dale slipped off the horse to make things easier for Douglas, and was a strong enough swimmer to reach safety. When Douglas remarked later that eleven men had been drowned in the creek, Dale replied that he was not going to be the twelfth. Dale also remembered that the only time that his companion spoke sharply to him was when he rescued Douglas's boots from the rain outside the tent and dried them. Obviously Douglas took waterlogged boots as routine.

To Roberts, Douglas gave a thought for the times in a letter written on 30 January 1898:

> if taking the World easy makes genius, Westland ought to turn out Homers and Shakespeares by the score . . . and the very cows, by which so many make a living, would often not be milked but for the roars of their offspring . . . this hurry scurry of modern life makes the said life hardly worth having.

Douglas may have felt his homelessness keenly as he aged. He complained that his relatives were usually grimly misanthropic in their letters from Scotland. His brother, presumably Sholto the banker, had sent him photographs of his home. 'I can't see that he has much to growl about,' wrote Douglas, 'if only he saw Castle Douglas on the Waiatoto, or my present bat-wing subsidised with sheets of iron. Yet I am comparatively happy and contented.' His happiness lay in his work and environment. When age and incapacity denied his capacity for work, he experienced a certain desolation of loneliness unsolaced by useful activity.

There was further work with Wilson that consolidated their friendship, though the younger man was often employed on the sort of energetic trips that Douglas could no longer do. In February and March 1898 Douglas made traverses at Waiho and in the lower Whataroa valley. He also worked on the Fox Glacier and explored in the Totara and Waitangi valleys.[24] From 1 May to 24 June Douglas made traverses of the Whataroa to just above its junction with the Butler, and of the lower Perth, but he could not reach the headwaters because severe frosts on the rocks made travel dangerous.[25] Then, as usual, he wintered in Hokitika with Roberts and continued on the geological map work.

From this time, with only one exception, there are no further letters from Douglas to Roberts or Harper. Fortunately the annual reports of the Survey Department continued to give loyal credit to Douglas and, with the accurate reminiscences of friends, they comprise a substantial record of useful work.

In fact, reports by Douglas were to be prolific for the next few years, giving evidence of his travels and continued work.

The Survey Report of 1899 noted that Douglas was still grading the Whitcombe track, where a flood in January had destroyed much previous work: '. . . in places the mountain appears to have gone into the river, leaving nothing but the bare rock'.[26] Later that year he made a 'rough topographical survey of the agricultural block in the Waitaha valley', and 'thoroughly explored and mapped a large area of unknown coastal country between the Mikonui and Poerua rivers'.[27] It was also in 1899 that he compiled a monumental report on the passes, swamps, towns, glaciers and geology of Westland. When in Hokitika, Douglas was given 'a bach at the back of the office', and it was there at the Survey Department that he wrote up his reports.[28]

But one significant expedition still awaited Douglas: up the Wanganui River in 1900. Companion to Douglas was William Gunn, son of a pioneer who in 1875 had found a Divide pass from the Perth to the Rangitata.[29] Douglas and Gunn did not reach the glaciers at the very head of the river, but from the confluence of the Wanganui, Lambert and Adams Rivers they climbed to the end of the Lord Range and mapped the fringes of others. Douglas's report contained his usual attention to topographical detail and showed his interest in forestry, wildlife and geology. His maturity of outlook was evident, and his reflective mind gave depth to his views. Oddly enough, the official Westland Survey Report gave no inkling of an important task fulfilled.[30] In later years the ranges were explored by geological surveyors and mountaineers. John A. Bartrum of the Geological Survey remembered that he invariably found cairns mapped by Douglas, a tribute to his accuracy.[31]

The Wanganui was Charlie Douglas's last major trip. In 1901 he completed surveys at the head of the Otira River near Arthur's Pass.[32] As usual he shunned Canterbury. In 1902 Roberts was promoted to Chief Surveyor and Commissioner of Crown Lands, Westland, and he reported that 'Mr Explorer Douglas' had made a detailed map of the lowland between the Poerua and Whataroa Rivers.[33]

The first part of 1903 was devoted to fieldwork to the east of Okarito, with more later,[34] but it is clear Douglas was only spasmodically active. A diary entry for New Year's Day reads:

> spending it at Murphy's, been rain, most of the week and done very little all last month, being engaged in recruiting my health by having a spell and regular meals. Am now getting better & hope to be able to do something this month. Rain all night and part of next day.

Two days later it was still raining and he was 'writing letters home . . . about time I did so'. Later in the month William Gunn joined Douglas again, and in

February and March they cut lines and chained traverses in the usual way until they had to meet Roberts at Okarito. In April Douglas was ill again, but he recovered and continued surveys by the Okarito Lagoon. His comments were mostly confined to 'rain all day' or 'fixing stations and points over Lagoon, mapping, sketching', with the odd variation such as 'Harrys bitch pupped' or 'Willie went to Okarito for stores'. On 20 May the diary closed.

The 1903 Survey Report noted 'Mr. Douglas's explorations of the coastal lands immediately south of the Whataroa River'.[35] During the winter of 1903 he must have been in Hokitika completing the second of the huge mile-to-the-inch geological maps for Westland. The first map was from Hokitika to Okarito, and the second from Okarito to Big Bay. One of them was eighteen feet long and five feet across. Both were cross-sectioned in places and hatched and shaded in colour. These maps were the culmination of his geological observations and were used in the New Zealand International Exhibition, staged in Christchurch in 1906–07, in the Geological Survey part of the Mines Department exhibit. Douglas received no credit for this work, but James Cowan, in his *Official Record of the New Zealand International Exhibition*, with reference to the West Coast section, did note 'an immense variety of minerals of various sorts collected by Mr. G. J. Roberts, Mr. Charles E. Douglas, the veteran pioneer prospector and explorer of South Westland, and other mineralogists and surveyors'.[36]

Probably Douglas gained great vicarious pleasure from these geological maps, and much later Mildred Mueller pointed out the importance they undoubtedly held for him. She wrote that the second one

> must be Douglas's Swan Song. It could only have been done by someone who had all the time in the world, and few duties; which was Douglas' condition for some time as he gradually became less & less able to do anything. It is beautiful – beautiful in colour and workmanship – detailed to the last degree. One can imagine that poor lonely-hearted man putting his soul into it – each detail of each valley, every river curve, mountain mass and mineral contents being put in with remembrance of the thrills and intense interest the discovery & exploration of each thing gave him. In doing it, he must have escaped from his office, in spirit, and re-travelled hundreds of miles, hearing and seeing again (as ageing people do, who work upon their past) all the loveliness, all the surprises, as well as the hardships that were theirs.
>
> I was glad to hear of that map – it was probably his escape from the lonely bewilderment that I believe was his towards the end.[37]

By October 1903 Douglas was back at Okarito, then to Whataroa Flat, and it was at this time that the second part of his 'Soliloquy Letter' was written (see pages 265–73). These are valuable and revealing documents. It is not known whether these letters were ever sent to Scotland in their original form, but the pencil drafts explain many things. By now Douglas hated writing reports and was completely cynical about tourists. He was not interested in politics; scientists were pests; his nerve and strength were failing; he mistrusted company promoters; and he needed quietness 'undisturbed by football or horsey maniacs'. He thought about a move to 'a small uninhabited island . . . or a hut in the most inaccessible part of the country'. If these revelations were not the whole truth, they were at least the unburdening of a man's feelings, the expression of a series of moods in which decline bred bitterness and disillusion.

Here was almost an end to the active period of his life that had contained regular exploration. Now in his sixties, such labour was no longer for Charlie Douglas. Ahead lay desultory work, followed by strokes, official retirement, and further ill-health, though the last years of his life were cheered by the devotion of a few good friends.

SIX

Last Years

From the early 1890s Charlie Douglas was affected by illness, especially rheumatics, no doubt brought on by his strenuous efforts over many years in the difficulties of the West Coast rainforest. By the beginning of the twentieth century, when he was over sixty, he needed the assistance of younger men to cope with his preferred life of exploration. After 1903, with the friendly supervision of G. J. Roberts, Douglas worked where he could for the Survey Department. Now, instead of exploring remote areas, he surveyed and filled in gaps, often on less rugged land where the government aimed to settle farmers. He also continued to work on fair copies of his earlier field notes and reports.

Douglas's working life was brought to an end by a stroke, which was followed by another. But the last years of his life were not as dismal as has sometimes been thought. Douglas lived in Hokitika, in reasonable comfort, supported by a government pension. He was probably frustrated in himself at not being able to roam as he might have liked, but at a time in life when he needed assistance, it was provided by good caring friends.

Douglas continued to be employed by the Survey Department after 1903. In the Survey Report of 1904 Roberts gave characteristic credit to the veteran explorer and surveyor:

> Mr. Douglas has thoroughly explored and mapped the wild, forest-clad hummocky country to the east of Okarito, and, as usual, furnishes much information of this tangled wilderness which is interesting and valuable.

Yet Douglas's writing on the Okarito district of October that year is rather dull. This is not so much a reflection of the lack of variety in the district, but rather a lack of the joy of life that so enlivened his earlier writings. Now and again the old traits of humour and good spirit break through the gloom, and infirmity does not take the edge from some aspects of his work. The topographical and geological detail remain meticulous, and the conscientious summaries of information continue.

That Douglas was still capable of contributing in a less active way to the work of the Survey was confirmed in the 1905 report, which stated:

> various blocks of forest-covered country . . . to be subdivided for settle-
> ment . . . Maps, accompanied by detailed reports were in all cases for-

warded for inspection and approval before cutting up the areas for public selection. Mr. Douglas greatly assisted at this, to him, very congenial work, and also furnished much valuable information about other localities.

His companion for much of this work was Jim Gunn, a brother of William, who had accompanied him up the Wanganui. Jim was eighteen years old, and many years later he gave his memories of working with Douglas.

> Our first job was to put on maps the location of all mineral deposits and report on any land that may be suitable for settlement, also timber belts. We used a prismatic compass, an Aneroid and field book, using what Douglas called a step traverse method. When we got back to some sort of base camp, we plotted the data on to maps, but most of the field work he took to Hokitika and worked on in Robert's office
>
> We first started down the Whataroa River and camped near the Heronery on the Waitangi River. From there we went to the Big Waitaha River. Our next location was at the five mile beach. We worked around the Okarito and Forks area for some months. Our next shift was to the Franz Josef Glacier and later to Cook River where we checked peak heights and the rate of the ice movement of the Fox Glacier. About that time we were joined by Arthur Woodham. We did a fair amount of climbing in that area, up to 7000 ft. From there we went to the Paringa, where we also did some hill work.[1]

This was probably quite taxing for Douglas, but friendships continued, and in between two of these trips he took his holiday with the Gunn family at Whataroa in January 1906. A visit to the area by Richard John Seddon, Premier of New Zealand, was recorded in a photograph of the two great men of Westland, Charlie Douglas and 'King Dick', taken outside the Gunns' home. Frank Gunn wrote:

> It was the last time we were ever to see Seddon in South Westland. The crowd, which had gathered to farewell him, had dropped back behind the camera, but as the great Statesman took his seat, with his wife and daughter, in their carriage, three local residents stood where he and Douglas had sat, and sang 'Will ye no come back again?' King Dick doffed his hat and stopped the carriage. He died about five months later.[3]

Jim Gunn and Arthur Woodham continued working with Douglas through 1906, and in midwinter they were joined by 'George' Te Koeti and Tommy Sieron. Gunn wrote about their time at Copper Creek, north of the Haast River in June 1906: 'Part of our work there was collecting mineral and timber samples for the Christchurch exhibition.' From there Douglas, Gunn and Woodham moved north to Paringa, where they took soundings of Lake Paringa and collected samples of lithograph stone from Abbey Rocks at the Blue River mouth. They also did some low-level climbing at the head of the Paringa and Blue Rivers. Their final camp was in a bush whare built by Douglas and Gunn south of the mouth of the Paringa. By Douglas's previous standards this was all quite straight-forward, but it was over-strenuous work for a man of sixty-six. Gunn had clear memories of the next events:

> While we were there a small steamer called . . . Douglas sent me on the steamer to Abbey Rocks to help load the lithograph stone, about 9 miles south and walk back to the Paringa. I was marooned there through flooded streams for one week. Six miles of the route was along the tops of coastal bluffs in very thick bush. It took me nearly 12 hours to travel six miles.
>
> When I arrived at camp Douglas had been ill about five days, could not walk and his speech affected. Woodham could not leave him. It was ar-ranged then to get him out. We got help from people at Bruce Bay. He was placed in a small flat bottomed boat which was towed up the Paringa river by men on horses to where the main south track crosses the river. From there he was carried to Condons Homestead at the Maitahi River, twelve men taking turns to carry him.
>
> Four of us (Jim Nolan, Bill Ritchie, George Koeti and myself) did the river work, including the Paringa which was up to our arm-pits and . . . cold. He was taken from Condon's to Bruce Bay in a light dray where Roberts had arranged for the steamer to call for us and take us to Hokitika. That would be in the spring of 1906.

Gunn gives a sad image of the grand old explorer, paralysed by a stroke and carried by his friends through places where he had ventured so often with vigour, but Douglas recovered quite well. Mildred Mueller remembers him pad-dling through flood waters in Hokitika towards the Roberts' house when she was on a visit there. And at Christmas 1907 he was camping near Dr Ebenezer Teichelmann's bach at Lake Kaniere, to escape the festivities in Hokitika. There he met an old friend and companion, Arthur Harper, who was holidaying in the bach with his wife and two children. Douglas was able to relax with Harper and the children before Mrs Harper charmed him and, overcoming his reti-cence, enabled him to talk freely.[4] The Harpers returned to Greymouth but must have sent photos almost immediately to Douglas. On 14 January 1908 while he was still at the lake, Douglas wrote his last letter to Harper.

> Dear Harper,
> Many thanks for the photos. I have got a good picture at last of this lake. The photo of you and I is like no doubt, but somehow or other I always look like an old clothes man in a bush photo, certainly I had old clothes on but that not the trouble, no doubt my phiz is not suitable to the surroundings.
>
> You cleared out in time. The mosquitos for a week after you left were lively. They drove out the two artists in a couple of days, then a Parson & some youngsters pitched a bell tent & were evidintly going to stop for a week or ten days, but in two days they had fled ignominiously.
>
> Ever since you left, picknicers have been here in droves & the launch &

all boats have been in use. Very few people have called on me, so I can't complain.

I found your knife on the island all right. I don't know whether you wished me to send it to you, its not much worth – still I send it. Sometimes a fellow takes an affection for a pipe or an old knife far beyond their actual worth. I know I am that way myself.

Hoping Mrs Harper & the youngsters have recovered from the mosquitoes. If ever you come here for a trip, come the beginning of March.

I am leaving here next Saturday for Hokitika. What I am going to next or where I am to go I haven't settled yet. At any rate I must leave the Survey for good and all. I think Ill clear away South with a Batwing & turn Hermit.

Yours truly
Charles E. Douglas

His work for the Survey Department was over, but this letter shows the kindly, whimsical Douglas at his best, observing his world and being helpful to a friend. His yearning to be far from civilisation remained strong, but it was not to be.

In early 1908 Douglas, through the agency of Roberts, negotiated with the Under-Secretary of Lands and Survey over the Public Service pension he would receive. A small confusion was created when Douglas gave 22 November 1880 and then 1 June 1878 as the date he joined the department, but its records showed he began to be paid for his explorations on 1 April 1878. At the time of his retirement Douglas's annual salary was £170 per annum, and his pension was fixed at £85 a year, to be paid monthly through the Public Trustee. On this he would be able to live comfortably enough, as he acknowledged in a note of 31 March 1908. He concluded with: 'I shall always look back with pleasure to my experience in the mountains of New Zealand and though I am passing from active work I do so with regret.'

A second stroke followed for Douglas, probably in 1908,[5] though whether it was before or after his actual retirement from the Survey is unclear. He may have burnt some of his notes and diaries at this time.[6] After the second stroke he was very ill and Teichelmann suggested that Harper not visit Douglas for a period so that neither of the men would be embarrassed by the occasion.[7] Harper, occupied in Greymouth with business and a young family, then lost touch with Douglas, whose official retirement from the Survey Department came on 30 June 1908. Roberts wrote a moving and sincere tribute to Douglas in his annual report.[8] Jim Gunn's last remembrance of Douglas was some two years after his first stroke, 'when he walked into a bar in Hokitika and put down 6d. for a beer. I paid for his beer and talked to him for half an hour. He could not speak well then.' This was probably after the second stroke.

But the old explorer recovered sufficiently to do more summer camping near Teichelmann's bach at Lake Kaniere. Hec Davidson and Ces Preston remembered him there, walking and talking, in late 1911. 'Preston is adamant that Dr Teichelmann arranged for Charlie Douglas to go out to Lake Kaniere every Christmas–New Year period from 1906 up until the time he was permanently hospitalised.'[9]

That Douglas survived more than nine years after his first stroke – until he was nearly seventy-six years of age – is perhaps to be regretted. It might have been kinder if death had claimed him by a swift end in the mountains. But until his last two years he seems to have been able, much of the time, to potter about fairly happily and there is no doubt that he was well looked after in the period of his illness and old age.[10]

He lived in a two-roomed hut behind the house at 20 Fitzherbert Street, Hokitika, that belonged to Jane Ward, widow of his partner in the Paringa in 1874. Douglas must have kept in touch with the Ward family after the end of the partnership and the death of Ward in 1881. He had been popular with the Ward children (who called him 'Duggel'[11]) and one of the sons, Bob[12], had been track-cutting up the Copland with Douglas in the 1890s. Jane Ward's nursing experience was valuable, and she did much to look after Douglas, assisted from time to time after 1909 by Arthur Woodham. Very close by and willing to give support were G. J. and Mrs Roberts, though Roberts himself died in September 1910, the year after he retired from the Survey. Members of the Macfarlane family were also regular visitors.

Douglas did have 'bouts of pain and the recurring frustrations of poor speech, limited mobility and rheumatism'.[13] Sometimes these were severe enough to put him in hospital. Records of the Westland Hospital show that Douglas was admitted as a patient from 4 July 1911 for forty-four days, from 3 July 1914 for thirty-four days, and from 5 September 1914 for twenty-four days. Dr Ebenezer Teichelmann, Superintendent of Westland Hospital and a mountaineer himself, gave Douglas personal attention and the best possible medical care, until he joined the armed forces in August 1915. Ces Preston reported that 'when Explorer Douglas was hospitalised in old age the doctor saw to it that he had his hot toddies at night, as his rheumatics played up'.[14]

Only in 1914 did Douglas's condition deteriorate to the point where his friends could no longer look after him at Jane Ward's place. Ironically, it was at this time that he received a bequest of £100 following the death of his sister Margaret in 1914. Perhaps the money helped in the care Douglas required. He was hospitalised from 10 October 1914 and well looked after in the Westland Public Hospital till his death there on 23 May 1916. Douglas died at the age of seventy-five of a cerebral haemorrhage, with the death certificate signed by Dr J. A. Doctor, who himself was to do some mountaineering. Two days later Douglas was buried in the Hokitika cemetery by the Reverend P. B. Fraser of the Presbyterian Church. William Wilson, the former surveyor now in business in Hokitika, held Douglas's papers, but there was no estate and no letters of administration were required.

Even on the West Coast the death of Charlie Douglas was almost lost in the war then raging in Europe. The *Grey River Argus* of 26 May carried headlines such as TERRIBLE STRUGGLE AT VERDUN FIERCEST BATTLE OF THE WAR. However, the *Argus* did summarise an obituary notice from the *West Coast Times* of 24 May. The full text of the notice, with all its inaccuracies, was:

> Charles Edward Douglas. Aged 83. We have to record the death of Charles Edward Douglas at the Westland Hospital yesterday evening. The late Mr. Douglas who was a member of a well-known and historical Edinburgh family, left Scotland at the age of 19 years. After a visit to Shotover (Otago) diggings he came to the West Coast and was employed by the Survey Department for many years in making exploratory and geological surveys in the far south of Westland.
>
> The very valuable topographical plans of Westland compiled by the late Mr. Douglas bear testimony to his ability as a pioneer explorer and his records generally should prove of incalculable value to the district in the future. This special knowledge of geology was of extensive value in regard to the mineral deposits with which Westland abounds and his reports on the possibilities of the West Coast are borne out by the many valuable plans which are now in the possession of the lands Department. His labours were principally confined to South Westland and there was no man who was better acquainted with that part of Westland. The work was frequently carried out under very great difficulties and privations but it is gratifying to know that his records have been preserved for future generation.
>
> That his ability was recognised in other quarters is shown by the fact that he was some years ago presented with the Gill Memorial prize for exploration by the Royal Geographical Society.
>
> Mr. Douglas retired from the service on a small pension and has been an inmate of the Westland Hospital for some time. His many friends in Westland will regret to hear of his death.

A genuine tribute, but on the wider canvas of a world war his death was minor news, even in Westland. Yet he was cherished in the memories and writings of his friends.

Then grew the Douglas legend, of a man who had been everywhere in Westland, whose exploits in difficult conditions were the basis of an important part of New Zealand's pioneering and mountain traditions, and whose writings had been lost. Future generations, among them John Pascoe's, were to be stimulated by the legend, by glimpses of his feats in recorded history, and by the mountain features that bore his name. He had died, but memory of Douglas and his deeds survived.

Selections from
the Douglas Papers

Charlie Douglas wrote extensively in field books, notebooks and letters, but little exists of his personal writing from before 1890. This means the energy and adventure of his youth and early middle age are not recorded in his own words. It is regrettable that accounts of his major trips up the Arawata and Landsborough Rivers in the 1880s, for example, do not exist.

Most of his writing that remains comes from the period after Douglas became a full-time employee of the Survey Department in 1888. From that time he seems to have become more prolific, perhaps because he was required to keep field books and send in reports, which appear in various manuscript and published versions. He also had more cause to communicate with officials. Douglas's writing in this period shows that he was starting to feel the effects of his age and years of physical exertion in difficult country. Towards the end of the nineteenth century when he was becoming less active, he also consolidated much of his knowledge of the West Coast in various wide-ranging reports.

These selections from the Douglas papers are here presented in chronological order. Most are dated, and the few undated pieces have been placed as accurately as possible. These selections form nearly half the total manuscript material available.

Douglas's original phrasing has been retained throughout. His inconsistent spelling has also been left untouched in most cases. Some punctuation has been added and editorial explanation has been included to clarify meaning.

Although he often preferred to be alone, Douglas valued his links with a great variety of people on the West Coast, and he liked to keep up with the local news. Every effort has been made to discover the basic particulars of people mentioned in the letters, and many have been newly identified from electoral rolls, Post Office directories, and records of surveyors and West Coast history.

SEVEN

Letter to Gerhard Mueller, 1885

Paringa River
12 May 1885

G. Mueller, Esq
Dear Sir,

I have just returned from a seven weeks starve up the Okura [Okuru], and in rather a delapidated condition, whether I have made any discoveries remains to be seen, but if merely getting across the Devide is anything I have succeeded, having got over that impassable wall in three different places, found out the Quartz Reef country at last – but can't see any Gold – and completed my chain of Saddles from Mt Cook to the Ark to my satisfaction if to nobody elses.

As I had to come up to this place to dig Mr Macfarlane horse along the road, I take the chance of the Mail to send up the Map, and a few sketches, the remaining sketches and a full discription of my Journey will come up in a Mail or two. In the Mean time, I'll give a few particulars which will enable you to fix in a sort of a way this wonderful Maorie Saddle [Okuru to Blue] – so called because the Maorie didn't go through – and two others which I found.

The Saddle up the Actor [Ngatau] River is reached by travelling through a nine Mile Gorge, not a very bad one certainly. Then a climb up precipices, for three or four thousand feet. It is passable for a month or two in the year, that is all. What river or branch of a River it leads down is doubtfull, the Young probably. I could see into Otago certainly, but could locate no know point. The height is I should say about 6000 feet.

The other branch which though the shortest, I call the Okura is the way the Maorie came if he ever did come through. Half a Mile above the Forks it Gorges and rises very fast to the Upper forks. I traversed up Princes creek till it became impassable – a second edition of the Burk[e]. My last shot which I made two miles long, I think you will find goes through a low Saddle and down the Valley of the Burk. I saw an opening extending that distance but couldn't get up any place to see what it was. What I took for the Burke Saddle last time I was up, was only the Gap of Broken Gully a small creek coming out of Mt. Action.

Following the Okura for five miles through a bad Gorge, I got at last to the foot of what looked like an available Saddle, so I started with swag to go down what ever river it led to, but got nabbed in a four days Snow Storm. Mr M'Farlane says the snow lay a foot deep on the Flat at the Wanaka, so you can imagine the fix I was in, three thousand feet up & no preparation made for such an event. When it cleared up, I had to stop four days till the Snow was hard enough to travel on. Then I found I was in Blue River. The Saddle No 1 is about four thousand feet high, and so steep that I believe a Tunnel 3000 feet long would strike 1500 feet below the top of the ridge, but you will see by the Aneroid heights, which up to two thousand feet can be depended on, that the Grade down would be far too steep for a Railway. Mt Glissa down at the Forks would effectually stop any less grade being formed even if the precipices of Mt Actor could be dodged. To get down Mt. Citheron side is out of the question alto-gether, as the cliffs come in many places down to the river, and on both sides the Avalanches in Winter must be something to look at. The other saddle from which I saw into the Young is although 5000 feet high by far the best for a foot passenger to cross the range, the ascent is easy on both sides, and if the snow is off, the best way to go over the range is to climb Mt Platea from this saddle, and follow the range down between the Blue River & the Young. I have marked the various branches of the Young with a A? as I am not perfectly sure what they are. The Block marked doubtfull, I couldn't see into either from the head of the Okura or the Actor.

The tracing of the Turnbull & its branch the Ino [Mueller], I took from various spots along the range and I don't think there is much to alter in my older Traverse. I was correct in the Turnbull. As for the Ino, it does come out of the Devide and my tracings are approxo to its course. This Governors pass I wasn't on, but I saw what looked like a brake in the range, which in position is about the place. Mr Stewart said he saw a saddle up the Young or Wilkin, I don't know which; if it is a pass, it is impossable as far as any use could be made of it. In describing the Turnbull & Ino Rivers, I think I told you the sort of Gorges they possess: and down the Ino a road would have to go from that saddle. To wind up: the four saddles mentioned are utterly useless for road or Railway, and will never be used unless by an Alpine Explorer or other Lunatic. Besides the Saddles, the Range can be crossed in many places, by the same sort of beings. As mentioned before there are no Glaciers anywhere that I could see and few extensive Snowfield. I am not in a very comfortable state to write any more about the Country at present. The last Trip has given me a shaking. It will take a few weeks to recover, so I'll reserve what more I have to say when I send up the remainder of the Sketches. It is hard to write with Cows roaring pots & pans clattering, and the shivers on a fellow.

With reference to the enclosed Voucher, I wish you would pay it in to John Marks [Haast storekeeper] Account in the Bank of N. Zealand. The Speciemens of Birch [beech] for Prof Kirk I will get before long as I am going up the Arawata with Mr M'Farlane to cut down a large Tree and send a Section to the Exhibition; the payment I'll require from the Prof'r will be a few seeds of the Falkland Island Tussock Grass if he has any.

I am going off tomorrow or next day to the Copper load [lode] Thomas Range to dig a lot out, and I'll try and get a box away in the Steamer for you as I promised. In the Same box, you will find carefully wraped up a block of Jet Black Quartz, with some metal in it; it is out of one of the Reefs I have found at the head of the Ino River and I wish you would get it Analysed and see what it is made of. It looks like something. I found seven Reef altogether, the True Kinds, runing No & So. cutting the line of strike & dip, and with hanging walls, soft casing &c. I saw no gold in them, but they are worth digging into with something better than a Toy pick. The country they are in is well defined, Castor & Pollux is the center, and they are visible in one branch of the Wilkin, the Ino, Turnbull & Actor Rivers, but no where else not even in the Okura. They are in a species of green Scheist, closer grained than what we saw up the Waipara River.

But I'll write about that some other time they are now safe blocked to exploration till after Xmas.

Your parcel to me is down in the bay I haven't seen it yet, but will find it all correct no doubt.

Yours Truly
Charles E Douglas

EIGHT

South of Jacksons Bay and Cascade

As with many of the Douglas papers, John Pascoe extracted selections of particular inter-
est from these two manuscripts and omitted the detailed topographical and geological
descriptions. Both manuscripts are undated, and Douglas did visit the area a number of
times, but 1890 saw his longest period in the Cascade River.

These extracts show Douglas's antiquarian interest, a sarcastic view of nomencla-
ture and settlement, and a little of his theories of glacial geology.

. . . Two Miles south of the Hope River, at Ironbar point, the traveller puts
down his swag lights his Pipe and thinks: for at that point close to the edge of
the bush lies a mysterious relic of civilization. The object of contemplation is a
bar of wrought Iron three feet long and four inches square, and the puzzell is
how did it get there; for two miles on either side the sea is a mass of boulder &
broken Water, so it could not have been landed from a boat. It is too heavy to
carry overland, even if there had ever been Lunatics enough in that lonely spot
to do it. Billeys innumerable have been boiled against it. It has been prised over
and sate on to gain inspiration, but all in vain, its secret is buried in the deep.

I have been witness in two or three instances of the singular & unlikely
objects the Sea will sometimes cast up. On Gillespies an Anchor was run out
clear of the surf, with a line attached to facilitate boat landing; next morning
that Anchor was high & Dry on the beach. In this case, a bag of stones attached
to weigh it down, in reality brought it up, but in the next instance the Articles
had no such assistance but a piece of string tying them together. A Whaleboat
loaded with sundries while attempting to cross the Haast bar got capsized &
smashed and the only things besides two Saddles & fragments of the boat
which were cast up, were two 7 lb weights and a bundle of horseshoes, but it
would be too much to ask, that a 3 cwt [hundredweight] mass of Iron came on
shore the same way.

The only possible solution is: that at one time it formed part of the ballast
of a small Vessell which had been wrecked near, & the block came ashore fast
to some of the Timbers. But it must surely have been long before the coast was

opened, as there is no trace whatever of any wreckage about, & it takes years for ships timber to rot so effectually as to leave no trace behind.

Those digressions about Iron bars and Moarie Middens I fear have very little to do with Geology, but the subjects of Dips & stratas, river beds, & sea-beaches is such a dry one that a little livening up now & again will do no harm.

The Cascade River

This name will always be a standing protest against the absurd nomenclature current in many parts of New Zealand. Here is a River that stands alone in Westland, as the only one that is in no hurry to gain the Sea. With its feeders and those of the Old man & Barn River I believe it possesses more than fifty miles of navigable waters coming under the influence of the Tides. Verily the Canal would have been a more apprioate [appropriate] name, better far if it had been called after the ubiquitous Smith or the World renowned Jones or Brown, or if some twopenny ha penny dignitary, some chairman of a School board, had gained a spurious Geographical immortality, by having a river called after him, in that case the name wouldn't be deceiving.

I confess it is not easy to give good names in a new country, espicially when a number are required. After exhausting all the Jacks & Jills, the Buggins & Biffins in the district, I had at last to fall back on Miltons list of the Fiends and Homers catalogue of the Ships. The Cascade was so called in early time, from the number of Waterfalls falling off the Plateau into the Sea, but surely some Surveyor might afterwards have given its Moarie name, or manufactured one that would sound like Moarie; however it is too late now the Cascade it will be called to the end of time.

In January 1953 John Pascoe was particularly impressed by a place where the whole torrent drops 150 feet, an unusual feature for a main stream, and he wondered whether this was the source of the name.

To those people who only know Westland streams as foaming Torrents or rapid muddy rivers flowing over unsightly plains of shingle, a sail in a boat or Canoe, up the Cascade will be a bright spot in their existance, once experienced never to be forgotten, espicially in the early spring when the banks are yellow with Goai [kowhai] blossom, hanging in gorgeous festoons over the Water.

In that glorious future to which Westcoasters are always looking forward too, when the 'Something is bound to turn up' does turn up, when mines will be opened of fabulous richness, and when industries yet undreamed of will bring peace and prosperity, Churches Gaols & the Tax Collector to South

Westland, there may possibly be a Township formed at the mouth of the Cascade – Sandfly would be a good name –

If this ever takes place the inhabitants thereof, will be afflicted or blissed – according to haste with two well defined crazes. The first will show itself periodically in sending up the river a party of men instructed to find the Frenchmen's Cave, & bring down the Gumboot & the two Kegs [*a tall story Douglas told of hidden riches – see Appendix 1*]. The second craze will take the form of a chronic mania for Aquatic Pic-nics. At the Warfs of Sandfly will be seen the Poetic Gondola & the Unpoetic steam launch, the Unsociable Rob Roy Canoe & the still more unsociable cigar boat, while the Amateur built Flattie & the ponderous Dug out will add effect to the scene and assist Fever & Ague to fill the Cemetry. The talk of the inhabitants will be watery & boat racing & regattas the order of the day, but I doubt if the Scullers of Sandfly will ever be able to fully develope their powers, unless they race in Armour. Beach himself couldn't do justice to a race, if a Sandfly was enjoying its self on each of his elbows, and another was sinking prospecting shafts in his nose.

The great objection most people would have to the Cascade as a place of residence could be summed up in two word 'Mosquito's & Sandflies', but the Philosophical mind can derive instruction & amusement from even them, which more than counterbalances any annoyance they may give. As an encourager of early rising, and an enemy to sedentry habits, the Sandfly is more effective than all the homlies ever written 'Go to the Ant thou Sluggard' says King Solomon, or somebody, but the Sandfly is far superior to the Ant: he goes for you. At the first streak of day he proceeds to business; with a fiendish skill he soon discovers a hole or a weak spot in the blankets, in he goes followed by all his relations, and up you must get. If the Mosquito is not such friend to Virtue as the Sandfly, as he meanly attacks people when they ought to be asleep, he at least has been the cause of many vigerous additions to the English [language], and he promotes the manufactures of Gauze & Scrime [scrim]. If the night is warm, and he has gone into partnership with a few industerious fleas, the Mosquito is master of the situation, but revenge is sweet and all past miseries are forgotten, when a fellow gets under a Mosquito proof netting, and a flea is not to be had, then he can listen with delight to the Where-iz-ee of thousands of exasperated blood suckers.

Some people are never content but will insist on improving on Nature. A Gentleman in Hokitika of an Acclimatizing turn of mind, and who had heard about the Cascade once kindly offered to send me down a Jar of Leeches to introduce there. He said they would thrive gloriously. I explained to him that we had quite enough of that sort of glory already without stocking the Waters of Southern Westland with such bloodsuckers. To fight Mosquito's & Sandflies is bad enough but for a fellow to get his legs covered with Leeches every time he forded a stream would be too much altogether.

But I must start on the Geographical again, and leave Mosquitos & Sandflies to fullfill their destinies; if their place in creation is small, no one can say they neglect their duties, which is more than most men can say . . .

Then the Eels! Ye Gods think of them. Not the bull headed, black backed whiskered Vagabond that tastes like subextract of bog water, and is palmed off on a swindled Public as an Eel, but the long elegant formed light coloured Silver Eeel; a fish that eats like Salmon and is only found in large clear running streams never in Lakes or bogs, or Lagoons. Prejudiced people have come down to the Cascade who shuddered at the verry thought of eating such water serpents, but in a week or two they went back full of Eel & gratitude, confessed they had discovered a new pleasure, and left the place with regret . . .

I have now tried to explain in a sort of a way some of the Natural features of the Country south of Jacksons Bay. If I have failed it is not from the lack of ideas, but the inability to at present put those ideas together.

Perhaps the best way for anyone to write on such subjects would be to climb some high Peak. Sit down & try to imagine what the Country looked like during the Glacial Period say. Somebody or other says "To the Dreamer of Dreams comes flashes of light", and sitting on a hill Top, day dreaming in the Sunlight, a sort of Mirza like trance comes accross one, & countless ages seem to roll back, and the country altered to a scene of more than Arctic desolation. Not a bird, or beast, not a Tree nor Flower nor Tuft of grass, but Glaciers compared to which the Great Tasman is but a streak. Moraines alongside of which the Cascade Plateau would be a Molehill, hills, Mountains & Spur shattered & torn from summet to base & piles of Debris extending far out to Sea.

Yet the same Summer Sun was shining then as now, the sea had the same shells, the climate appeared to be the same, but over the land the Demon of Desolation seem to have past verily. It must have been a queer Country to make money in (almost as bad as now) but things that appeared at one time mysterious gradually cleared up. I could see how Schists from Mt Alba & Castor & Pollux could get to the Arawata, how Olivine could be found at the Mouth of the Haast, and Drift get on to Open Bay Island three miles out to Sea. I could see how the Gold found lying in the Gullies near the Sea from the Paringa to the Big bay might have come down the Haast or Arawata, or might have travelled from what is now far in the Watersheds of Otago & Canterbury.

Charles E. Douglas

NINE

Letters to Mueller
and G. J. Roberts, 1890

A first brief letter in early 1890 shows the continued emphasis on saddles across the Main Divide and something of the difficulties faced in the organisation of survey trips. It also indicates a difference between the ideas of staff in the office and the practicalities of those in the field. At this stage Mueller was still making efforts to bridge the gap.

Cascade River
Feby 1890

G. Mueller Esq
Dear Sir

I hear per last Mail that you are coming down some time in March for your Trip up the Okura, & I wish you would drop me a note, as to where I am to meet you & somewhere as to the date, or near as possible. On overhauling my Camp fixings, I find that I have nothing but a Bat Wing & two flys, & where to get a 6 x 8 Tent I don't know storekeeping down here is nearly extinct, so none are to be brought, & those who have Tents darn't unroll them or they would fall to pieces. Couldn't you send one down to the Haast per overland Mail. The other things, Blanket for you, Billys &c I can supply.

As for the stores I dare say, between Harris & Kron [Cron] all that is wanted can be got on the Haast; Topsey & the Rabbitt invading Army will supply the rest.

Mr Robarts [G. J. Roberts] says in his letter that you are going up the Okura, up Princes Creek & through the Saddle into! where! I see he has still a hankering after that imaginery route. There is no doubt that a Saddle exists at the head of the Fish; for that matter there is a fine wide Saddle between Mts Cook & Tasman. Why not go up the Turnbull & down the Actor? There you will see four Saddles through the range. I can then show you Quartz reefs in Galore, & the whole length of My Central Valley from the Ark to Mt Sefton, with all its Saddles lying like a Map before you; only to see this latter, would require clear weather & an extra day to Ascend Mt Ino.

It will be rather stiff Swagging this Trip whatever route you take, & I was thinking it would be better if I took a 50 lb. of Flour up to the Actor & Okura Junction before starting with the others, but as for that Ill wait till I hear from you. If you only get the weather we have had lately, the Trip will give you more to fill in Maps and reports than you dream about.

Yours truly
Charles E. Douglas

The next letter is undated and its opening is missing. It was written to G. J. Roberts and filed with 1898 letters, but internal evidence suggests it dates from some years earlier, probably 1890. James Hector was knighted in June 1887 and Gerhard Mueller moved to Auckland in April 1891, so the letter lies between those two events. Henry A. Gordon was Inspector of Mines around 1890. The clearest indication of date is the comment on 'last years Survey report', which must refer to T. N. Brodrick's 'Report on the Glaciers of Mount Cook' published in the AJHR, 1889, C.–1A, p. 32.

. . . to enable me to develope what I had only found traces of, and to prove many theories which I hold with reference to the country, but which from want of funds must remain in the Speculative stage. If Mr Mueller can manage to get the money as you suggest, good & well, but I have awfull doubts, and will give you my reasons. In my days of Innocence, I believed that all Government Departments were filled with bands of Patriots animated with one impulse: the unselfish desire to advance the interest of the Country at large. But it gradually dawned on me that the different Departments were at Loggerheads & intensely jealous of each other. Interests of the country be blowed, its the Interests of the individual office we look after. Sir [James] Hector as you wisely remarked would talk of the Insolence of an Amateur middling [meddling] with Geology & put his Veto on it, & Sir Hector is a Knight, & I believe the Son in Law of another & talk of Democracy & such like humbug. A handle to a mans name is a powerfull lever for both good & evil, espicially the Evil. How could he sit down & keep his hair on, if another Depart[t] – as would be the one case – had an unknown individual out in the ranges, who was sending in Maps & cross Sections flatly contradicting those elaborate Maps which the Mighty Knight has for years foisted on a deluded Public? Why can't the Survey get a Member Knighted or even made a Squire, K C M G, you would be on more even terms? Is the Depart[t] cursed with too much honesty to ever be offered manufactured honours?

Then the Minerological part of your programe that is the Mines Department; who or what is this Depart^t is I have never been able to make out. The Minister of Mines, is evidently a Dummy, like a Lord of the Admiralty at home & the Department means H A Gordon, from what Mr Macfarlane told me of his interview with the Minister. The Mines they intend to develop in future is the Gold & Silver in the Pockets of Tourists. No more roads for Diggers & to Diggins but Tracks &c to Waterfalls & Glaciers. This would certainly meet one of your suggestions, & I don't think Gordon would object to me, but the Depart would want the work done in their name. Now although I have tried Gordon to see if his department would assist me, and I am at him at present to get what Mr Mueller wont give me, that is An Aneroid Barometer, Clinometer Compass & a map of the Southern Alps like what the Survey gave Pauline [Robert Paulin, prospector and explorer]. Yet as you justly remark, I would far sooner work for the Westland Survey, then be bound down by Gordon's Modifications; his ideas of the work wouldnt be comprehensive enough for me. Yours are as they should be; they take in everything even to inveigling Tourist into the Country.

Then the feelings of the Survey[or] General has to be thought of. With that thirst for Paper Collar occupations which unfortunately distinguishes the rising Colonial, hundreds of young men have gone through an Apprenticeship as Surveyors, and found when too late that the country has no room for them. A man in the position of Percy Smith must of necessity be pestered with scores of such applicants. It makes a fellows hair stand on end to think of his fate if he allowed an outsider, a non passed C.E. [Civil Engineer] to get a billet, in which if the Salary was not great, anyone who thirsted for it could get his name up, and in which the Scope for good square blowing would be practically unlimited.

These are some of the reasons which make me doubt whether the Surveyor General will agree to the proposals in your report, at least as far as I am concerned, but try by all means. Even if another gets the work, he couldn't very well help taking me on wages, and although it wouldnt be pleasant to be bossed by some Juvenal Theodolite [young surveyor] & have to do not only all the hard work, but most probably have to supply him with Ideas, yet things have come to such a pass with me that I must get something to do or leave the country. I would have cleared out last year after Bullock Creek prospecting, but I had hopes that Mr Mueller would have sent down the Skeleton Map I wanted, for me to fill in during the Winter & be done with it. I don't like to leave the Coast till that is done, but Map or no Map I must go & that before long, I have only earned £5 this last fifteen months & my Garments would do for the Prodigal Son.

I got the last years Survey report from Wellington and I see that I was right about Mt Cook; that pass called Bakers Saddle at the head of the Hooker Glacier, is evidently the pass I suggested must exist if neither the Cooks or Karangaroa Rivers drawed from Mt Cook. Had Brodrick managed to get from the East side to the Top of the pass he would have found no Snow or Ice on this side & could have landed on Cooks River bed with little trouble. [*Baker Saddle actually leads to the Copland via the Strauchon.*]

To fill in the Map on this side, you will now have to do what I said long ago, that is widen the Douglas Glacier, & make the Neve what it really is, three times larger than any Snowfield in Westland. I am certain that Mt Copeland is it Western boundary, & the Stream which you thought might come from Mt Cook, drains the Small snowfield on the Western side of that Mountain. Mt Copeland is actually below what is called – but falsely – the line of perpetual Snow, & the large Neve is wholy independant of Mt Sefton. Yet from causes which I'll explain at some future time, you needn't be afraid that I am wrong, but this place has to be visited again & I only hope its myself will do it.

I hope Mr Mueller will come down and do those saddles up Okura. Some Cockney Tourist or Perambulating Theodolite from the East Coast will be discovering them. I see in all the new Maps that part of the Country is marked unexplored, now that is one of the most carefull traverses I have done in the Country, & why it is marked unknow I can only guess.

It is now about two oclock in the morning & I must close & get ready my Swag for a start to the Bay. The Weather is good, I have nothing particular to do & I intended to go up to Trig T N before long, so I'll leave my camp on the Jackson & go up next day when Ill do that sketch for you as well as I can.

I have an awfull lot more to write about but must put off to some other time. I don't know what is wrong with me, but I cant write nowadays without a painfull Mental effort.

Yours Truly
Charles E. Douglas

P.S. Many thanks for the Tobacco which I received all right & appologies for not acknowledging it sooner.
C E D

In early July 1890, when Douglas was spending part of the winter with the Macfarlanes, he wrote letters to Roberts and Mueller, rather different in content and tone. Both concern survey mapping, but the letter to Roberts also has more digression and a substantial geological focus.

Cascade River
5 July 1890

Dear Roberts

I am not very sure whether I am owing you a letter, or whether it is the other way, but which ever it is, doesn't matter so here goe's. I have commenced on large paper, and will try to fill it some way, there are a good many things I wish to write about, various subjects come into my head at once & among the lot is concerning prospecting, so, as the Newspapers say, We will start on that subject.

I have now been overhauling this awfull country for nearly fifteen years, & have finally come to this conclusion: that as far as alluvial Gold is concerned prospecting is just a waste of time. No field of any extent can ever possably be found in Southern Westland. So we can leave the Dredge Cos [companies] to sweep up the leavings of the Diggers & make money if they can. The Digger himself can die out, his usefullness is ended. The Cockatoo [small farmer], whether the Beef or Potatoe variety of the breed, can follow suit; unlike the Digger he never was of any use either to himself or anyone else, and it was a great mistake ever to bring him into existance. As for Reefs and other Minerals, they have to be searched for systematically, my prospecting all along, has simply been trusting to luck. One man in such an extent of country can do little else than find indications of where metals may be.

And now I am going to give up all further looking for anything new, & confine myself to the three places where the show is good; these places are the Mariners Peak belt, the Thomas belt, & the Ino belts. In all my Travells, these are the only places where I have really found Lodes with anything in them, and as I can't carry on this life much longer, I may as well finish what has been a hard but still a glorious existance in washing up & seeing if I have really found anything worth opening. As for the Coal and Iron my opinion is this; the country is not ready for them yet, it is all book talking about half million harbours at Paringa & Jacksons Bay, with smelting works & Coaling Mail steamers.

'After me the Deluge' says the present Colonial, so for present benefit they would exhaust their coal mines – which say what they like are limited – & invite foreign capital to walk off with their natural resources, forgetting in their blind greed that those resources should be held in trust for future generations, if New Zealand is ever to be one of the great nations of the Earth.

I am well aware that fools look on the study of History & the rise of nations as nonsense, so much time wasted, but if the people of the Colonies would study it a little, they would learn that no nation ever attained too greatness, unless they had self sacrifice as one of their virtues. We think we are doing a great stroke sending away thousands of Tons of Coal from Greymouth. When the day comes that we require coal for our manufactures, the mines will be worked out, then we must buy it back from other countries at a higher figure than we sold our own. The most of the money that comes in for coal does us no good, those who really benefit are the capitalist who borrow money from over-wealthy Britain, who at present is in reality sucking the life blood of the World. If our Coal fields were of immense extent, or if we were advanced enough in manufactures to use our own Coal, than by all means develop every Coal field & Iron mine in the country & turn sellers instead of buyers, but our Coal fields cant possably be large, & our Manufactures are still in the distant future.

My advice is keep our Coal & Iron for the future even though the present generation has to live out at the Elbows, but I suppose it is no use talking. New Zealand is in the position at present of a boy shaving for a beard, they want to be big before there time, forgetting that Nations like men must creep before they walk, and from their out of the way position on the Globe, they must husband their resources & develope a mental energy with self sacrifice as a leading National feature, & those qualities must be far ahead of what the Anglo Saxon has yet produced, before they can even be half as great as the Mother country. But enough of this rigmarole, let us again to business.

The opening of mines of Gold Silver & other metals are a different thing altogether from Coal & Iron, sell them by all means, the Noble Metals as they are called, are like Bank Notes. They represent cash and are a very good thing to have, but their value is a myth. They exert little more than a transitory influence on national advancement, so run them in by all means, work them out & be done with them.

That payable mines of Silver, Antimony, & even perhaps Gold exist in the three belts before mentioned I am certain, & now you have extended the field of operations in hinting at Tin. I am very doubtfull in the matter of Gold in Quartz in Southern Westland ever being found payable, but my reasons for thinking so would take too long to explain at present, & Gold or no Gold I will always look for it.

The Tin specimen you sent down opened my eyes considerably. Are you sure it is a Valuable Metal stuck through the Muscovite? If it is, then as I told you before, I know mountains of that glassy looking stuff, & if I reccollect aright, the same black looking ore was in it. That is the first thing to look after, and when I am up in the Paringa district I may as well overhaul it & the other

Reefs & Lodes I know of. I know the Reefs you speak about up on the Blue River end of the Thomson range, and away on the narrow ridge between Blue River & the head of the Thomas, is another patch I found year ago and payed no attention too, who would ever look for metal in such glassy looking stuff.

The other Belt is the one I got copper in, I call it the Thomas Belt, but in reality Mt Diomede & Citheron are the places to look. According to my Theory, the line ought to cross the Burke River, and on coming down with Mr Mueller, there was the reef indications about 3 miles above Strachans Creeks. Whether he noticed it or no & held his tongue as I did I don't know, but I don't think Mr Mueller when Travelling keeps his eyes open to anything outside of filling up maps.

No Three Belt up the Ino is the last I discovered, & I have only touched the edge of it; it is evidently the same line of reefs that run accross the country to Skippers.

Now I'll tell you what I am going to do this Summer, & I want you to assist me if you can. Every rock that I think may contain something valuable, I'll send to you, & I want it Analaysed without proclaiming the fact to the four corners of the Earth. Don't be afraid that I'll send up chips from boulders or boxes of Rubbish. Every speciemen will be from the parent rock, and although the usefull & the useless in metals are often very much alike, yet we must chance that a fellow can't carry a Laboratory with him, even if he knew how to use it, a Lode when found is always worth testing, even if Iron & Sulphur are all it contains.

I intend if possable to overhaul the whole of these places this Summer. The Burke I am going to tackle when ever the steamer leaves. If Mr Mueller gives me the Job to put up the Enamalled Plates on the Haast Track that I suppose will be £5 or thereabouts, which will pay my Tucker on the Trip & something to spare if someone else puts them up. Then I'll have to wait till the Survey has payed in the £12 to Harris' Account, before I can venture to get Tick for Tucker. This Trip wont take so very long, as I know exactly where to go & look, on both sides of the River, & your assertion which I am almost sure is right, that Strackans Creek can be crossed low down, has relieved me from thoughts of the aggravating climb up to the Grass & then down again.

Coming down from the Burke, I'll away up the Waitoto [Waiatoto] for a couple of weeks, to put up a Whare & cut a Track through the awfull Gorge of the Axius [Te Naihi] so as to be ready after X.mass to tackle the supposed Pass. Whether there be a pass or no, I must get accross the range & get behind the Ino Reef country. I am not going up the Waitoto with a few weeks Tucker, but will take up stores for six months, & punch them up to as close to the Axius & Waitoto Glaciers as possable before I commence work. I am not going to be stuck, as I have so often been, just when I gained the ground where my work should commence.

This Trip if I don't brake my neck will be a glorious one. No human being has even dreamt of going into the country around Alba, Castor & Pollux & Aspiring. I find my Brains getting stagnant, having no new country to visit, but the map of the East Side of the Range Mr. Mueller brought with him, & a few glimpses I have got of the country showed me that here was a place unknow, with plenty of room for unknow Alpine Lakes Waterfalls & Glaciers.

I heard Pauline [Paulin] – & for that matter other people – saying that the Westland Survey was far behind that of Otago & Canterbury in correctness &c. I dont know what it is down country, but if their side of the Southern Alps is all done like the map I saw lately, Westland needn't blush, & I shouldn't be a bit surprised if my Trip this Summer doesn't revenge you on them for Prigging Mt Cook, by annexing Castor & Pollux & perhaps Alba & The Dome. There is something wrong about the Axius River, its course & headwaters are still as mysterious to me as was the Copeland [Copland]. I know it drains the Castor Snowfield, but the main branch comes from some unknow spot away behind that mountain, but time will show.

After coming down from my preliminary Trip up the Waitoto, I'll be ready for the October Boat, at the Paringa, & the Stores of which I'll give a list to Mr Macfarlane, is all the assistance I'll require to Prospect the Paringa. I'll finish Mariners Peak first from Blue River, as I go along, with Tucker brought from the Haast.

This letter is an awfull jumble I know, but I can't help it, I am writing with Jack Zielian [settler at Jackson Bay] clattering about. I have no place where I can write in peace, & I am getting out of the Art of Letter writing, I can't collect my ideas some way, so I'll close & write an account of our Trip through the Burk next mail, when I'll be more at leisure.

Yours Truly
Charles E. Douglas

P.S.   Could you send me the first time you write two or three of the enclosed size of Brushes? I have plenty of all the others, Paper Paints &c.
C E D

Cascade River
8 July 1890

G. Mueller, Esq
Dear Sir,

I send by this Mail the Maps of the Burke & the Turnbull also about a dozen Sketches. I dont know whether Mr Robarts wanted me to plot out the Traverse of the Haast from Grassy Creek downwards, but as I sent up the field book, I thought I might as well leave the mapping till I had got the Ruler &c which has not come down yet. I had to plot with a Carpenters foot rule & the scale puzzeled me. 48 chains to an Inch sounds queer but I couldn't help it. If the Maps won't do I can easily do others when I get the Tools.

In the Traverse of the Ino [Mueller], Mr Robarts told me to join on to Mts Ino & Selbourne but in no single instance could I get both at one time. If Mt Illion is fixed by the Survey, then the Forks are right, as I got both that hill & Mt Ino at that spot.

As I had none of my old field books to go by, I had to put in the Turnbull & the Okura approximately from memory. Point A the bearings from which I put on the Map, is the Cairn I put up when Traversing the Actor; it ought to be able to fix the head of both the Actor, Turnbull & Ino.

As I told you before I couldn't get through or over the fourth Gorge of the Ino, but the head of that river is put in from a sketch plan I took from Cairn A, and is tolerably correct.

The trip up the Ino with a discription of the country may as well be kept till I get down the big Map & Version books. As I intend to write a full account of all the rivers in Southern Westland, I have jotted down on the Map any items of importance which I daresay will do in the mean.

You will notice I have marked a lot of Cattle feed through the first gorge of the Turnbull which wasn't in my first Map.

I knew there was a small run up their, but at that time, feed was not so scarce as now, & a two mile track to cut was a heavy item. Now things are different, feed is so scarce & the Settlers are quarreling like Ancient Greeks. And I think by a little generalship, Government might get the run taken up at double the upset price. Sixteen pounds stg [sterling] per annum is too much in the eyes of the Settlers, but two runs of £8 each would make them bite, especially for the upper one, get a bid for one run & you have them. The combative instinct is roused, the citizens of Okura are only prevented from Murdering the inhabitants of Granville [unknown paper town?] by a gallows & vice versa.

Okura would pawn its hide to raise money to spite Granville & so would Granville to spite Okura. So much for that hint.

I have a dozen or so more Sketches to send up but must wait for My Spectacles before I can do any more. The Field book is all ready to send, but I'll keep it till I see if the Maps will do. The Sketch of Mt Bertha is not so good as I would wish. I can't see colour properly at present, however I'll send you another.

In case Mr Macfarlane has lost the list of what I wanted, I renew it

    1 Parll Ruler

    1 Flat ruler in 10ths

    6 H & HB Pencils

    1 Pair Compas's with pen, if you have none then buy one if there is any money left, & you have never sent me copies of the Tourists Guide. I have nothing more to say at present, & don't know where I am going next till the Steamer comes, most probably I'll give the Burke a few weeks prospecting.

Yours Truly
C. E. Douglas

TEN

Waiatoto Exploration, 1891

Douglas's explorations in the Waiatoto valley were the most strenuous and sustained of all those for which a full record exists. His journeys in the 1880s up the nearby Arawata and onto surrounding ranges may have been harder, but they occurred when he was probably at the peak of his fitness and experience. In the Waiatoto Douglas began to feel his age a little, and he was also very much on his own at a time when companionship might have made the exploration more enjoyable and less burdensome.

The Waiatoto expedition of 1891 is recorded in two forms in the Douglas Papers. The shorter version (Item 22) is given with only a few small omissions, covering the period from 29 January to 5 April. Then follows the longer version (Item 46) for the activities from 5 April to 3 May. Omitted are the rambling dissertations on the history of mankind, featuring Babo Smith, River Drift Jones, Mastodon Robinson, Glacial Epoch and Botanical Browns, and the AK Kadan Mystery. They have a certain charm but are both dated and confused. The focus here is on Douglas as an explorer.

G. J. Roberts
Fitzherbert St
Hokitika

Diary of a Trip up the Waitoto River
by
C. E. Douglas

1891 Thursday 29 Janry
After waiting for nearly a fortnight for good weather, and no flood on the River, made a start today from Hendleys with a Camp & part of loading. Pitched the Batwing on Sea side of Dochertys Creek as I couldn't get accross it, the bridge being four feet under water, then tramped back again to the Ferry, to listen with admiration to the Awfull Cuffers of Wm Hendley – may his shaddow never grow less [William Hindley, ferryman at Waiatoto]. As a narrator of tough yarns he is gifted far above the sons of men, & his versions of History & Biography throw a new light on English Literature. When on those subjects a

fellow has but one defence against him that is manufacture facts & prove them by ficticious Authors, but it is in fiction pure that Bill is unapproachable. He is compound of the Ancient Mariner, Sinbad the Sailor & Baron Munchausen, the button-holing pertinacity of the Mariner in making a fellow listen to his yarns whether he will or no, the Fictional powers of the Arab, with that strict adherence to Varacity which distinguished the baron, & if digression is commendable then he has that quality bordering on genius. His stories always put me in mind of those Rivers which rise no one knows where, then they flow on for miles in a steady defined channel, till entering flat country they branch into a hundred mouths & finally dissappear in the Sand.

But long may he and others rule the Ferries South, but for their excentricities we would have nothing to talk about. Can anyone explain why Ferryman are in general Characters, do ferries make them so? Or are they a special case born to create Ferries & how is it that they are in general sociable & talkative, while the Tollman, who's occupation is about the same is a gloomy Misanthrope?

Friday 30 Janry

Good weather at last and the River down to nearly its Snow melting level. Started in the canoe – The Surveyor General – with remainder of load. Load consists of two Batwing Tents & two flys – can be pitched as a 6 x 5 Tent or halved making two Camps to stage Tucker. A bill hook, half axe & Pick, Field books Compass Drawing & writing material, A Pea Rifle and Betsey Jane to catch Birds, and about 100 lbs of assorted Tucker.

As the Waitoto [Waiatoto] River for the first few miles, has no beaches to track boat or Canoe along, & very bad poling ground, it was paddle paddle all the way to Dohertys Creek, which place I reached towards evening & camped for the night. No birds to be seen, so have to exist on dry bread, or catch Eels for a day or two, till I get out of the blighting bird destroying influence of the Special Settler [from Jacksons Bay].

Nisson & Egglings homestead [settlers at Waiatoto, also spelt Nissen and Eggeling] still looks flourishing, as they still have some fat cattle to sell now & again, which is more than others in the same trade can say. They appear to be going in for fruit as an industry. The idea isnt bad, & might pay; at any rate the Trees won't run away into the Bush and get lost like Cattle, & if the worst comes to the worst a fellow might pass a dreamy Lotus eating existance very comfortably, living on strawberries & cream & drinking home made Wine & Cider. No tearing through wet bush after cattle that in your secret soul you know will never be caught, no anxiety about the Hokitika market & selfish prayers that the Otira pass may be Snowed up, but an Arcadian life of innocence with but one black spot, the annual call of the rate collector.

A little above Egglings & on the opposite side of the River is the homestead of the lamented Mr Cassey [Casey] – a lot of real hard work, and well done work at that, thrown away, the hut in ruins & the Grass paddocks distroyed by a very common mistake, overgrazing.

Saturday 31 Janry
Rolled up swags & started. Better paddling than yesterday, till entering the hills, when I had to carry load for quarter of a mile, take the outrigger off the Surveyor & drag it by main force through & over rocks. One great advantage of a Dug out is, it tracks just as well bottom up as any other way. Got to the round pool when tracking & poling commenced properly, the Surveyor with a double line tracks splendidly. I only wish I could take it up to Mount Aspiring. Pitched No 2 Camp rather early in the day but was getting tired & hungry. Got a Wood hen & a Piegeon, & must lay in a stock of Birds tomorrow. Bread & Jam is verry good no doubt but not the thing for swagging, & the River is too Muddy for Eels; at least I haven't caught any yet.

At the round pool, the spur from Selbourne comes to the River, & opposite the Camp the cliffs for a few chains are sheer down but not very high. I believe there is a Cattle track over the top, but didn't examine it. The Rock is Gneiss, with a strike No-East & So West. Dip 60° West. I call this Rock Gneiss, but in places it resembles Schist, & may be what M'Kay of the Geo Depart[t] [Alexander McKay, geologist] call Gneissic Schist, though it appears to me to be the same rock as the eighteen mile Bluff Haast river, & which Sir [Julius] Haast call Granitic Gneiss, who's right? I'll send speciemens up to Hokitika, but whether I'll ever know what they are called is doubtfull, having sent three boxes of speciemens to that City, and never got the slightest hint as to what they were or whether I was right or wrong in the names I gave the various rocks.

Sunday 1 Feby
Started on a Tour of inspection up the River to get birds, and also to see how far I can take the Canoe. Soon got all the Birds I wanted as Piegons are plentifull, & found I couldnt get a boat further than Palmers Creek. Above that there is a short rocky rapid, but impassable to anything but a Rob roy, or some ship that can be carried overland. So will shift Camp tomorrow, drag the Surveyor into the bush, and cut a Track over Watney spur, as there is no getting up the River on the West side without some sort of blazed line, to swagg the Camps along, although I have traversed the River to sediement flat years ago. I will carry a traverse line along with me, to enable me to locate speciemens if I find any, & sketch in the two sides of the River as I go along.

Monday 2 Feby

Shifted Camp to a spot about 20 chains below Palmers Creek, as that is the most convenient place to start a Track over the spur. Before hauling the Canoe into the Bush I crossed the River & overhauled the lower part of Palmers Creek. It takes its rise from the back of Mt Selbourne out of the usual rounded basin, covered with snow for six months of the year & with grass the remainder. It Gorges about a mile up & the rocks in the Creek bed are Gneiss & Contorted Schist. No trace of any metals or even metaliferous rocks.

How is it that the Okura [Okuru] Turnbull & Waitoto Rivers unlike all the other rivers south, Gorges & tumbles over Cataracts & rapids near where they leave the hills. Is it because the belt of Gneiss crosses their beds at these places, or has part of their Ice flow gone another way at some distant period?

The Paringa & Maita [Mahitahi], smaller rivers than the Okura & Waitoto, have denuded their beds to very little above sea level for miles into the ranges, yet their Neves are nothing compared to those of Castor & Pollux & Aspiring, which have poured Ice down the Waitoto. The Okura Ice flow certainly at no distant date – Geologically speaking – flowed down the Burke to the Haast. The Turnbull barely taps the Devide & that at a comparatively low place, but surely the Waitoto ought to have been able to gouge out its bed? Is it possible the Ice flow went down the East side through some depression reserved for me to discover?

Tuesday 3 Feby

Heavy rain came on early in the morning and continued all day. I thought this weather was too good to last, however its one comfort I have got the Canoe & Camp up before it came on.

Lying in a Camp all day with no one to talk to but Betsey Jane, & her conversation is rather one sided, with no books to read, & perhaps not in the humour to fill in sketches, a fellow has to think on something, or go cranky. And queer thoughts come into my head at times. I often ask myself in amazement what impulse drives me into the Wilds. Had I remained at Home in the Old Country, I might now have been the respectable Father of a family, passing the same Lampost – on the road to office – the exact same minute day after day, perhaps even standing at the Church Plate on a Sunday with a benevolent smile & a White choker. A comfortably situated old Foggy. A tooth in a Wheel of a Mercantile machine, a perambulating Ink bottle, Ledger & blooting pad, with just sufficient thinking powers & education to gabble on the topics of the day, but with my Reasoning powers completely dormant. But such a life was not for me, 'the impulse which drove the Bravest & best of Old Rome to face death and danger on the banks of the Danube & the burning Desarts of Asia &

Africa' that same impulse drives the Britan to do likewise & plant his flag all over the World, indifferent as to whether the danger to be faced is from prowling Savages, fever smitten Jungles or Artic snows. When he does Emigrate, the Average Briton generally makes an effort to settle down, & become what the World calls a respectable, usefull, benevolant, patriotic &c citizen, & when he dies his most flattering requiem would be to be able to say he left half a million of Money.

The impulse drove me out into the World, but the desire to then settle must have been omitted in my moral character, as here I am after thirty years wandering, crouched under a few yards of Calico, with the rain pouring & the Wind & Thunder roaring among the mountains a homeless, friendless, Vagabond, with a past that looks dreary & a future still more so, still I can't regret having followed such a life and I know that even if I & thousands besides me perish miserably the impulse which impells them to search the Wild places of the Earth is good, one or two are bound to add something to the Worlds stock of Knowledge while so doing, & even a small grain of Knowledge is cheaply purchased at the expense of a thousand ordinary lives.

Fools think that Knowledge can only be got from books & men, & call me a Fool for wasting my life in mountain Solitudes, but if in so doing I have found nothing new in Thought or worth giving to the World, I have at least gathered glimmerings of Truth as to how nature works, glimmerings which if they bear no fruit in this Life, may in the next where darkness will be light.

Wednesday 4 Feby

Rain all day, could do nothing outside, and inside the Mosquitoes & Sandflies made things over lively. However filled in some Sketches, and as the evening looks like clearing up, got things ready to start track over the spur.

I am perfectly aware that the Mosquito & Sandfly have a purpose in this World, but why don't they attend to it? There destiney is to keep down Microscopic Insects, who I believe would otherwise taint the Air, & give us Fevers instead of the present bad Temper, so Science says, but there sphere of use is when they are in the Grub state. Why don't they stick at that and not trouble innocent unoffending Prospectors who can't carry a Curtain? The Mosquitos are worse this season than ever I saw them, and make a fellow think irreverantly of Old Noah, if he gave them a passage in the Ark, in early days. But hold on, a brilliant idea has just entered my head. Perhaps, the Butterfly, Locust, Mosquito & others, are enjoying their heaven, their reward for strictly doing their duty when in the Grub state. A percentage who don't loaf, but do their best, as a reward blossom into winged Insects & enjoy a higher existance for a brief period, so don't let us growl at them and call their existance useless.

Thursday 5 Feby

Started to cut Track over the Spur but didn't get finished it is further than I thought & hard to get a passage down the Cliffs.

What on Earth is up with the Mosquitos. Is it because they have caught me in the bush for the first time with short hair? In most cases daylight clears them out, but today I have been Billhooking all the time with a regular glory of the Wretches round me. Filled in some Sketches and tried to write something but had to give it up, the mean Villians insinuated themselves inside my Spectacles, and defied fate.

Friday 6 Feby

Carried main part of the Swag over the spur, & left it under a rock, then spent the day trying to get down the Cliffs. Think I have succeeded, but it was too late to make down, so came back to Camp, filled in some Sketches. I wish I was out of this & up where I could see about me, & have something to write about. If not, my Diary will degenerate into the usual style, 'Mosquitos very bad, got up dressed, & then went to bed again'.

Saturday 7 Feby

Shifted the Camp and all the Tucker over the spur. Found a very good get down, & cut Track out to the River. Not very well today, and punching two swags very nearly made me brake down, so Camped early.

This is a very peculiar spur from Mt Watney, it is hard Gneiss and all the way through the Gorge it is sheer down into the river – say two hundred feet – steep as it is, the trees find cracks & holes to grow in, it being covered with Bush, the rock showing only as you travell along it. About twenty chain lower down the River than where I have brought the Track, is a long steep crack in the Cliff leading down to the River bed, when I was up the Waitoto seven or eight years ago I got off the spur down this Crack. I distinctly remember going down with a heavy swag & Topsey made fast to my wrist with a strap. Verily I must either have had more courage or less sense in those days, as I wouldn't dream of facing that place now I doubt it is the courage failing me. I feel now and again that my Nerve & Grip are not what they once were. It is funny that the older and more useless a fellows life becomes the more he tries to take care of it.

The two Nissons passed up the River on the other side with Cattle & down again the same day.

Oh! The Mosquitos!

Sunday 8 Feby

This being Sunday took things easy. The Nissons up to the Forks with a mob of

Cattle. Baked a weeks bread & sketched the Gorge & Palmers Creek. If the Mosquitos don't knock off their attentions, Ill have to go down to the beach for something to cover my neck. Splendid weather but birds scarce not high enough up for hens and am sick of Piegon stew.

Monday 9 Feby
Shifted Camp & part of Tucker to near the Forks, saw the Nissons going down the other side with a few Milk Cows. Yelled the compliments of the season to each other and passed on. From about Casseys Creek the River becomes very wide, and with a few exceptions runs slow, but it would have been little advantage to get the Canoe any further except to cross & recross when necessary, but for that there is not much need at present, & when it is necessary I'll manage it some way.

What a very thin range it is between the Waitoto & Arawata. A little more Ice punching and it would have been a Craig & Tail, a chain of rounded hills. From Watney all the way up to Fingalls head, the range is nearly perpendicular a hard solid Gneiss, & on the other side towards the Ino [Mueller] it is the same rock, but the range is not so steep except near Palmers Creek. On the beach opposite the Camp, which is composed of very small Gravel, the Laminated Schist predominate which shows that the line of brake is not far off. The Valley of the Axius [Te Naihi] & the Depression between Hyperia & Lucifer no doubt will be where it runs. The peculiar contorted nature of the rock on those hills may be caused by the Fracture between the Gneiss & Slates, though the lower reach of the Waipara River is rather far up. I thought the brake would be the low depression nearly opposite Callerys flat, but time will show.

Must climb some of the hills as I go up to get the proper strike & Dip of the Rocks – that is if I can – the outcrop low down is often deceiving.

Through the Supernatural meanness of the Survey & Mines Depart[t], I am without an Aneroid, so I must guess the heights as I go along. At the round Pool, say 30 feet above Sea Level, through the half Gorge the River rises 100 feet, & up to this Camp say 70, making the height here 200 feet above Sea level.

The Ferrets have not got among the Birds on this River evidently, as Kakapo's are squealling about in hundreds. Will have to tie up the Dog if I don't want the Camp full of Corpses in the morning. But what is up with the Blue Ducks. When up here before they were in hundreds, now I have only seen one & he travelled as Old Nick was after him. No appearance of Rabbits yet and am not anxious about them.

Tuesday 10 Feb
Punching up remainder of Swag, what a weary heart braking thing it is, staging

swags going over the same ground twice or thrice. A man to be fit for this Mountain Life ought either to be able to pack like a Mule or else live on Air.

I notice today that at this place the river commences to rise about five o'clock in the evening; the rise is very slight only a few inches. The nights are so warm that there is little difference between night & day melting of the snow. This is wonderfull weather, not a cloud in the Sky since Saturday, and the Hills as clear as if looked at through an Opera Glass. Perhaps the bad weather is collecting its energies to be ready for me when jammed up among the Glaciers. However I cant complain yet, there are indications of a change brewing.

What a comfort it is to find I am gradually leaving the Mosquitos behind; when I went down to my last camp they were prowling about in Clouds, & no doubt cheered when they saw me coming, thinking I was going to stop and feed them. If such beings use profanity there must be some talk going on at that Camp tonight.

Wednesday 11 Feby

Punched a Camp to above the Forks & came back again, if a good day tomorrow will be finished with this double work. What a mockery on our boasted Knowledge is this swaging; here am I as Tennyson or somebody says, one of the heirs of all the Ages, carrying a load on my back like – like I was going to say an ordinary Savage but that gentleman would have more sense, & have a Squaw to do such work – no, like an ordinary White man, where is this boasted progress we hear so much about? A Savage doesn't know the powers lying dormant in nature but I do – at least I ought to – and can't apply them. Every waterfall – and their name is Legion – I have passed on the road contains powers, that, if properly applied, would carry me comfortably & safely to the top of Mt Aspiring, & I have burnt enough of Wood on this Trip the Gasses of which contained power to send my Swag to the Planet Jupiter. Verily we are but on the Threshold of Knowledge, and can't be called Intelligent even – till our Servants are the forces around us & not our own backs or that of our fellow men.

It is sometimes amusing to speculate on the What might [be] ahead of a fellow on a Trip like this. I have just seen the Axius & to my surprise it is evidently not a Snow River. It was Winter when I was up here before, & both it and the Waitoto were equally clear, & the difference in Volume of Water was not near so great as now. Why the Axius, instead of being a half as large as the Waitoto, is not a fifth. It is evident that the Glacier of Castor & Pollux does not flow as I thought, or like the Paringa & many others it is a dying Glacier & sends down no Sediement. No Glacier up the Axius increases the chance of an available pass through the ranges, but time will show. There is still too much snow on the hills for that Trip yet.

Today has been hot enough, but the back ranges have been clouded all day. The effect of the shade has been that the River did not rise till two hours later than yesterday & the rise was much less.

Thursday 12 Feby
Finished Swaging Camps and Tucker at last, but find I must away to the beach for a few odds & ends that are necessary before tackling the head of the River. Better run short down here than away up where perhaps a few hours is equal to weeks of work. Splendid Weather only hope it will last.

Friday 12 [13] Feby
Started for the beach reached Hendlys a little after dark.

Saturday 13 [14] Feby
Got up to the Okura & sent on my order for stores.

Sunday 15 Feby
Stores came down too late to make a start.

Monday 16 Feby
Heavy Rain all day.

Tuesday 17 Feby
Started with about 35 lb of a Swag got to Hendly baked a cake & a few loaves. Showery most of the day.

Wednesday 18 Feby
Away up the River got to where I left a Fly and Blanket. Fed the Mosquitos.

Thursday 19 Feby
Rolled up and reached Camp above the Forks towards evening found everything right. Weather looks threatening, but am now ready to tackle the Mountains at any time.

Friday 20 Feby
Heavy rain all day. Filled in Sketches and Philosophising.

A few pages back I said some thing about the Mosquito, wondering why he didn't remain in the Grub stage & otherwise abusing those cheerfull, buzzing Insects.

Science says that the Trunk of those interesting bloodsuckers is the remains of an organ, of no use now. But in a past age when the hugh crawling reptiles & Mamals, the Ossarosse's the Mastadon, the Glyptadon – the – the Pentagon – the Octagon & others of awfull appearance & still more awfull names walked the Earth the Mosquito feasted on, yea perhaps nagged & finally distroyed, those monsters. Now when they are gone Kitto [mosquito] still retains its Trunk an emblem of past greatness, as it is only one in the Million who ever get a chance to use it in those degenerate days. That is one Theory, but I have another much more probable: the Trunk instead of being a survival is in reality an after thought of nature's given to the insect for a noble purpose. After profound study I have come to the conclusion that the Mosquito & also its Cousin the Sandfly have been great Moral Engines in advancing the human race. That is how it was.

Away in the early ages of the Earth, man lived in warm countries & ran about naked. His food was easy to get, & although his brain contained the Germs of progress, that progress was dormant, as Man was awfully lazy. Nature seeing this Man, this paragon of Animals who was destined for better things, sprawling under a Cocoa Nut Tree waiting for the fruit to tumble into his mouth, determined to alter things. She developed the Mosquito, sharpened his proboscis, explained to him his high mission, & one night she introduced a few Million into the camp of Pre-Adamite Jones Smith & Co. Gracious! hadn't both parties lively times of it. It is more than probable that the introduction of profanity into human speech dates from that eventfull night.

It is impossable to imagine what would have been the result had not Pre Adamite Brown conceived the idea of stitching Palm Leaves together and putting them over him. Seraphic Bliss! He slept that night in comparative comfort. Mans dormant brain had started into activity. Clothes were invented. The Mosquito did it.

Brown who developed a genius for Tayloring was a bad hand at climbing Trees. So he agreed with Robinson to make him a coat payment to be made in Nuts. Robinson had no more idea of Tayloring than a cat has of its Grandfather, but his climbing & fossicking abilities stood high. Barter & the division of Labour had commenced. The Mosquito did it.

Pre Adamite Buggins in a Claw-hammer Coat & sea weed neck tie gained thereby the smiles of the lovely Miss Pre Adamite Jones, completely crushing Robinson, M'Pherson & a host of others who were only togged in Palm leaf Monkey Jackets. Decorative Art in Dress had commenced & Love on the civilized modern basis; admiration for the Garments, not the being inside was soon in full swing. The Mosquito did it. But there was still something awanting. Nature had another look at the Paragon & found that he was still addicted to lying in bed of a morning, & still given to sprawling under Trees during the day.

So the Sandfly was invented; an Insect who ceaseless activity & fiendish skill in discovering holes & other weak spots in Garments amounts to Absolute Genius. There was no more sleeping in of a morning after this, & man, once up, found he had to fly round & work at something to gain relief. Regular work & industry had commenced; the Sandfly did it. In future I will always look with respect on those usefull Insects and never injure them so long as they will skirmish in reason.

Saturday 21 Feby

As the weather looked threatening this morning, I didnt shift camp, but as it cleared up a little towards evening, Sketched both sides of the River, took shots at Peak from Point A at the Forks.

I am begining to think that what I called Mt Datames [Datamos], is in reality Mt Duncan, & that Datames is the Peak near Fingalls head. If so, then my central valley brake comes in right, instead of being down the Waipara, which I always thought too far inland & with too high a saddle. It crosses the low depression nearly opposite Callerys Flat; that is where the line from Ino saddle to the Ark runs at any rate. If this is the case, then there is a large open flat above Sediement Flat, the one Mr Mueller & I saw from Point T Waipara Traverse; it looked so like the other one & the hills were clouded at the time that I couldn't be sure. The dissappearance of the Hyllus Glacier certainly puzzeld me and it does yet.

Climbed up to the fall on Mt Duncan & got a speciemen of the Rock, Gneiss Strike No East & So West, Dip 25° So East.

The falls would be a magnificent sight, but for one defect – they want Water in them. I suspect Sutherlands fall, & many others there is so much blow about, have the same defect. It is not everybody who can see a Waterfall with the magnifying Orbs of Pauline [Paulin], who saw the fall up the Arawata one hundred feet wide – exactly fifty times more than us ordinary Mortals can see it with our degenerate eyes. He Photographed it, & people say a camera can't lie – can't it by Jove? If they said it seldom speaks the Truth, it would be nearer it. I'll allow the box & chemicals to have a high moral character if allowed – but the manipulater can demoralize it if he likes, & make an otherwise honest box travell the downward path, in company with the Horsedealer the Promoter of duffer C^os & other descendants of Annais.

Sunday 22 Feby

Started for the head of the River with one Camp; and a fortnights Tucker. Traversed to about a mile up Sediement flat where I camped. It was nearly dark before I got through the [Bush] Lawyers & Flax Swamp which edges the River on the South side – its the last time I go through that den again. The River on this side – the Western – is the same so I'll try and Ford tomorrow. The Camp is pitched anyway, as the night is fine. But this place wouldn't do if a flood came on, an almost impassable Swamp between me and the hills & not a Tree big enough to scramble up, but nights are short & I can chance it. Ill describe the journey after as I am too tired to write now.

Monday 23 Feby

Sketched in the Pickle Haub [Pickelhaube] Glacier & the flat, surely this can't be Castor & Pollux. It looks a Mean Mountain to what it shows from the Thomson range & Cascade Plateau. Roberts says in the Map it is, so he is very likely right. Mountains alter so much in this country that a fellow often makes Mistakes, & I thought its Glacier would be far larger. It is a high up Glacier, at least 4000 feet, & the Hyllus runs perfectly clear, so it is a dying out comparatively motionless mass of Ice. The name Pickle Haube is a puzzel. Who or what is it,? is Pickle &c the name of some celebrated German Professor or was he a Mongol General, or is it the name of a New Sauce, invented by some Philanthropest to make Rabbit Stew more palatable than it is? I must enquire & get a bottle. [*The peak is named after a distinctively shaped German helmet.*]

Took bearings all round from Point D & carried Camp & Traverse line to head of the Flats. Those Flats are much longer than I thought, being nearly 2$\frac{1}{2}$ Miles & from 30 to forty chain broad in the open. There is no grass worth speaking about on them, they are just open river beaches covered with fine gravell & Silt, & flooded all over at times. The Ford was high but better than I expected, the Water is so muddy & this river is bad for quick-sands & sunken Snags, so I had to feel my way with a stick. A capsize coming back wouldn't matter so much as I'll be light, but going up is different. The rise of the River up to here is as follows: 200 feet at Axius Junction; from there to entrance of long rapids say 20 feet; rise to foot of flat 250 feet to head of Flat at Camp 20; making this place 500 feet above sea level.

The steepness of the hills espicially along the Haast range is something wonderfull 40 Degree's is the usual Angle & that on the East side of the River.

Find I have an addition to my Camp, in Eggling Dog Poker. I suppose he saw his way to a glorious hunting with Betsey, & kept out of my sight till too far away from home to be sent back. He is a good Dog & will find his own Tucker, & more if wanted.

Tuesdy 24 Feby

Rain in the morning, but cleared up about mid day. traversed to the upper flats a distance of about 3 Miles. This is the Flat sure enough we saw from Point T,

& had the day been clear we would have seen the whole course of the River up to the Glacier – at least the Eastern Side.

The flat is something the same as the one below, very little grass or Scrub on it, but the Shingle is larger, & the river has deeper channels still the whole flat is flooded at times, by sudden rushes of Water, caused no doubt by slips further up. Sketched in what at present Ill call Mt Datames & the depression into Arawata. Datames shows on this side the peculiar fracture shown in former Sketches of Bel & Hyperia. This is evidently the brake in the formation. As Hyllus & Datames & all the Drift in the River bed now show the Laminated Schists – Mt Aspiring Slates – The strike on Datames is No East & So West with a Dip of 25° So East – this is 3000 feet up. On Mt Hyllus the Dip is perpendicular & the Strike No East & So West, but near the Hyllus river the dip on this Mount appears to be So West. But as I am reserving the Geological till I come back, this statement may require altering. I can't carry rocks going up, the Swag is heavy enough already, and planting speciemens in bags the labels are bound to get wet. Plenty of Kakapoes. Poker & Betsey had a dozen lying round the Tent this morning, they are not very fat but good enough for soup.

Its a Knowing Dog Poker, when I hung the birds up, & was going to walk away, he looked ernestly first at me, then at the birds & then walked to the Fire, & looked at me again. I took the hint – he wanted one roasted.

I must eat plenty of birds, and spare the Flour as I don't know what is ahead of me yet.

Rabbits are showing up but not very plentiful. What is up with the Blue Ducks? They are very scarce, & so wild that the Dogs can't catch them & they wont let me get within shot of them. On the Haast & Okura, the Ferrets are pitching in to all the Birds, is it possible that an AEsthetic bred of those vermin have come into the Waitoto a breed too refined for Vulgar game but must have Ducks alone?

The drift in this river shows a variety of rock that have come down, Schists Chloride [chlorite] & otherwise, Quartz of great variety but nothing in it but Iron Pyrites, some Muscovite Jasparoid Slates, & a few others I have seen before but don't know their Names, but all belonging to the Slates. I must keep an eye on the various creeks going up & try & find the In Situ of some of those rocks. The creeks are now getting better defined, but few cut very deep, which is a bad look out for outcrops, besides they run mostly with the strike not accross it.

Strange there is no trace of Copper or Galena yet, the reefs in the Waipara ought to crop out on this side of the range, though I have my doubts whether the Galena & Copper Mr Mueller was blowing about in his Waipara report, come from Lucifer & Hyperia. They may have come from the Mt Eros block, & none showing in the Waitoto, almost confirms that opinion of mine. Copper shows in the beaches near Palmers Creek, & I know it can't come from the hills there, so perhaps the Axius is its original home, but Galena I have got no trace of as yet.

Wednesday 25 Feby
Started with Camp, as the hills were clear. Sketched up & down the river, took bearing &c, just got up to the foot of the Flat when it came on a Deluge of rain. I couldn't find a safe ford, having no time to look about me, so camped on the East side close to the Fan of a large Creek. How big this Creek is I dont know, but it is the last chance of the Castor & Pollux Glacier coming into the Waitoto, unless the Pickle Haube is it.

If I have to keep this side of the River, which I hope wont be the case, I'll have to bridge a few Creeks & Torrents going up to the Glacier, some very ugley gorgy looking gaps are looming up at the head of the flat.

The night looks in for a storm, but I am in a splendid Camping place. Hens [weka] & Rabbits Galore, Wood good & all safe unless the hills slip away which isn't likely. Writing this a la Maorie with nothing on but a blanket, my only shift of clothes drying at a roaring fire, & the rain is coming down in Torrents.

Thursday 26 Feby
Rain all day, till near evening, when it cleared up a little & I got a splended view of Mt Aspiring & Glacier. They are not so far away as I thought – one Camp more will do the River. The Glacier & Gorge looks a most dismal sight, every rock an Inky black. The Glacier appears to lie in a regular basin surrounded by high precipices.

Tomorrow if it is a fine day I will Traverse the Creek up. It is an open Creek, not very large & about a thousand feet up ought to be a good place to fix a Cairn take bearing & Join on to Mt Aspiring Hyperia Point T &c. If the weather permits, I'll then scale Mt Ragan it is high but not very difficult I think.

Filling in Sketches. There is something wrong with my drawing. Somebody or other say that when a man after long application at anything doesn't progress he has reached perfection, or is working on a wrong Tack? Now I know I am not chasing perfection, so it is evident I am on the wrong tack, but where is the right one, long as I have been drawing now, I know I haven't advance a single bit. The power probably is not in me. The Artistic is awanting. I am in the same boat as some I could name, who have been thumping at a Piano, day after day for years, & no better than when they started. In fact they appear to get worse, though that may be because listeners become less mercifull after prolonged

Torture & make remarks that are not encouraging. The actual drawing I might manage, it is the shading & coloring that sluys me [that I find difficult]. Whether my eyes are variable or not I can't say, but I can never mix colors twice the same shade. I have an idea that my principle fault is what is very common among Amateurs, that is being in too big a hury, wanting to see how the thing will look when finished. I would like to see a good Water colour drawer at work, were it only for a few minutes. I can pick up a thing by eye, never by ear to tell me to do this, & plaster over that & so on, is so much wasted time.

If I have no one down here to show me how to do it properly, there is one thing not wanting, that is Critics, & Critic often of a most maddening discription.

One chap says, why don't you color the Trees green, as they ought to be? I put on some bright Pea Green, and he says, 'Ah thats better, that as it should be.' Another has read about the deep blue sea & wants me to Color Water Ultramarine, & the sky ditto.

One chap much admired a Tree in a sketch of mine. The said tree I thought I intended for a Snowy Mountain Peak. I was requested to draw a Settlers Shanty once, but had sense enough to decline. In the first place I couldn't have drawn him on the Verandah to look like a human being, & in the second place even if I had been able, he never could have understood why I couldnt draw a life size figure on a four inch piece of paper.

I am not romancing. There is a man down here who considers himself educated, rather above the Common herd in fact who on looking over a map burst out laughing. On asking him the reason he said 'why look here, the Lagoon near my house is over a hundred yards long, & the Surveyor has put it down a wee bit of a thing not half an inch'. This staggered me, I thought he might be joking, but no he was in ernest, his brain that the Donkey was so proud of was that of an Animal. He could only take a piece of an Idea at a time, & far more people are so gifted than most men would imagine. However I was glad to hear his piece of Idea; at one time I thought I had fathomed the depth of human stupidity when I meet a man who started *up* the Landsbro' to get to the Sea, but this Special Settler showed me a lower depth still.

Talking of Sketching, I once meet a couple of most unflattering Critics, & in a most peculiar place. I was sitting sketching with my back against a rock, as is usual, when finished I held it at arms length to admire my handiwork, when in that mountain Solitude I was startled by a yell of derision. Looking up, there were two Keas peeping over my shoulder with there head cocked to one side, as I have see featherless bipeds do in a picture gallery. I held out the Sketch for them to admire. One came hopping along with his top knot up & one eye closed to examine it. He looked first out of one eye, then the other, gave his mate a dig in the ribs & gave vent to a Yell of derision. No. two came trotted along sideways, then struck an attitude, shaded his eyes with his claw if I reccollect aright, though I am not quite sure, then he sniggered, & gave a Yell that brought Keas round in dozen. What they thought exactly I don't know, but they evidently had a very poor opinion of my Talents.

Friday 27 Feby

Made an early start up the creek, found a place point G. about five hundred feet up, where I got a good view of Mt Aspiring, & Sketched it in as quick as possible, as clouds were fast collecting. Just got it & a few bearings finished in time. The three Waterfalls show on the Sketch are intermittant every hour or so. Great masses of Snow comes pouring down instead of Water. Some of the falls lasted as long as twenty minutes, & the noise sounded like low Thunder. I don't think the Glacier is of great extent, but from the size of the snowfield above & the Sunless den in which it is jammed it must be of immense thickness.

Although the weather didn't look very tempting, I made up my mind to make a run for it, & scale Mount Ragan, a hill that must be nearly 7000 feet. I got up the bed of the creek for a good way, then took the bush out to the open country. So far the Travelling wasn't out of the common, but the last 2000 feet look apalling. It wasn't a cliff, but a smoth slope of rock dipping towards me as I thought at an Angle of 60° but on getting closser, the Angle got less, and on arriving at the foot of the slope I found it was smoth as if chiseled by the hand of man, hardly a brake or a crack the whole way up, but the slope was only about 25 Degrees.

I had never tackled such a distance of sloping rock before. The puzzel was this: a fellow might get tired & want a rest, & perhaps not get one & so come down by the run again, or he might slip on a steeper part. My boots weren't very good, 25 Degrees don't look much but I found it quite plenty. I went up a few yards & slipped once, so I off boots, put them in my bag, & started as the Scotch would say in my stocking feet, & it was the grandest piece of climbing I ever did. I don't think I was more than half an hour getting to the Top [of Stocking Peak, to the west of Mt Ragan]. I could have done 10,000 feet of the same. The Summet was a Sell. I could see nothing. Sometimes I got a faint outline of a Mountain – perhaps the Dome Peak – with a Valley between, but whether the Valley was open or covered with Ice I couldnt say. Certainly Ragan, Platea & Mycalae send far more Ice that way, than into the Waitoto, so perhaps, what I saw was the Valley of the Maituku [Matukituki]. If it is, then it rises near Castor & Pollux, but of that I can't be sure. But of one thing I am certain & that is, whether it be the Wilkin or the Maituku there is a saddle say 6000 feet between Ragan & Arbela, free from Ice & Snow, & through this pass the

Rabbits come over from the East side in droves. I believe they come over to breed on the open Morains & slopes of the Sunny side of the range & then pour back again in swarms on devoted Otago.

As nothing was to be seen & the weather was getting thicker, I started down the way I came, got to the foot of the slope, put on my boots over what remained of the socks & reached the Camp. Boiled the Billy & then had time to Traverse the Flat to the head; it is about two Miles long & say 25 chain broad. The Rabbits are swarming at the head of the Flat. They are barking & killing all the Trees, & it is evident they have been up here for years. Perhaps they will gradually exterminate the Westland Bush as they did in St Helena & Assenscion. The trees off the ranges, all the little soil the country possess[s] will be washed away down the river & deposited at the Mouth – a bright look out for the Cockatoo's [farmers] – Breed Ferrets in galore, spread Poison as you like, this Island will never get rid of the Rabbits. What is the use of distroying them down country, when they can retire to the Wilds & breed in safety. People don't seem to know the Geography of this Island, or to enable them to borrow more money from home, they don't want to know. Why at least a fourth of the country will never even be inhabited, & consequently will remain a breeding ground for Armies of Vermin, who have been introduced in the country by the dense ignorance of the people.

The weather looks dickey tonight, but if fair tomorrow I'll make a rush up to the head of the River if possable & finish without shifting Camp.

Saturday 28 Feby
Heavy Wind all day hills covered with Snow to the two thousand feet level. Did nothing but cut firewood & keep myself warm. What a Funny country this Westland is. Yesterday it was semi tropical, & this morning I was awakened at an unearthly hour by the cold. Comfortable to find oneself suddenly in the middle of winter, with nothing but a Calico shirt & drawers within three days march, the River in flood & couldn't get down if I wished & nothing but a half blanket to sleep in. However wood is plentifull & good, birds in hundreds, and at the worst I can hang out for 10 days yet.

Sunday 1 March
Still raining & looks as if it meant to continue & hills packed with snow nearly to the Flat. If this continues will have to go & hunt tomorrow wet or dry & save Flour. My Tucker & spare Camp is on the other side of the River & if starved out would have to raft.

Finished the Sketch of Mt Aspiring doesn't please me it look hard & mechanical, however can't expect to draw cramped up in a batwing.

Monday 2 March

Unexpected fine day. made a start at dawn for the Glacier. Traversed & fixed the country & found the distance nearly double what I thought, however got up after an awfull scramble, & got back to the Camp after dark. The two Dogs in a delapidated condition – hunting Rabbits – & myself not much better. The Therma is a most magnificent Glacier Walled round by high precipices. The terminus of the Ice is say 2500 feet above sea level. The Moraine is one of the largest in Westland & for three miles & two thousand feet in height the River dashes through Glacial Drift, boulders like small Mountains, & Creeks running at right Angles. Very dangerous to cross, as there are no Spars long enough to cross them, & the rocks were slippery with Ice or slushy snow for half the distance. The moraine is covered with a dense mass of Ake-Ake, Holy Lawyers & giant nettles, with stings on them like Harpoons. The upper mile & a half to the Ice is open, at one time no doubt covered with Grass & Broom, but now a mass of broken boulders – and Rabbits; the Dogs went nearly cranky trying to nab Bunny, but there were too many holes for them to fly to. Poker has both eyes nearly closed & Betsey Jane has one eye left but her nose is scraped & bleeding trying to jamm a two inch nose into a one inch hole.

Altogether this has been one of the roughest days travelling I have had for years, & no one but a Lunatic will ever visit the Therma Glacier twice, unless a track is cut, which certainly wouldn't be a very hard job, if it was taken up the other side – the Western – of the Moraine. Had I taken that side I would have escaped the dangerous Creeks, & perhaps sluyed [avoided] the Nettles.

Tuesday 3 March

Heavy rain all day, could do nothing outside but getting wet to the Skin collecting fire wood. The snow is coming fast off the hills & there is a big flood on the river. Eesser Creek is coming down roaring on both sides of the camp, but it can roar, I am perfectly safe. Wont be able to get down tomorrow even if it does fair up. However take things easy & Moralize a bit for a change

On the Maorie Hen [weka]

I have often wondered if the assertion be true, that man is the only Animal with a sense of humour. I doubt it.

The Jack daw squinting down a Marrow bone is acknowledged to be one of the most comical scenes on Earth, but perhaps it is only man who sees fun in it. The bird might not. I haven't studied them sufficiently to be sure, but if I recollect the expression on the Birds countenance was one of anxiety not humour.

But no one I think will deny the Maorie hen a sense of humour, who has once seen the backward glance of that Audacious bird when dissappearing in thick scrub with an Ivory-handled pocket knife, or a long cherished Merscham [meerschaum pipe], & I believe they have other qualities in common with human beings.

I have an interesting family of them round the Camp at present, a father mother & three cheeky youngsters, & really how wonderfull they are in their ways. I can tell as well what they are saying as if I had the magic ring of King Solomon. The other day there was an unopened Jam pot lying outside the Tent. She came along turned it over, looked wise, pecked around the rim but could make nothing out of it. He came up & shoved her to one side, with a 'clear out old Woman what do you know about opening Jam Pots'? He propped the Jar of Ambrosia on its side & struck an attitude, while the Wife & family gazed in admiration as the Old man raised his shoulders above his head, then came down with a bang on the Tin. Julius Ceasar! What a discomfiture, his beak glanced off & buried itself up to the eyes in the Mud. The Youngsters sniggered, the Old Woman trying to put on a hypocritical look of sympathy rushed forward & said 'Are you hurt, dear, do let me straighten your proboscis & wash the mud out of your eyes & then try again I know you can open Jam Pot'. 'Try it yourself he yelled, you know I don't care for Jam' & he sneaked away to repair & wash his beak. Since then he avoids that Tin but she tapps it & looking steadily at him, remarks 'how good some people are at opening Jam Pots,' while the Young fiends make his life a burden, by their muffled sniggering.

He looks at me now and again with an expression which plainly says 'I wish you would clear out with your Jam Pots ye long legged featherless scare crow', & I wish I could clear out.

Wednesday 4 March

Heavy storm of wind & rain. Had to get up & put brakewind round the Tent before I could kindle the fire. It was blowing a regular Paddies Hurricane. Up & down & all points of the compass at once. Blankets and everything wet, but got on snug after a bit, & dried clothes &c.

Betsey Jane generally lies at my feet & the weather was so bad that poor Poker determined to try & get under the Tent also. He couldn't lie before the fire, there was no room so he commenced a piece of Generalship, to try & get Betsey out & himself in, but she knew too much for him & wouldn't budge.

Then he made an appeal to my feelings, he shivered & looked at me, then he craned his neck over, & evidently thought there was room for him between me & the back of the Tent; he looked with eyes that plainly told me so. He takes up as much room as a two year old Donkey, but the weather outside was certainly miserable, & his cute hints were too much for me & I let him in, & there he now is jammed behind & giving vent to his happiness, in occaisonal groans of satisfaction.

Thursday 5 March

Weather clearing up but putting more snow on the hills. Hope to get away tomorrow, as I am on quarter rations Flour, no Tea or Sugar but fortunately plenty of Birds & Tobacco. I have got awfully stiff and lazy lying cramped up in a Tent, that I feel the truth of the old saying 'The less you have to do, the less you do,' but the march down the River will liven me up again. Don't feel in the humour to write anything & besides I am nearly out of Candles.

Friday 6 March

Got down to Camp at head of Sediement flat. No use hurrying as I cant cross the River yet. Hope Ill be able to cross tomorrow as I have no fancy for going down this side if I can help it.

Sketched in the Devide from Ragan to Aspiring, collected speciemens & took bearings of the strike & Dip of the rocks going down. The River is going down very slowly and the Creeks are still high. Singular that what I called Glacier Creek, although high was running clear, going up it was low & white like a Snow River, will work out this problem at my leisure some day.

The strata on the hill opposite is Schist but of a harder nature than on the Devide Strike No East & So West Dip 25° So East.

The Devide from Ragan to Issus is soft Schist – Aspiring Slates – with a general strike of No & So. Dip 20° West. This Dip appears to be the same all the way to the top of the range. The Average height of the Peak I would say is a little over 7000 feet. They are topped with Ice in most places. Evidently the Crown of large Ice fields which flow principally to the East side.

Saturday 7 March

I am now safe down to my Camp opposite the Axius, among the Moral Engines again – the Mosquitos & Sandflys – but with plenty of Tucker & Candles, & with a Duff & Maorie Hen on the Fire. Very tired with my tramp but I intend to make a night of it.

This is about the first time I ever was on a Journey like this, & showed such bad Generalship as to have my Tucker on one side of a River & myself on the other; but the weather looked so tempting when I went up & I made so sure of being able to cross and recross on the upper Flats that I chanced it.

The River was very high, coming down which gave me a great deal more Bush travelling, & although I got it in four branches all nearly about a size, it was touch & go getting accross. I thought at one time I would have had to give it up & make down the East side, or chance being washed up on the right bank.

On the subject of Fording, how few people really know what precautions to take. I am not speaking of those Dunderheads who take the foot of a straight rapid, or cross at a certain place simply because that happened to be the Ford when they were there a few years ago. Such people are past speaking too. But take the men who do know a little, just watch them going into a River, they never look to see where the current they are going to cross runs to—where they would land if a tumble took place, and every man Jack of them partly unhitches his Swag with the full intention of chucking it away if a tumble does take place. Why the Fools unless they are carrying stones or Ironmongery, an ordinary Swag will float for two or three minutes, and is as good to hold on to as a small raft & if a man will only throw it off, but keep the straps in his hand, it gives a splendid purchase to enable you to gain your feet, if, as is more than probable, footing is there to be gained.

Today my Swag would certainly have sunk, as I had a Rifle, Axe, & a lot of rocks & very little else. But I had two good Billies, & I rolled them empty in the center of the Swag, with their lids tightened on with a strip of greased Calico, & I am sure that Swag would have kept me above water for half an hour. A bundle of Flax sticks broken into small pieces & jammed into a bag will float a man easily, but the Art in safe Fording is to always select a place with the current running into a back. You are out & clawing up on the shore almost before you are aware that you have got washed off your feet.

To show how a little thinking will in an emergency get a man over almost any river, take the following.

I knew a man on the coast named Nicholl, who was the best forder I ever saw & he couldn't swim a stroke. Going South from the five mile with a Tin pump on his shoulder, he came to the Waiho which was in high flood. There was no boat in those days – most people would have turned back, but not so Cousin Jack [a man from Cornwall]. He stuffed his Coat in one end of the Pump & his shirt & Trousers into the other, tied some flax guys round to keep all tight & to hold on to, then he took a rapid that struck well into the opposite side, waded in till carried off his feet, and whoop the Pump held athwart the stream, shot him accross at once his head & shoulders weren't even Wet.

Sunday March 8
Taking things easy. Filled in a few Sketches, & making ready for a start tomorrow. The hills are all covered with Snow, but the weather looks well. I had intended to write a summary of the Trip to-day, but will reserve it till I get to Castle Douglas where I have a Table to spread out everything & make up my notes. My notes are very like [Joe] Collyers day book, when he kept the Govt store on the Okura. I certainly never jot down on chips of Wood Shingles or pieces of Bark, but my notes are scattered over note books scraps of paper & backs of letters. There is one thing about this Trip I am pretty sure of: that is I'll

never see the head of the Waitoto again, unless some one hires me as a guide at £1 a day. There are no indications of any Minerals up it, till near the Glacier, which shows conclusively that the Mineral belt is under the Snow & Ice.

Monday 9 March

Started at Sunrise with one camp, leaving the other and a lot of Tucker where it stands. It will be some time before I get back I expect. Got down to the Canoe very tired, found it all right, fixed outrigger & started. How delightfull after a long days tramp to get swag & self into some sort of boat, & float away down stream with little effort. The evening was delightfull & I never got out, till I reached Hendlys a little after dark.

The Month of April

Been at home for nearly a Month, sent a Map away, & sluyed [avoided] the Equinoxal Gales for the first time. I have generally been in the Bush & got the full benefit of their discomfort. Every man woman and child, except Self & Collyer, have been down with this La Grip [influenza] – [*In the long version Douglas also wrote:* . . . when I was ready a week or two ago, that confounded old rupture laid me up till today Saturday the 4 April.]

Diary of a Trip up the Axius to the Lord Knows where, in search of a pass for a future Railway, or a Bridle route through the range to enable West-coasters to plunder Tourists.

Sunday 5 April

Got away from Castle Douglas with Camp and canoe, but as the Tide was out, went no further than Hendleys. Spent the day baking & listening to his Yarns.

I may as well give one to fill up this. Of course it would be impossable to give all his digressions, but here is a yarn he told me today. The subject was the size of some of the Maorie War Canoe. I remarked that some of them were 60 & 70 feet long. I might have added thirty or forty feet to them, but I knew he would do so.

'Look here Charley, he said, when I was digging near Nelson in the early days, I found an old Maorie Canoe embedded in the wash we were sluicing. There was only the nose of her sticking out, but I saw she was a boomer. We brought on a head of Water & soon uncovered her, & so help me she was a model, 138 feet long 15 foot beam & as sound as a bell. The Maories had only finished the outside, so we all started to work and Dug her out to about three inches thick.

'Maories Diggers & Old Whalers came for miles to see it, & said they had never seen anything like it before, and advised us to take it down to Nelson for exhibition or sale. We put skidds under her & tryed to launch her, but it was no good. So I sent to town for Canvas, decked her over so that she wouldn't sink when dashing into the water, & we ground sluiced her into the River, & then we filled her up with the chips – we were four days wheeling them in with planks & barrows – & I sailed her to Nelson. Sold the chips for Kindling wood for £40 & got £400 for the Canoe from a man who put a Donkey engine & screw on her, & took her to Sydney'. Here Bill looked over his spectacles to see how I was taking it, & then he said 'do you know what came over it'? No, I said, couldnt imagine. 'Well the New South Wales Govt bought it for a pleasure Yacht & I believe it now runs on the Neapean River'.

It doesnt matter what subject you start, Bill is ready & his inventetive powers are something extraordinary. Many of his Yarns are no doubt long since manufactured & ready like Sheridans Bon Motes, but I have tried him & found that his Improvisatoric powers stand high. I have got numbers of knotty points in History explained, & when I am going away I generally hint at something I want finding out, & when I come back he has it explained working round to the subject in the most ingenius manner, & bringing it out as if he had just thought of it. I have left him with the Mystery of the Man with the Iron Mask & wouldn't mind betting that when I come down he will tell me all about him & who he was – probably his great grandfather knew him well, & his father had the Mask hanging up in his Carpet factory.

It is a great pity that Bill's best yarns are not decent, a fault that spoils most of the Worlds best storys. Some one says that there are only fifty good stories in the World & thirty nine of them can't be narrated to Women.

Perhaps the stiffest yarn Bill ever told me, was about a skating adventure. It took place one Winter he was in Canada. Canadians as a rule are good on the Ice, but they were no where when Bill appeared. He took a bet – £10,000 – that he would Skate with a Basket of hot rolls to a neighbouring Town. The distance was forty miles, & he undertook to deliver them hot, and he did it & won. When he arrived at the end of the Journey, the Rolls were so hot you couldn't put your hand on 'em. He left me to work out the problem. Whither he travelled so fast that they hadn't time to cool, or whether his speed through the Atmosphere was such that they were heated, as a Meteor catches fire when entering the Earth Air.

At this point the narrative moves from the short journal to the longer version.

Monday 6 [April]

Started up the River at high Water, got the Tide to near Nissons and then started paddling and poling. The snow melting is now nearly over, and the River is very low, making navigation rather more difficult than before, as snags are now in the way which before were well under water. However as I made a short stage only to Dochertys Creek I got up early. Camped and laid in a stock of Eels so that I havent to stop on the road – hunting, this Dochartys Creek is full of them. They are barking and splashing in hundreds, and all the real big river Silver gentlemen. I wonder how a canned eel factory would pay. The first chance I get I'll solder up some Eels in Tins, keep them for twelve months, and then sample. I think I know the way to manipulate the preserving business. Cockneys they say like eels and the Lord knows there's enough of them to open a trade with.

Tuesday 7 April

At daylight this morning it came on to rain, so had to get up and pitch the fly. Turned in again, but had to get up in a storm of wind and rain and make a brake wind all round. Collected wood, skinned the Eels and salted them; then amused myself the remainder of the day drying my only shift of clothes.

Night coming on, and having no books to read, and no Sketches to fill in, think this is a good time to give my opinion on nomenclature as regards New Zealand, and also relieve my feelings of a grievance, which I was reminded of looking over Mr. Roberts latest tracing of this part of the country; that is, taking my names off a map without any apparent reason.

It has always been the acknowledged right of an explorer to affix names to places, and unless the said names are absurd or very inappropriate they are allowed to remain. I have no objection to my names being taken off, if those put in their place are more appropriate or sonorus, or even shorter, thereby taking up less room, but why should a name short and Sonorous like Hyllus be altered to Flannigans summit, who in blazes is Flannigan. [*F. W. Flanagan was Chief Draughtsman, Lands and Survey Department, from 1891.*] I think I know most of the great ones of the Earth, from the earliest times down, but I can't recall the Flannigan as one of them. No one of that name has ascended the Peak and acquired a right thereby to disfigure the Maps, then why should Mt Ino which surely is short and poetical be removed to immortalise that Cattle Duffing [stealing] Vagabond Soutar, at least I conclude it is meant for him.

Rosey peak for Clio is not so bad, but why alter it? A fellow traversing new country has to put names or Numbers on peaks and Knobs to keep the run of them, and suffers fearfull mental agony in so doing, and when he does hit one which is poetical, it ought to remain and I'll give a good reason for that further on. Let anyone site down and try to name say twenty natural features and see how difficult it is. If he can get in that number three names that are discriptive, he is lucky. Before long he has either taken refuge in Pointed or Broken Peak, Snowy Summit or such like names, which are applicable to fifty different mountains and become tiresome when almost every River has one of them, or in dispair he takes refuge in the Browns and the Jones. Just think of the suffering you are entailing on future generations, what Poet can stretch his wings when he has to tackle such names. I'll try and give an example of what I mean. A la Sir Walter Scott.

> Mount Percy Smith shall tumble down
> Ben Jones capsise and crush Mount Brown
> Ere – Ere – Oh! blowit
> Ere ever I become a poet

I often put absurd names on, but they are in places which don't require one after the country is maped. They are only intended to locate a certain point while traversing, but I never put a foolish name on a prominent Peak, or other natural feature which is of importance in the Geography of the country. The fact is the N.Zealand Maps are over-named, why should every Knob in a Mountain have a separate name, outside of the Survey Office? Mr. Mueller's Map of the Landsbro is a case in point, there has been no attempt whatever to get out of the Browns and the Jones here. Now a stranger to the country looking at that Map, would conclude that the long line of illustrious names which decorate it from Sefton to Brewster represents so many daring colonials who ascended these towering Peaks. He would never dream that sheer bad taste and poverty of Invention, put such everyday names on the country, never imagine that Government Clarks and Survey apprentices, supplied the illustrious names and that the towering Peaks don't tower at all, but are simply knobs on a Mountain Mass bearing about the same proportion to it that the teeth do to a Saw. Take the spur from Mt. Aspiring to Watney; there is Watney, Lucifer, Duncan, Hyperia and a host of other names, with perhaps the exception of Lucifer which does stand out, all the Mount this and Mount that are simply Nobs on a well defined spur. Yank them all off I say, and call it the Haast range and be done with it.

In the case of Mt. Rickarts which is but a Nob on the side of the Thomson range it is different. That Mt. represents a peculiar formation, but three fourths of the names could easily be taken off a Public Map and vastly improve it. No one can object to Mount Potts [*in the Rangitata watershed, named after T. H. Potts, a naturalist of the period*] horrible as it sounds, had the said Potts ascended it he would in that case be entitled to torture future generations and fill Lunatic Asylums with disparing Poets. There is a craving in weak minds for this spurious Geographical Immortality, that can't be stopped. The Country is hard up why not put a Tax say £10 per annum on all those who have a natural feature called after them, unless they claim by right of discovery. If names are absurd or inappropriate, yet sound well, Keep them on if their absurd meaning is not apparent to the General Public.

Eros is short and sonorous but its absurdity as applied to a very rocky mountain is hid in a dead language. How many know that Cupid and Eros are the same? Some of the Maorie names could not be translated to ears polite, yet how well many of them sound. Nerger is the only one down here with a good handy name, yet Nerger in Danish may mean Jones or Smith. My Brother at home objected to my Mts. Alpha, Beta, etc. and thought I had run out of ideas but I hadn't. They are absurd, more so than Eros, yet how many of the Public either now or in the future will know they are Letters and not names of celebrated Carthagenian generals.

Comments on nomenclature continued 18 May.

Wednesday 8th April

Still raining, took a run down to the mouth for a Billy lid left behind and to get Axe sharpened. Found Bill Hendly in a state of Mental Collapse. He could [not] even pitch a yarn, three of his teeth were aching, and, awfull to relate, his boat got smashed [in] last nights Gale, through risking his life putting a horseman over. All the ferrymen on the Coast have lost a boat some time or other; carelessness on there part as he says – now they have him. Collyer will be down to condole in a voice of hypocritical sympathy, and Bromart will forget to swear in his delight when he hears of it. However the boat is repairable. I gave him a hand to drag it up on the bank and came back to the Camp towards evening. The weather is clearing up and shows the hills covered with Snow. Surely the white Mantel is not coming on for the Winter yet?

Wednesday 6 May

Weather has been so bad that I gave up the Trip to the Axius till the steamer came down and have now got back to my Camp at Stoney Creek.

Thursday 7 May

As I have rather a heavy Swag to carry in one, I halved it and carried part up to Casseys Creek and came back to Camp in the evening. The Travelling on the East side of the River is far better. On the [east] the Nissons have cut a tolerable Cattle Track and there is no climb like over Watney spur. Prospected the Creeks on the road up but could get no indications of anything. Betsey Jane got two Kiwis in a log, nothing very remarkable; but the first one she hauled out and nearly plucked in the process was nearly black on beak, legs and feathers. I never saw or heard of one like it before. Another was still in the hole so I carefully hauled it out expecting I had found a new variety but it as the usual grey colour. The Black one is evidently a lusus naturae [fluke of nature] like a white Moarie hen. I must skin it damaged as it is.

Friday 8 May
Rain most of the day, so couldn't make a start. Filled in some Sketches.

Saturday 9 May
Fearfull storm of Wind and Rain, heavy flood on the River had to put up a brake wind all round the tent and make everything fast. 10 o'clock and Night wind a caution.

Sunday 10 May
Today has been the greatest storm of Wind and Rain I have seen for many years. The 'Surveyor General' is standing on end in the River but couldn't get out to it. I know this place I am Camped on has been flooded at some far distant Epoch, but I never expected the Adventure I had after dark. The River certainly was high, within three feet of the Camp which I thought sufficient, but at seven o'clock it commenced to rise fast and in a few Minutes put out the fire. I had just time to hurry everything into a bag blanket and make for high ground when the river appeared to come down in one big Wave. Hurrying back to the Tent to get the Fly off and secure some charred ends, I meet Betsey swimming ashore with the pup in her mouth.

I got the Fly off and found one boot, but no Trousers, Coat or shirt; here was a fix to be in. It was pouring with rain, bitter cold pitch dark and nothing on but Flannel and Drawers fortunately I had plenty Candles and Matches safe. And having found the Tomahawk I started an illumination and Pitched the Fly in a sort of a way. So far so good, but I must have a fire some way or other. Searching for dry wood in a dark bush was out of the question, so I had to go back to the Tent and dive in three feet of water for charred ends and a junk or two of rata. I soon got a Fire started, and made up mind to sit cramped before it till morning, but about 1 oclock the rain knocked off and the River went down as fast as it rose. So I lighted two candles and fixed up the Camp again, made a roaring fire of Rata, dried and the Blankets, and turned in about four o'clock.

Monday 11 May

Fine day at last, found my boot, shirt and Trousers and etc. buried in the mud. Spent the day washing and drying them, the Blankets and Batwing. The Surveyor righted herself and took a voyage up the River and into the bush along with the Tree it was made fast to. This is the first time I ever saw a boat which broke loose make up a rapid river instead of down. It gives some idea of the force of the wind. Last night some of the squalls actually lifted the water out of the River, and spin it along as dense spray. One time the Wind was roaring up the River, twenty yards in front of the camp, another moment it was smashing Trees on the slope of Watney, not a hundred yards behind, but singular to relate at the Camp I hardly felt it all the time the storm lasted.

I find although I got off so well, I have lost the paddle which I can replace up here, but I cant do the same with my Tea and Tobacco, which, with a Tin of Jam and a few odds and ends, are either now on the beach or perched on some river snag. So I must take a run down to the mouth tomorrow and get a fresh stock and see how many of the settlers are alive.

I wish I had an Aneroid the other day to see what warning it gave of this storm. I knew it was coming this way, on Thursday last when up the River I meet nearly all Nissons Cattle coming down, not feeding and sauntering but steadily pegging it in Indian file. They felt it coming and were making to the flats for safety. I have noticed this with Cattle many a time, but never saw animals travelling so eagerly before. I don't think Cattle born and bred in the bush are good barometers. They are no doubt so accostomed to nature's cantrips [mischief] and don't no where better to go, but tame and half wild beasts certainly become uneasy before any great climatic change; more so no doubt in Tropical countries where the changes are greater, but last few days storm was violent enough to give a forewarning to anything but dull headed Man.

Tuesday 12 May

Away down to the mouth. Took the Rifle intending to get some Birds on the road, but the Wind appears to have blown them away. Found Nisson and Eggling alive and very little the worse for the Storm but all hands were down with this La Grippe and looking as if some one had kicked them, on arriving at Hendleys and opening the door found the place a small Hospital. Collyer bent double with Lumbago, and Hendley so bad with the Cold that he imagined a blood vessel would burst through coughing and finish him before he had his Debts in. These pair looked miserable, and would no doubt have made each others Wills out before morning had I not arrived and livened them up a little. Baked a loaf and get some Tobacco so needn't go to the Haast.

Wednesday 13 May
Away up to Stoney Creek Camp again, got there at dark and made all ready to start in the Morning. Winter has now fairly commenced frosty morning and clear days.

Thursday 14 May
Shifted Camp up to Cassey's creek and found my stores damp a little but still all right. Found the black Kiwi and although it is awfully mauled by the Dog, took it on to skin it. On the road up also found my Satchel and sheath knife, which I lost coming down last Thursday. Never expected to see em again, as I had no idea when I lost them. The knife is an old friend. I have lost and found it repeatedly, and had it for years.

Friday 15 May
I have two good swags to carry from here up to the Axius, but I am so sick of staging that I put them both in one and crawled up to within half a Mile of the Forks where I camped for the night, one comfort I am among the birds again, piegeons and Kakapos are fat, and tomorrow I be among the hens [weka], it makes a wonderfull difference in the Flour, having Birds.

Saturday 16 May
Shifted Camp to over the Axius, as it is the Sunny side, and the one on which I must go up the River if possable. The Waitoto is still Muddie and is going down very slowly. What is the reason? The nights are bitterly cold; last night I had to fire up towards morning or freeze. Went up the Waitoto a few chain found the entrance to the Lake, a deep still channel, and had a look accross the River at my Camp. Could see the fly is up all right, but how the Tucker is, time will show. I don't know when I'll get across, but may try tomorrow, as I cant go up the Axius till I get my other Camp over, I seem to be in the discovery luck this trip. Hope it will continue. The Quartz Copper and Galenea evidently comes down either Casseys Creek or the Axius as at the Mouth of the former it is abundant.

This trip I found a black Kiwi and Y day I saw the birds I have not seen now for years and which I believe are unknown to Science; the N.Zealand hummingbird – at least I give it that name from its diminutive size – it is evidently a Troglodyte or Wren [bush wren or rifleman?]. My reasons for not catching it, I'll give further on when I have a wet day.

Sunday 17 May
Spell today, put a brake wind round the Tent for future use – laid in a stock of

birds and had a look at the River, it has gone down a foot since last night, but not low enough to ford yet, must try and get over tomorrow as a change is brewing and I cant see anything about to make a raft.

Monday 18 May
The first thing this morning went and had a look at the River it was still high, but as rain was coming on determined to chance it as I can't leave here till I get my other Camp over. The Ford was very broad and muddy so I took a pole to feel my way accross got over all right a few Inches above the belt and no quick-sands or sunken snags as I expected. Found my Camp standing the Tucker dry and everything right, rolled up and crossed over again and spent the day drying everything cleaning birds and baking to be ready for a start tomorrow, though the weather doesn't look well. There is one comfort I have now got my blan-kets together and will have a good sleep tonight the first for nearly a week. One blanket thin as a Mosquito net isnt the thing for this cold weather and keeping the fire in all night is disturbing. How well I feel that I am growing old. At one time I could have slept comfortably in the Snow with nothing but a single blanket, but now alass a cold night demoralizes me for the day.

Filled in a few Sketches and now will continue my remarks on Nomencla-ture.

When the Survey have yanked off three fourths of the names of natural features retaining only prominent Peaks large streams and suchlike the maps will look much better. Population as it gradually spreads will put on names when required for local purposes and it will not be the grown up people but the children who will in most cases do so apprivately. Children are natural in their thoughts and quick at picking up peculiaritys in anything they see. Grown up people when asked to name a locality commence to think in a crude way, with the result as shown in America, Ganges and Euphrates for little burns and Babaylong or Paris for one horse Villages, and in this country we have the awfull nomenclature of the Digger and the Brown and the Jones, the Pointed Peak and the Snow Dome of the Survey.

I will wind up by showing what I suffered many years ago from this cause; it may make Surveyor and Explorers pause and think of the Misery they may entail on generations yet unborn when calling a Mountain, Potts, or a Creek the twenty Mile.

If the following Odes are not written in the polished strains of Sappho or Pindar, who's fault is it, surely not mine? No, it was the Villanous names that squashed me, not the absence of the Poetic Fire.

Many years ago when I was a new chum in the country, I picked up a review of Burns Poems. This is what it said, if I recollect, 'the great secret of Burns popularity as a Song writer lies in the skillfull manner in which he has worked up the quaint phrases and incidents of humble life with the Sonorous Nomenclature of his Native land.' Ha! I thought, here is a country who's quaint phraseology and astounding Nomenclature wants but a Bard to make it immortal. Pen and Ink was handy, the Moon, Patron of Lunatics was at its full, so I dashed into song.

Ode to my Nannie

Down where the drunken Woman's Creek
Flows past the Cranky Man
There sitting on a Moarie head
I first espied my Nan.

2

Her Father keeped the dairy
In Peg legs golden Vale
He milked one Cow with crumpled horn
And one with Iron Tail.

3

Often having milked the pair
Half sprung he'd go to rest
Declairing on his soleme Oath
The latter was the best.

This would never do. I evidently have missed the connection with Burns some where. However try again, I might get Laurel in my hair yet.

To My Nan

Her beauty rare – Her golden hair
Her smile so sweet and tender
Her blushing cheek – like roses sweet
That blossom in December

2

Her stately pace – Her winning grace
'Her tip tilted little nose'
Her eyes so bright – Her Neck as white
As driven July Snows

3

With sidlong glance – she looked askance
My heart completely flaying
I felt alas – Like any Ass
Preperotory to braying

4

But Cupids dart – although so Smart
That this child nearly fainted,
Some courage put – Into my Nut
And we became accquainted

This is worse and worse. December roses and July snows sound strange to Anglo Saxon ears. I began to think it was Straw I would get in my hair before long, but one more trial

To My Nannie O

T'was sweet upon a Summers eve
To wander with my Nannie
To hop across the Roaring Meg
And climb up gentle Annie

2

O'er crackem back through Swipers Vale
Past Tinkers and past Taylors
Then along the winding Moke
And o'er the Drunken Sailors.

3

Through no Towns, squares and Square Town Streets
Those names inspired by heavern
And home return by Blue Nose Creek
And Gully twenty seven

4

To Xmas sports on Murder flat
We'd dander down the hill
And scramble through the Dead cat lead
To Sunny Snoggins Ville

5

But Oh Alas, Ah! Woe is me
My griefs I scarce can utter
She jilted me when Bristol Bill
Dropped dead upon the Gutter

6

And now Im left alone to weep
My sad untimely doom
And supple Jacks and Lawyers
Will cling around my Tomb

7

But first before that dire event
And ere my life be fled
Ill off into – oh hang it all
I'll off and shave my head

And the best thing to do.

Tuesday 19 May
Rain most of the day so could do nothing, filled in some Sketches got a few more birds and then started scribbling again.

Wednesday 20 May
Rain most of the day, but managed to traverse up to the so called Lake. It is not a Lake but a Lagoon Creek with open Swamps here and there. The route up is a dense mass of Ferns and Lawyers and in a high Flood it is probable the whole Flat is Flooded.

Thursday 21 May
Fine day. Traversed from four miles up the River and found the Axius Forks up at that distance. The forks are at the head of a beautifull Grass Flat surrounded by high Snowy mountains, a regular Alpine basin, the River up to rises fast say 1300 feet, but there is no Gorge only Cataracts and Boulders to dodge. But at the end of the Flat the left and main branch comes out of what appears to be an impassable Gorge flanked by high precipices. However I'll shift my Camp up there tomorrow and settle that point.

Friday 22 May

Shifted Camp up to the foot of Clio Creek. As the nights are bitterly cold, had to lay in a stock of wood, which is fortunately good and plentifull. The Gorge up above looks a sneezer, but tomorrow will settle it. There is any amount of Quartz, Chloride, Schist and Slates lying on the beach, but the Creeks coming up still show only Gneiss Wash so the Metals are further up.

Saturday 23 May

Traversed and laid off the Flats. Sketched all round and ran the line up the river for about three miles. Found no Gorge at all, but a succession open River flats with a few slight rapids; but although the River bed is comparatively open and wide, all hopes of a practical route from Otago through the Mountains down the Axius must be given up. The Mountains on both sides come down in towering precipices to within a few chains of the River, and in many places the Avalanches must even bound into it. Above where I knocked off, the river gets still narrower and the precipices of Mt. Tyndar and Urania are a caution to look at. From that point up, the River bend away to the South where if there is a pass it will be found but I doubt it is too high and Avalanches from Castor and Pollux will probably render it impassable.

In the long version of the 'Waiatoto' manuscript, Douglas gives two accounts of his climb to a saddle up the Axius [Te Naihi], and dates them differently, 24 and 25 May. There is some repetition. The first version does not focus on what he did on his 'terrible hard days work'. Neither story makes it clear exactly where he went. In the second version there is also an account of his preparatory day, probably Sunday 24 May. Other days are also incorrectly dated. Here all the diary entries are placed in chronological order.

Sunday 24 May

I had a mental debate last night as to whether to shift all my Camp up as far as the foot of the Saddle, if there is one – or leave most of it here and take a Flying Camp and see what was ahead. To go over the range and down the Wilkin is nearly impossable in my present sate. I have plenty of Tucker here certainly but I havn't a cent in my pocket – I am literally without a pocket – and would have to Sundown my way amongst strangers and might run a strong chance of being locked up as an escaped prisoner from Milford. [*Prisoners were working on the Milford Track December 1890 to August 1892.*] I have no Coat. The Hens stole my hat and my Trousers have only one leg left. In fact I am in thin ragged calico shirt and still more ragged drawers. The weather is cold certainly; I dont mind that, but if bad weather comes on, it just becomes a matter of site up all night keeping the Fire warm, when a fellow has only a Flying Camp, a Fly and single Blanket.

However I made up my mind to chance it, and at the brake of day I started with a Fly, single blanket, Tomahawk, Pick, some Tea and Sugar, six scones and four Smoked Hens, picked up my Traverse and in half a mile got another surprise; no gorge as expected, but another open grass flat, and there away up the River the Pass loomed out. The same depression I saw from Mt. Eleoner the last time I was in the Bay. Sketched it in, as I might not get another chance, and took bearings. The River now became open all the way, and I simply took it on a face, as the saying is, sometimes wading up it for quarter of a mile at a time, then a few chains of Beach to enable a fellow to come out and see if he had any feet on him. Gracious wasn't it cold wading this Sunless Alpine Stream. Betsey Jane fairley knocked up with Cramp, and I had to carry her over many of the Fords; rather good having two dogs to carry the Pup is growing, and its weight is an Item now, though I must give it credit it is quiet all the time.

Passing along the Cliffs of Calliope and Tyndar is a splended sight. They are almost sheer down, polished and furrowed by Ice but the Avalanches must be small, as they are too steep for snow to collect in any quantities, the Snow and Boulders don't reach the River if there is a flat of a few chains to come and go on, but some of the Slips [must] come uncomfortably near. Passing Mt. Tyndar the hills on both sides slope and are covered with Timber. The River still continuing open till the Gorge at Peg 51 showed up. The River falls about two hundred in fourteen chains, but there is a good sidling along the Terrace. A few chains further I reached the Forks, pitched the Fly and laid in a good stock of Wood. What a grand River the Waitoto is for wood. Here in the Sunless Valley where everything in the Middle of the day was covered with hoar frost and Ice, I got a good fire in no time. Perhaps the fact that I burnt the Oil I carry for my Rifle and used up a Candle and half a box of matches may account for my success.

The Saddle branch is much the smaller of the two and the get up looks tolerable, but I'll settle that tomorrow. Only I think I go up by Tyndar Spur. There is more chance of seeing something of the country as I go along. I have been sold every hill I have climbed this Trip through fog. Wonder if the fates will be propitous. As I couldn't get a good view of the pass at the Forks, and it was still early in the day, I continued the Traverse up the main branch, twenty chain up at point K got a good view, took bearings to the Sentenil lowest part of the pass and got a shot at a high Peak that Towers over the pass. Mount I don't-know-what, no doubt Mt Alba. Continuing the Traverse, the Actor rises very fast and appears to get larger the further I got up the Cataracts. Boulders and fallen Logs, got worse and worse till about a Mile up. I came to a sneezer of a Gorge, where the River turns away to the East, how far through the Gorge I can't say, probably it continues till the River brakes out of the usual Ice basin.

I see no evidence up the Actor that the head of the River is subject to Slips, or that there are any Glacier except of small size, however, I may know tomorrow, from the range opposite.

Got to the Camp at little after dark and amused my self keeping the Fire in. I have no Diary book with me, I left it at the other Camp so can't write anything about the Jones and the Brown. Night looks fine, and my luck may be in. I wonder if I am going to annexe any of Otago this Trip. Making a rough calculation of my bearings and distance from the Mouth of the Axius, according to Mr. Roberts Tracing, I should be a good way into Otago at this Camp, and my Traverses are all short 10 P Cent at least, and the size of the Axius up here, makes it look Dickey for the Ownership of Castor and Pollux, but that I cant tell till I get down to the Beach and plott out my work.

I am almost sure there can be no pass up the main branch. In no single instance have I found a saddle at the head of a main stream, it is always at some small branch miles below the head. Then again there must be Snowfields of some extent round Castor to block the way, whether the Axius passes that mount or not. At any rate it must be at least 5000 feet, as from a few glimpses I got from Mt. Ragan there was no depression under that height and in the direction where the Axius is heading then was a maze of high Peaks. The Pass up the other Branch appears to be not a pass, according to the usual acceptance of the term – a narrow gap through the hills – neither is it a Saddle unless the low part to the left is one. The pass is simply a level depression in the range, averaging say 4000 feet. The part to the left is lower, and may be called the pass proper. The Bush line nearly touches it, so it will be about 3500. This said depression which I call the Axius pass and somebody may call it the Scroggins yet – is very like the Flatest part of the Thomas Range, is well grassed, and I should think is about three miles long.

Sunday 24 May [Monday 25 May, first version]
This has been a terrible hard days work and I got home at dark regularly knocked up, but I think I have settled the pass effectually. Starting at early dawn, I continued my Traverse up for seven Miles to where the River branches, one stream coming from the Saddle. The other and larger one probably drains Castor and Pollux, but about a mile up I came to an impassable Gorge and had to give it up. The winter is now fairly on, and it is not safe to be jammed on an Alpine stream like the Axius, the upper five miles of who's course must be filled in with Snow for Months, and the Avalanches coming over the Cliffs of Calliope and Tyndar, might finish a fellow and no funereal expanses to pay.

Although I did not see the head of the Castor branch, yet I am sure no Saddle exist that way. In no single instance have I ever found a Saddle at the head of the main stream; it is always drained by a smaller branch. Then again the Avalanches of Castor and Pollux must run in that direction. At any rate if their is a saddle it cant be under five thousand feet, as I saw no lower depression from Mt Ragan up the Waitoto, and again the nature of the Gorge would render one useless if it did exist. The pass up the other branch is neither a pass, according to the common acceptation of the term, neither is it a Saddle. It is simply a level depression in the range averaging say 4000 feet high. One part of it to the left is slightly lower than the rest and may be called the pass. The Bush line just bearly reaches it, so its height may be say 3500 feet. The depression which I call the Axius pass (you can call it the Scroggins if you like) is very like the flatest part of the Thomas range, so well grassed, and I should think is about 3 miles long, and over the centre a ghostly looking peak showed for an Instant, towering high above the pass. I got a bearing to it and it will most probably be Mt Alba – this Mt. Tyndar is I think a peak I called from the Okura Traverse, Mt Lacconia, but I am not sure, and this Alba is perhaps Mt. Lycia.

I tried in vain to ascend some of the Peaks in this district to get a view, the Worst is easy to get up no doubt, but nothing of the head of the River can be seen their, and the ridge further on is impassable. I got up Mt. Clio, but could not get along to Urania, which is the peak to ascend, but I have crammed it all round and cant see a place a cat could climb to the Top. Calliope and Tyndar will never ascend [except] with a Balloon or some expensive contrivance. As for the get down from the Pass I will explain, by Map and Sketches, how it may be passable to take a steep graded Bridle track through, but a graded road or a Railway can never be taken there is no room for them. The precipices on both sides of the Axius would represent miles and miles of Galleries cut in the solid rock. I could easy get with a swag on the pass.

I have Tucker enough to carry me down the Wilkin, but a snow storm may come on any hour, and what would be the good taking a rough dangerous journey just to say that I went through? I never was given that way. Had the route up the Axius been available, had the pass not been so high as to be snowed up for at least four months in the year, I would have gone through in spite of any Snowstorm, but as it is I'll away off to the Beach tomorrow and consider as finished what I believe will be my last journey on the Souther Alps of New Zealand.

Monday 25 May [second version]

This has been a day of Adventure, and although I saw little, yet I got sufficient to settle the Pass in a sort of a way. What is down the Wilkin four or five miles below the Saddle I cant say but it appears to be a wide open Valley for that distance. No doubt there will be some sort of a gorge lower down, which prevented the enterprising Inhabitants of the Wanaka district from exploring the pass along ago. As the long narrow depression I was on must be a prominent natural feature from many parts of Otago, Gorge or no Gorge, it must be too low down to be an obstacle to a Railway Grade. There may be obstacles in the Valley, I didnt see as I only got a glimpse for an Instant in the lull of a Blinding Snow Storm.

The night was too cold to get much sleep, so I boiled the billy before daylight and made ready for a start carrying nothing but Compass & field book, and leaving the Pup rolled in my Blankets safe from the Hens. The morning broke well enough, the Wind had a nasty soughing sound that was suspicious, and there was a black haze covering Alba and the Spectre. But Tyndar Calliope and all round was perfectly clear, and when I started I had no idea of what was in store for me. The Climb up the spur was good and in about two hours grass was reached, but a change had come on, the haze had thickened and most of the Peaks were covered. I just got a glimpse into the head of the Axius, and saw a piece of what must be Castor and Pollux, and a small Snow field the head of the River, but that was all there was no use taking bearings as I saw no fixed points to get them from, and push on. Was the road getting down the other side of the spur? Snow commenced, and by the time I got on the ridge running to the Saddle, it came on a hurricane of wind and Snow. The Squalls that came up through a depression, no doubt at the head of the Ino, were something to be remembered, and I debated whether to hook it down again, or make for the Sentenil which distinctly loomed out every now and then. I had the wind on my back if I went on, and I knew I could always brake down Saddle creek.

So I chanced it, and in an hour or so I got not on the Sentinel, but on the ridge from Mt. Alba, but I could see nothing. I waited half frozen and got a look down, and saw the Valley of the Wilkin for a moment, and also found I had passed above the Saddle and was looking down the other side of it. The Specter and the other end of the pass was invisible, so I couldn't see the length of it, but I saw that Saddle Creek winds slightly round the Sentinil, and the pass proper at the head of it is in that direction. This depression appears to be a sort of Triangular affair, three streams going totally different directions about the one point. The only other example of the kind I know in the country, is at the head of a branch of the Pike where Barringtons and Hidden falls Saddles, from the Watershed between, branches of the Dart, the Holyford, and the Pike.

While waiting in the shelter of a rock I got a glimpse of Specter, but I was so cold that I couldnt get my compass out, and couldnt have held it if I had. The Wind was getting worse, and the Snow was already ankle deep, and I saw if I remained any longer I would become a Specter myself. So I made a bee line down the Saddle Creek at a run, and I am doubtfull if any human being will ever go down that creek at the rate I did. How splendid it was to get down out of the wind. The Climate appeared to suddenly become tropical by the contrast. When well down the creek with a safe run ahead of me, I stopped and had a smoked, and began to see the narrow escape I had of dropping from exposure.

In side my shirt held by the belt was a beutifull all round Bustle of snow that drifted in, and fast as I had come down, there had not been heat enough in my carcase to melt it, and there was another small patch unmelted in my only pocket, and the Compas satchell was full of fine snow. Had I remained much longer I no doubt would have become sleepy and lain down to waken – Where – I believe the reason I escaped both this time, and on other occaisons, was the Idea of perishing never entered my head. Nothing is so bad as Terror for lowering a Mans stamina. I got down the Creek to the Camp much better than I expected. It looks worse from away down the River than in reality and a Bridle Track could be carried over the Pass without much difficulty.

I found out three things this Trip.

First the Saddle is better and thinner than I expected though I doubt it is higher.

Second I found the Quartz Reefs on Tyndar spur and in the Saddle Creek, so the line of mineral country from the Ino [Mueller] runs as I thought. It would be an inducement for a Railway to come through this way. A Tunnell would be sure to tap the Reefs.

Third. I have often heard of a Swiss Alpine Hurricane a Termenté as I believe it is called [*tourmente de neige*, blizzard]. But this is the first time I have experienced a real one, and I have no wish to experience another unless I am better clothed than I was today. There was no Snow down at the Camp only rain, but as it might turn into snow before morning I fixed rafters under the Fly, and made all snug for the Night.

Tuesday 26 May

Fine clear morning, not a cloud in the Sky, but the hills covered with snow to within a thousand feet. It is evident that last nights storm was only local, manufactured by the Spirit of the pass for my especial benefit. According to Tradition, those beings object to mortals intruding on their solitudes. I am not much acquainted with Spirits, unless they are enclosed in Bottles, but there is one thing about these guardian beings that has always puzzled me; that is the amount of atmospheric energy they can command and the stupid manner in which they missdirect it.

The spirit of the Cape hovered High over Di Gama's ship raised an awfull storm and shook his fist at the Navigator. Surely a tenth part of the energy expended in raising the wind, would have enabled that awfull being with the streaming hair to go to the Coast of Africa, pick up a boulder and drop it on the

Intruders. I didn't see the Spirit of the pass but if he was there and raised y days hurly burly to scare me away, he made a useless fuss about. He might have knocked me into the Middle of next week with half the labour.

I didn't see any use stopping up here any longer. I had enough of Tucker to carry me over the Saddle, and down the Wilkin but I have explained before my objection to that Trip. My Compass is almost useless fairly worked out. It still acts for a rough Traverse, but for fixing Peaks with anything approaching accuracy it is useless. If I had an Aneroid and Good compas, and the pass had been lower and more easy Available, I would have chanced it.

A Bridle Track would be snowed up on the Wilkin side for at least four months in the year. As for a Railway, I explain that further on the way people out here look at engineering difficulties, it may be considered as impracticable, at present, though the fact of the pass being there ought to be keep in view. If ever a Railway is wanted accross the range, it would be by far the most direct rout from Wanaka to Jacksons Bay, and if a grade can be got from Wanaka side up. There is no Engineering difficulty all the way on this side, that couldn't be overcome by men who understand the work.

So I started off for the beach, and consider as finished what I believe will be my last exploring Trip in the Southern Alps of N.Zealand. It is not my fault I allowed Winter to be before I got up here. I have been hanging about the Waitoto for months, waiting for the Snow to come off the hills. Not last years stock, but snow that has been falling all summer dissappearing every storm, but the winding up of that storm always put on a fresh supply. I can face old hard snow when necessary but this soft slushy unstable new fallen stuff is murder to travell in. Got down to my Camp at Urania flats, pitched the fly, and made right for a good sleep the first for three days.

[Wednesday] 27 May

Shifted away to Camp at the mouth of the Axius. Just got down as heavy rain came on, found everything right, but found alas I had left behind a small bag containing Needles, Thread, Pocket Knife and worse still my Spectacles. If a storm doesn't come on, I must lose a day going back for them. I wouldn't mind about the other things but the Spectacles! horror. When I first started artificial eyes, I was reccommended to buy at least a gross of them, as I was sure to lose them everyday, but these are my first and I never lost them before, though they have tumbled into the Fire and Potts of Soup and been trampled in the mud a score of times. Once I just got home in time to arrest a Maorie hen in the act of trying them on.

The older a fellow gets, the more things he finds he can't do without. The more little nicknacs he has to look after. If I only carry on long enough, I may waken up some morning and find that one Maorie hen has walked off with my wig, and another is away in a dense bush calmly contemplating my new set of grinders and wondering what he can do with them. It is one blessing fashion doesn't penetrate into the Wilds. I carry a comb yet, and at one time I owned a hair brush, but as the latter weapon was always getting into the Ashes or Mud and putting more soil into a fellows hair than it took out, I discarded it. Imagine having to shave in a Batwing every morning, and the mind shudders at the state the Razor would often get into, and the unholy uses it would be put to when the Baccy knife was amissing. There once came a chap South prospecting and he brought an umbrella. I still live and might even survive if I met a man in the Bush wearing a stove pipe hat and kid gloves, but I don't think I would live long if I had to do so myself. I was never intended for formal society, though not naturally unsociable, but there are somethings connected with Civilization I can't get over. I might be prevailed on to wear gloves, to cut my hair like a Jail bird or even to mount an expanse of white shirt as wide as an Ethopian Serenader, but no human persuasion will ever prevail on me to crown my head with that Horror the Stovepipe hat and walk about in that fearfull atrocity the Claw Hammer Coat.

[Thursday 28] May
When fossicking about the Camp today, I found the Bag containing my Spectacles and I had brought it after all, but on unrolling my Swag last night it had tumbled to one side unnoticed; that's a weary trip up the River saved. It has been heavy rain all day so amused myself filling in Sketches [and philosophising].

Friday 29 May
Took half the Camp down to Casey's Creek and came back to have a hen hunt, but only got two and a pigeon. Clear frosty weather hope it will last for two more days, then I am done with the River.

Saturday 30 May
Shifted Camp down to Casseys Creek and picked up the other Swag. Will put them both in one tomorrow and try and get down to the mouth as this weather cant last, and two more days I will be out of everything but rice and Tea, I have calculated the Tucker this Trip very well, but I would have had more Flour had it not got twice wet.

Sunday 31 May
Rain all day, so didn't Travell. I might have got down wet through but time in Westland is not of such importance as that.

ELEVEN

Letter to Roberts, 1892

This letter was written shortly before Douglas began his exploration of the Copland valley. As usual he is sceptical about government officials. He also shows how well developed his understanding of the mountains of Westland has become. Even though he has done no real exploration in the area, Douglas guesses correctly that the best pass from the Hermitage to the West Coast will be between Mt Sefton and Baker Saddle, which is where the Copland Pass lies.

Waitoto Lagoon
17 Febry 1892

Dear Roberts,

I commence this letter on a large sheet of paper, but I am sure I wont fill it, as I must write an other letter when I send up the Sketch Map of Cascade country, which will be next mail for sure. I have it nearly done & it isn't such an elaborate affair, but I have been fossicking among my old books to see if I could get any data by which to fill up the swamp as I saw little of it from the road line & didn't see the necessity of climbing up the Plateau the only place where I could see it properly. I know I had some Sketches of the country somewhere but havent found them yet – they mayn't be in existance or you may have them up in the office.

I think I have given all I can about the proposed road line in field book &c which go up per this Mail, so I need say no more on that subject, but proceed to something else.

So you had a dive at the Surveyor General [S. Percy Smith] concerning my noble self. I dare say if he had a free hand as you remark, he might do something towards developing Tourist Track &c, but all Gov. officials from the highest to the lowest appear to be crossed by some mysterious higher power. We hear a good deal about freedom & the rights of man the beauties of Democracy & such like Cant, but no one dare act or think now adays apart from routine. Richard John [Seddon, not yet Premier] great as he imagines himself to be, when an election is near, has to crawl & cring to every ignorat shirtless vaga-bond who happens to have a vote. Even the Governor [Lord Onslow] daren't have told the people of Westland his opinion of them & there country if that opinion was adverse. I am beginning to think that Maori Bill was right, when he said he was the only sane & free man in the country.

I am very doubtfull if the Surveyor General does get an advance of Money to explore via the Hermitage & West Coast, whether he would be allowed to give the Job to me. No! Somebody who has influence will be sent, some Sur-veyor with a large party, or some Ministers son or nephew who will explore the country through a Telescope & come back with as many accounts of his hairbreadth escapes as that Bather Geo Park. Speaking of Park, I wasn't aware till I saw it in the newspapers, that you and Mr Mueller quite agreed with him that there is a pass up the Waiho via Mt Burster you must feel pleased. I don't know who it is that writes under the name of Sunbeam but Moonshine would be a more appropriate non [nom] de plume.

With regard to this recconaisance Survey over to the Hermitage, I have something to say – whether I get the Job or not – you say go up the Karangaroa or Cooks – at any rate start from the Western side of the Alps. Now there is an axiom in War, always get your base of operation as near the enemy as possable. In this case the enemy is the Hooker Glacier, I think it is called, & the Eastern slope of Mt Sefton both close to the Hermitage, that is the place to start from; once get to the crown of the devide from there the route to the coast is noth-ing. It is down between Mt Copeland [Copland] & Little that the route lies, down a stream I think you call Kaloolah or Bones creek. New Zealand Glaciers are too lively to carry a track over them, so I have little faith in a route over the Glacier via Bakers pass, it will I think be from the pass along the sidling to-wards Sefton. However I have no map of the country to exactly point out a route I have never seen. There is one thing I am going to do if the Survey don't send me out this season, that is sneak through the Wilkin pass in a week or two, & sun down [swag] my way to the Hermitage & have a look at the place on the quite [quiet]. So I wish you could send me the latest tracing of that part of the country, & I don't want anyone to know I am going that way. Bye the by, some time ago you wept over the horrable name of the Axius. The name I thought sounded fine, it didn't enter my head about this vile habit of punning which affects mankind, so yank it off if not too late. The pass may as well have a good name, as some day it will be a regular route through the range. So call it anything you like but the Douglas.

You have sent me down a fine stock of drawing material; I could start a stationers shop with less. I have got what I never could get before, a Cake of White & a drawing pen that will draw. Mr Mueller never would send me a Cake of White. He said people used it to blurr over mistakes. He needn't have been afraid of me. I never was skillfull enough to cover my blunders either in maps or in anything else.

I have no more to say, except that you needn't send me any more mapping paper. I have enough for two or three years, drawing paper is what I want, & you say you will get me some so all right. When I wrote up for some, I thought there was plenty in the office I didn't dream that you were sending away for it. About Mr Mueller sketches I explained to Mr Strauchon [John Strauchon, then Chief Surveyor for Westland] about them & I think the best way is say nothing send me the paper necessary & get the duplicates, but to get them all you would have to send me back one of my field books which contains the Sketches of the Arawata & the Pike [Pyke], but as I told him is no hurry that is long winter nights work.

Yours Truly
Charles E. Douglas

P.S. With reference to my Voucher for Wages £15. I wish you would pay £12 on to Harris Account, & could you not send me down the £3 in notes in a letter? It is so long since I have had money in my pocket I am curious to try how it feels.
C E D

TWELVE

Copland Exploration, 1892
Karangarua Note, 1895

For many years the Copland Pass has been a standard alpine and even tourist route from the Hermitage, near Mt Cook, to the West Coast, but it was discovered relatively late in the nineteenth century. Douglas was involved from the beginning of formal West Coast exploration of this route and he found it difficult travelling up the Copland River, which is a major branch of the Karangarua.

The main focus of the 1892 instruction to Douglas was to examine Baker Saddle as a possible mule or horse route to the Hermitage, and because of this and heavy snow he did not thoroughly explore the very head of the Copland, where it adjoins the Main Divide. However, from as far as he went into the headwaters it was clear there was no snow-free pass over to the Hermitage. Later events concerning the first crossing of the pass are covered more fully in Appendix 2.

There are several sources for the Copland exploration, and they show something of what happened to the original work of an explorer-surveyor like Douglas.

1. *Douglas's pencil diary in journal form.*
2. *Pencil draft of letter report by Douglas to John Strauchon, Chief Surveyor for Westland, edited a little by Roberts.*
3. *Ink draft of this report, further edited by Roberts.*
4. *Final report printed in AJHR, 1893, C.–1, pp. 42–47, further altered at head office. The end result was still credited to Douglas, but it is rather different from his original and it is doubtful if he had approved all the changes.*

The material that follows is from the draft report to Strauchon, written at the Karangarua River. Here, as usual, Charlie Douglas shows the multiplicity of his observations. He writes about where he went and how he got there, as well as commenting in detail on the topography, geology, birds and trees of the Copland valley. At the end he considers the merits, or rather demerits, of Main Divide crossings over Baker Saddle and Broderick Pass, arriving at the correct conclusion that neither route was suitable for a 'mule or Horse Track'.

Karangaroa River
8 June 1892

J. Strauchon Esq., C. S.
Sir,

I have the honor now to write out full particulars of my trip up Copeland and Karangaroa River. If I have failed in the main object, to discover a pass available for Mule traffic to the Hermitage, the Survey will now have the block filled in for good, and Adventurous Tourists who cross the range will at least know what they have to contend with before reaching the Coast. The Traverse of the Copeland has taken up far more time than anticipated, but the Country was of such a nature that tracks to get the Camp through the gorges were absolutely necessary, and the want of Fords fit to cross and spars to bridge the Rivers made matters worse. The Copeland is the only River in Westland that I have been forced to clear my way with Bill hook. Other rivers were bad, but a crash through could always be made somehow.

The Traverse is necessarily very rough, and may in places be out far more than is usual with my surveying, but fortunately on the watershed of the Copeland I had a number of peaks, fixed by triangulation with very good angles, in most cases to check my work, and the bearings to peaks were always taken twice and marked if they varied.

The Aneroid heights were taken every day, and at every station camp etc. I enclose the whole of them with the time of day by watch and they can be worked out in the office more accurately than I have done on the Map. With one or two exceptions the Glass was steady, and there was little difference in the readings at the various points going and coming.

The Sketches sent, take in nearly the whole country on both sides of the Copeland and are drawn more for topographical purposes than to show Scenery, and as soon as possible you will receive the book with the original bearings as they were taken.

I have also given all information about Timber, Fords, Tracks, Land and Geological features, noted possable passes, Scenery and all I can think may be of interest to some and of practical value to others.

H. [Harry] Cuttance of Okure [Okuru] and Betsey

Through the bad weather, it was about the middle of March before We got fairly started from the Ferryman's at the mouth of the Karangarua. The River was high at the time but the Fords were good as they generally are on this River and Scotts Station was reached. The owner of this place has evidently an eye to the future as he has 'Aorangi Hotel Tourist resort' painted on the Weather Boards with a sketch of some unknown Mountain Scene as a sign. This was all very well, but a skull and cross bones under the Sketch looked ominous. Whether the bony grinning object was a piece of Egyptian Philosophy or simply intended as a caution to the Tourist I don't know; he didn't know himself.

From this place to the Forks of the Copeland, a distance of 6 miles, the travelling is along wide open river bed with occaisonal stretches of bush tracks to escape unnecessary fording. At the Forks, the River beaches cease and the usual mountain stream commences.

The first 3 miles up the Copland is tolerable travelling. The river rises in that distance some 300 feet with high flat terraces on either side most of the way up, but 20 chains above Architect Creek, the gorge commences and the river rises 1200 feet in 2½ miles. This is not a true gorge, as in no case do the cliffs approach nearer than ten chains. Perhaps the best discription of it is a natural sluice box very badly paved. On the North side, there is a well defined terrace some 300 feet above the river bed, running up to the Flats. This terrace is rolled wash, with morainic drift dumped on the top, but on the south side from the cliffs to the river bed the hill sides are covered with immense boulders tumbled and tossed about in chaotic confusion. The occaisonal glimpses a traveller gets of the river while peeping through between or under boulders like small hills is in my opinion the best scene on the Copeland for beauty. The river cataracts come rushing out of the most unlikely places, and over rocks worn into fantastic shapes by the action of the water. Away thirty and forty feet up, snags and fragment of trees perched on rocks or caught fast in trees show the height of the river in floods. Some idea of the size of the boulders can be formed by one I measured, it is a mass of rock fallen from above and stands on a ledge five hundred feet up and away from the River. It is a flat square 300 feet of a side – 1200 in circumference and 120 high with large Rata trees growing on the top.

Those trees, like most which grow on such boulders, in course of time find a want of either water or soil, so nature has ingeniously supplied the want by causing the trees to send roots down the face of the Rock to the ground below. A little above this boulder but in the river bed is another curiosity, 'The Chair'; it is a large rock hollowed and shaped like a chair, it would just fit the Statue of Memnon only he would have to tuck his legs up. [*A reference to the Colossi of Memnon, the remains of an ancient Egyptian temple at Thebes.*] The Forrest in the gorge is a mixture of cedar, Totara, Rata, Kamai [kamahi] and usual underscrub. The Cedars and Totara are in many cases of immense size, but they are too much scattered to be of any market value, except for local consumption such as bridge, cribb work or snow sheds in the event of a track ever being brought down the Copeland. Totara of a certain sort is common enough in Westland, but the real article, all heart and no sap, is much scarcer than people suppose, so the presence of it in the Karangaroa and branches is worth noting.

At Boulder Camp and Cave Camp are two other blocks very nearly as large as the one I measured. The first is a true ice born Erractic and our permanent camp was completely sheltered under it. It is composed of hard granatic gneiss and probably came from Mt Stokes [Mt La Perouse] when the icefield extended to the Karangaroa Flats. The wild cattle had evidently appreciated it, and before we could Camp work like the cleaning of the Augean stables had to be gone through, showing they must have used it for years. The wild cattle are getting scarce not only on this, but in all the other rivers; shooting down, want of feed too and plethora of Bulls being the cause. Those left might afford sport to Tourists who care naught for wet dense scrub and mouth full of spiders caught in the chase. But then, beef is little good, and the glory of shooting a bag of bones cant be very much. And the danger which give a zest to sport is almost wanting, unless a fellow deliberately rushes on the horns of a West Coast bull when cornered, he doesn't show much fight.

After a weary rough scramble through the Gorge, the Flats commence. These are only about two miles long and a mile broad from the foot of the hills. They are partly open river bed and partly Ribbon wood and Ake Ake scrub (one peculiarity of the bush is it has a lean up the River, showing that the winds almost all blow up) – scrub with low grassed Terraces running parallel with the River. In ancient days it has been a glacier basin, then probably a lake which has gradually filled with gravell. Aniseed and other mountain plants show how little effect sun has on the flats. Such basins are very common up West Coast rivers. In fact every large stream has one or more of them, some well grassed and others so. So those in valleys running north and south may be of some value when population forces its way into the Mountains, but those like the Copland lying East and West are almost useless unless in a very wide valley, as for five and six months the year they are practically Sunless. Those above 2000 feet level are some times snowed in for months. However they are a Godsend to travellers, the delight of breaking out on one of them after miles of scrambling in dense bush more than repays all the trouble, and then the Scenery can be appreciated. Occasional glimpses of Peaks and Glaciers through dense foliage may be very pretty and verry Artistic but they are aggravating to ordinary mortals.

The scenery from the Copeland Flats is splendid; to the North Mt Lyttle [Lyttle Peak] towers up looking far higher than it really is. The peak is a well formed Tent ridge and the slopes of the mountain are covered with a splendid Glacier of the third class. This Glacier is very steep and is continually sending down masses of snow and blocks of Ice and rocks.

In severe winter the Snow slope from Lyttle comes down to near the Flats, as shown by gravell and small rocks lying on the top of boulders in that peculiar losely packed way which only melting snow can give. When in that state the scene must be magnificent; a towering peak and a Glacier terminating in a long serpent like slope of white snow flanked by dark bush and still darker cliffs. If a road was only through this country, Winter would be the time to visit it. Not to cross the range, that would be rather dangerous, but to see what the Mountains really looks like when clothed in white (then is the time to hear the Avalanche and to learn what driving snow really means. It is not by trotting out of a comfortable hotel and back the same day that natures wonders can really be seen.) Let some enterprising Tourist or alpine explorer just try up a Westland River in the winter and the glories of the mountains will show themselves to his eyes. The extra dangers at that season are mostly imaginary, though the extra discomfort is certainly not.

About thirty chain below the Cuttance [Lyttle] Glacier the Ruera River forks and recieves a branch which drains a Glacier [Marchant] on the southern slopes of Mt. Copeland, but I only saw the top of it from point H. The creek didn't look a bad one to go up but little was to be gained by the journey. The days were closing in and time was pressing. Before leaving the Ruera there was one pecularity worth a passing notice. The Main Copland ran the usual dirty white glacial water, but the former stream was nearly as black as water coming out of a Coal pit. I never saw water so coloured in any stream in all my travells, and the cause was a puzzle for a while, but an examination of that part of the Ruera fan which had been cut by the Copeland showed that an outcrop of the very soft dark Schists must be under the Glacier and the grinding down of it coloured the water. This variety of Schist shows in the Waikupakupa River but I thought it died out there such is not the case but the outcrop must be very small, on the so. side of Copeland ranges.

Away on the south side of the flats is one of the wonders of the Copeland, namely the Sierra. The Jagged peaks and broken face of the Wakatipu 'Remarkables', all that I have read or seen of rugged ridges or mountain, sink into insignificance before this wonderfull sight. A range of broken shattered cliffs, topped by a serrated ridge looking as if some Giant with little skill and a very bad file had attempted to make a saw out of the Mountains. 'The Splinter' [Splinter Peak] is an immense slab of rock pointing along the ridge, but its end standing out from the solid hundreds of feet; other points and slabs look as if the slightest shock would send them tumbling into space. Wherever a glimpse can be obtained of the slope to the southward, masses of snow show the presence of a large snowfield over the ridge. The whole ridge is unmistakable evidence that no Earthquake of a severe character has shaken this part of the Island for ages, as such a shock would have brought most of the jagged tops down to the foot of the cliffs. The sketch sent with the map gives a very poor idea of this ridge, but no doubt it is better than no Sketch and will at least give some idea of what I have faintly attempted to discribe. Other countries may show better Glaciers, higher mountains, than the Copeland but I doubt if anything like the Sierra can be seen away from the Moon as seen through a large Telescope.

Near the top of the flats Scotts Creek comes over almost the only waterfall on the river. The Creek rises from a small elevated Glacier on Scotts Peak, and is only interesting for the fall 50 feet high, and the Snow shoot from the Glacier a narrow sloping Gorge commencing just above the fall. This shoot has piled the Creek nearly to the Flats with shattered boulders all sharp and Angular as they fell from the cliffs. Kiore Flats [Welcome Flat] the name and Rata.

Leaving Kiore Flats, the river runs for a short distance over stoney beaches and among rocks, but on the little rise, till all at once it brakes out through a narrow Gorge, rising in cataracts three hundred feet in a few chains. The travelling now becomes difficult, instead of the Schist and gneiss boulders of the lower gorge which at least give good footing, the slippery Torlesse Slates come in, making progress up to the Forks rather slow. It is not so much the greasy nature of the boulders, as the fact that numbers of them are 'rockers' which makes travelling rather dangerous. The bush on either side also changes. The Cedars, Ratas and Totaras are still there, but they tower as solitaries above a dense undergrowth of various discriptions of mountain scrub, a jungle hard to billhook and that can neither be crawled over nor under. Opposite 'Big Slip', the terminal moraine of the Strauchon Glacier commences and runs up to the Forks, as an almost perpendicular face of Drift 600 feet high, cut but very slightly with small watercourses.

This moraine abuts on the lower end against the precipitous spur from Mount Price [Price Peak] and at one time no doubt filled the whole Valley. But it has been worn to its present form by the action of the Copland and Raureka Rivers. A road could never be taken either down it or along the face. It is standing safe at present but remove the Trees, and down it would come in immense slips. The whole valley is remarkably free from 'land slides'. The Big Slip is the only recent one on the river of any size, it has come entirely from above, a height of nearly two thousand feet and has not only filled up the river, but the rocks have bounded hundreds of feet up the other side. This slip is I should say from the size of the scrub about ten years old, and at the time it fell must have completely blocked the river, but not for long. Such slips contain too much rock and too little earth to dam those dangerous bodies of Water so fatal in other parts of the world. The rocky spur from Prices Peak mentioned before must at one time have sent down great masses of rock, as on that side down to the flats the slope is piled with boulders like the south side of the lower Gorge, but it is at rest now and the cliffs look as if they could fall no more. At one time the Westland Rivers must have been subject to slips larger and more numerous than in the present day. A slip coming down into a river bed is a rarity nowadays, but up every river there is evidence of whole hill sides having come down, sweeping all before them, at what date this took place is hard to say. They are now covered with full grown Trees, but all appear about the same age. As if some exceptional commotion had take place along the coast, perhaps a very wet season combined with an Earthquake shock at the right moment did the business.

The River all the way up to and near the Glacier is unfordable and unjumpable and up the Marchant [upper reaches of the Copland River] for two miles it is the same, so as we were on the wrong side of the river and had to go up to Baker's Saddle somehow, it became a question of throwing a spar accross, but here was the difficulty. A good place to cross had no spar handy, and vice-a-versa. At last near the middle Forks we found a large flat rock standing in the middle of the river and away 300 feet up the hill was a Cedar spar about fifty feet long. This we cut and lowered with the rope and after some manoeuvering it was proped up against the rock at a considerable angle. I scrambled up hauled up the swags, and the next thing was to get Betsey across. The spar was too steep for her to walk, so we made her fast to the middle of the rope and it was haul away, and I'll never forget the imploring look and howl of that valuable animal as she felt herself launched into space over a foaming torrent. The other end of the rock was a short spring into shallow water. The swags were launched over, the Dog prefered to jump, and the Copeland was crossed in safety.

From the Strauchon Glacier down to the Forks, the Copeland [Strauchon branch] has cut a deep rugged channel through the moraine. The south side has a comparatively gentle slope from Round Peak, but the north side is almost as steep as the terminal face. The river is passable travelling considering the country and rises very fast to the Ice. Then along the Ice to the foot of the saddle the rise is slight, some 400 feet. Near the lower end of the Ice is a broken hill point K some 200 feet high composed of moranic Drift. From the cairn on this point, a complete view of the Strauchon Glacier, Mt. Cook, Stokes [La Perouse], and Banks Peak [Sibyl] can be obtained. This glacier which is one of the first order is fed principally from the eastern slopes of the Stokes and Banks Peaks and its size is out of all proportion to the snow fields at its head, but as it lies in a sunless valley and the winter drift into the Saddle, exposed as it is to the full sweep up the Copeland of the southerly gales, no doubt accounts for the large mass of Ice. From its terminus, to the ascent to the Saddle, the glacier is so covered with Debris that it is hard to believe when necessary crossing it that beneath you are hundreds of feet of Solid ice. Here and there in round holes or cracks where a cavern roof has collapsed the ice can be seen, but otherwise the walking, but for the absence of vegitation, was just the same as coming up the moraine.

To the right the _____ a small glacier on Banks Peak has broken the regularity of the terraces, which run from the ascent of the saddle to foot of the glacier. Those terraces are about 200 feet high, and are by far the most difficult and dangerous part to travel, worse than any I have ever seen. The Torlesse slates dont pack as well, they are packed with drift so losely that the greatest care must be taken going up them. Once on the top, good going being covered with grass and small patches of scrub, stunted. The slope from Rugged and Banks Peaks is gentle for a thousand feet up, but further on the cliffs from Banks Pk come and sheer down two thousand feet up. The cliffs of the Copeland Range being the same height on the opposite side, form as it were a frame for a picture of wonderful grandeur. The blue ice slopes of Baker's Saddle in the middle distance, and the gleaming brows of Mt. Cook in the background are about 150 feet high and are flat on the top, but they only extend from point K for about 40 chains when the cliffs from Copeland cut them off. Between that Spur from Copeland and Stokes are two small glaciers of the perpendicular class. The first one is down from a comparatively low saddle Maurupeka [perhaps Cuttance Pass] forming an interesting but impracticable route into Cooks river. The other is simply a slope of snow and ice from the ridge seperating the southern slope of Mt. Stokes from the Copeland watershed.

The trunk of the Strauchon glacier is flanked, as said before, by towering precipices, but once past them the ice stream widens out and is feed from slopes of snow on either side. A face of clear siriac [serac] ice leads up towards Baker's Saddle, the ascent to which it would be best to attempt from the middle for a few hundred feet, then edge away towards Stokes, but at certain seasons the falling rocks and Avalanches must make the enterprise very dangerous. Near the top the Snow field is almost flat and although this has been an exceptionally season for hills clear of snow I saw no outcrop of rock anywhere on the Saddle except one block well up the slope of the Stokes.

The Marchant [upper Copland] River

This stream come out of a second class glacier [Copland Glacier], feed by the snows of Banks Peak and Raureka. Proceeding from the middle [forks], the River bends away to the south for about a mile and then to the right. The peak of Mt Sefton towers in immense precipices with its glaciers hanging as it were on the top of Cliffs 2000 feet sheer down. From the foot of the cliffs to the river, the valley is filled in with a slope of old debris rising two thousand feet in about a mile and over this slope in places avalanches are continually coming down almost to the river bed. High as Sefton is, it is too steep on its northern face to hold a river and glacier large enough to reach the bed of the River, but the continual denuding of the rocks has filled in the whole valley of the Marchant from the glacier to the Forks with this slope of debris except where the avalanches have come down. The whole country is covered with scrub that defies discription. Fortunately the rocks are not like those in the [lower] Copland. They are smaller and better packed, so when any sort of a track is cut through the scrub the travelling would be tolerable, but to hack through that jungle a fellow would need to carry a grind-stone to keep tools in order.

Forced by the slips from Mt Sefton to coast along the base of Round Peak, the Marchant has cut a trench through the Drift for about two miles, when the terminal moraine of the Marchant [Copland] glacier comes in from the North. Although not so wide as the Strauchon Moraine, this one is very nearly as high at its face, but it is far more cut into ridges. A branch coming off Sefton joins the river just below the terminal face of the Main glacier and has assisted in rounding off the country at what might be called the upper Forks. This south branch is a small one and sends no ice to the Forks, but the drift from it and a small elevated glacier on Mt Raureka evidently has periodical fights with the main Glacier. Crossing the debris of this branch there is an open spur which leads to the crown of the Divide, a height of I should say 6000 feet above sea level. The top was bare of Snow when I saw it first, but it must be remembered that in ordinary seasons the usual Winter fall might not melt and this pass [Copland Pass] may thus be considered as covered with perpetual snow (note that snow fall prevented more explorations). [*The ink draft report added:* We saw this pass when it was bare but a heavy fall of snow prevented further explorations in that quarter, and although the snow came off most of the hills in a day or two it never left the pass or higher peaks.]

Geology

The Geological features of this part of the country are not of very much interest. The variety of the Rocks are few and they run with a regularity of Dip and strike that appears to be characteristic of the Southern Alps round the Mt Cook block. Some twenty five years ago, when I prospected from the Lower Forks up as far as Architect Creek, there was a little payable gold at the Lower Forks and on the River up to the Creek gold could be got all along the edge of the banks. The gold was very fine and in those money making days the prospects were not considered payable. Since then, a party built a Hut some twenty chain above the Lower Forks and set in to work. What they got, I never heard but the result was evidently not encouraging as they soon left and the place was deserted for years. Four years ago, I went up again to try and get through the gorge and found two men living in the Old Hut and digging along the edge of the river, they soon left disgusted and no one has been up since. Both parties told me they prospected the river for miles and got a little gold etc.etc. But I have my doubts about their veracity. A few chains above Architects Creek is the gorge where no one but a Lunatic would look for gold. The flats above don't show even a colour and they never saw them, and above Architect Creek I never could get the slightest indication of gold or any other metal.

The whole country at the head of the river is composed of the Torlesse Slates and the non metaliferous Granitic Gneiss lower down, with the exception of the patch of Schist on Mt Lyttle. There are no Auriferous rocks in the country and in the Creek and river beds there is not the slightest trace of Reef Quartz or Iron stone belts. Note absence of Lightning strokes on the Hills like up Cook and Waiho Rivers. Any gold that exists has come down Architect Creek but whether it came from the head waters around Lyttle and Copland or through the Anontio's Saddle [now Whales Saddle] from Cook River it is hard to say. I believe it came through the Saddle in ancient days, when the ice flow from the basin of Cook and Tasman poured not only down Cook River but into the Karangaroa.

Up the Copland, the Gneiss is the main rock with an average strike no.E and So.West and a dip of 80 West. Above the Middle Forks the strike is nearly the same but the Dip is East I didn't find the junction of the Torlesse Slates but it is some where in this locality.

Note of Speciemens brought down.

No. 1

At Shelf Cliff Gneiss Strike No.No.West and So.So.East Dip. 25 West.

No. 2

Cliffs below Prices Peak Gneiss No.East and So.West dip. 80 West.

No. 3

Scotts Creek 2000 feet up No.East and So.West. Dip. 80 West.

No. 5

Spur from Mt. Scott 4000 feet up Strike No. and So. Dip 25 East.

No. 6

Banks Peak, 5000 feet up Torlesse Slates Stroke North and South Dip 25 East.

On the other side of the Strauchon Glacier the Strike is No. and So. and the dip is perpendicular. The Torlesse formation up this river is not so well defined as it is away north and the nature of the rock is different. It hasn't the dark appearance of the Slates of Mt. Tasman, but looks as if it were merging into the Gneiss gradually. Another feature is the almost total absence of Rock Crystal on the debris of the glacier, the Balfour and Fox Glaciers are strewn with blocks covered on one side with a sugary coating of Crystals. Red, white and green and masses of pure Silica two feet long and six inches in diameter can be got on the hills, but no such thing shows in the Copeland. A few minute Crystals I certainly saw but they were not noteworthy.

About a Mile below Architect Creek are several Mineral Springs coming from the foot of the cliffs. Their temperature is above the other waters, but they could hardly be called hot springs where they emerge from the shingle, though no doubt they are true thermal springs, yet the long distance they travel through loose drift mixing perhaps with other waters may perhaps cool them. A reserving of Hot Spring and Mineral. If sunk on no doubt they would be warm at any rate they smell bad enough. Up through the first gorge is Therma Creek, a large evil smelling stream the water is cold and tastless, but in the still pool thick scum blotched with tints of yellow and red lies on the water. This can be skimmed to one side like cream and the clear water is seen beneath. What the mineral components of the creek are I dont know but they are certainly strong. Such cold mineral springs are very common, all along the ranges but they are seldom so large as Therma Creek. Whatever is in them they are totally different from the redish springs which come out of bogs.

Ornothological

No Kakapoes outside the Birch [beech] North of the Maita [Mahitahi]. Years ago the Karangaroa and other rivers in Southern Westland were celebrate for their ground birds, no prospector need carry meat with him, even a gun was unnecessary nothing was required but a dog, almost any mongrel would do. The Weka prowled round the Tent, anexing anything portable and the Kiwi made night hedious with its piercing shriek. The Blue Duck crossed over to whistle a welcome. The Caw Caw [kaka] swore and the Kea skirled, Piegeons, Tuis, Saddle backs and Thrushes hopped about unmolested. The chorus of the Bell bird was heard in the dawning and all were tame and inquisitive, but now all this is altered. The Digger with his Dogs, Cats, Rats, Ferrets and Guns have nearly exterminated the Birds in the lower reaches of the southern rivers. The cry of the Kiwi is never heard and a Weka is a rarity. The Blue Duck once so green [inexperienced], is as carefull of himself as the Grey and Robins are extinct. But the Flats of the Copeland put a fellow in mind of old days; it was full of birds all tame and inquisitive as of old. The Kiwis were of larger size than usual and very light in colour, some were completely White on the Belly and many of the Wekas had white feathers, and they were larger and more like the East than the West Coast Bird which as a rule are smaller and darker than those of Otago and Canterbury.

The Robins ate out of your hand and the Bell Birds sung its chorus in a style only now to be heard below Jacksons Bay and the Blue Ducks were as tame as of yore. Before we left the Copland and coming away we saw the Tracks of a Cat. Such is the result of the advent of the white man a few more months and pussy will extend operations and the small birds will vanish for ever and worse and worse the Ferrett is on his way up from south.

Land Timber &c

In the lower reaches from the sea to the hills the Karangaroa wanders over a wide river bed with large patches of open grass land adjoining suitable for sheep but very liable to floods as they stand very little above the river but the great width saves them to a certain extent as Mr. Scott who has had sheep on them for several years has lost very few from that cause. Still there is a risk. The grass toped hills carry sheep and keep them in good condition for about eight months in the year, but there extent is limited as the spurs leading back to the main ranges are impassable razor backs. So if Sheep farming on this and other rivers is ever carried on to a payable extent, settlers must clear land below on the flats. Away from the river the Bush Islands on the Karangaroa are easily cleared and grow very good grass but they are always liable to be washed gradually away.

Towards Saltwater River the land is good but heavily timbered for a mile back and then open swamps extend in patches to Cook River. These are reclaimable by burning and cutting ditches to carry off the water and I believe it would pay better to attack them than the bush. They would take longer time to lay down in grass as they must be dried first, but the expense is nominal compared with bush or scrub clearing. Similar country extends on the other side of the river towards Hunts Creek, but it is much dryer and covered to a great extent with Black Scrub which is easily fallen and burnt off, the only draw back is that such country when cleared and not properly drained in a few years is choked with rushes. Whether Sheep pasturing would have a beneficial effect on it has not been fairly tried yet.

Further up the river, the hills gradually close in but still all the way to the Forks are terrace flats with good soil but in most cases heavily timbered. At the Forks the terrace flats taking in both sides of the river, are about a mile wide and are covered with Red and Black Pine, Rata and Totara. Some of the pines are large and with splendid barrels, but they are sparsely scattered and like the

Cedars and Totaras up the Copeland they are really of little value except for local purposes. The only forrests of marketable timber are about six miles from the mouth where the Totaras are growing in thick groves, but they are immature Trees and as a lasting timber young Totara, however large they may be, are no better than mountain birch [beech] or Kaimai [kamahi]. On the hill sides for three or four miles up the Copland and Karangaroa are plenty of large spars of ino [hinau], but whether this is the same as usefull No[rth] Island Ino I don't know. I have never seen any of it used too in Westland so I can say nothing as to its lasting properties. This is all the timber of commercial value I have seen on the Karangaroa and I consider it one of the poorest rivers in Westland in that respect.

If poor in forrest trees, the River away in the mountains shows an extraordinary variety of scrub. Holly, Fuschia, Ake Ake and other Trees, which in many parts of the Coast are merely bushes grow here into respectable trees. Holly one foot in diameter are comparatively common and the Mountain Heaths grow into small trees, even the Bush line is higher than I ever saw. Up at point B the Scrub line is close on ? 5000 feet, nearly the limit of vegetation, and all along the range from the sugar loaf to Sefton it almost entirely displaces the grass which generally commences from 3500 to 4500 feet.

I know nothing about Botany or Horticulture so my opinion on the subject is of little value but I wonder if the Heath which grows on those hills, the Lemon Scrub and other Shrubs and flowers could not be cultivated into Garden plants. The heath is a true one with small waxy looking bells and I dont see why if it got fair play it wouldn't hold its own with some of the Italian rarities I remember at Home in ancient days.

Another tree, I dont know the name of though I believe it is of the genus Heath, has a smooth brown stem and the branches are topped with a bunch of blue green foliage like the Cabbage Trees [probably a *Dracophyllum*]. It is very common all along the ranges close to the grass line and might be introduced as an ornamental tree in gardens or parks, the curious fantastic shapes it grows or can be made to grow into would commend it to those who fancy such ornaments. Although strictly a mountain tree I have seen it occaisonally growing down to the sea level so climate is no object I expect moisture and shade is all the Tree requires to grow in any temperate country.

As for flowers up the Karangaroa they are comparatively scarce. The Mountain Lilly, aniseed Hemlock and Cotton grass, about sum up the lot. No Eddelwiss was to be seen and many Flowers common in other parts of the country were either scarce or altogether absent; perhaps the scarcity of grass on the high ranges and height of the Bush line is the cause.

Charles Douglas, bank clerk, Edinburgh, October 1858.

ATL, F-147805

Charles Douglas about the time he emigrated to Otago in 1862.

ATL, 75-24101-01

The Douglas family in Scotland, about 1870. From left: Sholto, Martha, Margaret, James (brother), Fettes and Rosa.

ATL, F-56766

Above: *Charlie Douglas, A. P. Harper, their swags and Betsey Jane in the valley of the Cook River, March 1894.*

Photo: A. P. Harper, ATL, F-18450

Below: *Charlie Douglas in a bush camp above the Franz Josef, 1893–94. This shows the 'batwing tent', where the tent itself was pitched to one side of the fly so a fire could be lit under the fly as well.*

Photo: A. P. Harper, ATL, F-50864

Above: *Charlie Douglas and Betsey Jane, 1894.*
Photo: A. P. Harper, ATL, 75-241-17

Below: '. . . the pictures in which I appear are decididly actionable. The bivouac up Craigs creek would do for a witch scene with one of the hags at the mouth of the cave with a blanket round her, hatching villany.' So wrote Douglas to Harper on 10 July 1894 about this shot of him drying his socks by the fire in a tributary of the Cook River, March 1894. The photograph of Harper at the same site was probably taken by Douglas.
ATL, F-117070, F-56739

Douglas and his mai mai at the mouth of the Wanganui River, 1893.
ATL, C-22545
Charlie Douglas relaxes at base camp in the Karangarua valley, late 1894.
Photo: A. P. Harper, ATL, F-56781

Above: *Douglas, Andrew Scott and three Scott children at Karangarua, 1894. The churchwarden pipe would have been a luxury not taken into the bush.*

Photo: A. P. Harper, ATL, F-55446

Right: *A. P. Harper and Douglas at Karangarua, 1894.*

ATL, F-55444

Below: *Douglas as the blind man with his dog at Karangarua, 1894.*

Photo: A. P. Harper, ATL, 118142

Douglas washing his shirt in a glacial river while his towel dries on the rock behind.
Photo: A. P. Harper, ATL, F-55445

Betsey Jane, Douglas and Harper in a dugout canoe, probably after their exciting trip down the Wanganui River in October 1893.
ATL, F-25539

Above: *Douglas, Peter Westland, Betsey Jane, Mrs Westland and her friend, known as 'Chooks' or 'Dolly', February 1894. The party was on its way to what became known as 'Lady Westland's Look Out' or 'Christmas Outlook' above the Franz Josef Glacier. Peter's Pool, a kettle lake in the valley below the Franz Josef Glacier, was named after Peter Westland on this visit.*
ATL, F-56774

Right: *Mattias Zurbriggen and Edward FitzGerald about to set off for an attempt on Mt Sefton, 11 January 1895.*
ATL, G-3232

Above: *A Survey party on the Cook River flats, probably mid-1894. From left: Dick Beck, Alf Good, unknown, William Wilson, Charlie Douglas and Bill Boyd, the cook.*

ATL, 75-24101-22

Below: *A group of Survey staff in the late 1890s. Standing: James Smith, C. J. Pfeifer, A. D. Macfarlane. Seated: E. J. Doreen and Charlie Douglas*

ATL, F-56779

Westland Survey staff, 1895. Standing: A. D. Macfarlane, William Wilson, James Smith,
F. J. Harrop. Centre row: J. B. McIntosh, W. G.Murray, David Barron, G. J. Roberts,
Charlie Douglas. In front: C.J. Pfeifer, E.J. Doreen.

A group of Maori at Bruce Bay in the early 1900s.

Photo: Dr E. Teichelmann, Pascoe Collection, Hocken Library, 152

Left: *Ruera Te Naihi, the Waiatoto ferryman, late in life.*

Below: *Kere Tutoko and Gerhard Mueller in Hokitika, 1866.*

Above: *G. J. Roberts, Leonard Cockayne and Charlie Douglas near Arthur's Pass, 1897.*
ATL, F-123682

Below: *Douglas, Cockayne and Roberts sitting on a pile of firewood at the Bealey.*
ATL, F-56747

Above: *Tourists at the 'Iron Hut' built by Douglas at Fox Glacier, 1897–98.*

A. C. Graham Collection, Macmillan Brown Library, 470M-N

Below: *Douglas (right) on the Fox Glacier in the 1890s. The other surveyor is probably James Smith, and William Wilson would have taken the photograph.*

A. C. Graham Collection, Macmillan Brown Library, 96-2

Above: *Charlie Douglas, veteran explorer.*
ATL, F-55448

Left: *Arthur Woodham.*
ATL, F-56778

Below: *Joe Collyer and Bill Hindley at Okuru, early 1900s.*
ATL, 75-24101-25

Above: *Richard John Seddon, 'King Dick', and Charlie Douglas in relaxed pose outside the Gunns' home at Whataroa, January 1906. The coach belonged to Jock Adamson, who held the mail contract from Ross to Gillespies Beach between 1886 and 1913.*
ATL, F-56757

Below: *The last-known photograph of Charlie Douglas, at Lake Kaniere, January 1908, with A. P. Harper and his son Tristram.*
ATL, C-24064

Above: *A sketch by Charlie Douglas, looking south-west towards Big Bay from the ridge between the Cascade and Gorge Rivers.*
ATL, D-P056015

Below: *A view south over Lake Alabaster towards Mt Madeline. This sketch, looking towards the Hollyford River, shows the furthest south Douglas reached in his explorations.*
ATL, F-56810

Above: *Arnott Point from the south.*
ATL, D-P057025

Below: *Looking north from Whitcombe Pass.*
ATL, F-56822

Above: *Douglas sketched the Lambert Glacier and Mt Lambert from the Lord Range while up the Wanganui River.*

ATL, F-56815

Below: *The mountains from which the Okuru River flows, with Mt Ellis prominent.*

ATL, D-P058022-E

Above: *This 1892 sketch shows the low point of Fitzgerald Pass at the head of the Copland River.*

ATL, F-56799

Below: *The view down the Copland River from Welcome Flat.*

ATL, D-P058031

Above: *An 1880s sketch from the upper Arawata valley, looking over the Bonar Glacier towards Mt Aspiring.*
ATL, D-P056006-E

Below: *Mt Aspiring (left) above the Therma Glacier, from the head of the Waiatoto River.*
ATL, F-56785

Looking north over Haast Pass from above the Makarora River. One of the few sketches Douglas did outside Westland, though it was not far away, just over the pass.

ATL, F-56814

Above: *A sketch by Douglas from the Westland plain, looking into the gorge of the Twain River (later renamed the Douglas).*

ATL, D-P058048-E

Below: *On his trip up the Copland valley in 1892, Douglas worked hard to try to find a route over Baker Saddle to the Hermitage. This sketch by Douglas, looking up the Strauchon Glacier to Baker Saddle, with Mt Cook through the saddle, shows why no straightforward route was possible.*

ATL, D-P058047-E

Above: *Looking towards the Olivine Ice Plateau from the Arawata River. The Andy Glacier is prominent and Ark is the distant peak in the centre of this Douglas sketch.*
ATL, D-P056026-E

Below: *Mts Castor and Pollux from above the Waiatoto River.*
ATL, D-P059060-E

Above: *Mts Tasman and Cook, sketched from Craigs Peak.*
ATL, D-P058046-E

Below: *Looking up the Copland valley from Welcome Flats.*
ATL, D-P058030-E

A drawing of the hot springs at Welcome Flat. Douglas must have sketched this after the discovery of the springs to show their vicinity. The government was always interested in hot springs that might become tourist attractions. Douglas noted the types of vegetation and recorded that the spring water was 150° F at the springs, 100° in the swamp, and down to 70° where the springs stream reached the main Copland River.

*The range of Charlie Douglas's activity in South Westland, from Hunts Beach,
over the bushed coastal plain, to the foothills and mountains.*

Craig Potton

Above: *The site of Three Mile, south of Okarito. Breakers, bluffs and the lagoon exit for Cockabulla Creek show some of the hazards of coastal travel in South Westland.*

Below: *The Haast River in flood, a familiar sight to Douglas.*

Craig Potton

Above: *The wanderings of the lower Cascade River, restricted on its northern side by a lateral moraine from a previous age.*

Below: *The Arawata River, showing the braided nature typical of the lower reaches of South Westland rivers, though few are as long as this river.*

Craig Potton

Above: *Looking down the Copland River to the Karangarua River.*

Below: *Mt Sefton dominates this view up the Copland valley. Welcome Flat is in the foreground and the Copland River curves round to the left towards Copland Pass.*

Craig Potton

The Track

Now I come to the main object for which I was sent out, that is the practability of a route for a mule or Horse Track via Hooker Glacier and Baker's Saddle and I am sorry to have to state that in my opinion the Route is impractable. Impossable I wont say, for it would no doubt be possable to tunnell a route under glaciers and snowfields, but that sort of work can be put to one side at present. It is a great pity as a route through Bakers Saddle would be the most direct one possable through the Southern Alps and open up some of the most splended scenery around Mt Cook and the alternative route of which I will speak further on is much longer and not so convenient in many respects. I am well aware that in many of the mountain regions of the earth Tracks are taken over the most impossable looking canyons along towering cliffs under Galleries and through Tunnels, but how to take a Track over a sloping Icefield continually swept by Avalanches is a puzzel unless the route is carried under ground and such is Bakers Saddle.

The Strauchon Glacier is flanked by towering cliffs, then it widens out to the Saddle in the snow fields from Banks and Stokes [La Perouse] both fields coming from the top of the mountains down to the glacier without a break in their flow. But as some enterprising explorer may consider that I am wrong and that a route through the saddle is practable, I will give the best road [track] line. From the Saddle to Flats of Karangaroa there is no difficulty whatever, two short bridges over the Marchant R and Architect Ck are all that would be required, beyond the usual sidling cutting and level crossings. I have examined both sides of the River the whole way up and the line marked on the map is the best route to avoid Natural obstacles. Of course if a road ever comes down the Copland, modifications would be made. If a road is never made through Bakers Saddle, one may be made some day to the head of the Copland at any rate a practical route laid down on a map is always useful. No one can tell what may turn up in a new country.

From the crossing of the Main South road to Architect Creek it is unnecessary to say anything. The route is on river or terraceflats the whole way. At Architect Creek a bridge would be required either for foot or horse. The creek is rocky with no fords and a level crossing would never stand for any length of time. There are two suitable places 60 or 70 feet about twenty chains up from the Mouth. Leaving this creek the track keeps the North side of the Copland to the Kiore [Welcome] Flats. There is a comparatively flat terrace running with the slope of the river and about 300 feet above its bed. There are very few creeks to break the regularity of the terrace though some might require culverts or level crossings.

Crossing the river at the first ford on the flat a few chain above peg 4 the road line is on the South side of the river up to Tekanu [Tekano] Creek where the river can be crossed in two or three places with a short bridge 60 feet on rock ? boulder abutments. From this point to the Saddle is along the slopes of Round Peak to the lateral moraines of the Strauchon Glacier and thence on to the Saddle. Through the flats no road is required, but from the foot of the Cataracts in second Gorge, the road would require to be of a very steep grade say from 1 in to 1.8 up to the Forks. The sidling however is good with no large creeks or any formidable obstacle to overcome. 'The Big Slip' above the Cataracts can easily be crossed if another fall doesn't take place which isn't very likely.

The Alternative route is as said before is not so convenient and much longer than that by the Hooker but it is a practicable route with few difficulties beyond what any one has to contend with in a new and mountainous country like New Zealand. I dont know the Country from the [Lake] Ohau up to the Saddle, but Mr. Brodrick is satisfied that it is a good route into the Landsbro [Landsborough]. Up the Landsbro, the route can either be taken down as soon as possable to the River bed taking advantage of the Grass flats, or it could be carried on a comparative level from the Pass to the foot of the M'Kerrow Glacier. The former would be much cheaper and would avoid some heavy cutting in crossing various rocky creeks. A few short bluffs would require to be negotiated but the distance round or over them is very little, and there is no necessity to carry the route so close to the River that floods would carry it away.

Arriving at the foot of the M'Kerrow Glacier the only real difficulty on the whole route has to be faced. There are no foot or horse fords on the Landsbro all the way up. Just below the glacier there was a ford when I was there five years ago, but such fords can never be depended on. They are seldom or never permanent so near the Ice. A bridge would be required and there are several sites, one about 40 chain below the glacier with bed rock on both sides, and a span of say 100 feet is the best and by using some of the large boulders which are high above flood mark much shorter spans could be obtained. Then comes the main part of the work. 40 chains of rock cutting from the end of the glacier along the cliffs to the Saddle. Seddons? [Karangarua Saddle] These cliffs are nearly perpendicular and just at the lowest point of the Saddle 4400 feet they are only one hundred feet high so that the actual climb up is not much [glacial retreat has much increased this]. When up the heard of the Landsbro, we had only one day to lay off the whole country and no doubt when on examination the cliffs might find a better way up and save a lot of heavy rock cutting.

Once on the Saddle which is a flat grassed ridge with a small tarn near the summit, the route would be down a wide open [Karangarua] valley to the Gorge at the bend. This is a place where the river drops about a thousand feet in cataracts and falls in a distance of half a mile. No Track could be taken down the river but on the south side a rocky terrace, flat on the top, starts from about the top of the fall and ends in a sloping spur at the head of M'Gloins Flats – a ledge evidently intended by nature for a roadway. Note the Spike on Ryan's Range. From the McGloin flats to Forks of Copeland and Karangaroa it is all plain sailing. One creek would require a short bridge that is all. The track would require to be taken down the south side of the river to about 2 miles below the Forks as the fords in general are bad and there is no necessity to cross till then. As Bakers Saddle may be considered impractable This is the route I would strongly recommend as a Tourist Track. The scenery up the Landsbro is splended. Mt. Hooker, Dechen with its dome of snow and immense neves, Strachan and Fettes with their towering cliffs and the wonderful canyon like the Gorge of the Zara [Zora] are worth travelling to see. A couple of hours climb to point H on the Dwarf peak will disclose Mount Sefton with its snowfields, the Valley of the Karangaroa clothed with green forrest and the M'Kerrow and Douglas Glaciers, with the wonderfull low ridge between them then away down to the Coast is the Gorge of the Twain [Douglas] the affluent of the Douglas Glacier, and then the Traveller can sit and wonder how such a small stream and narrow gorge could have carried the Ice flow from Sefton, which came down to the flats at one time.

In the summer of 1894–95, Douglas and A. P. Harper were directed to explore the main Karangarua River and tributaries such as the Twain [Douglas]. The aim, as in the Copland, was to find a relatively easy route from the West Coast to the Hermitage. Douglas's illness meant that Harper did most of the exploration, and it became apparent that in the vicinity of the Hermitage, the head of the Copland River offered the best possibility for crossing the Main Divide. This was confirmed by the crossing of FitzGerald and Zurbriggen on 24 February 1895, and that of Harper on 13 March. Douglas wrote little on the Karangarua explorations, because he felt it was for Harper to do so, but he did comment on the route to the Hermitage.

The track up the Marchant and over to the Hermitage is more feasable, a good sort of track could be taken that way but there would be a brake in the middle where a glacier has to be crossed. That small piece of ice ruins the whole route at present as a horse track. Then again although a horse track could easily be taken up to the foot of the Saddle [Copland Pass] by the route marked on my map of the Copland, to make a permanent road up to the saddle would require not ordinary, dry stone building to prop up the road but mortar & dressed stone masonery and where are you to get the building stone from. The immense snow fall in winter at the height the saddle is would obliterate every season any ordinary road formation.

And again as long as there is a stoppage half way accross the ordinary tourist will not go that way. It would only be used by the more adventurous Alpine travellers & they are not numerous enough in the country to go to the expense of a Horse track even up to the saddle. My idea is to make a foot track – benched when necessary from the Forks to the foot of the Saddle then a few cairns to guide people in a fog over the range, and let travellers walk the whole job would not cost much. A Wire bridge over Archetect creek, and an iron hut either at the foot of the saddle or on Welcome flats would be all the expense outside the actual track cutting, and a man could be sent for a week or two in spring to see that all is in order it would be a fine piece of exercise for the road overseer.

THIRTEEN

Fragments from the Whitcombe and Mikonui, 1892

The reports by Douglas on the Whitcombe, Mikonui, Gordon [Kakapotahi], Waitaha and Wanganui Rivers between 1892 and 1900 are largely topographical. A comment on reconnaissance surveying and two examples of Douglas's digressions from 1892 are given here. The latter are both on his favourite topic of birds, and the account of the kaka colony combines observation with satirical humour.

As a general rule in traversing up a river bed little of the scenery of the country is visable. Gorges river bluffs & gigantic boulders with the water dashing under or over them can be admired, but as far as Snowy peaks, snow fields and glaciers are concerned, a fellow might just as well be in a tunnel or railway cutting till near the heads of most Westland Rivers. A climb of three thousand feet through dense bush on to the open grass, is a labour certainly, but once out of the bush & with a clear day all trouble is forgotten for the time being, the climb up a spur is seldom so bad as it looks from below, & if a spur is taken which stands well out from the hills, more can be seen of the country in ten minutes than could be gained with a months toiling down in sunless gorges.

I have been nearly thirty years knocking about the wildest parts of this island & thought I knew a lot, but at this place I found I didnt know everything. Crossing the sandy flats were a number of mysterious footprints; two toes like a Maorie hen [weka], with a faint mark of an inner one & a long spur behind out of all proportion to the toes. The whole thing was four or five inches long and answered to no bird or animals footprints that I know of. Could it be the Notornis [takahe, see pages 224–25] we thought? When in Hokitika I heard a legend about that bird being in existance on the Whitcombe saddle, but the Dog paid not the slightest attention to them, which it would have done in the case of a large ground bird like the Notornis, even if it had never seen one. A Westland bush dog is never afraid of anything it meets in the wilds & if a stranger it gives instant chace.

The tracks were numerous & so were the Crows, & it came in to our heads that perhaps they owned the footprints. After some trouble we managed to hunt a Glaucopis, whats his name [orange-wattled crow, or kokako], out of a patch of scrub & made him run accross the sand & the mystery was explained at once. He runs as it were on his hands & elbows, a thing I never knew before.

. . . you can never make New Zealand like Britan. The difference in the vegetation & seasons prevent it, & it is not to be desired. Eating plum pudding & roast goose, with thermometer 100 in the shade, simply because it is Xmas is nonsense, & to get up any sentiment over a blackbird that only skirrls, or a red brest sitting on a Tu Tu bush, sneering no doubt, swearing at the mosquitoes, is still greater nonsense. We have birds quite as amusing in their ways as any at home, & birds that only want a little cultivation to sing as well, and they are just as preatty as any in northern countries. While on the Mikonui we were camped on a hill side in a regular roosting place for Caw Caws [kaka] & to listen to them & imagine what they were saying was as amusing as studying a rookery of crows.

From dusk, till about an hour after dark, here is a continual chattering & quarreling. Newcomers jostling each others of their perch, skirrling, keyhacking, growling & swearing goes on, till gradually the Colony settles down to quiteness, only broken at intervals by some juvenal tumbling off a branch, or a crusty old foggie growling because his wife has trood on his toes, or is trying to wheedle him out of a new bonnet, or the Caw Caw substitute for that article. Finally all is silent, & the unfortunate mortal camped below thinks he will get to sleep at last. Sad mistake. There are beings who appear to be created for no other purpose than to spend their lives in being a nuisance, they are both human & ornithological, and among the Caw Caws they flourish in glory.

The first nuisance is the benighted, late from the office father of a family Caw Caw. He is always alone & when miles away heralds his approach with a loud Key-hack, which his family & intimate relations answer with prolonged skirrls. There is no hurry with this gentleman, no swevering from his path home, but a steady plodding attention to buisness, which, combined with the infernal signals that he makes to notify his coming, make a fellow wish he was in the pot. One comfort: his arrival only make a local commotion, not like number two who rouses the whole rookery.

No 2 may be called the 'wont go home till morning Caw Caw'. There are generaly three or four of them together, & their progress through the Atmosphere is the reverse of steady. They skylark together in the air, sing snatches of what they no doubt call songs, & gyriate about among the trees, as if looking to see if any Pub was still open. They rouse the whole camp & for ten minutes all is uproar, & every note & screech known to Caw Caw can be heard at once, mingled with the cracking of twigs as the inebriates seek their perch.

Next comes the Serenader Caw-Caw. He has no particular time fixed when to begin, or when to stop. It all depends on the state of his lungs & perhaps the temper of the community. Perched on the top of a high bushey pine he enlivens – as he imagines – the still hours of the night by whistling his national melodies with the power of a locomotive, & with all the confidence of the Amateur Cornet player who feels himself safe from bricks & shot guns. A shot fired in the directions only rouses him to fresh activity – he is never hit. He puts on extra steam & varies his song with improvisatore embelishments.

Assisting the Serenader but not quite so loud comes the Spooning Caw Caw. Tuckele! Tuckele! softly gurgles one fool up a tree. Tuckele! Tuckele! replies the other away in the distance. Tuckele; Tuckele; Keyhack, Skirlygee; says she. Tuckele, see-scratcher, Keyhack he-hou, tuckie ta ho, says he, & so on all night long. They are too engaged or don't notice the enraged yells from the neighbouring trees by Caw-Caws, who are no doubt telling them in flowery language to dry up or put their head in a bag.

Last & worst of all comes the Orphan Caw Caw – fortunately he is scarce. This is a young bird who's mother has left him hid in some bushy tree, & forgotten all about it. Terrified for bogles, or hungry for supper, he commences about dark & continues till dawn screeching changes on every word in the Caw-Caw language, & innumerable others of his own invention.

The benighted one comes early & although he notifies his approach with unnecessary frequency, he is soon quite [quiet].

The Wont go homes are quite enough when they once get to bed.

The Lovers can be shut up by cat calling whistling & making a noise.

The Sereinader I believe could be stopped by sustained volley firing in his direction. Some of the shot might tickle him, but nothing less that a thunderbolt will stop the orpan [orphan]. He is a Ventriloquest & is not in the tree he appear to be in, but where, is the puzzel?

FOURTEEN

Letters to Roberts, 1892

Gordon [Kakapotahi] River
29 Sept 1892

Dear Roberts

I had no time to write to you when I came down the Mikonui, so I take the first chance viz Allen passing to write a short account of my recent wanderings.

We got down on Wednesday evening to Hollys place wet through, & had to keep ahead of a fresh coming down the gorge, but I managed to join the traverse to the Main South road & on comparing it with the map the distance is nearly the same, so much for that. I carried the line from Sunbeam creek over the hills & joined on to D M, & the end of survey line from Ross, but I could find no trace of the Mikonui water race anywhere not even an old blaze.

The Saddle [Douglas saddle] into Doctors creek from the Mikonui is a well defined brake between the Maita slates, Granites & Sandstones, & the older schists & is evidently the same brake so well defined in the Southern parts of Westland. I made the height 1150 feet & when you correct my Aneroid reading I don't think there will be much alteration. Away up the South branch of the Mikonui a small creek comes in from the West. This creek is evidently the line of brake, & I think there is a low saddle [Truran Pass] along the foot of Dickies spur, quite distinct from the wide depression inland of Mt Rangitoto [?Mairs Saddle]. It does not show on the map, but I saw an opening from the top of the hills & I am certain an opening through to the Gordon is there, at anyrate I am going to settle it. We ran short of stores up the river, so I left a cap with some few eatables on the Mikonui flats near the Forks, from which I will overhaul the South branch when I go back.

The weather has been so bad for the high country that I have given it up for a week or two, & will do Mt Rangitoto & the lower parts of the two Waitahas at present leaving stores at one or two places, so that when the weather clears I can get on without having to put off time packing.

If you get out the Big Telescope & aim it at the hill Cropp has his sheep on, you ought to see a Cairn (K). It is five feet high & ought to be visable for miles round. I got hold of a few of the main range peaks from it & saw well into the saddle near Derwent Craggs. You will see by the Sketch, that the Creek wheels round to the back of Buttons peak & probably round behind Mt Fridda [Frieda], that there is no practictable pass in that direction the depression if there be one must be far above the grass line.

I didnt ascend Mt Brown, as I intended to tackle Mt Bowen instead, but the snow has been packing on more & more every day & I had to give it up. Mt Brown wouldnt have done at anyrate, as I couldnt have seen into that creek near Mt McWhirter from it, so must try & see over either from the Gordon or South branch of the Mikonui.

I am gradually getting the run of the country & the Geology of the same. The headwaters of the Mikonui is all the Auferous slates, but it appears to be a belt barren of minerals, as I saw very little trace of Quartz of any kind and the serpentines & green fellsprs of the Pass river are entirely absent. They no doubt are only a small outcrop on the Eastern slopes of Bowan from the brake at Doctors saddle down seawards. The Maita slates are the prevailing rocks, broken with dykes of granite & another rock; I forget the name of at present, but will find out when in Hokitika next time. We had no pick or dish to try prospects, but in the lower gorge of the Mikonui there have been people digging at some time or other, & when the track from Ross to the flats is made, Diggers will have more chance to work the ground as they can go down two thirds through the gorge with ease. It is the last mile or so of it that is bad to get up.

I got the stores all right at Fergussons, but the other lot that should have gone to Allens Hut up the Waitaha, is now up at Rangitoto, & as there is more than I want for the Silver Mine and Gordon river I'll have to pack some of it back again, unless the weather is very bad & we have to use it up there, but it can remain for a little till I see. In making out the list of stores I forgot all about Baccon, butter, & cheese so had to send Cropp in to Ross for them, that is some 17/- more on the account with Woolhouse.

When leaving Hokitika I ordered a small steel prospecting pick at Burns, the Blacksmith, & told him to take it to you when finished. It isnt in the swag at Fergussons, perhaps it is up Mt Rangitoto. If it didn't come, then never mind at present, I'll get it for the next trip.

I dont know how my account stands, but as a cheque will be due for £10 at the end of this month, I wish you would pay that amount into the account of Arch^d M'Bryde [Archibald McBride, storekeeper] Gillespies beach. His Bank is the Union, I think, or if not the Bk of N Zealand. If you can't find out, I wish you would send a cheque down to him, he has been bothering me lately & I suppose Ill have neither peace nor rest till I get out of debt some way, but pay my stores &c first & if there is not £10 left then let him have what there is. I am never much troubled in my mind making Shanty keepers wait, but I suppose they must be paid some time.

How did the Photo's turn out? You might send one or two to let me see them. It was no great loss having no camera. As far as I have been I have seen no scenery or anything wonderfull; the whole road & birds seem to have left the country.

I will write again when down from Rangitoto so no more at present.

Yours Truly
Charles E Douglas

P.S. Is this of interest? [*newspaper cutting on Exact Surveying enclosed*]

Gordon River
28 October 1892

Dear Roberts

I have just finished the Gordon river & Rangitoto today and am away off to-morrow morning up the Waitaha so I write only a few lines. Besides, I will be in Hokitika in a fortnight or so. Fergusson is to pack the Camp and stores up as far as a horse will go, and if this weather will only last I'll soon do the Waitaha, as I have now got the run of the country, but I am very doubtfull if I will be able to get accross the range to see down the Whitcombe. I have found no place as yet either up the Mikonui or the Gordon where I could get up, but I may find a weak place some where the snow is too heavy on the hills & its slope is too steep. I very nearly got on to Rugged peak but was stopped by a precipice & had to give it up.

The Gordon has been an awfull river to traverse for the gorges. Miles of it had to be done in pieces, but I think I have got it nearly right. It is a good deal longer than shown on the map & Prices river must be shortened a bit, but I must see the head of the Waitaha before I can make sure. I needn't go into particulars. In fact I can't. I am nearly knocked up marching all day & have to leave with Fergusson at daylight tomorrow & take advantage of this, the first spell of fine weather we have had.

As there will be another cheque due the end of the month, I wish you would send me down £4 of it to Fergussons. I have had to get boots, packing to pay for, beef butter &c. This trip will cost more than the Whitcomb one as there are neither birds nor fish to be caught in the country. However I have got two Kiwi egg for you. If I can only get them up without smashing them, & if I can get a live bird towards the end of the trip, I'll bring it up also.

Yours Truly
Charles E Douglas

FIFTEEN

Letter to A. P. Harper, 1894

Cooks River
10 July 1894

Dear Harper,

I have been away up Fox glacier with [William] Wilson, which is the principal reason I didnt write to you sooner. Certainly chronic lazyness may have had something to do with it, but that neither here nor there.

Your Photos came to hand all right, & I am well pleased with them. Whether my relatives care for snow & ice I dont know – probably not – but they can't criticise them as Alpin scenes. I don't see how they could be any better. By far the finest, in my opinion, is the one of the Fox looking down the glacier. It is splendid with its light and shade, but the pictures in which I appear are decidedly actionable. The bivouac up Craigs creek would do for a Witch scene with one of the hags at the mouth of the cave with a blanket around her, hatching villany. The blind man and Betsey jumping in front of me are good as Photos if they are intended to represent the two most disreputable tramps I ever saw. Do you mean to say I have that general appearance? A Witch with a blanket on a tramp without – well I suppose chemicals can't lie, I must be careful to keep out of sight of the Police.

Wilson and I were up Ryans peak, for a week or ten days, and I managed to hack my way along to the next peak, where I got a splendid view of the [La] Perouse glacier, all except the terminus. You can tell your friend in the Old country who objected to the small size of the Balfour neve, that it is even smaller than the maps make it. The Perouse goes right back to the ridge close to Tasman, & where we thought it branched into the Balfour, the ice is five hundred feet below the Balfour range. This peculiarity – a large glacier with a small neve, is common in Westland and can easily be accounted for.

I have plotted out the Balfour, and it turns out to be much larger than was expected. From the terminus to the foot of the cliffs under Tasman, is a little over six miles long, and at its broadest fifty chains, but thirty chains may be taken as the average. Its actual area is however comparatively small, as it receives few feeders & those of no extent. My measurements have all been corrected by Theodolite, so they cant be far out.

The experiements concerning rate of flow of Fox ice have not had time to develope yet. We put cairns & black flags all over the ice, & got the Theodolite to bear. Four days showed a progress of about three feet per day, but we are going up again in a fortnight or three weeks, when a more accurate estimate can be made. It no doubt will not travell so fast as we made the Waiho [Franz Josef], but it is travelling. I see little or No change at the terminus, but the glacier is rising fast up above. Your flag opposit r is now invisable, & the next point will soon vanish. The ice close to r is now high above that point, & the first icefall above the base line G appears to be coming down bodily, but that may be only an optical delusion.

The ice is now very bad to travel on, as slippery as glass with mysterious points that appear to exist only where a fellow happens to tumble. You ought to have seen Wilson and I on the glacier; only one axe & no tacks on our boots. I dont know his injuries but my hide is bruised considerably.

You talk of coming over in August via some pass through the mountains. I think you had better leave it alone. Your pass into the Perouse is practically impassable & I very much doubt if anyone could come by way of Waiho & Victoria glaciers those short days. Fyfes route [from the Mueller glacier to the Landsborough] may be passable in August, I dont know, but if you did get through, & were unable to get down the Kanrangaroa, you would have a seventy mile tramp through bush before you reached tucker at the mouth of the Haast, as you couldnt find the passes into the Paringa or Blue River.

Now to business. If you are coming back, by all means send over any necessaries or luxuries you can get in Christchurch. You know well enough what is wanted, & if you want money to buy them, let me know & I'll tell Roberts to send it. There is a good chance of the *Waipara* coming to Bruce bay in August, which time would just suite. You say you will be up the Waiho in Septr. If so, then I'll be up the Copeland getting things ready for say the end of Septr; quite early enough to tackle that place. As for getting stores from Hokitika landed in Bruce, I am not settled about that yet, I don't know what is to be done, whether the district will take a month or four, and if I am stranded with stores that have to be packed away down to Haast it wont do. Besides the packing will be much heavier, if I dont deal with the natives, and I dont care about investing in a Horse till the Haast is tackled. Up here the inhabitants are Horse copers to a Man & mokes get mysteriously lost. However I have written to Roberts as to how long we will be about Karangaroa & Bruce bay, & if it is going to be a long job then I'll get stores down.

Another thing I have something to say about & that is Fyfe coming over. I dont know whether you and Roberts have made it up to get him. I have written to enquire & told him distinctly that if another man is to be put on, he must be a West coaster who knows the country, a bushman, & above all a swagger – one who hates scenery & would have all mountains rolled into undulating vallies – otherwise I clear out altogether. I know well enough what it would be, you two would be climbing peaks for your own glory. I would have to keep camp & do the Surveying. Climbing peaks & walking up glaciers may be all right for the Alpine club reports, but it is useless for laying off the country. We were sent out to fill in details of country who's general outline is already well fixed & known, not to have our name in the papers as Alpine lunatics. Their again, look at the talk on wet days in camp, shop – shop. As far as I am concerned, I don't want another man for the trip it means extra baggage. If they would let us hire a man now & then when we wanted that would do. A man who would swag a load up on to the grass & clear out without helping to eat this load.

I dont know if I have any more to say. I'll write in a week or two when I have been up the Fox & let you know some particulars.

As for my Photographing I know nothing as yet, except that some of the plates are spoiled. There are so many bolts & screws about the Camera that I found I had to get drilled into it, as far as bolts & screws & shutter are concerned I am now all right, but the exposure has yet to be tested. I have sent no plates up as yet, and wont send any till I have finished up the Fox. I got a splendid day up Ryans peak & took to giving 1 second exposure with medium stop – that ought to do.

Betsey Jane is now gathered to her fathers, when on Ryans peak I sent her back to camp as there was some rock climbing to do & have never seen her since. She must have tried to follow me & gone down a crevasse or over a precipice peace to her ashes.

If you come over could you not get me a pup, either Lurcher Retriever or Setter in Christchurch, as small a variety as possable. A pup untrained is the best both for Kiwis and Kakapoes, it yells and leaves you to dig the birds out. An old dog works silently & finally fetches an unrecognisable mass of blood and Kiwi feathers. So try and bring something canine, & mind this, a pure bred pedigreed dog will not stand the Westland bush, whether its so much wet, or whatever is the reason, but I have never seen one live long unless it was simply a house animal out say once a month.

Yours Truly
Charles E. Douglas

SIXTEEN

Fragments from the Balfour and Cook Rivers, 1894

These manuscripts are mainly topographical in content and here just two small extracts are printed: one about the vagaries of cages for crossing rivers; the other an ironic view of mountaineering.

The so-called wire bridge, is not a bridge, but a wire rope along which an iron cage runs backwards & forwards. The trip accross is decidedly interesting, espicially to strangers to such primitive appliances. Getting into the cage requires some skill, as it has a nasty habit of starting off when only half the passenger is aboard. Once in, he sits down on a sort of gridiron suggestive of roast missionary, & lets go the hook and away he sails along the rope. At this part of the journey a stranger generally brakes out in pleasing smiles, but the inhabitants know better. The gridiron gets slower & finally stops about half way. Then comes trouble, the wheels refusing to revolve, the rope cut the hands while hauling on it & the traveller wonders where he would be if the hauling rope broke, & left him hanging like a guy over the middle of the river. It doesn't matter who he is, whether Parson, Quaker or Presbyterian elder, he can't reach the other side without using objectionable adjectives. I have crossed on these wire cages scores of times, & with all sorts of people, and in no single instance did the man who put them up, the road overseer, Chief Surveyor & all Gov officials in general escape without vigorous expressions being hauled at their names and memories . . .

However primitive those bridges are they are decidedly usefull, but the road overseer ought to examine them occasionally & see that they are safe. The main rope is all right for years, even if the hauling ropes broke any one not an idiot, could still work himself accross, but the spindles of the wheels are very likely to corrode, as no one ever thinks of oiling them. But there is no use talking about it, unless a flood mercifully carries away the whole concern. Nothing will be done till somebody disappears, but then we have J.P. & cornors [coroners] & what are Cornors for unless work is found for them to do. Even Mr. G. Mueller, the first introducer of them, fell from grace for a time when crossing the Pyke river & relieved his feelings by shouting out. What he said was 'Oh bother', but it sounded different in our ears. There was certainly some excuse, the cage was a large one & G.M. pulling at the wrong rope got his fingers under the wheels . . .

The Fox Glacier

. . . As I have written this report for the benefit of the Survey, not the Alpine club, for the benefit of those who consider a glacier not as a vehicle for self glorification, but as a subject that may be of some scientific interest, I have refrained from giving any narrow escapes unheard of sufferings or awfull perils we encountered, partly because we didn't experience any, but principally because there is enough of this Globe trotter literature knocking about already concerning the awfull escapes towering precipices, & peaks moving glaciers & awfull avalanches.

What earthly interest is there in mentioning that Jones fell down a cravesse [crevasse] and got up again minus a tin of soup & his ice axe, or that Smith would have been killed, had he been where an avalanche had fallen. Had Jones gone down & never come up again, then I would note the date & record particulars with pleasure. His appearance at the terminus some half a century later would be of great value in determining the exact rate of flow & number of bumps a foreign body would get travelling down a glacier. Why shouldnt cliffs tower & peaks stand errect? Do people expect them to lie flat? Avalanches are like wild pigs – not dangerous unless you foolishly get in their road. An ice cave is blue, what other colour could it be? If I ever find a glacier brick red, then the Universe will know it.

Charles E. Douglas

SEVENTEEN

Letters to Harper, 1895

After their explorations in 1894–95, which had been punctuated by Douglas's illnesses, he went further south, and Harper worked on reports and maps in Hokitika for a time. The pair corresponded, partly to sort out their joint affairs, and also, no doubt, because they had become friends. Douglas devotes considerable space to photography, which clearly intrigued him, and gives a further brief explanation of his philosophy on nomenclature.

Bruce Bay
25 April 1895

Dear Harper

I had a barney with Ryan [storekeeper at Gillespies] about your share of account – a subject he had no business with – and as he said you were going to write to me about it I send this note up ahead. It makes very little difference to me, whether you pay in to him or Scott, and to save more bother to yourself you may as well pay in to his account the sum of £7 which is half share of the stores I got from him for the late trip. The remainder you can pay in to Scott. If you have already paid the whole amount to the latter, then it doesn't matter; let things rip. Ryan has got paid for the only account he has presented me. He might at least present my private account before talking about no money being paid in.

This is an infernal district to have anything to do with. I hear that Scott has been blowing at Gillespies that he has been keeping me the last four months & I paying £1 a week board all the time. Whether Scott really said it or no doesn't in the least matter down here.

I am now on my way South, have taken three days from Scotts to Bruce Bay & will no doubt take as much more before I am down to my Whare at Waitoto. Rheumatics are getting bad again, riding a horse again I suppose, but they are not very bad & I don't care two straws if once I get down. If I can't walk, I can take exercise in a canoe, on the Waitoto & shoot ducks & swans.

Apologising for any bother you have had with Old Ryan, and hoping to hear from you soon.

Yours Truly
Charles E. Douglas

PS I send dates of glacier measurement. I have got a pup from the Maories and Eggs is now promoted to be cattle hunter & probably sheep worrier to Ritchie [at Bruce Bay].
C E D

Haast Beach
10 May 1895

Dear Harper,

I just got down here three or four days ago and found your two letters awaiting me. The Cheque for £6-14-0 I will send up to Ryan which will save more bother; as you told Ryan you have nothing to do with his account with me. Our joint account was I consider paid long ago by Mr Roberts with the £24 my first two orders. The other two still lying in Hokitika can remain for a bit. I am never in a hurry to pay whiskey accounts made with a three pointed pencil, and old Paddy might at least produce the account before he kicks up a row about it.

I can't tell where the missing half plates are. I sent up all that were open by steamer, except one package which you got yourself, and that if I recollect was a packet of ¼ plates. The only open packet I had after you left, was one containing some half spoilt films you had up the Waiho. That packet I have overhauled last night, and found only 6 films that have apparently not been used as there was paper between them. I opened a lot coming down, to take the Maories with, but none of them had been touched before I opened it. The other packets are just as they came from Hokitika, so where can they be? I overhauled everything in Scotts before leaving, to make sure nothing was left behind. I took ½ doz photos before leaving Gillespies. They went up in the box I think, and were rolled up in a piece of yellow cloth, can the missing ones not be there?

I had some great fun Photographing the Maories. I told them I had only three exposures for the lot, so they must devide into three parties. Next day one came to Ritchies, and said they were all ready, so down I went and ye gods what a sight. They had evidently been practising attitude, and were dressed in gorgeous array. Gnatu [Katau Te Naihi] and family were standing round a table propped against a stump. On the table was a large battered Bible & the head of the house wanted to stand in the attitude of Gladstone excited over the Irish question.

The next crowd was Kellies [Kere Tutoko]. He was good, covered with a beautifull Maorie mat, and his attitude was also good, but when I saw Bill I fainted. He was standing stiff as a poker, a new suit of hand me downs on, a mere in one fist, and an umbrella in the other. His wife had a gorgeous tint parasole and from the way she held it, it was evident she wanted a portrait of it not herself.

After a lot of trouble I got them into some sort of order & if I have only hit the time, the lot ought to be interesting. Though I doubt if they will be pleased when they find that the glorious tints of red & yellow checked shawls wont show. Wilson is to develope them & if any good I'll send you some up. He is getting on splendidly with his photos now & I am sure will make a good amateur. He is carefull, learns all he can, and takes an interest in the work, so is bound to get on. Carelessness I know very well will prevent me from ever being any good at it. I was bad enough at home, but now I am fifty times worse. However never mind, if I can only manage to hit proper time & stops, I care little for the rest. I can get others to develope for me, and the less I have to do in that line the better for my pocket money. Every baby, cow, pig house &c is gaping to be taken and people think the process costs nothing. Before you go away, be sure and send me down a few of your photos of scenery and a few portraits of myself.

I send up by this mail the remainder of my Cooks river report and Mr Roberts wants me to write something about the Karangaroa, but I think that is your work. You have done all the work this last season, so why not get all the credit? To get my name to the front is of no earthly use to me now, and I never had any Ambition worth speaking about.

Hoping you are getting on in town and that I'll here from you before going away. I am going down to Waitoto, & will be there for some months so address to that place.

Yours Truly
Charles E. Douglas

Waitoto
8 July 1895

Dear Harper,

I was beginning to think you had cleared out, and left me Photoless, but the arrival of half a dozen & the promise of a batch next mail has revived me. The one of the Kea is fine, only it really has the appearance of a bird at least as large as a Christmas turkey. The camera case was too small a one to be along side of it. The one of yourself is like as they always are when taken naturally. I certainly prefer your portrait photos to the proffessional studio ones, although probably the Public would not have them. I have never as yet seen a shop Photo that at all resembled the person it was intended for. You will hear people say 'Oh! how like Smith that is' while the fact is they only Recognise Smiths watch chain, necktie or whiskers. If Jones was in the habit of walking about in a Roman helmet, and you put that helmet on Smiths photo, nine out of ten would say it was Jones to life. I don't say if a fellow wants to send away his picture that he should be taken in a dirty apron, leaning against a battered doorway, but he should be as near as possable in his every day attire & never in new clothes. If a fellow who never combs his whiskers does so for his Photo, then he will not only feel combed whisker, but look combed whisker. You remember Blanchard's picture you took at his place? There is a something mysterious about it, because the cause is invisable. That photo looks gold ring and nugget pin. Robinson of the Wanganui looks soaped imperial, and all proffessional photos look 'I have a new set of clothes which dont fit and just washed my face' cut which there is no mistaking.

I was not having a dig at you more than anyone else concerning the barrowful of ice in a gully. I was only entering a mild protest against giving small things big names, and giving what in my opinion was the cause of it – the desire to strike an attitude as the discoverer of something however insignificant. A laudable desire no doubt in big things, but not otherwise is this thirst for discovery. A patch of ice stuck on a hill side is no doubt a glacier, but it doesn't come up to preconceived notions of one. What would you think of calling a stream that runs a gallon of water an hour a River, or a pond that would be crowded with a score of Sticklebacks a Lake? I must certainly plead guilty to having so named small things, but that was in the distant past, before I found out that Mr. Mueller and others had no more idea of sarcasm than a horde of Chinamen.

An enthusiasm for mountaineering, I would certainly not call a petty vice, it is only when it becomes a hobby that it is so & if that hobby is ridden to death, then I am not sure if it doesn't become a big vice, and I don't think such is necessary. I know mine doesn't pay either mentally or materially, and they all have the same result whatever form they take.

I have no more to say at present, but will write when the photos come. I have taken none myself, as I am keeping the camera for certain objects.

Yours Truly
Charles E. Douglas

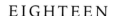

EIGHTEEN

Letters to Harper and Roberts, 1896

This sequence of letters from Douglas is one of his best and most informative. As usual he is discursive and sometimes cryptic, but together the letters give an excellent insight into what occupied both his days and his thinking. G. J. Roberts was still his superior in Hokitika, but A. P. Harper had finished exploration and was working as a lawyer and mining agent in Thames.

Paringa River
29 August 1896

Dear Roberts,

I have very little to write to you about, not having fairley started to work, but as I am going into Black River tomorrow and might not show up for a few weeks, I write a short note just to let you know how things are getting on.

I got landed on Paringa about one oclock on Tuesday afternoon, after rather a prolonged passage for a hundred miles. The weather was good and I got everything into the futtah [whata] all right, but couldn't get accross the river, as there was a fresh on & no appearance of the only inhabitant. However towards evening Hawkins [miner and ferryman at Paringa] showed up and took me over. Next morning it was blowing too strong to get the goods over and the Maorie ['Bill' – Ruera Te Naihi] did not show up till long after dark. On Thursday we got them over, opened the boxes found everything right, and made up loads for next day, when I started up the river & camped opposite O'Rourkes [Hugh O'Rorke, a landowner at Paringa]. It has been raining ever since, but has now cleared up for good weather and I am off tomorrow to start fairly to work. I did a little fossicking round the bluff and on this side of Paringa hill, but saw nothing I didn't know before, except perhaps that the granite belt is wider than shown in my map.

As was intended at first, the Maorie was to start a canoe while I prowled about, but Hawkins sold his boat to Bill for £2, so we will take it into the Lake & I'll allow him say £1 for the use of it when we get there, which wont be for some time yet. I'll now take Bill with me and don't intend to make any secret of it that I am going into Black river to finish the Survey of that block, and over-haul the forrests of Yellow & White pine on the flats.

There is still too much snow on the hills to traverse up the Paringa, and it dont appear to be coming off, but there will be plenty of time, as I can do the Lake and that block first.

After crossing the Hokitika bar, Wilson & self started sketching along the coast. The sea was very heavy all the way, and it was drawing under difficulties; what results Wilson got I dont know, but I send you my performance such as it is. We saw none of the back country and only pieces of the hills near the Coast, and near Okarito rain came on and darkness stopped all work. Coming up I sketched in as far as Bullock creek, but as the Captain kept too close to the shore all the way to Paringa I could do nothing. If ever I go up in the Steamer I'll try again, or perhaps do what is better, get the camera and a lot of Snap shot plates and bang away all along. If they are not good for pictures they may give an outline from which a sketch can be taken.

I send up besides sketches, two franked envelopes – inclosed in them you will find a lot of letters which belong to the Office. How they got among my letters I dont know. I also send up pay sheet for August Bill wants his sent down in Cash if possable; he says and very truly 'cheque no good. Me owe three different people me give cheque to one the others growl. Man who gets cheque he no change you take it out', but in this matter of sending money versus cheque you please yourself.

15.9.96

I forget now when you started Bill & self on the paysheet so I leave it to you to fill up. Bill started from Bruce Bay on the 26th and I allow him two days extra for packing. Talking of this packing, I am going to keep one of his Horses. Whether will I allow him a day extra each time he packs, or pay him so much for the use of the horse while I have it, say £3 for all the time Ill be on the river. I have not spoken to him about this, but will wait till I hear from you. In the mean time, allow him for the two days packing he has already done.

The goods were all right with two exceptions. I ordered some 10 lb German sausage from Perry and 3 bottles painkiller from Linneman. Neither have come, so see if they are down on the bill.

While on the Okura [Okuru] I borrowed a £1 from Bill Hendly, & wish you would pay him if convenient, and Mrs Bow bailed me up for Ferries or something & Bill gave me a pound cheque. I never looked at it with my usual care-lessness, but handed it to her. It turns out that Bill gave me a £5 cheque, in mistake; he was to stop it when he got up, or at least was to find out what it was, so please let me know something about it. If it really was a £5 then I must bear the loss, as I know he will never get it from her, but this is a matter that must wait. I am too much in debt for stores to pay for stupidity at present.

There is nothing particular I want or will want till steamer time at least, except a pocket knife to sharpen pencils. I lost mine on Okura, and when you send down any papers please stick in an almanach of some sort.

If Mrs Roberts would mount a few of my Photos and give one to Old Mueller, one to Mac [Macfarlane] and one to Marks [Haast storekeeper] I would feel obliged. It might be the only representation of the Douglas they may ever see.

Writing this letter cramped up in a Batwing and with swarms of sandflies about has been awfull work, so I will draw to a close for the present and will write whenever I get back. So live in hope, but dont build castles in the air at least dont make them too big.

Remember me to Mrs Roberts, Mac and the whole lot, and hoping the lumbago will only keep away for a few months at least.

I remain,
Yours Truly,
Charles E Douglas

Paringa River
21 Septr 1896

Dear Roberts

I just write a few lines, as I'll be done with the Black river block in a few days, when I will send up a full account of my recent doings, with Map filled in &c – a box of speciemen will be in waiting for the steamer when she comes down. So you must keep your hair on till then. I send you by this mail a bag containing a speciemen of Pyrites, which you must get tested they are from a belt & in situ. Many of the speciemens sent up will no doubt be considered rubbish, but I cant help that, one speciemen of which I will send up a good lot, must be well tested. It will be a new departure if there is anything in it.

I cant for reasons you know of, say much or in fact anything at present. Next mail you will get full particulars, but dont get excited, I havn't found anything that I am aware of yet.

When I landed here, I found a Tobacco famine raging, so I will be out of that valuable weed before the steamer comes, so I wish you would send me down a lb of twist overland, and I wish you would send me a £1 next mail for incendal [incidental] expenses in the shape of a piece of Mutton or beef now and again.

I will want a few more stores down next steamer, but not much as I brought a good supply last time, however I'll give you a list next mail. Hoping you are all well, which is more that I have been. The rheumatics have been troubling me a little, but they are waring away with a ducking now & again.

Yours Truly

Charles E. Douglas

P.S. Be sure and acknowledge receipt of parcel containing speciemens they are address Chief Surveyor Hokitika.

CED

Paringa River
1 October 1896

Dear Roberts

I have just shifted to this place after having overhauled all the Paringa & Hunts hill block, have been up every creek & gully where there was any chance of an outcrop, & along the sea face to Eureka Creek. That creek I will do over again, also the one half way along the bluff, and the Melaphyra on the South side of the river, but this I am leaving to the last as I intend to be at the mouth for a few days waiting steamer. The big box of speciemens I dont let out of my sight till it is safe on board. In the meantime I am prospecting the spurs from Mt Kinnard & intend to take a flying camp up the river & get some speciemens of lodes I know of out in time to send away by this boat.

There is no use my going to overhaul the reefs at the head of the river at present, as hardly any snow is off the hills yet, & I see it will be better for me to go down & overhaul Maorie Bills creek, & that little block before taking to the mountains. Up the Paringa there is really little prospecting to do. Tommy [Law] & I did that years ago. All I have to do is to overhaul what we then found. Certainly I have acquired extra knowledge since then, and may have to do some extra prospecting.

What I have found in Black river district will be best know by the Map & box of speciemens. There are four or five quartz reeks numberless leaders, and a few lodes of something that looks like nothing, & but may be something. I pounded a lot of speciemen & certainly could get no gold, but some of the reefs have pyrites both in them & their casings & that may be indications of something better lower down. It is certainly a wonderful block of country for its size, containing old & recent conglomerates, Slates, two seperate belts of granite, sandstone & shales, Limestone breccias & a belt of Lithographic limestone of good quality mysteriously situated between the Volcanic breccias.

The face of the bluff from Black river to near half way creek & the point over the river which Dr Haast called Melaphrys, are identical in structure with the moranic bluffs all along the coast, but in this case the drift is cemented into a rock harder than any granite, but the process has not altered the shape or otherwise of the boulders sand or small stones of which such bluffs are composed. Whether this has been caused by the direct action of heat, or whether the gasses of the limestones when it was distroyed by the volcanic outbrake penetrated through the loose drift of a moraine & cemented it by some chemical process, I don't know. I am inclined to the latter.

One thing appears to be certain, that there has been two eruptive periods a long time apart. The first which formed the green conglomerates showing at Black river point & in patches up No 3 creek Dry creek & other places was evidently anterior to the Limeston coal & sandstone age. The other which must have been of comparatively recent date, probably after the so called glacial age; the Limestones sandstones & drift on which it has acted are by far the most recent formations in Westland. Now which of these outbrakes jumbled up copper, antimony & perhaps gold & other minerals into the rocks of the block, that is for experts to settle. There is no doubt the metals are there, whether payable or not I for one can't say yet.

There are speciemens from two belts No on bags. No 9 & 17 No two Creek, & No 2 No 3 Creek, which I particularly want you to get examined by some expert. What is it? Is it a felspar a quartz or a species of granite? Those dykes or reefs are twenty or thirty feet wide & their position in the dark Maita slates is well defined. Why I am so particular in wanting to find out what they are is this: if they are mineral bearing, then I knows lots of them in the Slates all down the Coast. They are in general not far from the granites, which makes me suspect they have something to do with that out crop. You & I with scores of others have walked over such belt, and never paid any attention. They look just like a lighter coloured Maita Slate at first glance & it was only when I examined a piece with microscope that I noticed the difference.

In your last letter you mentioned about the Antimony away North, & gold being found in it or near it. Now the prospecting of Kinnard & I up Paringa was after this same Antimony, of which their are large belts in that district. So at least, the so called Experts of Hokitika said, & that ours ran 20 Dwt [pennyweight] of gold and 30 p cent of Antimony. So I am going to have a look at them again: they certainly don't look like mineral belts as far as I remember, & their was such a lot of lying, pointing, and underhand work going on over our discoveries, both in Hokitika & Paringa, that I never knew what to believe still there may be something in it, & I will have a run up to the Old galena mine. Though it is doubtfull if I can find the place, as I never worked their & paid little attention to what people were doing, as I knew even at that time that what we had found was only indications of what might be.

I send up the monthly voucher, and a list of some more stores I want down per Steamer. I have plenty of stores yet, but I want the Steamer to call this time & she wouldn't perhaps come if there was nothing. O'Rourke has some goods also to make up something worth coming ashore for. I will certainly be out of Tobacco, Candles and matches, but as for the others, I want them as I don't know where Ill be the next steamer. Don't forget the calico, I didnt bring down enough and had to cut up my spare tent to make bags for speciemens. 3 Yds good calico X 3 Yds of any cheap sort. I am as deaf as a post, that is what I want a syringe for, a lead one preferred & the spectacles get any cheap sort. Get Mr Macfarlane to try them what suits his eyes will do for me.

Bill the Maorie wants 200 lbs flour and 50 lb Sugar landed for him at Bruce Bay. Could you manage that for him & take the price out of his cheque?

That is about all I have to say. You will get full particulars by the Steamer which I hear is to leave on the 19th. We have had splendid weather down here, with frost every night. Looks as if Winter was only coming on, but this weather is good for flying round the country & long may it last.

This is an awfull shop for back-biting & scandal; all are at loggerheads with each other, but I suppose the poor devils having no other occupation in their leisure moments. There is not a book or a newspaper in the district, dont suppose they would read them if they had any.

There is no fears that Dan Hawkins [miner and ferryman at the Paringa River] or anybody else in this district will visit Black river, so fear not, except prospectors who come from North. If ever you hear of any party coming down this way always let me know. As long as no one knows whats in my letters, or in boxes going away, I dont care two pins for all the inhabitants in South Westland.

Yours Truly
Charles E. Douglas

Paringa River
5 October 1896

Dear Harper,

The reason why I have not answered your letters is not because I have turned proud, or fallen in love or gone insane, or got into gaol, or had no time it has been simply through sheer lazyness. The immortal Tupper* says 'There is a demon who shapes the destinies of man, and his name is Tomorrow'. That sable imp must have presided at my birth as I am always putting off till next day and so on, & so on.

After you left Karangarua river, I managed to get Bill-the-Maorie to pack me down to my whare on the Waitoto, where I remained all the winter. I had to move about, to cook & gather firewood & the rheumatics gradually left me. In the spring I made three attempts to get to the head of the Waitoto but failed. The whole valley was packed with snow, as it was the heaviest snowfall we have had for years, and the frost actually froze the eels in the shallow lagoons. For months the sea was so calm that no shell fish came up on the beaches & the gulls were starving, with the result that a mob of them pensioned themselves on me, & I daresay I was missed when leaving.

Roberts sent down word for me to go along with Wilsons party up Cooks river if I was able. As I was to carry no swag I agreed & was up on Ryans range Scotts hill & Fox glacier for six weeks Photographing, except on the Fox. But I have seen nothing of the results of our work. Photographs have a habit of mysteriously vanishing in Hokitika. We went up to the foot of the ice fall of the Victoria glacier, at least we thought we did. The fog was so dense all the time that nothing was to be seen. The Fox was in splendid condition for travelling on, and just as well it was. You would have fainted had you seen our order of March, every man going his own road. One man had a rope but no ice axe. That was Wilson, he was in the worst places he could find & generally a few hundred yards away from any body else, another would start yelling to find where his mates were. I prayed Wilson & the party to keep in some sort of line if only for the sake of effect, and in case the Gods got out there thunderbolts, but it was of no avail. Going up that steep face to the Victoria was worse. I found the only safe place was to climb into the bush and let them roll rocks down on each other. I dont mind being honourably killed on a hill side but to have some fool

---

* Martin Tupper (1810–89) was an English versifier whose name became synonymous with pretentious twaddle.

up above assisting was too much.

I suppose you have seen by this time, the last years Survey report [for 1895–96]. It gives the Fox glacier with trimmings and I suppose that will be the last exploration of it for some years to come. I at least dont want to see either it or that district again, unless the present inhabitants get exterminated. The law which prohibits people from murdering each other ought in my opinion to be modified in the case of the Okarito and Gillespies district.

If Gillespies is bad, it cant hold a candle to the Paringa in the matter of quarrelling. there are three parties on the river all Irish and the excitable brand at that. How any are alive is a mystery. 'Lookee Charlie' says one pointing to an enemy over the fence. 'Do you see that ruffian he's the biggest thief & liar South of the line. I would have shot him long ago, only he aint worth hanging for.'

Interview the ruffian and he says 'By the hole o my boot I wonder to see you speaking to that rogue up there; he is the biggest thief and liar ever created, the only one that can beat him is the vagabond down the flat. He is the champion scheamer & liar on the coast he would skin his own father and make shoe leather of the hide.'

The Vagabond down the flat wonders how the two up the flat have not been hanged long ago, and lives in blissfull hope that such will be their ultimate fate. I never go up or down the river but I meet some of them prowling about trying to pounce on a stray beast that has got through their rickety fences. But they have one good point among them; they are not always looking out to plunder strangers as they are to a man away North.

The reason I am down here is this I have been six months in Hokitika making up my geological map of Westland. It was a ponderous undertaking for one man to draw out a map eighteen feet long & five feet broad. It took me two months to arrange my old tracing & collect field books &c before commencing. It is now finished, but is sealed up either till I die or finish overhauling the numberless reefs & lode I know of & which are marked down in the map. There is a prospecting boom on at present, and I am not quite so green as to show the public my discoveries, till I find out whether they are any good. So I am now as it were washing up as the diggers say. Whether I'll be able to finish I am doubtfull, as I am braking up fast, and whatever happens I'll come out of it a cripple. However never mind. I'll keep on as long as I can crawl, and let the end when it will. Then no doubt some fraud will get hold of my map & notes & get any credit that is to be got out of them, but in that case they had better be carefull as most of my work has a duplicate in the Old country, and my relatives may have more care for the credit of the family than I have, and polish them up not perhaps for publication, but to hand over to those who know what to think of them.

So you have settled down at last and going to study human villany in a proffessional manner. You will have splendid opportunities at the Thames [gold-field, as a lawyer] among mining expert, ditto advocates, diggers with theories salting & smoking prospectus & such like. Truth, it is said, lives down a well & can be drawn up when wanted. But on a gold field engineered by Syndicates & promoters, she gets down the deepest shaft or some where towards the centre of the earth & never comes up. The Digger & prospector as a rule is reticent but honest, he wont cheat his mate & seldom his employer if working in a mine for wages, but his honesty is only as a rule in small things. Let him get into a position where there is a prospect of gaining thousands, and he would try to beat the Angel Gabriel.

In my own quite way I have learned a lot of the seamy side of human na-ture, and in no single instance have I ever meet an uneducated man who could stand even the prospect of sudden prosperity. People laugh at the pride of birth & higher education, but people, thats the mob, are generaly wrong; these are the only two things that may keep a man square when the temptation comes, as it does more or less to all.

If I find anything valuable while out this time, I dont intend to have any-thing to do with floating Cos [companies] or such like. I sell all I may find for a fixed sum & have nothing more to do with it. I never hungered after money, the article is really of very little use to me; if others make a fortune let em, it is no fault of mine if people lie & cheat themselves to perdition.

You gave a very vague address the Thames, but I daresay this will find you all right. My knowledge of Nor Island Geography is misty. I am not sure whether the Thames is a town, a river, or a volcano. If I remember the old name of a diggins in that quarter was Coromandal.

I must now close hoping you will excuse my long silence and that you will write some day and let me know if you have survived Fitzgeralds book [*Climbs in the New Zealand Alps*, 1896] which I believe is out or soon will be. He evi-dently is the real discoverer of N. Zealand, not Tasman as so long supposed. Speaking of discoveries a chap named Mathieson [Donald Matheson] has been writing to the papers about his wonderfull adventures in the Landsbro. He evidently found out that river, the Otoko pass, Brodericks saddle &c.

Yours Truly
Charles E. Douglas

Paringa River
18 October 1896

Dear Roberts

I dont know how her Majestys mails are carried down here, but there has been no mail from Hokitika for a month. I believe some of it is reposing at Gillespies, some at the Maitaha [Mahitahi] I only hope the mail going north has arrived safe, and you got my letter and parcel.

After leaving Black River, I went up the Paringa, but there was too much snow on to prospect the head of the river so I overhauled the Kaitara – with no result – and brought down some ore from the big lode up Ironstone creek. I only gave the place a flying visit to get a speciemen out for analysis. There is a galena leader & some more things to overhaul up that creek before I am done with it & that will be when I overhaul the reefs up the Paringa. The stone may only be iron, but it looks very like some silver and antimony ore I saw in Town, so get it tried. If it is something besides iron & that goes even a small percentage, then it ought to pay as it is easy of access and a boomer in size.

In my last, I said I had found nothing as yet. At least I cant see gold in any of the reefs found, but I send up per steamer a big box full of speciemens & some of them may show at least valuable indications. You said send up everything, & I am doing so, taking the risk of being called an ignoramus for sending up so much rubbish, but unless a fellow is an expert or has a few chemicals with him, it is difficult to say what is rubbish now a days. I suppose the only difference is: a man sends up a rubbishey rock with nothing in it, is called a fraud. Another gets the same stone in another place and it happens to have metal of value in it, then he is a very clever fellow. The saying that nothing succeeds like success applies to prospecting more than anything else, except perhaps politics.

I could get none of the copper and gold like the speciemen once in Hokitika. Some of the quartz contains pyrites with traces of Copper. In the vicinity of the breccias in Dry creek & Dryburn the reefs are only small leaders, but there are signs that a very large reef evidently runing Nor & So. runs near the head of No 3 Creek, & those two latter streams as their beds to near the head are strewn with large boulders of a laminated quartz, but to find it the spurs must be trenched. It I am certain, runs into the volcanic rocks near the sea, and out of it the mysterious speciemen may have come. If the Dutchman did pick it up in Black river country, then most likely he found it on the fan of either Dry creek or Dryburn. I searched all the creeks and gullies for an outcrop of this reef, but it was no good. The heads of the creeks run comparatively level and are filled with boulders & show little or no outcrop of the main rock. Whether the speciemens sent up show indications sufficient to warrant the expense of trenching, I leave for experts to settle, but my verdict is for the present *No*. Unless some one gets the scent of the country all the reefs & leaders are safe at present. The inhabitants here have neither the requisite knowledge or the energy to go prospecting. Of course if a prospecting boom starts South and even one good payable reef found, things would be different. But unless something is found in the speciemens sent up that I dont know of, the Black River block can lie dormant for a while. I would like if possable to finish the district and get far away south first.

There is no doubt the country is a very interesting one geologically, but I think south of Paringa will be more so. That is a block I know little about and don't think a single speciemen showing the nature of the rocks has ever been brought.

With reference to the reefs up No 2 creek & out of which the bag No 5 came out, I really dont think much of them unless No 9 is a quartz reef. No 4 reef is a large one certainly, but the quartz does not look promising – if there is anything in the bag No 5 sent up, then it might be worth while opening out, but don't think that the whole reef is full of pyrites. The bag really contains all I saw in the face in the shape of a small patch in the center of the reef. The top casing shows pyrites a little, and small patches are to be seen in the boulders down the creek. This reef shows also in Junction creek, but I could not get down to overhaul it without a rope and somebody above to look after it, the creek being gorgy with a succession of waterfalls, but the blocks up that creek show no more indications than those in the main creek.

What makes this creek so hard to prospect is not so much the cliffs gorges and slips, but the general absence of them. The main creeks show the bed rock only in places, the blind gullies are worse & slips are rare. The bush is no worse than usual, but in the loose rocks & remains of drift on the spurs & gullies cover everything. This is particularly a country for trenching, when good indication must just be found.

As for the box of speciemens, they are all in bags and numbered, and each creek has its speciemens enclosed in another larger bag with name written on it, so by consulting the memo & map no difficulty will be found in locating anything. Every speciemen except two specialy marked – not in situ, are taken from the solid.

The map is rather rough, as I had to do it down here with too many curious people about wanting a glimpse of it, so I just dashed it in at intervals when no body was looking. It will do however and shows the locality of the speciemens and nature of the country. If a better one is required, it can be made out at any time. I suppose both it and the memo of speciemens will go off with the box to where ever you are sending it, but I am keeping a duplicate of the memo for future reference.

Remember to be sure and get some information about Spes No 9 & 17 No 2 Creek, also No 1 Ironstone creek. If metals of value are found in either of them, then my future movements will be materially altered.

Open the box before sending it away. The map is inside, and if you open any of the bags, be sure and not get them mixed. I have kept everything in duplicate and depend entirely on the numbers to find again the exact locality of each speciemen.

When I get rid of the box and the steamer is away, I intend to go up to the head of the Lake, and overhaul Maories Bills Gully and the fall into Blue River. How long I'll be away will depend almost entirely on the weather, but Bill will take a run in for the fortnightly mail, so by watching when the South mail goes down, any one you may send will find my where abouts. But I hope there is no occaison for that yet. Let me be ready for a plunge south first.

I would like to know what sort of beings will be sent down, if they are of the brand of Messrs Cassey & Hyndman [miners from near Kumara], I'll none of them. So you must explain who they are, and exactly what I have to show if any one comes down.

The Mail has come in at last or rather two of them at once, and all letters papers & parcels came to hand. Any amount of Newspapers, a lb of tobacco, package of Arsenical soap and £1 for which many thanks. The Tobacco came just in time to prevent a famine – for one who once smoked, your skill in purchasing bad tobacco borders on genius, who did you get it from? However never mind, it came in very handy, and what is left will be usefull to lend people who want a smoke on the cheap.

I enclose Bills account for packing, & only charged shifting camp. I am not particularly able at present to carry a swag & dont want to knock myself up the first go off, otherwise the camp would in more than one case have been carried on our backs. But as long as I am in a place where I can use a horse I'll do so, and pay the difference myself, but there will be very little more horse carrying. Once on the Lake and among the hills the Pilgrims progress business commences. By far the heaviest work will be carting out rocks, if I have to bring out large speciemens of everything I know.

So you are a grass widower at present, you must be happy. I wish when Mrs Roberts comes back you would send me down a Photo of myself, and how about that Survey group taken before I left? I dont mind if you purchase a couple for me, one to send home and one to send down to me, but there is no hurry over that.

My rheumatics are still troubling me, but I have only lost two days since starting with them, and these two days spell was a mistake. However bad they are in the morning, I find the best way is tramp about, the rougher the country the better. Bill & I were four hours in a pelting rain floundering through a White pine swamp about as bad a one as I ever was in. Finished off by fording the flooded Paringa four times, & I have been better ever since.

It is this way, I can see if this is going to be a hot dry summer, I have to cave in, if not, then I'll be all right. I believe the hill tops are the best for my brand of rheumatism.

I have no more to say at present, but will write again soon. Remember me to Macfarlanes & all.

Yours Truly
Charles E. Douglas

The following part of a letter to Roberts is undated but placed here as it was found. The references to the dog Betsey Jane suggest it was written in 1893, but Douglas did have more than one dog of that name. Other details, such as the syringe, 'Bill' (Ruera Te Naihi) and sending up the October voucher, link it to the other letters of this sequence, and it must have come from Paringa, where Dan Hawkins ran the ferry.

[Paringa]
[October]

[Dear Roberts]

. . . Betsey Jane caught a Kiwi & Kakapo. We brought them down, but the soap didn't come in time, but we will get you some up the lake. There appears to be plenty about the country yet, and anything in that line except harrying birds nest, I get you if you want.

Although the month is not done yet, I send up the October voucher. Bill wants you to give his to his Misses as he calls her. He is very soft, she will get none of it, that old ruffian Kelly [Kere Tutoko] nabs all stray coins, and would get Bills clothes and blankets if I would let him. For the first week or two Bill lived principally on tinned fish and Lea & Perrins sauce. His eyes fairly bulged with joy, when the boxes were opened and he saw oblong boxes with a picture of a herring on them. They are all finished now & I dont get any more for a while. Eels, hares & whitebait are now the go. The beef here is not worth eating, so it is just as well game is far more plentiful than I expected, and we have two good dogs that bring in everything they catch.

I got two bills from Christchurch for newspapers & which I enclose. I wish you would send over two post office orders in my name for the amount. That is about all I want till Xmass; that's to say if you have sent per steamer, the spectacles and pocket knife. If you have forgotten them & the syringe, please send them overland. I have only one pair of glasses left, and if they are broken I am stranded at once. The syringe I really require, although at present deafness is a blissing. Dan Hawkins talks away for hours & I dont hear a single word. He says he thinks I am a splendid listner, though I hear nothing. I know perfectly well what the yarns are about; prosey old stories spun out to interminable length about a bear hunt in California or an episode in the life of a Tom Cat he had some forty years ago. You know the sort of yarns I mean, which come out of an old Foggie who's life really has been full of incident, but who has forgotten all only a few of the most trivial remaining in his memory.

NINETEEN

Letter to Roberts, 1898

This discursive letter shows that Douglas, in spite of his earlier ill-health and somewhat depressed view of the world, was still planning future activity, including the exploration of a number of West Coast rivers. Mining was declining significantly on the Coast, but Douglas seems to accept that tourism was, to some extent, a valid activity. Photography still features prominently in his life and he is concerned that glacial change should be accurately measured.

Waiho Glacier
30 Janry 1898

Dear Roberts

Now that I have got through with the Fox for the present at least, and punched my way through to here, it is about time I wrote the long letter so often promised, but whether this will really be a long one I dont know as I have really very little new to speak about. Things down here are in a dying state but as a matter of fact they appear to be no worse than they were twenty years ago. Diggin certainly on the beaches is nearly a thing of the past, but people are settling on the land in a sort of a half hearted way, as if they had doubts as to whether they won't all be stumpted when road work stops. The old ones take more interest in the Old age pension bill and the price of coffins than anything else. Even whiskey fails to rouse them as of yore, and the young ones are talking Klondyke, but havent the pluck to go there. The only really hopefull being I have meet south of this is Andrew Scott of Karangaroa, who believes in the future of Southern Westland, which is more than I do to tell the truth. I have some faith in Sardine terrace, but it can only be a small concern at the best, and it represents almost the only piece of ground that may pay, from Gillespies down to the South Pole. Up here at the Waiho, Mapourika is nearly played out, at the Forks of the Callery ditto, and all eyes are now turned to this Waiho great extended sluicing Co which I believe will end in a collapse six weeks after the water has been brought on.

Gordon, a digger here, is going to bring the Waiho on to the Hospital point, and sluice away the hot springs. He [Andrew Gordon, settler and miner near Okarito] can certainly get the river on it has a fall of 225 feet from the glacier, but I cant see where the ground is. Another chap, a blatherskite name Batyen [W. H. Batson?], has applied for twenty head of water out of a lake on the South side of the Waiho and is going to work the flats with elevators &c. Do you know anything about this lake? I never saw it down in any map; it is some way opposite the Forks back of the broken hills the Glacier track goes along. Is it worth cutting a line into and fixing it? I expect it is a small edition of the Alpine Lake and may run a sandhead of water when not in heavy flood. On the Beaches I hear Fiddian [Samuel Fiddian, farmer and miner at Bruce Bay] struck a patch of surfacing at last, & Ned Gibbs [farmer, miner and store-keeper at Waikukupa River] has been getting good gold for several month on Sandfly beach. He is working it as a family affair, all the youngsters from the baby upwards assisting. Their is some talk of the Alpine Lake being brought on to the three mile. Another collapse for Mac [Duncan Macfarlane]; as usual they talk of five or six heads of water, why if it was half whiskey it wouldnt require Ike Pherson to drink all that comes out of it! The lake was usefull no doubt as a storage reservoir in the old days of the Alpine race but no more.

I have now given you all about the diggin. Now for something else. We had splendid weather up on the hills with [William] Wilson, as you no doubt know, raining down on the flats while we were up above the clouds roasting. The whole country was covered with snow, which really was an advantage, as we got on to places that would otherwise have been impassable. It seems you want me to write another report on the Fox, so I must keep as much as I can of information for that, and get on to something else. I am sure I don't know what more I can say about that glacier except to note its recent retreat. Am I to write about our trip on the hill tops to fill up a report or is Wilson not going to do it?

Last mail I sent up a rough report on the Cooks and Waiho track. With the exception of a new piece of road at Waikupu there is really very little to do to open it. I hear Donovan [James Donovan, storekeeper at Mapourika] is going to spend some money clearing it out to the Omaru or Waikupu, but the new deviation will be beyond the funds of the county council, as I expect, unless they all [want] a very steep and awkward zig-zag. The new line would be about a mile long. They ought to open this road, it would at once throw the Franz Josef and the Fox into one trip, and would be used by the cattle men. It will certainly not open up any land for settlement, but its continuation South of Cooks will render accessable more land than any of the Southern roads has yet done. The country has come to this, the rising generation must either settle on the land or clear, there is no get out of it.

You must have had a grand trip this time, up in the North Island. How did you like a fortnight in the office in Wellington? It must have been too like the old country for one who has been most of his time in easy going Westland. Is it Herbert Spencer who says that we must take the World easy, work less and think more to reveve the age of Shakespeare, in this Victorian age? I dont know, if we think much, but if taking the World easy makes genius, Westland ought to turn out Homers and Shakespeares by the score. Anyone who has seen the mail travelling South, will agree with me about people not being in a hurry. A packer comes just when he feels inclined, and the very cows by which so many make a living, would often not be milked but for the roars of their offspring. But perhaps their are other places in N Zealand just the same, and long may they be so. This hurry scurry of modern life makes the said life hardly worth having, but enough of Philosophy.

I got the photos all right, a number of them have been sent home already, so I am keeping most of them for myself. I dont see why I shouldnt have an album of my own, and give Wilson some coin to get me one a big chap if possable. I'll fill it some day, and perhaps some day may have some sort of home to put it in. I got from Wilson a small album of his photos, which I sent home, and that will do them at present. This mail I send up two dozen exposed plates, which I hope will be a success. Tell Mrs Roberts that I am sorry most of them are not Artistic but for topographical purposes. They are all different views of the terminal face of the Waiho glacier, are all taken from fixed cairns; at least the cairns will be fixed when I get the chain down. They are all taken either early in the morning or towards evening, and the stop was 32 with from four to six sec^d exposure. They ought to give you an idea of the state the glacier now is in and the rapid retreat at the terminal face. I have got the place all ready to run the chain round and will join all on to the Sentenil. The next lot of photos will be artistic, and possably please Mrs Roberts better, but if some sent are bad, keep a copy neverless, & if possable send me down copies before I leave so that I can mark their position and bearings. They will come in handy years after we are dead, and if you could only get a copy of Pringles early photo of the glacier, it would complete the set. [*Thomas Pringle, an early Dunedin photographer, took the first known photograph of the Franz Josef Glacier, in 1867.*] I dont know where he took it from but it must have been near point r. Harpers photos are nearly worthless for future reference, as he never took the bearings of the camera or fixed or even noted the point he took them from.

I got a letter from home lately. It is without exception the most cheerfull one I have had from my relatives for many a day. As a rule their letters are full of a grim sceptical missanthrophy, wondering what they or anybody else were created for, and always looking at the dark side of things. Every one of my relatives have been this way, and I often wonder how I am so exactly the opposite to them in almost everything. I send two Photos that came in the letter. I don't know where they are, most probably they are views of the place my brother [Sholto] lives; if so I cant see he has much to growl about. If he only saw Castle Douglas on the Waitoto, or my present bat wing subsidised with sheets of iron. Yet I am comparatively happy and contented, and perhaps he is also if he would only confess it.

This Iron house was a good deal of a puzzel at first, as most of the numbers got rubbed off, and the angle irons got bent a good deal in the packing. It looks rather a flimsey thing, the angle irons are too light for such a large building, but as I dont know much of iron work they may be all right. It is certainly a very ingenious shoe Davidson [Hokitika engineer] has put on eight of the uprights, no fear of them drawing in a wind, but it was a puzzel to sink holes in a moraine without dynamite. However we have managed it all right & the house will be ready in a day or two, but there will be a lot of work cutting drains and making everything ship shape.

It will be very usefull as a shelter, but as a work of Art, it is the most hedious looking house I ever saw or dreamt about, when finished I'll send up ONE photo of it but no more.

When the traversing round the glacier is finished, and that wont take long, Ill shift on to the Totara according to instructions. You said nothing about the track up to the outlook. It has completely grown up, so I'll spend a day clearing it out. It is by far the best view of the glacier in the locality up at lookout point.

So you had a talk with the Surveyor General about filling in details on the Westland maps. Is he going to let me [go] down to the Waitoto & Arawatta next spring? If I get up those two river, I'll give you something for the Tourist guide, and I do want another shy at that big map I was at before. I have a mighty lot to put in it, before it is even half complete.

In traversing the rivers north where do I commence, at the main road or foot of hills or where? And are the Waitaka [Waitaha] & Poerua to be tackled before the Wataroa & Wanganui, are they worth it? I forget what the Waitaka is like, but the Little Wanganui or Poerua appears to be only a straight shoot down from the hills. I hear a great deal here about the impassable gorges of the Totara, but they can't be a patch on the Waitaha & it was very far from impassable.

I must now be drawing to a close. Not that I have nothing more to say, but it is hard work writing in a bat wing with no table, and wind blowing the candle about. I got the two cheques and statement of account all right, also [Alf] Dale's cheque which I have given him, and enclose the two pay Vouchers. I sent two up to Mr Murray [W. G. Murray, Chief Surveyor, Westland, 1898–1901] so they can be distroyed. I also enclose two photos, & Rentons bill for

Plates which please pay at end of month. [Renton was a Hokitika ironmonger and merchant.] I want nothing down I can think about, except the chain and you might send me down a piece of red calico, if there is none in the office then invest in a red pocket handkerchief. I want it for a lantern to shift plates with.

I have enough of Illfords to finish this place. If I can manage the dozen Isocromatic, are they not good for taking flowers spider webs & such like? I got a couple dozen $1/4$ plates, of this Iso let me know what stop to use and what exposure. When will my new camera be out? Mind and dont send it down to me; let Mrs Roberts experiment with it first. I hope it is a handy one, as this big half plate one I have makes me groan to carry it.

Ill start at once with report on Fox, and will have it up in plenty of time. I suppose you want the same about the Waiho. I have no tools so can't map here, but send me down a rough map of the place.

Yours Truly
Charles E. Douglas

Whitcombe River
5 March 1897

Dear Harris

When I left your place on the
Heart last Dec. Mrs H gave me a commission
for something in the medicine line. but till the
other day I couldn't recollect what it was
I knew there was something but what was the
puzzel. somebody in the camp spoke about
Chlorydine + then I remembered. so I wrote down
to Roberts to send down a bottle of it and another
of Eucal — how do you spell it — and no doubt
you have got them by this time

I was nearly three weeks in Hokitika
before starting to work. so saw all the Xmas.
entertainments. and nearly exhausted the
brewerys. however I didn't spend much and
kept out of the hands of the Police

TWENTY

Letters to the Harris Family, 1897–99

After the original publication of his book on Charlie Douglas, John Pascoe received further relevant material, including letters written by Douglas to 'Harris', then a settler just south of the Haast River, towards Okuru. This would have been William Harris, who had been storekeeper at the Haast in the early 1890s and whose address at the time of these letters was listed in the electoral rolls as Haast Beach. His wife was Mary and the couple had a number of children.

These letters are the most relaxed and gossipy of all those written by Douglas which still exist, and refer to many other West Coasters. They were not written to his social or employment superiors, but to a well-known friend, and Douglas could be as sarcastic about others as he liked, perhaps to the point of scandal-mongering. They should be taken with a few grains of salt, and it must be remembered that Douglas never sought to offend! More important than their content, these letters show Douglas was not always a loner and that he kept in good contact with friends and acquaintances in South Westland.

The full text of all the letters is published here, though a few words are obscured in the originals and the third letter is undated. The others were written in 1897 and 1899, and seem to be part of an extended correspondence.

5 March 1897
Whitcombe River

Dear Harris

When I left your place on the Haast last Decr, Mrs H gave me a commission for something in the medicine line, but till the other day I couldn't recollect what it was. I knew there was something but what: was the puzzel. Somebody in the camp spoke about Chlorydine & then I remembered, so I wrote down to Roberts to send down a bottle of it, and another of Eucal – how do you spell it – and no doubt you have got them by this time.

Opposite: *A page from one of Charlie Douglas's letters to William Harris.*

I was nearly three weeks in Hokitika before starting to work, so saw all the Xmas entertainments, and nearly exhausted the brewerys. However I didn't spend much and keept out of the hands of the Police.

I have been up once or twice to the Hospital and saw Yankey Dan he is a sort of fixture there, runs messages down town and if he gets lively they put him to bed for a week & plaster and blister him.

Sam Fiddian was told by the Doctors that he couldnt live more than a month, and his spell in the Hospital certainly reduced him. but Sam is a philosopher he cleared out & boarded with old Bell remarking that if he had to die he preferred dying with some tucker in him, and when I left Hokitika he appeared to be getting all right. The Hokitika Hospital is getting very mean in the tucker line. I expect they are starving the patients to force them out when this new pension racket commences. Speaking of this pension I think the best way is for all hands to swear to sixty years of age, and go in for the £25 per annum. It would just keep a fellow comfortably in baccy and beer. Unless something turns up on the coast all hands will have to become pensioners, or purchase a pistol and few charges.

I saw Old Wise [George Wise, mining agent] pretty often in Hokitika and he was there when I left, but I have heard nothing about him since where he is or what he is doing. Perhaps Buckland is going to throw him over or perhaps the latter gent is going to do nothing with Sardine.

How has Wilsons Mica reef turned out I have heard nothing about it – a failure no doubt. The great mining boom appears to have collapsed since Ziman left, and now people talk of Seddon & the poors rates [old age pension, advocated by Seddon and introduced in 1898].

Hoping you are all well & that you will drop a note some day

Yours Truly
Charles E. Douglas

P.S.   How is Scully getting on remind me to him – and don't let him leave unless he leaves his books behind him. [*Duncan Scully was a miner and settler in the Whataroa–Okarito region.*]
CED

10 July 1897
Whitcombe River

Dear Harris

I think it is about time your last letter was answered, were it only to enable me to make some remarks on the present Matrimonial boom.

The Alliance between the Crone [Cron] and the Condon clan will make a powerfull syndicate of land grabbers in the Southern districts. Condon is a sort of human cuttle fish spreading his tentacles over the Maitaha [Mahitahi], Paringa & everywhere else. The Crone will bring into the firm that limpet like tenacity which sticks to everything he can get so between them they ought to own the whole South unless which is probable they quarrel.

Nisson I hear has got off one of his daughters, Theresa no doubt. I wonder how she feels with a daughter three inches taller than herself. It will be diffi-cult to maintain a proper dignity with a family larger than herself. I wonder if Harry plonked down £50 to the old man. That is what I heard was the price Nisson put on his Angels. The payment ought to be the other way. How are Joe [Collyer] & Hendly getting on like two acts no doubt. Tell Bill not to swear against beer or spirits in his old age, it isn't worth the trouble – the peg ought to have been put in fifty years ago. Then people might believe him. And tell him from me that the Hokitika beer is now good. I have tried it. The summer before last the Tasmanian hop cropp was a failure, and the brewers had to use Aconite or some other poison as a bitter, hence the awfull stuff last season. When I came up from South I was nearly murdered by it, but now hops are cheep and beer is good. I have tried it.

There is going to be a great clearing out of the old hands I fear up in Hokitika & I doubt there will be one of them [left]. It is not le grippe but a phases of that complaint that takes the form of a rheumatic fever. It seems to puzzel the D^{rs} and attacks old chaps in preference to young one. I suppose the young ones will say that is quite fair. When I left Hokitika [William] Fowler the draper [Michael] Murphy the butcher, [Joseph] Churches [merchant and hotel owner] & a few more were all given up and Mac [Duncan Macfarlane] for the first time I ever saw him that way was awfully down in the mouth and well he might be. What will his family do if he goes. I hear that Maggie Mac is going to marry [Joseph] Grimmond [mine and sawmill manager in Ross] whenever he comes back from the old country. I doubt there will be a hitch. Why didn't he marry and take her a trip to Britain. If it is not to take place till he floats the Kanieri water race, she can wait till doomsday, as the like of Grimmond could never float anything on the London Market, with Ziman who knows all about the spec hand in glove with all the moneyed men.

As for myself I have behaved wonderfully. I was up here for five months without leaving the camp, and when I did go down for a fortnight instead of seeing the Record celebrations I cleared out with Roberts to the Bealy [Bealey] to do some sketching & Photographing, and when I did come back I had only three days to sample the beer so hadn't time to get locked up.

I will be up the Whitcombe for three or four months yet and then I believe I am going to the Waiho to lay off tracks for Tourists. After that I dont know what I am going to do. I daresay if the Survey have any more tracks to lay if in bad country they will keep me on but of that I can't say. [W. G.] Murray can see what neither Mueller, Barron [Chief Surveyor, Westland, 1895–96] or any of the bosses could, that it pays to send someone a head who knows what rough country really is and how a road can be taken almost anywhere. This job I am on was condemned as an impossible route through the ranges and but for Roberts & [John] Smyth[e] [surveyor] nagging at them it never would have been started. The Colliers Gorge in Whitcombe river was the block that was said to be impassable, precipices towering up from the river for hundreds of feet made it look awfull to those who didnt know that every precipice has a top to it somewhere. Yet I got a dray road route through it in three weeks with a good regular grade and not a bit of rock cutting the whole way.

I simply put maps and instructions to one side and carried the road over the top of all obstacles, and the best of it was I got through three hundred feet lower than the old survey trial line. The track I am to lay off up the Waiho runs up along the glacier & is another of Muellers impossible job. I have no fear I'll get through it as easy.

I suppose you saw in the papers that I had got a medal from the Royal Geographical Society. It rather took me by surprise as I didnt know they had ever heard about me. The prize is a medal and £35 in cash. A fellow isn't supposed to draw it in money but get it out in a piece of silver plate with inscription telling my many virtues, or take it out in instruments. Now as a silver salver or ornamental fruit basket would not be a very usefull object to carry in the tent with me, I must send word for them to send me one of those new photo machine, that can [take] eighty views one after the other and instantainily. No bother but touch the button, so when I come down get out your smiles. I'll bring plenty of chemicals so can fix them up on the ground, but when I come down is the question. I might be down early next year as I hear something about a botanical expedition going South then with me as leader. I know as much about botany as I do of Astronomy but thats nothing.

However whether I come sooner or later I will finally be down to Waitoto [Waiatoto] even if only for a spell. So I wish you would look after my hut some one might sneak off with the iron & I dont want to have a new hut to build at present. The Old hovel will do me for a bit.

I have no more to say at present hoping your road making job will continue and remember me to Mrs Harris & all the young uns.

Yours truly
Charles E. Douglas

P.S. I forgot all about it – I saw Wise every day while in town & had great talks with him about Sardine [mining claim] & other places. There is a hitch some-where. Wise evidently holds the ground & Buckland & it looks as if the Robinsons [who] were in it are trying to work him out of it. Wise evidently has no money & the [???] are trying to [???] him out and jump the [operation?] themselves. I hope they dont as I would sooner trust Wise than a cartload of Bucklands & Robinsons.

Wise has been putting out feelers trying to find if I knew of something down South but I am not ready for that yet, and he must introduce me to someone better than Joshua Gibson [Hokitka businessman] if he manages to float Sardine. I'll then lay him on to a spec or two which I think will pay. But I am awfully suspicious of those Syndicate men espicially since the revelations I heard from Auckland – if they are all like him then I want nothing to do with them but Wise seems a better sort.
CED

❖

Hokitika

Dear Harris

Your letter only came a short time ago so I have only a few minutes to scribble a short note. I can't even get some paper, but never mind.

I send down a rough tracing Turnbull river showing the correct position of the upper flats and the boundary of Nolans run – you will see that his boundary is along way below anything you want.

As for Murdocks Cattle [perhaps Murdoch McPherson, a settler at Okuru] the only thing I can see for you to do is to pound them, but as the nearest pound is Okarito, and the risk and bother of taking a mans cattle that distance is too much, so either apply for a pound in the district or do as Old [Band?] did get your yard proclaimed a gaol. I suppose Mac is the one to apply to. This as far as I can see is the only remedy you have.

I didnt find the Photos till the other day so can only send you down a few but will get some better ones shortly. The first two I took of your crowd were exposed on the same plate – I enclose the pleasing result, but it isn't fixed so will fade away in bright sunlight. As for the others I took, I havn't found them yet so you must waite a bit. I have only a few minutes to catch the post so must close.

Remember me to all and hoping to be down by August steamer when I'll make the place howl.

Yours Truly
Charles E. Douglas

P.S. I have no idea who got the watch, has A. Campbell [Archibald Campbell, a miner at Haast] not it. If you can't find it never mind. I'll bring one down when I come.

If the Dog comes up make it fast aboard with something, it wont bite. Or get it in the hold.
C.E.D.
Will write again soon

❖

20 March 1899
Whitcombe River

Dear Harris

You complain that I, in the land of beer & skittles dont write. Now that is the very reason for my neglect, all the time I was in Hokitika I never really had time to write, what with drinking beer, visiting and trying to escape visiting my time in Hokitika was fully occupied. Since leaving I have been up here for four months without a chance [some?] three days journey from any mail: French or the Russians may have taken Hokitika for ought I know. When I'll be down I dont know but am writing on the chance of getting this letter and several others away someday.

I have very little to say about myself since I saw you last having been pitched forked all over the country – up Cooks & the Waiho, then on to the hill tops with Wilson then down to Cooks again. Then up the Wataroa to get half frozen then three months in Hokitika varied by a hurried journey to the Otira, getting as usual half killed by the jolting of the Coach – curse these coaches, and doubly cursed the snobbery that wont allow a fellow to walk if he prefers it. Even a china man when travelling up here must use a bike a horse or a trap, and look as if he liked it, and was accustomed to carriage exercise all his life. Now I am up here, finishing the Whitcombe pass [track] and then I am off to the Rakia [Rakaia] and [will?] make my appearance on the Coast somewhere down the Wanganui either entire or in pieces.

This job I am on has been a caution it has averaged all through one day working and five days packing tucker the rising generation cave in at once when the beef steak and onions run out, and to go for a day without dinner means death. It is not put on; you would be surprised how weak and heart broken they become when tucker runs short what would happen if it ran out altogether the Lord knows. I wonder how some of them would like to go through what you & I have done yet they talk as if they were a superior race to the old worn out Digger.

I suppose you heard about Yankee Dans death. One of the Wards and myself found him lying in Mother Bells potato garden in a fit, we got him to the Hospital but he died an hour after. It may be some consolation to him in the happy hunting grounds to know that the last whiskey he tasted on earth was poured down by me. The Dr was away no one knew what was wrong with him, so I took the case in hand and poured down his throat a jorum of the universal remedy. The Doctor said whiskey was a bad thing to give in a case of Appoplexy but philosophically added 'it didn't matter'.

There was a good few at the funeral, not that one in ten knew Yankee Dan but if the day is fine a funeral is a good excuse to take your girl out a walk in the cemetery. I always somehow manage to extract humour even out of a funeral and I got it at Dans. The Rev Mr Douglas was the [Presbyterian] parson in attendance, and you ought to have seen the holy horror of the Revd Gent when the coffin came to the grave carried by four of the [worst?] non church goers in Westland. Tomy Law & self first, and two other companion heathens behind. He glared at us collectively then fixed his eye on me and preached a Sermon, not the nearly a few words style but a regular sermon, on the glorious chances we were throwing away in neglecting our duties to our church, or his perhaps he meant; there is no doubt he fairly caught us – as we couldnt clear out very well – and fully expected a bob from each of us at the evening service that day, but alas we adjourned to Hansen's [hotel] instead.

Bones died a few days afterwards a most senseable ending he had, as he died in the Doctors place and saved the bother of an inquest. He left his money some six hundred pounds to Bob Dee [formerly of Haast] so Dollars will no doubt be back to the Coast sometime in July or August that is if the Alaska climate hasn't [got?] him, if it has then there is a nice [little?] law suite on the board.

What an awfull fraud that Klondyke has been, and such impossable yarns have been talked about it. People dont seem to think at all now adays but take everything for gospel that is seen in a newspaper. How could a man carry down country a potato sack full of nuggets on his back, yet I saw that gravely asserted as a fact, very little Arethmetic would show the thing to be impossable as the load would weigh some tons, then the stories about Mail cans, flour barrells &c being used to put the gold in, why all the gold that has as yet come out of the Klondyke isn't so much as come off the West coast in one year, and Diggers hadn't to purchase water tanks & flour barrells to put it in. There is no doubt there is gold in Alaska, but the present rush is simply a Steamboat swindle from beginning to end.

I thought I would be down your way this Autumn, but I can't perhaps I'll be down in Spring I would rather work in the Jackson bay district for £1 a week than up here for £3, but I must go just where I am sent. The Survey have proclaimed my section at Waitoto a cattle reserve so I am again out of house and home.

I dont want to buy land in N. Zealand except in the cemetery, but I suppose I must put up a whare somewhere down south as a refuge when I am no longer wanted on the Survey what may take place any day. I only wish they would send me down to where their is really some prospecting and exploring to do, not like up here where it is nothing but overhauling well know country getting it ready for colonists who will never come.

I couldnt send Strands [magazines] for a long time as they got collared, but I now send three and will continue to send them with some sort of regularity if possable.

Mind me to Mrs Harris & the family &c.

Yours truly
Charles E. Douglas

TWENTY-ONE

Features of Westland

The problems of presenting the Douglas Papers were never so marked as with his wide-ranging survey of South Westland, completed about 1899. Published in full, they would total 53,000 words and repeat much information given in other reports.

The series includes diverse subject headings: Passes, Lakes and Tarns, Swamps and Lagoons, Bluffs and Beaches, Islands, Towns, Waterfalls, Canyons and Gorges, Glaciers, Geological. They are illustrated with sketches and all together give an unrivalled picture of Westland between the 1860s and the end of the century.

These manuscripts have been used elsewhere to help create the story of Charlie Douglas's life. Here only samples of interesting observations are given: 'Whitcombe Pass' and 'The Thomson Range' from 'Passes, Lakes and Tarns'; various digressions from 'Swamps, Bluffs and Beaches'; 'Jacksons Bay' from 'Islets, Towns and Glaciers'.

Whitcombe Pass

From Brodricks pass to the Whitcombe, a distance of nearly one hundred miles, all the passes are Alpine; that is to say glaciers and snowfields have to be crossed. There may possably be sub Alpine passes up the Wataroa & Poerua as these streams have not been traversed, but there is little likelyhood of any existing.

The Whitcombe is one of the old Maorie routes from the east to the west coast, when on the hunt for greenstone. The first Whiteman to cross was [Henry] Whitcombe, the surveyor who came through in the early days of the gold rush. Whether an official account of his trip was ever published I don't know, but his field book and diary must be in existance in some Survey safe, as Louper [Jakob Lauper] the Swiss who travelled with him certainly brought them out. Whitcombe appears to have got over without very much trouble, but was drowned in the Teremakau [Taramakau] river when on the Coast Journay to Greymouth. Louper who managed to cling to the old canoe got ashore and buried him on the beach. Whitcombe was the first of those Westland surveyors and explorers who perished in the wilds leaving nothing but a name on a peak or pass.

[Lauper's account of the trip was published in the Canterbury Provincial Gazette

of 6 July 1863. Nearly a hundred years later, John Pascoe edited the narrative, which was published in Christchurch, 1960, as Over the Whitcombe Pass.]

After Whitcombe, I know of no one who crossed this pass till Mr Roberts came over from the Rakaia to Hokitika in the eighties. After him several parties have been through traversing and chaining the river and laying off a foot track over the range. This track which is benched on the sidlings is now within a few miles of the saddle & no doubt will be finished shortly, then there will be no difficulty crossing over the range from Hokitika to Ashburton.

Although the Whitcombe pass is 4000 feet high, it keeps very free from snow most of the year, the summet being exposed to the warm Nor Westers. In appearance it resembles the Haast pass, almost level on the top, but it is destitute of timber or even scrub, and the depression is not so wide. Originally the pass may have been much lower and probably U shaped, but the debris from the Sale glacier has filled it up it may be for hundreds of feet. The route down the Louper to the Rakaia a distance of about three miles is through open grass country with occaisonally patches of scrub and presents no difficulties to a traveller.

The Thomson Range [Northern Olivines]

There are no lakes or tarns on this range from the Ark till Mt Collyer is passed, when lakes Lebe [Leeb] and Clarke are reached. These are two real mountain tarns. They are gems of beauty & for surroundings are unequalled in Westland. They are about a mile long and from fifty to sixty chain wide. There shores are diversified by open grassy slopes, scrub covered hills, and precipices rising out of the water: for a background they have the distant Mt Aspiring, with Mts Lucifer and Bel, & the waters are an indescribable deep blue. The lakes are separated by a ridge 1500 feet high, height above sea 3300.

Crossing the Awarua another short beach leads to a long boulder lined bluff. This is the place where a few men have been digging from the earliest days of the Coast. Little gold has been got on the beach, but on the sloping terraces in the scrub a considerable amount has been obtained at various periods. The work was very heavy on account of the large boulders that had to be shifted, and it is doubtfull if the gold from Big bay payed the men who worked it more than a sort of Starvation wage. But there is a fascination in living in such places, away from all communication with the outer world which attracts many people – espicially the failures. As one of the inhabitants said 'There are plenty of birds & fish, no taxes, no bother about clothes, no coal, firewood, or gas to pay for, no churches, charities parsons, lawyers or doctors to bother; splended health, your lord of all you survey, what more does a fellow want.' Perhaps he was right. There is no use philosophising on the subject.

A lonely grave on the South beach is a gentle hint to all, that Westland rivers are not to be played with. These graves are a feature at the mouth of every river in the country. People in the early days were buried by their mates, just where they were cast ashore. Now there is a senseless craze that everybody must be buried in company inside a proclaimed cemerty, with the result that the absurdity is often witnessed of a pack horse, laden with human remains stuffed in a potato sack, travelling fifty or a hundred miles up the coast. In the early days people had some idea of the fitness of things – whether intentionaly or not doesn't matter – and the prospector and explorer who had led a solatary life was buried like an Old Sea King on bluff or beach close to where he fell. And it is to be hoped they will be allowed to remain, and not, as was once or twice suggested, be carted to Hokitika & planted in rows like potatoes in the cemetry.

[Rafting]

I might as well say something about rafting, an art which most people in Westland imagine they know all about. Yet I havent seen half a dozen good rafts made in the country, and it has been more by luck than good management that so few people have been drowned off them. There are five different kinds of rafts by means of which almost any river can be crossed. They are the Oblong raft, the A shaped, the Moki, the half Moki and the catamaran.

No 1

The Oblong raft is the most common variety. In fact this shape has been almost universally adopted. It is however the most unweildy of them all, and far more dangerous and in my opinion is a floating absurdity – espicially when – as is the general rule, – the cross spars which bind the raft together are placed under instead of on top. The oblong is a still water conveyance, as in a slight current it becomes unmanagable. However it has one advantage. It is easy to make and can be made any size to accommodate passengers, for from some unknown reason people seem to prefer being drowned in company, to the comparative safety of every man making his own raft. Any material that floats will do for this raft, and for No 2, but flax sticks if they can be got are superior to all drift wood. The next best is dry totara or green lightwood. Other drift timber gets waterlogged very fast, and if the distance to cross is great there is danger of the raft sinking.

No 2

This is a one man raft, or at most a two man, and is far superior to No 1, as it is managable in not too strong a currant. It is simply no 1 only shaped like the letter A, the man sitting or standing at the broad end, the pointed part being slightly out of the water. So long as the crosspieces are placed, above and not below, and the pointed end well lashed, this raft can be poled or paddled with a fair amount of speed. I once sailed down Lake Brunner and then paddled across it on a raft of this discription and really it was safer than a boat, it could neither sink nor capsize.

No 3

The Moki [or mokihi] is a Moarie contrivance, and requires flax sticks for its construction. It has a wooden Keel from which the flax bundles are built, forming a leaky but unsinkable canoe it is however rather an elaborate contrivance to make, and requires teaching.

No 4

The half Moki is simply No 2 made with three bundles of flax sticks with this difference: the two outer bundles are slightly smaller than the center one, and instead of being lashed level they are slightly raised forming a boat shaped floor to the raft, the hollow between being filled up with more flax sticks, and all lashed tight. This raft requires some skill to handle in a current as it is rather cockly, but it can be paddled almost as fast as a canoe. For a current, it is certainly the best of all except perhaps No 3, but I would not recommend nervous people to try it be content with No 2.

No 5 The Catamaran

This is no doubt the safest and best way to cross a river that is anyways rapid, but it is seldom used even by those who have seen it tried. Its great objection is you have to sit nearly to the waist in water when astride it. The floating qualities of New Zealand timber is not sufficient to enable a fellow to sit cross legged on a small spar, and a large one is unweildy.

The Catamaran is simply a dry totara spar, eight or nine inches in diameter and twenty feet long, with another spar half its length as an outrigger. The passenger sits straddle legs about six feet from the thick end, with his feet well together, then paddle away. The thin end of the spar out [ought] to be well out of the water. The whole affair is wonderfully balanced, is quite safe and can be paddled across almost any current, and can dodge snags better even than a canoe. An ordinary telegraph pole would be about the thing to make this contrivance with.

A number of years ago, there was a digger on Hunts beach who used to cross rivers in flood with a single spar without an outrigger, but he must have had some acrobatic knowledge I wot [know] not of. I have tried this way but never could manage it.

The bark canoe is very difficult to make, and is never safe, so I need no more than mention it, but a word about canoes or dug outs as they are called. People have read so much about Robinson Crusoe taking eighteen months to make a canoe, that they never think how quick one can really be made by a good axe man. Two men ought to be able to make a dug out that will carry three or four men and their swaggs, accross or down any river in Westland, and out to sea for that matter in a couple of days or even less. The ship probably would not be very neatly finished, but it would be all that is necessary for practical use.

To sum up, almost anything that will float can carry a man over a river. Floats can be made out of sea weed, bottles, barrels, even grass and rushes. Lake Titticca [Titicaca] in the Andes is navigated by boats made out of rushes and plastered with clay. Alexander the great crossed part of his army over the Oxus on bags stuffed with hay. I once crossed Lake Mapourika in a Canoe that had no stem to it, broken off in fact. The place was made up with turf and earth, on which I sat to prevent the water washing it away. In the early days the Haast river was navigated in a bakers dough trough, sluice boxes, tin pumps and various other impossable looking contrivances have all been used for crossing Westland rivers.

Jacksons Bay

From the Holyford [Hollyford] to Jacksons Bay, no Township was ever laid off, partly because there was no inhabitants worth mentioning and partly because there wasn't room for one, but Jacksons Bay as a town had a short though not very brilliant existance. A settlement on the lines of the Holyford, only on a more liberal scale was started at Okura [Okuru] Waitoto [Waiatoto] & Arawata, with Jacksons bay as the main city. Town sections went at high prices. A Store, a Public house and a Gaol were built – the latter always a sign of prosperity. A Jetty was started [but not finished, a significant handicap to the settlement], the neuclus [nucleus] of a harbour where mail steamers, and battle ships were to coal up, but Alas the land was no good for settlement, the coal and other minerals could not be found, and in a few years the township ceased to exist. When I last saw it there was an old whare and the Gaol still standing, the latter building had both doors open with a reproachfull look about it, as if inviting some one for mercys sake to come in and be locked up.

TWENTY-TWO

Birds

*This study of New Zealand birds, completed about 1899, is the most substantial mono-
graph by Charlie Douglas, and there is continuing value in it. He gives insight into the
habits and changing numbers of New Zealand birds more than a hundred years ago, and
enables people of the present to make comparisons with the past.*

*The original also included opinions and observations on exotic and sea birds, but,
like the section on fishes, they are not reproduced here. The focus is on the birds Douglas
knew best: those of the bush, rivers and lagoons.*

Modern scientific names are given from Barrie Heather and Hugh Robertson's Field
Guide to New Zealand Birds *(Auckland, 1996), and also included is a comment on
the manuscript written in 1953 by Dr R. A. Falla, then Director of the Dominion Museum.*

*Douglas did not make a special study of birds, but here he shows how much he
observed in the course of his life. Sometimes he is very accurate; at other times he lets his
imagination roam free. He is unsystematic, discursive, often entertaining, and at times
quite incorrect. Douglas shows some of the attitudes of Victorians who assumed the
world was for the benefit of humans. However, he is also searching for an understanding
of the ecology of his natural world in a way that few others even attempted in his time.
He is clearly familiar with many bird-catching techniques and often used birds for food,
but he is also aware of the impact on birds of humans and the predators they have
introduced, such as cats, dogs, rats and ferrets. What he has seen in his lifetime is enough
to make him a conservationist in quite a modern sense.*

The Land Birds of Westland

Writing about the birds and fish of New Zealand is but going over old ground.
So many books have been issued on the subject. Still one who has been wandering about the country, and studied the birds in their native haunts for over
thirty years, may be allowed to know something about them, beyond the dry
discriptions of Science; discriptions which are only for a certain class, not for
the general public. Even a dry subject such as Ornothology may be made more
readable by being enlivened with a little humour and short stories discriptive

of the habits of birds when in their natural state of existance. To most people a bird is simply a bird. To me, it is a living creature with its likes and dislikes, a creature in most cases with a measure of intelligence few give them credit for. Take for instance the Weka. No two birds are really alike. They have their differences in intellegence in their ways and habits, and all other birds except perhaps pigeons are the same, even what we call the most stupid have different degrees of stupidity. No two birds of whatever species are actually alike.

Before proceeding in my discriptions, it must be understood that I make no pretentions to Science, and will give the birds, not their scientific name, but the name they go by in the country – however inappropriate those names may be, avoiding Scientific terms even when I know them, and will write: not as for a book or a magazine, but as pleases myself. And it also must be understood that I am writing of Westland alone, both as it was and is, in regard to bird life.

There are few greater mistakes that people, not only in the Old Country but even in the Colonies, fall into than that New Zealand is destitute or comparatively destitute of birds and fish.

A man may be thirty years in the Colony, and still know little about it. He goes home [to Britain] and is considered an Authority on all subjects connected with the natural history of the country. While it is a fact, that with the exception of a few surveyors, prospectors and an odd explorer, not one man in a hundred has ever been out of his own particular district, a radius of say thirty miles, which to him is New Zealand – with a hurried gallop to Town once a year, and all his time in the country, never half a mile in the bush, and he knows the mountains only by telescope.

The Canterbury plains and open parts of Otago have few native birds, as it is not their nature to frequent such places, but the bush, except near long settled districts – is swarming with various kinds of birds. The lakes, bush, creeks and lagoons are full of ducks, and on the river flats and mountain ranges, wekas, keas, ka kai [kaka], and blue ducks are to be got almost without trouble. From the sea beach to the snow line, bird life is to be found. As to another common assertion, the want of song birds, the song of the robin, the chorus of the bell bird, and the tui, and the plaintive flute like note of the crow, will compare favourably with the birds in any part of the World. Many who ought to know better lament the vocal silence of the woods so unlike the British Islands, let those people get up on a summer morning and they will be defened with melody.

In places that have been long settled, and where every house and hut keeps a lot of half starved cats, birds cannot be plentiful, but to assert that because they are not to be seen about a town, they dont exist anywhere – is nonsense.

The Bat

This part bird, whole animal is unique in its way, as being the only mammal indigenous to the country. According to native tradition, the Maorie rat [kiore] was brought by them from whatever part of the World the traditional canoes came from, and such may probably be the case. The Norway and black rat and mice, came out as free immigrants – or rather stowaways – and received a crown grant of the whole country on landing. Rabbits, ferrets and stoats had their passage paid by a far seeing paternal government, but there is no evidence that the bat was imported, so he ought to be proud of himself.

The bat labours under one great dissadvantage in this country, he has no ruined castles or old towers to haunt: still no doubt they are quite comfortable in a hollow tree. They have the usual bat habit of camping during the day in a bunch, clinging to each other. It is rather startling, after kindling a fire against a hollow tree, to see a bundle of astonished bats tumble into the fire.

Although strictly a night animal, they are often to be seen in the day time, but only in the dark sunless gullies. The bat never was plentifull. Still a few are always to be seen both summer and winter shortly after sunset, and they often come down a fireless chimney, or get into a hut or tent dazed by the light.

In moral character, the bat is not so innocent as one would suppose. They can steal. In a camp in the bush I was puzzeled to find baccon, butter and any sort of fat, nibbled as if by mice, elaborate fixings were put on the futtah [whata] but with out success, till late one night having occaison to go for some stores, a lot of bats flew out. The mystery was explained. Still it is not often the bat steals and when he does, there is not much harm done.

Ground Birds
The Apteryx

There are three varieties of this singular bird in Westland, the roa, the kiwi, and another which I have called the giant kiwi, as it is feathered more like a kiwi, than a roa. What its real name is I dont know. The Maories in Bruce Bay seem to have known it only by tradition, and couldn't give it a name. Before the West Coast was opened by the digger, all those birds of the Apteryx family were supposed to be, if not extinct, at least nearly so, but this was soon found to be a mistake, and now every museum in the World has their stuffed effigies, and some of the zoos have them alive. Whether they breed in captivity I don't know.

In the nineteenth century there was no uniformity in the common names of the various members of the genus Apteryx. *In particular Douglas does not make a clear distinction in the following passages between 'the kiwi' and 'the roa', and it is not certain exactly which bird each is.*

The Kiwi
[Brown kiwi?, tokoeka, *Apteryx australis*]

From the fact that bank notes, postage stamps and advertisement chromos, generally have a portrait of this unholy looking bird on them, it is evident that the kiwi is the accepted national bird of New Zealand, on this subject I will enter more fully when treating about the Weka.

There is no occasion for me to give a discription of the Kiwi and the roa, as their singular appearance, and large egg are well known all over the world, better known than perhaps any other bird in the country. The kiwi was at one time common all over Westland, almost as much so, as wekas, but the advent of cats, dogs and ferrets along with the huntings for science, have thined there numbers, and before long it will only be found in the Sounds, and the wilder parts of Westland, where it will exist long after the roa and giant kiwi are extinct. Neverless it also is doomed to final extinction, not altogether from cats, dogs etc. who accelerate their fate. No doubt neither will it be through want of food. The same feed that existed a thousand years ago exist still, but like the moa, the mamoth, and the mastadon, their use in creation has come to a close, it is only certain types of insects and shellfish, that appear to be everlasting. Birds, and beasts and even races of men have to run their course and finally dissappear, giving place to some higher type.

The kiwi is certainly not of high type. It looks like a being one would expect to see in the moon, Mars, or some dying out Planet. When running about in the moonlight, it looks like a ghost of a bird, espicially if it has just been digging in a rotton log, when its beak is often luminus-phosphoresent.

When breeding, the kiwi lays as a rule two eggs, but in no single instance did I ever get two chicks, and never saw remains of either of the eggs. What they do with the spare one and the shell of the other is a mystery. Is it kept to feed the solatary child?

How they hatch there eggs, which are almost as big as themselves, is another mystery. I have only once caught them hatching or gammoning [pretending] too; it was in a hollow log and both birds were asleep, not sitting on the eggs, but curled in a ball alongside of them. I think most of the heat required comes from decaying matter. The leaves and such like they lay their eggs on – their was nothing the wildest imagination could call a nest. When asleep the Kiwi is a singular object. They stick their long beak between their legs, and repose as a round feathery ball.

In combat the Kiwi never use their beaks except to make a slight cracking noise, but fight with their feet, a la Lancashire. Harmless as they appear, they can still kill each other, but they could not be called quarrelsome birds, unless a few from different holes are put in the same cage, then their is war. Perhaps they do fight, when meeting each other in the bush, but as they have no battle cry like the Kakapo, and many other birds, but fight silent, no one knows what Donnybrokes may be going on in the silent forest.

In captivity they are rather difficult to keep alive, many dying in a few days, but when they get over the change they are easily tamed, and will eat almost anything. It is in captivity that their dense stupidity can best be seen. If put in a room, they will go tramping round close to the wall using their beaks as a walking stick. If a box or a tub with water in it, is put against the wall, he doesn't go round, but if possable kiwi climbs into the tub, through the water, and out again, and so on for hours, never thinking to avoid the tub and the water, if he can get round the back of the fire so much the better. Never mind a singeing.

I once tamed one, and after while he did develope a faint glimmer of intellegence. He turned into a day bird, would jump on the table, and help himself to whatever was on the plates, and at night he would jump on my bunk and try to get inside the blankets. If he did succeed, he gave a peculiar girning; a cry I never heard before.

As for eating a kiwi. Just before they commence breeding they are very fat and good eating. Still I must confess it requires some considerable practice to get the acquired taste. They have an earthy flavour, which to many would be dissagreeable. The best definition I ever heard about roast or boiled kiwi, was a man, remarking it tasted as he should imagine a piece of pork boiled in an old coffin would be like. The egg has slightly the same flavour, but is not to be dispised. One egg makes an excellent fritter, covering an ordinary frying pan.

Altogether the kiwi, except in a museum as one of the last of the pre-Adamites, is of neither use nor ornament. His intellegence is on about the same level as a spider, and it seems almost impossable to develope it. No doubt like every living thing, it has its uses in creation, but as his work is done in the dark, it is not apparent enough for people to give him any credit for it.

I said the Kiwi was of no use. Here I am in error, they are usefull in a garden, catching grubs, slugs and worms. They dont scratch up flower beds, like domestic fowls, or pull up plants by the roots to see what the end is like, as do Wekas. I believe if there one virtue was only known, they would run the toad off the field as the lord of a hot house or closed in garden. Then again, almost the first kiwi caught on the Coast was purchased by an enterprising publican, who found it attracted more custom to his house than half a dozen auburn haired barmaids.

The Roa

[Okarito brown kiwi?, *Apteryx australis*]

There is little to be said about this bird that does not apply to the Kiwi. There habits are identical, the only difference being that unlike the kiwi which is to be found all over the Coast, the roa is to be found only in certain localities, namely between the Okarito river and the Waiho and between the Waitoto and the Arawata; these are the only two places they are to be found till the Hollyford is crossed. I believe a few have been caught near Nelson, and no doubt, like the Kiwi, they were at one time to be found all over the country. The puzzle is how did they dissappear from every place but those mentioned above? They must have dissappeared from other parts long before the advent of the digger. The Maories have no explanation to give. Sometimes I think they had vanished ages ago, and were only to be got in the Sounds, and that either the old time Maories or the whalers brought a few up by sea and turned them out in the two places mentioned. Still this is only an idea of my own.

Birds only being found in certain localities, where although the feed and surroundings are the same, yet ten miles away there are none of that species, is no more singular than a patch, say, of black birch [beech] growing close together, and not a relation within a hundred miles. Or a tree forming the main forrest on one side of a river, and not a trace of it to be seen on the other. Birds certainly have a power of locomotion that a tree has not. Although a roa or a kiwi can't swim, as far as I am aware – yet accidents of floods could not help taking some over any river on the Coast. Many no doubt would get drowned. Still some must have got accross and populated the other side, but in all my wanderings I never got a trace of a roa, except in the two places mentioned. Although to mortal eyes the soil, the vegetation and feed appear alike, there must be some subtle difference in soil that we don't understand. This is the only way I can account for the localising of certain species, whether animal or vegetable. Even some birds with their power to shift readily and safely from one part of the country to another, still confines themselves to certain districts.

The Mountain Kiwi

[Great spotted kiwi?, roa, *Apteryx haastii*]

I have very little to say regarding this bird, as I have only seen two of them, and being pushed with hunger, I ate the pair of them, under the circumstances I would have eaten the last of the Dodos.

It is all very well for science, lifting up its hands in horror, at what I once heard called gluttony, but let science tramp through the Westland bush or swamps, for two or three days without food, and find out what hunger is. Besides at the time, which was many years ago, I was not aware that it was an almost extinct bird. Had I known so, I would at least have skinned it and kept the head and feet.

The bird was a third larger than the bigest roa. It had the grey feathers of the Kiwi, but much coarser more approaching those of the roa, its beak had more of a curve, and its spur was very long. Otherwise it resembled a roa more than a kiwi.

On asking the Maories about this bird, they could give it no name, but said it was an inhabitant of the mountains and that its spur could kill a dog. The two I caught were camped under a bunch of ferns, in the center of a large swamp between Karangaro and Cooks river. Another bird of the same species was caught some time after by a digger up Cooks river. I didn't see it, and dont know what became of it. These are all I have heard of as having been caught in Westland, and although I have hunted the place since with a good dog, I never again got a trace of the bird. One I believe was got recently on Stewarts Island. Whether it was the same bird, I don't know.

The Mountain giant kiwi must be either very rare, or perhaps it is now extinct. May be some still exists down in the Sounds, that handy place for locating anything you can't find. The Sounds certainly are unexplored, and it is impossable to say what rare birds may yet be found their. Although I don't believe a new bird will ever be found, either there or in any part of New Zealand.

The Weka or Maorie Hen
[Weka, *Gallirallus australis*]

In a new country that has hopes of someday becoming a nation, people should be carefull how they select a national bird or beast. The lion and the eagle have already been annexed by old countries, although their courage and usefullness is rather apocryphal. Canada takes the beaver, which is good, it is a fine emble[m] of industry, and its hide suggest bell toper hats. Australia has adopted the Kangaroo, which is also good; it is an animal characteristic of the country, its tail makes good soup, its hams are passable and its skin makes shoe leather – so the shoemakers say – so it is of some use. The beaver and the Kangaroo will pass; but the Kiwi which New Zealand has adopted is neither use, nor ornament, and has not a single good or bad quality to reccommend it.

Why did New Zealand not select the Weka? Here is a bird full of good qualities and who's vices lean to virtue's side. Personal valour of a high order. An undying thirst for knowledge – unthinking people give it another name –

which causes it to annex everything portable about a hut and carry it into the bush to study at leisure. An affection for its young, that would face the Prince of Darkness in their defence. And above all an intelegence apart from what we call instinct, far higher than I ever saw in a bird. It has one fault which it shares with some other New Zealand birds; it is a cannibal spareing not even its immediate relations.

At one time the Weka must have been the main food of the Maorie, and they had the sense to protect it, which is more than the whites ever did. When the Maorie made a raid on a river, they allways left sufficient birds to restock it again and they left that river alone for three years. However seeing the way whites slaughter the birds with dog and gun, they are now not so particular, with the result that the birds are not plentifull as once was the case. There general breeding grounds being on the open river beds between the mountains and the sea, where they were easy got at, the bird had little chance to keep its numbers with men and dogs after them, in season and out. If the society that looks after the game would make a close season for four or five years, the weka would be as plentifull as ever. They can hold their own against cats and ferrets. In fact I believe they actually keep those animals down and may possably exterminate them; it is quite a common occurrence for the hens to walk off with young pups and kittens when the owner is away. I have lost a good few pups that way, and there is no doubt that it was the weka that exterminated the wild cats and dogs that once flourished south of Jacksons bay. It was not want of food but the impossability of rearing a family that finished them. From this it can be seen that the weka's pilfering abalities for which he is so much abused has its uses, and that it is really a public benefactor in his own particular way.

Here is an idea of mine, and that is that the weka could be made of far more use to the world than at present. Away in the Antartic and South Indian ocean are numbers of uninhabited islands on which shipwrecked mariners often die of starvation, or at least live miserably. Why not put Maorie hens on those islands? They would have no enemies in such places, they are easy to catch, good healthy food, and will live and thrive anywhere eating and digesting anything from a jam tart to a pea rifle cartridge. Some of the birds were introduced into the Aucklands I believe but there are other islands south of New Zealand then there is St. Pauls, Kerguelen land, the Crozets and numbers of others on which I believe this bird would thrive. Whether they would live in the tropics is doubtfull, but such places don't want them, they have fruit and fish as a rule. A roast weka would be a godsend to a shipwrecked sailor after living for weeks on seal or penguin.

To thoroughly understand the Weka, its virtues and its vices, its wonderfull strength, and still more wonderfull intelegence, the bird has to be studied in its native wilds. If not shot at, or chased by dogs, they soon get tame, and take possession of hut or tent, as if they were put up expressly for their benefit. It is seldom one is alone, generally having his wife with him, and all the better if they have a young family to provide for – or rather they make you do that. At first they certainly are a bother, walking off with everything they can carry, and inspecting with their beaks all articles they cant lift, but after a while when they are thoroughly satisfied they leave things alone.

The Weka generally lays five eggs although I have seen seven, but that is rare, and they seldom rear more than two or three young ones. When sitting or looking after the chicks they will face anything. I have seen them by sheer cheek and audacity route an experienced bush dog, and when grass happens to be set on fire, where they are sitting, they will die rather than leave. When hatching, the two birds take turn about sitting, and have very regular watches. I watched a pair for days and found their time was almost exactly four hours. Once I kept the cock bird over his time, by a judicious expenditure of bits of butter. She commenced yelling out for him, and as he didn't come, she did, and chased him to his duties. That cockbird was literally henpecked. When the young come out, the old ones starve themselves feeding them, holding the grub, worm, or whatever it is in their beak, which the son or daughter deftly removes and swallow. It is interesting to watch them, and it is a beautifull family picture to see the two old ones, and two or three young ones, standing in front of the fire, with their wings spread out enjoying the blaze. This standing before the fire is not uncommon and wild birds will often do the same, robins thrushes and wrens all can appreciate a fire even if they saw it for the first time.

As wekas are very fond of butter and jam, they soon find out the tins those articles are kept in, and make desperate efforts at burglary, they bang at it with their beaks and will get inside if possable. A very good amusement is to leave an unopened jam tin on the ground. They turn it over and over bang at it end way round ways and everyway, and the manner in which that tin is kicked about is a caution. The only rest it will have is in a waterhole. What a hen wants stealing a bill hook for is a mystery, but they often do this. They will even attempt the axe, but that is too much for them. There strength combined with some knowledge of mechanics can hardly be believed unless seen. In one instance two wekas actually wheeled or handspiked a piece of baccon weighing eight pounds, thirty feet into the bush, and uphill at that. How they did it is still a mystery to me, but next morning after long search there I found it, their was nothing else but my two hens that could have done it.

We have been accustomed for ages to have dinned into our ears as a fact that man alone has reasoning powers, and that what a bird or animal does is

entirely instinct; this is all nonsense. Everything that has a brain has something above instinct that more or less guides its actions. This we must call
reason, the reasoning of man and that of animals is a mere matter of degree. It
couldn't be instinct that started the hens on the jam pot. Once I laid a pan of
boiling fat down on the ground, never thinking the hen would touch it, but he
did, down came his beak into the pan, he jumped with a squeal of agony, then
rushed outside and buried his beak up to the eyes in the cool wet mud. If that
was instinct from what ancestor did he get it? I must have been the first man he
had ever seen, and that pan and fire he could have had no acquaintance with.

I once heard a story illustrative of weka intelligence, although I can't exactly vouch for the truth of it, however here it is.

An emigrant came out to Canterbury with a little money. He purchased a
block of land and started to make his fortune farming. All went well till he
commenced potatoe planting, then trouble loomed ahead, almost as fast as he
planted them the wekas dug them up, and replanted them in their own peculiar way. The farmer was desperate, he made a scare crow one of those stuffed
effegies that farmers at home still pin their faith too, although it is an object of
derision to any bird of experience. Next morning the figure was on the ground
and a number of wekas were engaged finding out what was inside. Then that
farmer tried one of those windmill racket affairs, worse and worse; the noise
brought all the hens round to see what the row was about, but next day brought
the last straw, getting up earlier than usual the farmer saw what dumbfoundered
him. A hen was as usual digging up the seed, and handing them to his family
for future use. Just as he arrived, Maorie had finished a row, and could it be
believed? That bird cocked his eye along the line he had just skinned, took a
left half turn, and deliberately paced the distance to find where the next row
commenced.

That farmer bundled up and sold everything at a sacrifice. He said, farming
might be a noble occupation, a healthy occupation, but when a man had to
contend against such intelligence it would be far better to go to a town and
turn burglar or politician.

With this tale, I will close the account of the weka. A volume could be
written about them and their funny ways, and long may they flourish in the land.

The Notornis
[Takahe, *Porphyrio mantelli*]

This almost extinct bird may possably exist in considerable numbers in the
Sounds and country back of Lake Te Ana [Anau]. If so I think it will be local-
ised in certain places like the roa.

At one time it no doubt flourished all over Westland, that is if we are to believe the Maories; but it is almost impossable it can now be in the country. I have been all over Westland from one end to the other, and always with a good bush dog, and if the bird existed, I could not possably help finding it. Besides myself there have been surveyors, propectors and cattle hunters also over the country, and no trace of the bird has been found. That singular drumming noise heard at night in Southern Westland is the Ka Ka po [kakapo] courting cry. Not the Notornis as some people wished to believe.

The Maories say it was a Passbird found high up in the Mountains. This I don't believe, it may no doubt have crossed the ranges at times, like its relative the Swamp hen [pukeko], but on the ranges is not where these natural haunts must be. It is decididly a swamp bird like the bukaka [pukeko], and if ever found it will be in the Lake and lagoon covered plateaus which are said to abound in some parts inland from the Sounds. It is to be hoped if they do exist no one will find them. Science would soon exterminate them in the interest of museums.

I have not seen a notornis except in a picture and dont know to what family it belongs, the rails most likely, so I have bracketed it between the Weka and the swamphen.

Douglas was not entirely correct, in that the takahe is not specifically a swamp bird, but he did predict where it would be rediscovered, in a valley west of Lake Te Anau. Dr G. B. Orbell found it there in 1948.

The Swamphen
[Pukeko, *Porphyrio porphyrio*]

This is a sad example to man, bird, or beast, not to attempt too many accomplishments. Jack of all trades and master of none would well apply to this foolish fowl. An ambition to excell in all ornothological gifts has been its ruin, and made the bird an object of derision to the feathered creation. It can fly, walk, dive and swim, but can do none of them even tolerably well. It flies with a contorted jerky motion, but only for a short distance, alighting on any tree handy, and staggering among the branches as if intoxicated. It walks as if troubled with corns, and in runing it often stumbles. When swiming it looks like a domestic fowl tumbled in a water butt and wanted some kind friend to rescue it. It diving is still more absurd, putting on the airs of a grebe, it turns its head from side to side with a knowing look then goes down, with a disordered splutter of legs and wings, coming up at once with jerk like a cork.

Occasionally I have seen them perched on a tree stretching their necks and making a fearfull noise, which shows probably they are going to add singing to their other accomplishments.

Besides being a jack of all trades, this bird has a variety of names, no two people being agreed as to which is correct. The Maories called it the bu-ka-ka – is this spelling correct? Some people call it the coote, from some fancied resemblance to the water hen of the Old country. Swamp hen it is generally called in Westland, but I have heard it also called bald pate and New Zealand turkey; the latter name the most absurd of all, as it has not the slightest resemblance to that bird, either in appearance or habits.

The small tuft of white feathers which swampy no doubt thinks is a tail. He is evidently very proud of cocking it up and down continually when walking. When the bird comes out on an open space walking like a man with tight boots, its little white tuft bobbing up and down with a jerky motion, its head and body continually bowing and nodding, with the antics of a French dancing master the swamp hen forms a strange apparation.

Like the weka, this bird can be snared, but not so easily and it will tame around a house, espicially if there is a stable with corn about, and it astonishes the domestic fowls with its antics and impudence. The only thing they are afraid of are hawks, who catch them in the open or when flying accross from tree to tree. Swampy, when he sees a hawk, makes either for the water or the scrub squealing all the time. Dogs also catch them very easily. An experienced dog when he trees a hen doesn't go barking and howling. He simply sits down, the hen gets tired waiting, comes down to the ground and is nabbed at once.

The swamp hen is tolerable eating and makes good stock for soup and appears to be one of the few birds that increases with civilization. In some parts of Otago and Southland they were becoming a nuisance and a price was put on their heads.

A page back I was writing irrevently [irreverently] about this bird's flight. He really must at time fly with a sustained flight, as they can cross the main range, but many must perish on the journey as I have often found them dead on glacier and snowfield.

Ducks
The Paridise Duck
[Paradise shelduck, putangitangi, *Tadorna variegata*]

History and tradition are silent as regards the origin of this name. The bird is not particularly gorgeous in plumage. It voice is not angelical in sweetness they can neither sing nor whistle, and their cry is only slightly superior to the music of the bagpipes. The name may be a corruption from some unknown language where it may have had a meaning.

It is called a duck, but it most decididly belong to the goose tribe. It lives on grass and oats when it can get them – its cry is something like that of a goose only it does not hiss, and they often join geese about a house, never ducks.

If not shot at or otherwise disturbed and there is a grass paddock handy, they soon become comparatively tame. When their eggs are hatched under a domestic fowl, and the top pinion of one wing cut off, the young will grow up about a poultry yard like other domestic fowls, never leaving the place as they can't fly. In this state they become fat and are very good eating but I have never heard whether they breed in captivity.

If shot at or otherwise disturbed, the Paridise duck soon becomes very wild, and remarkably cute, keeping a sentry like crows. It is aggravating after painfully crawling gun in hand through wet grass, and swamp making sure of a fine pot shot, to find that a confounded drake has had his eye on you all the time. He says Krayzanque, the other birds reply and all fly off with a cry too much like a laugh to be pleasant to the disappointed one. I consider it mean in the bird, after you have crawled quarter of a mile in hopes of a shot, to wait till you are almost within range. The wretch might have sung out when he saw you first and so saved all the trouble.

When hatching, the paridise is not particular where it makes its nest as long as it is hidden. In among thick scrub near the waters edge in a flax bush or often up a tree, they don't mind which. How the young get down from the tree without being killed is a mystery, but they manage it some way. As the young bird cannot fly for months after they come out: the old ones develope wonderfully intellegence in protecting them from dogs and men.

A man who has never seen the dodge will be walking along a river flat, when he sees a poor wounded drake fluttering along the ground. Ha! he says to himself, I'll have that bird for supper. Down goes his swag and with a handfull of stones he starts in persuit, but somehow, however fast he runs, that bird always keeps the same distance. If a stone is thrown it always lands where the bird was; if that man stops for breath, or to think, the bird stops also, and spreads its wings out as if in the agonies of death, stringing the man on to make another dash, but always with the same result. At last when he has gone a mile or so, the duck comes along, she had been planting the young ones and comes to tell him its all right. He gets up with nothing the matter with him, and both fly away with a derisive laugh, leaving the man to curse his stupidity, and to wonder if he will find his swag again. I don't suppose a man would be taken in twice with this dodge, but most dogs never seem to tumble to it, but keep after the bird, putting on terrific spurts in the vain hope of catching it.

As the young of the paridise ducks are full fledged and grown before they can fly, they are easily caught. Almost any dog will do, and when in the water the birds can be driven ashore in mobs the dogs being ready to receive them. Just before they can fly is the time; the young ones are good to eat they are then fat and tender.

Strangely, Douglas makes no mention of the distinct differences between male and female paradise ducks in terms of appearance and call, but perhaps they were so familiar to him that it seemed too obvious.

The Gray Duck
[Grey duck, parera, *Anas superciliosa*]

Unlike most New Zealand birds this duck is shy by nature probably he knows he is good to eat stuffed and roasted, consequently he always sleeps with one eye open. It brings nine to ten young into the world, but seldom rears more than two or three, eels being the cause. It is quite a common occurance to find a duck with only one leg, an eel got the other, and I have often found young birds inside the fish.

The gray duck tries to protect its young when on land by using the same dodge as the paridise, but not so successfully, as the young generally take to the water, where the enemy really is. This bird and the blackswan are the only two I know who convert themselves into what might be called an ornothological perambulater. They are often to be seen swimming with some of the young on their backs it is rather a pretty sight, and I have often wondered if any human being would shoot them while so imployed.

As the gray duck is a shy bird and rises very quick it affords more of what is called sport than any other – in the country – except a quail. A home country sportsman would have a fit if he saw the delebrate pot shooting in Westland. Imagine having to throw stones at a bird so as to get far enough away to fire without blowing it to pieces, or on pointing a gun at a Kea Kea to see the audacious bird cooly land on the muzzel and yell defiance.

The Blue Duck
[Whio, *Hymenolaimus malacoryhnchos*]

Generally called the mountain duck, as it is mostly found in the rocky torrents up to the grass line, it is what is called a soft bill, and its colour is a light grey or slate with brown mottles on the breast. It is about the size of a grey duck, and its prevailing characteristic is stupidity to an amazing degree. This combined with what appears to be a fatal thirst for admiration is its ruin, and makes it an easy prey to dogs and men, and nothing but the inaccessible places it frequents saves it from being exterminated.

If the bird would only hold its tongue. I know of none who's plumage is so well adapted for concealment, the light grey with the mottled breast and white tipped beak being the exact shade of the granite slate and quartz fragments lying on every riverbed, but a desire to show off is its ruin. I have often walked within a foot of them, and would never have noticed the birds if not attracted by a plaintive whistle, and on looking round there they were, stretching their necks, whistling and hissing, evidently thinking themselves swans and worthy the admiration of the universe.

A green hand in such a case, if he had a gun, would at once let fly and think himself clever if he got one. But that is not the way to do: look around up and down the stream and see if there are any more, if so drive them together, then sit calmly down, take a good lean on a rock and fire. If the birds wont go close together throw stones at them. If any fly away after firing dont get excited, and run after them, but load the gun, pick up the slain and have a smoke. Soft bill will soon come back to see what all the row was about.

This discription of the blue duck only applies now to the very wildest districts. In places where they have been much disturbed they develope a caution which shows they are not so stupid as imagined; there tameness and so called stupidity is simply the result of living in a country where for hundreds of generations they had few or no enemies.

When the blue duck means business he can fly at a speed few fowls can equal. Generally however they seldom fly more than a few score yards. Often when fired at and missed they will only splutter along the water for a few feet and quietly wait till you load again. They will tumble over a waterfall in the most reckless manner or allow themselves to be swept among rocks and snags, coming up twenty chains below whistling and wagging their tails with the calmest indifference. A dog who knows them, simply runs up and down the banks barking and making as much noise as possable. Bluie gets bothered and takes to the shore where he is caught at once.

Altogether the blue duck is an interesting bird to study and it is well worth anyone's while to spend an hour watching them and their ways. They are good eating and as they are easy to catch, and frequent parts of the country where other birds are scarce, they are very acceptable to survey parties and explorers.

The blue duck lays from four to five eggs and when the young are hatched they take to the water at once. The old ones take great care of them and display a faint glimmer of intelligence when swimming accross a rapid using their bodies as a brake water for their young, and if going up stream, one bird goes ahead to brake the force of the water, the other following behind to shove them along.

One peculiarity of the blue duck is there general habit of peging off the ground on a creek or river where they intend to breed. Whether they learned this from the early diggers, I cant say, but every pair of ducks keepts two or three hundred yards of the river to themselves and woe betide any stragglers who invade their dominion.

I once came down a creek for about four miles, and for the fun of the thing, drove every duck and their young one ahead of me, with the result that on reaching the flats there was thirteen pair of ducks with a numerous offspring engaged in a sort of Donybroke. They fight with their wings trying to hit with a spur on the tip, but with all their fighting they don't appear to hurt each other much.

On going up the same creek next day, I found to my surprise that every pair was back to their own ground again with all their young with them.

I dont know much about the domestic relations of ducks, but both the blue duck and the paridise appear, once they pair, to keep together till one or other goes to their long home. When a blue duck with young swimming about looses its mate, the survivor attends to the family, but if there is no family he, or she goes on the travell. Whether they annexe somebodies hubby or wife or whether they capture some forlorn batchelor or spinster, I dont know, but duck or drake is never solatary for any length of time.

The Teal duck and Widgeon

[Brown teal, pateke, *Anas aucklandica*,
New Zealand scaup, papango, *Aythya novaeseelandiae*]

There are two varieties of this duck; the brown teal and the black teal or widgeon. They are apparently the same bird, common to most parts of the world, so no discription is required. In the bush creeks in lakes, lagoons and marshes they swarm like vermin, going in flocks of hundreds in some places, and they can be driven ashore and hunted with dogs like the paridise duck, with this advantage, that both young and old will leave the water.

They are good eating, easy to catch, and are a happy chubby little bird troubled with few cares about danger from men or dogs. Tame and stupid as the blue duck is, you have at least to walk to them to get a shot, but in waters where they have not been disturbed the teal will follow a boat or canoe imploring the occupants to shoot them.

The Spoonbill

[Australasian shoveler, kuruwhengi, *Anas rhynchotis*]

This is a bird I have seldom seen in Westland although they may be common in other parts of this Island. They are about the size of a grey duck, with dark plumage, and a few of the white and bronze feathers of the paridise duck. The bill is soft and wider at the end than the base, somewhat resembling a spoon, hence their name. They are very shy, and the speed they fly at is extrordinary, going past with a whiz like a bullet out of a gun. In shooting allowance has to be made for this speed.

[Methods of hunting ducks]

Having now finished an account of the ducks in Westland, I may as well give a short discription of how to catch them, otherwise than shooting, or with a dog. Before the introduction of fire arms the Maories appear to have had only a few ways of catching ducks, whether the net was introduced by the white man I dont know but I have never heard of the natives using nets for ducks their only way was noosing them or killing them with stones or spear neither are a very sure process. Noosing is only practicable in certain waters on the arm of a lake or a narrow still creek or lagoon, and it is done this way by stretching a flax line accross the water where ducks frequent. On the line are tied a row of flax nooses three inches in diameter, each loop slightly overlapping the other. The line is tightened, till the ends just touch the water. At night, or day time for that matter, the ducks swiming along get their heads in the noose which tightens on their neck, and soon either strangles them, or holds them till taken off. I daresay the Maories got good hauls this way if birds were plentiful, but generally two or three get caught ahead of the main mob, and their splashing either frightened the others or irritrivably tangle the line, with its row of loops and so renders it useless.

Another way is called driving. To get a good haul a dog or two is required, and it only succeeds with young paridise ducks and teal, and requires certain waters. Just before the young ducks can fly, select a long narrow lagoon with a sandy beach, or a small patch of grass at the head of it, get into the canoe and zig-zag up the lagoon, splashing with the paddle and making as much noise as you like. Gradually as you approach the end, you will find droves ahead of you. As they get jammed, the old ones will fly away and as the young ones can't, they are obliged to take too the shore. Then is the time to let the dogs out, and you can assist by dashing among them using the paddle as a club. The load of birds caught this way is wonderfull. The great trouble is to get the dogs off. They get so excited and would slaughter till knocked up.

Trolling ducks is a North American Indian method, and is done in the following way. Go quietly with gun and amunition to lake or lagoon where ducks are known to be, peep through the grass or scrub, if any birds are to be seen, wave your hat or kerchief for a few seconds over the intervening bushes, then drop down for half a minute, taking care not to show yourself. Keep repeating the performance till you have attracted the birds attention. They will draw together from all quarters, and bear down in rows towards the object that has attracted their attention. When once they have started their curiosity is so great that it matters little whether you are seen or not. Keep on waving till you can see the eyes of the birds. Then – ! The best gun in such a case is an old tower musket, loaded with a handfull of powder and shot and paper in proportion, then take aim where the best row of heads are, shut your eyes, commend yourself to your patron saint, if you have one, and pull the trigger.

If properly loaded, the distructive effects of an old musket both before and behind is something fearfull. The great objection to using a musket is that it requires two to work it, one fires the other gathers up the slain, and watches where the old howitzer comes down. The man who fires is generally prostrate for the remainder of the day.

Trolling ducks is well enough, now and again, but the birds get very shy, and it is seldom more than two shots can be got at the same place. They will remember their fright for long after and sheer off at the slightest motion in the bush . . .

After having mentioned such contrivances for capturing aquatic birds, it will no doubt be supposed that I have that thirst for blood, which we are said to derive from our barbarian ancestors; a thirst which as we cannot now gratify at the expense of our fellow man [is] expended in slaughtering dumb animals, but such is not the case with me. I never kill bird or beast for sport, and hate to see anyone doing it. If I want a bird for food, I take the surest method of doing it. I have lived for weeks on dry bread, rather than kill birds knowing they had young, and cannot see why any living thing should be destroyed simply to afford amusement to a lot of cockneyfied sportsman who dont require them for food and who for one they get, leave three wounded to die miserably. Necessity is the only plea for taking life, and those individuals who shreik and yell at an unfortunate hare flying before the hounds, or who gallop like lunatics to see a fox torn to pieces have different ideas of humanity than I possess.

The Grebe

I dont know whether this bird has any relatives in the British Islands, but there is a Grebe on the Swiss lakes which may be allied to it.

There are two varities in Westland, differing both in size and plumage but in habits identical.

[The Crested Grebe]

[Australasian crested grebe, puteketeke, *Podiceps cristatus australis*]

The crested grebe is a beautifull bird, and sits the water as gracefully as a white swan. It is slightly larger than a grey duck. On the neck and breast and all under the waterline the plumage is white with a sheen like satin and its skin is in demand for mufs trimmings and so the unfortunate bird was hunted for that purpose.

Although their wings are small they can fly with great speed and a sustained flight, but it is only at certain seasons they do so, preferring very sensebly to trust to their wonderfull diving powers to escape danger, for which they are always on the look out. Knowing by experience that the vain maidens of New Zealand are thirsting for their hide.

At one time the grebe was almost exterminated. Then a law was passed protecting them for all time, and they were gradually recovering themselves when the fish hatcheries found out, or thought they had, that the greb distroyed fish, and war was again proclaimed with the result they are hardly ever seen, except in the far South where they are likely to hold their own as no one can get at them.

I wonder people don't use their reasoning powers a little more. At the first opening of the Coast, the shag, the grebe, the heron and the crane were far more numerous than they are now, yet the whitebait, mullet and grayling held their own with ease. Why can't the trout and salmon do the same now that fish enemies are scarce? Yet some ass sees a shag or crane helping its self to a few fish, and he at once makes to the papers to ventelate his feelings. The result is the fiat goes forth that a race must be exterminated. I hold we want an Acclimatisation society and game laws, but let those who engineer such societies have at least a little knowledge of the birds, beast and fish they make believe to legislate for.

But to the grebe again. There must be something wrong either with its head or eyes. When watching an enemy, it keeps first one eye then the other, fixed on the object for a few seconds. Then it turns its head to give the other a chance, so on back and forward as if one eye couldn't trust the other. I have watched them many a time and thought that one or other of its eyes were defective, short sighted in fact, and that in the excitment, the bird always forgot which was wrong, but it would be strange if all grebes were short sight in one eye. The more probable reason is the bird has a double brain one for each eye; the two are always at loggerheads and cant trust each other when danger is near.

At one time I thought the grebe was stupid bird and was always shy and on the look out for danger, but an experience I once had with a bird altered that notion.

One day five of us were in a boat on a lake, when about two miles from shore a crested grebe showed up. It was fired at, with the usual result, a splutter of shot where the bird had been. For curiosity we determined to rung that bird down before it could reach the shore. One got to the bow, with two double barrelled guns and amunition handy, the other four took to the oars. The moment the bird appeared it was fired at, and the boat pulled in the direction it was supposed it would come up. This work continued for about half an hour, the bird sometimes making shorewards, sometimes towards the center of the lake. At last from keeping under for more than a minute, it had to show up every few seconds, but only the point of its beak was to be seen just to get a gasp for breath, and down again suddenly it disappeared altogether. We waited and waited but there was no appearance.

It could not have flown away, or got to shore without our seeing it, so we concluded it had sunk dead to the bottom. By the merest chance some one happened to look over the stern of the boat which overhung considerably, and there was his lordship peacefully taking a spell with a satisfied grin on him. To our honour be it said we let that bird go.

I never saw or heard of any aquatic bird trying this dodge, except in one instance in the Old Country. A sea diver called the Marrit dose the same thing around fishing boats, but his hiding is more to see what he can steal out of the nets as they are hauled in.

The grebes mode of nesting varies according to the nature of the lake or lagoon he frequents. Sometimes they nest up trees overhanging the water in a flax bush and sometimes, but not very often, they make a floating nest and actually moor it to a snag or the bank.

Once I found a grebes nest with eggs in it. I took the eggs and placed to round pieces of quartz in their place. Looking at the place two days after, the nest was torn down and scattered over the country; the bird had evidently got in a passion at being the victim of such a miserable sell.

The Small Grebe
[New Zealand dabchick, weweia, *Poliocephalus rufopectus*]

This bird is two thirds less in size than the crested one and is not so fine in plumage, otherwise it is the same in habits. It always was a comparatively rare bird and is a very curious little being, quite tame in the presence of man. If you dangle your leg over the water and keep still, they will come up and peck at your boot.

The Shag
Douglas does not distinguish different shags clearly enough for them to be identified.

This is another bird, the origin of whose name is lost in the mists of antiquity. I have heard the same name applied to the British Island cormorant. No doubt that is where the name came from. They are undoubtedly the most repulsive birds in creation, and have a satanic leer in their yellow eyes would give a nervous fellow the shivers. The bird would be more appropriate than an owl in a picture of Leonora and the spectre horsman, and if stuffed and standing well upright they would give a fine finish to a hearse.

There appears to be two or three varities of the shag with habits and appearance the same, differing only in size. The king shag, as it is called, standing over two feet in height, but they are very rare. The shag generally builds there nest in communities high up on trees, but often they make their nests on the ground, and no doubt when the ferrets get at them, they will build on the trees altogether. Not that they would be afraid of ferrets themselves. It would be a brave dog or ferret who would tackle a shag, but they would take to trees for the sake of their young and eggs. The nest is often left to take care of its self, while the old ones are away feeding. The nests are the usual careless construction built by many birds who have few enemies. A few sticks huddled together, and added too as the young come out, is all they consider necessary. The three or four eggs they lay are white and oblong shaped, varing in size according to the bird, but although oblong is the general shape, it is a matter of indifference to the bird, sometime the egg is round, sometimes even lobsided.

The shag is one of the few New Zealand birds who are honoured by having a price put on their head. Half a crown is I believe the value put on them. Near fish hatcheries, they are no doubt more distructive to fish, than any other bird except perhaps the cranes and bitterns, and it is heartrending to come suddenly on thirty or forty shags suning themselves on a river bank, and if startled they will throw up enough of white bait to supply a ministerial dinner. The birds of the air and the fish of the sea were created for mans benefit and it is preposterous that a bird should be allowed to live that creates such havoc. So we say. But I should like very well to know the shags opinion of a certain long legged biped, who manures his onion beds with whitebait when he cant sell them. No wonder that when flying past a white man or a chinaman, the shags look over their shoulder at them with a glare of demoniac hate in their eyes.

I can understand how a grey duck may have an intuitive knowledge that it is good eating, and be shy in consequence, or how other birds may become so from experience. But that the shag, a bird that no white man would eat if he was starving, and for any purpose except baiting an eel pot are not worth a charge of shot, a bird that is seldom disturbed by man and is too powerfull to fear hawk, kite or any other New Zealand enemy, should be shy and always on the lookout for danger puzzles me, but such is the case. Perhaps they do think their flesh delicious, their hide more valuable than sable, and that every museum is thirsting for their stuffed effegy.

Perhaps in times of famine the old Maories did hunt them remorslessly. The old native was rather partial to strong tasting and smelling food. As with the penguin, gull, ganet and such like birds, to eat shag requires a prolonged training. They have plenty of flesh on them, but the taste is suggestive of red herring with guano sauce.

The shag is generally found in the lakes and lagoons near the sea and they will go out to sea occasionally, and enterprising individuals penetrate many miles inland where water exists. With all their clumsey appearance, they can fly like the wind and think nothing about crossing the snowy mountains, and they can dive and swim under water almost as well as a grebe.

The White Crane
[White heron, kotuku, *Egretta alba*]

From the ugly to the handsome is an easy transition – birds like men suffer from that unfair judgement which makes the good and the beautifull synomous [synonymous] terms. Here is a bird as useless as the shag, for any human purpose – unless to ornament a pond – a bird that distroys more fish than any shag, and eating dead sheep and other carrion that a respectable shag would scorn. Yet being handsome, it is admired and protected, while the other is a pariah dispised of gods and men.

The crane with its snow white plumage is certainly an ornament to a sheet of water, and if they do distroy fish what does it matter? They are as much entitled to a share of fish as we are.

Like the heron, it does not weigh much, being only a collection of legs and feathers, and those feathers have been its distruction. It is a shame that a race of birds should be almost exterminated for the sake of a small tuft of feathers, where the birds tail ought to be. That tuft is really all that is wanted the rest of the skin is generally thrown away.

The Crane breeds in comunities on high trees, and at one time they were plentifull all over the coast. But their principal breeding ground near Okarito was distroyed by one of the inhabitants who cut down the trees they had been building on for centuries. The vandalic act was done not to get at the birds, but to spite somebody else, who wanted them preserved. After that the birds scattered and before long only a few solatary ones could be seen.

If not disturbed, the same bird will remain about a district for years and become tame. I had one walking about my garden as if it was the owner, but it is bad policy to tame birds espicially if they are rare. Some fool is sure to come along and shoot it for its skin – so he says – but the skin is generally thrown away in a few days. At least that has been the fate of any I have seen, they never get as far as the bird stuffers.

When not hunting for fish, the crane is to be seen perched on a high tree, one with a dead top prefered. There he will site for hours meditating and digesting the pint or two of whitebait inside of him. When hunting, they prowl about shallow pools standing in the water as still as if they were stuffed, but with one eye open all the same. The height of crane happiness is to get a shallow pool where the fish have been left by a flood, and can't get away. Then he throws caution to the winds, he knows he has them, and proceedes to empty that pool as fast as possable, in case some shag on the prowl comes to assist.

If suddenly disturbed the crane rises with a loud trumpting cry. Legs, wings and head look as if they were in each other way, and that the bird was going to tumble to pieces in its efforts to escape. But when once fairly started on the wing, it stretches its legs away behind – to do duty for a tail – and sails away arching its neck, and turning its body gracefully about. A wonderfull contrast to the shag who was roused out at the same time and got steam up at once and is plying his pinions at a rate, and with a determination as if he didn't intend to stop till he got round Cape Horn.

The only chance the crane has of surviving, in Westland at least, is in the far South where they have started a cranery, when I first found it there was only one nest. Two years afterwards there was five. As the place is a clump of trees in the middle of an almost impassable swamp and in a country with no inhabitants, and not likely to have any for years to come, the birds will have a chance to again spread over the country. Where the place is, and how I got into it I decline to say, leave the birds alone by all means. There are one or two birds supposed to be extinct but are not so, although very rare. There whereabouts is my secret and will remain so, when a bird or beast is nearly extinct Science and Museums offer high rewards for their capture. If it is the last of the race so much the better. As a speciemen, there is an expidition away at present to the wilds of Patagonia in hopes of murdering the last of the giant sloths.

Some one has remarked that if the Venus the Apollo or the Mooses [Muses] were distroyed some genius in sculpture might arise to give the World others, but a bird or animal species once distroyed can never be restored on earth. So give the few rare birds a chance of existance.

These lines incorporate the essence of Douglas's conservation philosophy. The white heron nesting colony he refers to, first discovered for Pakeha by Gerhard Mueller in

1865, still exists today on the Waitangiroto River north of Okarito and Whataroa. The colony was vandalised in the late 1870s and not given sanctuary status till 1914. Only since the Second World War has it been properly protected and enabled to flourish.

The Blue Crane or Heron
[Reef heron, matuku moana, *Egretta sacra*]

This bird is much smaller than the white crane and in general appearance and habits it resembles the home heron to which species it no doubt belongs. It is said to be a native of Australia and not New Zealand, and therefore a bird of passage. I rather think it is a bird common to both countries, as I have seen them all the year round.

It is a solatary bird and very rare even at the first of the Coast; now only one or two are to be seen below Jackson's Bay. It is generally to be found near the sea coast prowling about among the pools in the rocks at low tide.

The Bittern
[Little bittern, *Ixobrychus minutus*,
Australasian bittern, matuku, *Botaurus poiciloptilus*]

There are two varities of this swamp bird both exactly alike in plumage and habits differing only in size the small one is not a fifth the size of the other. The small bittern I at first took for a young bird and it was long before I knew different. Even in the early days it was very rare or at least seldom seen. I can't recollect seeing one for years now. Although I don't think they are extinct it was always a very shy bird and good at hiding itself, and their native haunts were in such impossable swamps no wonder it has seldom been seen.

The large bittern frequents the same sort of place, and are not so rare, and as they dont appear to hate civilization like the other one, they are often seen, and are widely scattered from one end of Westland to the other prowling among the rushes at the edge of lagoon and bog holes. They walk with a crouching sneaking sort of gait, and if startled will take to the bush and up a tree instead of flying. At which they are not very expert, rising very slowly their legs dangling down as if they wanted to shake them off.

Although strictly speaking a fisherman, they are not above eating dead sheep or birds. When frogs spread over the country as they are sure to do, the bittern will be in clover, and bliss [bless] the man who first introduced them.

The Red bill

[Variable oystercatcher, torea, *Haematopus unicolor*,
Pied oystercatcher, torea, *Haematopus ostralegus*]

This is one of my favourates from their cuteness and queer ways. To what class of birds they belong too, I never enquired. No doubt the plovers, or snipes claim it as a near or distant relation.

The red bill has a long red beak, and long legs of the same colour, the plumage on one bird is jet black, on the other black and white. They gather in large flocks in some places. Sometimes only small flocks are to be seen, but they are never solatary. They evidently like each others company. There usual haunts are the sea beaches and mud flats, of tidal rivers and lagoons. Running along the edge of the water ready to pick up anything eatable, their legs when running go at a great rate, but as they take very short steps their gait is what might be called toddling. I dont know whether they can swim, but they fly very fast, being able to get full steam up almost instantly, like most of the duck and snipe tribe.

The red bills are amusing birds to watch, one will run alon[g] the beach ahead of the others, then he will suddenly stop and hang his head to one side in a meditative attitude. The others will run up to him, and hold their heads down as if listening to some profound remarks, then another will stamp his foot, and run ahead a few yards and no. 1 will run up and listen to his side of the argument.

In the Okarito flats, when the tide goes out, it leaves large mud flats bare, or rather it is not mud but a stiff clay sediement. In this deposit there resides a crab about the size of a shilling, who makes a hole running straight down for a couple of inches, and then bends at right angles for two more. The crab feeds about till alarmed when he takes refuge in his castle.

Those crabs are a source of mental anguish to the red bill for sins comitted in some past existance. It would appear as if they were compelled by some invisable power to stand at a crab hole and try to catch one, a thing they never by any chance succeed in, but there they will stand for hours on the flats with a patience worthy the highest admiration. While enduring their punishment, the head of the bird is slightly turned to one side to enable it to watch the crab with one eye, while the other is on the look out to see if his mates are successfull, and every now and again they give an angry stamp with their feet. The moment a red bill is seen to bury his beak up to the eyes in the mud, all the others crowd round him in hopes he has caught a crab at last. While the disappointed one cleans his beak and tries to explain how he nearly caught the vile crustacean. The birds then all suddenly rush back to the holes they had been watch-

239

ing so carefully, for while away the crabs had come out of their holes and were complacently eyeing them.

A scientific gentleman once told me that red bill stamped his foot to bring the crabs out to see what the row was about, but I believe that to be nonsense. The stamp is one of anger caused by the crab, who knowing he is safe is quietly chaffing red beak. No doubt asking him why his bill wasn't made to go round a corner. They stamp their foot the same way when arguing on some obstruce [obtuse?] subject and in places where neither crabs nor worms exists.

When shot at once or twice, the red bill is able to tell the exact range of every gun in the district, keeping just out of range with perhaps a slight margin for contingencies. I once cleared a lot out of a lagoon by using a wire cartridge. They lost faith in their judgement of distances after that, or became doubtfull what my powers of distruction might be.

Often the only way to get a shot is to walk along using the gun as a walking stick, and making believe to be admiring the scenery or looking for shells never looking at them. The birds will after a time fly close to you, when a good flying shot may be got, but no one will do this dodge twice with the same birds.

The best shot I ever got at red legs was on a lagoon. There was a large log on the bank, where the birds would stand in rows sunning themselves. So I got a canoe and covered it with boughs, then lying down with musket ready, I let the dug out drift towards them. When close enough, I started up and fired, going overboard at the same time with the recoil, but had the satisfaction after getting myself out of the water of doing the same for thirteen red bills. This dodge did not clear them out, but if a tree or bush was seen floating towards them they were off.

The only way I ever could snare redbill was by leaving flat nooses on the ground making them fast to a peg, but this way is not very sure, they are very irregular in keeping their footpaths and it requires a great number of nooses to catch any.

The Snipes

There are a good many varities of this bird, the largest being the grey snipe [New Zealand dotterel, *Charadrius obscurus*], it frequents the sea beaches and river flats during the winter, but in summer I have often found them in the mountains, almost to the snow line, where they lay their eggs and rear their young. But what they feed on in such high latitudes, I don't know. Perhaps they fly down to the low country every day. With their extrordinary speed of flight, they could fly from the top of Mt Cook to the sea in a few minutes.

Besides this snipe, there are a number of other sandpipers, plovers or whatever they are called, with the usual habits of their class. In stormy weather, they fly about the sand hills on the beaches in dense mobs. At least at one time they did, but like a great many other birds they are retreating to more favoured localities where they are not shot at.

There is one little snipe with brown bars across its breast [banded dotterel, *Charadrius bicinctus*], which frequents the open river flats. It is said to be a bird of passage it may be so to a certain extent, but some are always left behind as they are to be seen summer and winter.

The Black Snipe
[Black stilt, kaki, *Himatopus novaezelandiae*,
Pied stilt, poaka, *Himatopus himatopus*]

This bird is evidently allied to the red bill, and is a singular looking object; a small round body perched on long slender legs. One bird is black the other, black and white. Like the redbill to which bird they bear some resemblance in plumage, antics and habits, it frequents the same places lagoons and mud flats, but it isn't afflicted with an order to catch crabs like red bill. It has always been a rare bird in Westland at least. A pair trotting about now and again in certain localities, represent the black snipe both now and thirty years ago.

The Kingfisher
[Kotare, *Halcyon sancta*]

I will now finish the aquatic birds with this pretty little fisherman. It is almost the same bird that exists in the old country, only not so gorgeous in plumage, and is about the same size with a beak large enough for a turkey. It frequents the edges of lakes and lagoon, where small fish are to be found, perching on the limb of a tree with exemplary patience, looking as if it was admiring its beak, but in reality keeping an eye open for its prey. When its chance comes, it make a dart down to the water like a flash of light, its colours showing in splendour the fish that has attracted the birds attention is doomed; it never misses.

The king fishers is sparsely scattered all over the country, and appears to hold it own against cats and other enemies. So they will remain, unless like its home relation, they are slaughtered for their feathers to busk hooks for fly fishing.

Parrots

I now come to a couple of birds, the Kaka and the Kea kea who appear to be peculiar to New Zealand, or if found in other countries not so widely distributed. I have heard that the Port Philip parrot is identical with the Ka Ka, if so then the bird is not peculiar to New Zealand.

The Kea and Kaka are not true parrots, but a sort of connecting link between them and the cockatoo, and their scientific name is Nestor; why called after him I can't say. I never heard that the Homeric Nestor had a hooked nose. He was celebrated for his wisdom, which those birds cannot lay much claim too, unless cheek is a form of wisdom. Perhaps the name was given them, because they are always chattering and like to hear themselves talk, which was rather a failing of the prosey old grecian whenever he got a chance.

The Ka Ka
[Kaka, *Nestor meridionalis*]

Or as it used to be called in parts of Otago, the tomahawk, from its habit of digging into rotton trees for the large white [huhu] grub. The bird is about the size of a pigeon, and was evidently the last Nature gave the finishing touch too. When she had coloured the plumage of all other birds making some green, some blue, some red, using every colour and shade of colour, she wiped her palette on the Kaka and the Kea. Redish brown is the prevailing shade on the one, a dirty green on the other, but all colours and shades of colour have a fair show. The head of the bird is large in proportion to the body. It eats like a parrot holding its food in one fist, and can raise a slight crest of feathers like the cockatoos but it is only a burlesque on that birds.

The Ka Ka is very easily tamed, and when caught young can be taught to speak – in a sort of way – but it is not a desirable bird about a house, being much addicted to mischief, taring everything it gets hold off, giving vent to fearfull yells, if disturbed in its amusements, and in the still hours of the night they liven up the place by whistling their national melodies with the power of a locomotive.

The Ka kas generally travells in mobs, up and down the country according to the feed but a few are always left behind and no part of the bush is ever entirely deserted by them. As the rata blossom is a favoure of theirs, and is three months later in high country than on the flats, the birds work their way to the heads of the rivers towards the end of autumn, at that time they are very fat and good eating. In some rare instances the feed fails all over the country. Then they will crowd round civilization on the chance of picking up something. They will even come inside a house and can be seen in dozens perched on a fence in a starved state, with no energy left in them and can be knocked down with a stick. But as they are too lean to eat, it is only mischief to kill them in such cases.

They live very daintily, sucking the honey from the rata and flax blossoms, or digging into rotten logs for that epicurean morsel the white grub. When tamed they dont require to be caged or tied up like parrots, seldom going far from the house. The reason being the other Kakas consider them as renegades and mob them accordingly.

In captivity they are best fed on bread and sugar, but they will eat most things handy, often dying through nibbling paint off a wall. For recreation place a long wand like a fishing rod, fast in the ground at an angle of 30 or 40 degrees, for the bird to swing on. Perched on the end of the rod, the bird will require no other earthly felecity, see-sawing up and down for hours, and giving vent to his feelings in skirrls of happiness.

The Maorie manner of catching Kakas is simple and effective. They use a decoy bird if one can be got, then they select a tree that has a bushy top. The Maorie then gets a number of pieces of wood shaped like the letter L tying them to a long sapling. Thus on the top is a sort of flat noose with string, long enough to reach down to the end of the upright, so as to enable him to tighten the noose when required. The rods are fixed on the tree so that they and noose are just above the branches. He then ties the decoy bird in the densest part of the foliage. All is now ready for business. The captive bird yells out, and all the kakas for a mile round hurry up to see what the matter with him alighting.

The moment the darkie sees a bird on a noose, he tightens the string, which catches it by the claws then he draws it down towards him. The yells of the astonished captive brings more birds round in an excited state. The bird caught is killed by a bite on the head and dropped to the ground and the wand and noose put up again. When once the birds get excited, it keeps an active Maorie or whiteman busily employed hauling in and killing. The birds are not in the slightest degree afraid of the man, and he can relieve his feelings by yelling as much as he likes.

I know a Maorie who got over a hundred Ka Kas in an hour or two this way and might have caught more, but frantic with success he tumbled off the tree among his dead birds. He wasn't hurt however and looks back on that day as a bright spot in his existance.

To those people who are too stiff in the joints, or too timid to capper among the branches of a tree forty feet from the ground, the best way is to get a double barrelled gun and sit under a tree with the decoy bird. In general, your decoy bird will make noise enough, but if not, give him a whack on the head and stirr him up in the ribes with the ramrod, he will soon start swearing. As the Ka Kas come round you can blaze away. There are not so many caught this way as the other. The noise of the gun scaring them away after a while, but then all you have to do is to shift to another tree some distance away. These are the two best ways to catch Ka ka, when they are plentifull as they are at certain seasons. Single ones can be caught with a noose, or caught with a piegeon spear, but those ways are not very sure. Without a decoy the birds can be collected by imitating their different calls, or making a scraping sound with a file and an old match box.

In mentioning decoy birds which are used both for Wekas and Ka kas, it is certainly a mean way to use one of their countryman to decoy the other to their death. No wonder the free birds have a down on renegades. I have seen a sheep in a slaughter yard leading his innocent relations in droves to the killing pen, popping through a wicket made expressily for him when he had the unfortunates fairly penned. That animal didn't have any pangs of conscience to trouble itself with. I have often wondered what its reception will be in the next world when it enters the Valhalla of sheep; rather lively times he will have or ought to have.

At some seasons the Kakas become so fat they cant fly, but must make for a tree and climb up to safety. At such times, they can be caught by dogs who whip them off the ground with evident delight. Once up the tree the bird is safe. They display considerable ingenuity, when climbing keeping the barrel of the tree between them, and the enemy – with a possable gun – peeping round with a comical expression to see how the land lies, and mocking the man or encouraging its self with derisive yells.

The Kea Kea
[Kea, *Nestor notabilis*]

This bird is slightly larger than the KaKa, with green as its prevailing colour, instead of brown, otherwise it is very nearly the same in general appearance, but in moral character and vocal abilities it is far inferior. It frequents the mountain ranges perching like a miniature condor on dizzey precipices.

Unlike the Kakas, who have a dozen different cries, the Kea has just one, weird, Key-a Key-a, hence its name. Sounding like the wail of a lost spirit, the cry is rather a startling sensation while climbing a dangerous precipice, suggesting a possible corpse lying a thousand feet below, with the kea standing on the head picking out the eyes. That is just what they would do if they got the chance.

For curiosity and impudence the kea takes the record among all the feathered creation. The moment they see a man coming into their haunts, they flock round and follow him, as if they were afraid he was going to steal some of their property. Or perhaps they have hopes he will brake his neck. When walking, two or three birds are pacing along in front while a few more bring up the rear. The rest are flying from rock to rock shouting there war cry. If he sits down, round they come hopping about within a few feet of him. They will often alight on a gun barrell or a stick if held out to them. Many a time in the mountains, I have had to get up in the early morning to save the tent fly from being torn to pieces by the Keas, and a survey trig with new calico on must be a regular godsend to the birds.

Keas are easily knocked down with a stone or a stick, but they are too knowing to be snared in the ordinary way. I once laid a large noose flat on the ground with string attached and a piece of white paper in the center. Standing back a few yards I waited in hopes the birds would see the paper, but they also saw the noose and not one would cross the unknown danger they walked round it in a critical manner, looked at me and skirled. At last a more venturous one suddenly grabbed the line I held in my hand, gave it a jerk which carried the noose away from the paper, which was at once carried away with a triumphant yell.

Every time a fellow goes among the ranges he sees some new antic or piece of impudence among the keas. They have taken to sliding down the roofs of the iron huts government have put up for tourists, taking time about at the amusement. Once I was reposing on a large flat rock, when five keas visited me. Two stood at one end of the rock, evidently waiting for some sort of performance. The other three placed themselves in a row almost at my feet, then one started an attitude and hopped and skipped towards the other two at the end of the rock, but was received with a yell of derision. He stepted to one side, as if in the sulks. Then another one did the same, and was received in the same manner, and so with the third. Now can anyone tell me what those birds were doing. Were they dancing the skirrls being the music? There is a bird in Australia that I believe dances in front of his house, but I am not aware they have musical accompaniment. Or were the birds courting, the two by themselves being elegable young ladies, the others forlorn batchelor showing off their paces, they put on airs enough for that purpose. However their performance mustn't have been satisfactory as they flew away and left them disconsolate.

A Maorie once told me a good way to catch Keas was to get a sheet or yard or two of calico and lie down under it. The birds mistaking it for a patch of snow alight on it and are easily caught by hand, so the vile aboriginal said, and as the arrangement sounded feasible enough I tried it, but instead of catching the kea, the kea caught me. The moment I grabbed the birds leg, beak and talons were through the calico, and I was obliged to confess that the sheet was correct as a trap, but that an ordinary mortal would require to be sheathed in plate armour before commencing business.

In parts of this island, where the kea has a price put on his [head], they may be shy, but any I have seen are as curious and audacious as mentioned. They are so easily tamed that when caught and tied by the leg, they will in a few hours, eat butter or fat out of your hand – and it also if they get the chance. Some people say they can be taught to speak, but about this I am doubtfull, having tried them but with no results, and never heard that any one else succeeded.

They are not a desirable bird about a house. Mischievous as a Ka Ka is, he is primeaval innocence compared to a kea kea. A good industrious bird will in a few hours make a wreck of a hut, tearing the thatch off the roof, digging holes in blankets, towels, clothes and smashing plates etc. They can work with an energy and skillfull knowledge of weak points in garment which is astonishing.

Unlike the Ka ka who live on nector and ambrosia, the Kea will eat anything berries, roots, mutton, beaf and carrion of all discriptions. It is said to be a bird that has changed its nature from a vegitarian to an omniverous prowler, but I am doubtfull of this. Mutton didn't exist in New Zealand at one time so Kea hadn't a chance to get any, but I am certain he didn't always live on roots as is said. The reason the kea has a price on his head is they are accused, whether justly or unjustly, of killing sheep, digging a hole through the living animal to get at the Kidney fat. But I am doubtfull about this yarn. I never saw one standing on a galloping sheep, although I have seen them pecking at one that had died from natural causes, and any shepherd I have asked about this Kea vice laughed at the idea. They no doubt acquired a taste for mutton in the back country of Otago, where beef and mutton was run up a high pole of the branches of a tree to keep it fresh and from the rats. From that they took to dead sheep; every hill side had always a few lying about. Besides, how could the birds do it, a sheep is not such a foolish animal as not to roll on the bird and crush it by sheer weight. Kea couldn't possably get his claws out of the wool in time. Once a bird landed on my dog's back but with fatal results. The dog tumbled a summersault, and had him before he could disentangle. himself.

It is said that only one keas's nest has ever been found. Whether this is really the case I can't say, but it is probable, few people ever go to the home of the birds, and they no doubt build in such inaccessable places, that not to come accross their nest is not so very surprising.

Although the kea's wings are rounded like those of a weak flying bird, they have wonderfull powers of flight and a generalship in using the wind to assist them.

I have seen them coming straight up the face of a precipice with a hurricane blowing, and not loosing an inch of ground, and the only evidence of effort was a quivering of the wing feathers. This may appear wonderfull, but it was generalship, the bird keeping a foot or two from the precipice was in reality working up in an eddy.

Paroquets
[Kakariki]
[Red-crowned parakeet, kakariki, *Cyanoramphus novaezalandiae*,
Yellow-crowned parakeet, kakariki, *Cyanoramphus auriceps*]

I have a hazy sort of recollection that at home in the bird fanciers I saw a small green paroquet with a scarlet head. If it was not the New Zealand variety it was very like one. What they are kept in cages for, I can't say, unless it is because they can learn a few words supposed to resemble English, such as 'good day moik' 'pretty cocky' etc.etc. They are oftener seen in cages than any other bird in this country that is a native, and they will live for years in captivity though their destiney is generally the same as most cage birds; the cat gets them.

At one time the paroquets swarmed all over the country like sparrows devouring grain and distroying gardens, but now they are extinct in many localities. They vanished all at once, as if they had migrated in a body to some other and safer country, where cats didn't exist. As cats hunted them remorselessly, the bird afforded grimalkin a delicate and easily acquirred food. No watching for long aggravating hours at a rat hole, with perhaps no result except an occasional glimpse of the rodents whiskers, but a sudden spring among a flock of paroquets and down with one in each claw. Probably when the cats die out, as they are doing, the paroquets may recover and ornament the bush again. They are the only brilliant plumaged bird in Westland and are a beautiful object when free in their native woods, and even if they are a nuisance at times it would be a pity if they became extinct.

Hawks

There may be more varities of this pirate but I will only mention two, they are scattered all over the country, both now and in the past, but were never a very plentifull bird, and as the small birds dissappear so do they.

[Australasian harrier, kahu, *Circus approximans*]
The large hawk has hard times no doubt, as his flight is slow and clumsey for a bird of prey. Small birds often mob him. In such cases he clears out as fast as possable, as they are too quick for him, and he can't get a crack at any of them. So he lives principally by plundering nests. A tame duck, or domestic fowl is a

godsend to him and he will eat dead sheep in an emergency. I have never seen him attack a living sheep, but if he gets a young lamb away from its mother, that lamb's eyes are out in a few minutes and no doubt the hawk finally kills it.

The expanse of wing of this bird will scarcely be believed. I shot two on the Haast; one was eight feet four inches from tip to tip, the other was six feet nine inches, but with all their expanse of wing they have very little lifting power, as a large hawk can only lift a duck for a few feet, so no one need get up any of those legends about birds carrying babies out of cradles, as the eagle is accussed of doing.

Derek Grzelewski, in an article on Charlie Douglas in New Zealand Geographic *No. 32, 1996, gave a comment on this hawk description: '"A hawk with pterodactyl-sized wings"? "No hawk has a wingspan of eight feet four inches and nests on a crag," says palaeontologist Trevor Worthy. "Douglas was a thorough surveyor and I think we can trust his measurements. It is likely that he shot a pair of Haast's eagles. And as no one has ever seen them since, it is possible they were the last of their kind."'*

Hawks generally build their nests on a very high crag or terrace, laying the nest on the ground; at other times they may occasionally build up at tree but not often. No doubt as ferrets and dogs get more numerous, the hawk will take to the trees. Altogether they nested on the ground simply because at one time they had no enemies.

Anyone robbing a hawks nest had better keep his hat over his eyes and show as little of his face as possable. The bird will fight desparately for its young and will follow the plunderer for miles.

[New Zealand falcon, Karearea, *Falco novaeseelandiae*]
The other hawk is much smaller, but swifter and more distructive. They often hunt in couples, and anyone going near their nests will know it. The birds will make a swoop for the face, then sheer off, coming on again instantly, not both at once, but one at a time. I have never been actually struck by one, but have had my hat knocked off; dogs are attacked the same way and the birds will strike them repeatedly. When the dog finds he can't get hold of them by making frantic jumps in the air, he clears out as soon as possible.

The Owl or Morepork
[Ruru, *Ninox novaeseelandiae novaeseelandiae*]

There are apparently two varities of this bird. One [unidentified] is small and must be very rare, in Westland at least as I have only seen one, and that was five and twenty years ago. [*Possibly the laughing owl,* Sceloglaux albifacies, *last reported in 1914 and now considered extinct.*]

The best known is the larger one, called the Morepork by the diggers and settlers from its peculiar cry. Like hawks it is sparsely scattered all over the country. It is about half the size of the pigeon and is simply a brown owl, with no marked peculiarities to distinguish it from any other bird of its class. It cry is a very distinct more-pork which must have been unpleasantly suggestive to a boats crew when landing on a cannibal coast. I rather like to hear them hooting and tooting on a still night, chaffing each other. Their cry might not be considered musical, or lively, but it is better than the shreiks of the Ka Ka, the drumming and squealing of the kakapo, or the where iz ee of the mosquito, and it relives the monotony of waiting under a tree for daylight to imitate their cry and getting an answer in return. The death like stillness of the New Zealand bush after midnight is as depressing as gazing on a deep black pool of water in a gloomy cavern.

The morepork can be easily tamed and it will hunt mice and rats about a house, roosting in the day time in the darkest corner it can find, but it will resent any undue familiarity, such as handling it when in repose.

Like the bat, the owl can sometimes be seen in the daytime, but in dark bush and cloudy sky, just after sundown, is their general time to start on the prowl.

I don't know how they fight each other, if they ever do it, but I once had a tame one attacked by four rats, and it defended itself by lying on its back and fighting with beak and claw, and it was the rats that did the squealling, not him.

The Kakapo
[Strigops habroptilus]

This bird was no doubt common at one time all over Westland, but now it is confined to the country south of Bruce Bay. The last bird found north, was somewhere about the Mikonui river near Ross, and that was many years ago. Since then, I have not heard of any more having been found and have never got a trace of them outside the mountain birch [beech] country which extends from the Maitahi [Matitahi] river to the Hollyford, and up the Landsbro river to its source.

At one time the Kakapo swarmed in that birch country from the sea beach to near the snow line, and in two instances I have caught them on a snowfield, as they were trying to cross the Divide. They may manage in some cases to get over, as a few are occaisonally to be caught on the east side of the range, but no doubt the ferrets have finished them long ago, as they are fast doing on the Western side.

The early explorers in Westland were often puzzled, when going up a narrow bush spur to find a beaten track as if sheep or some other animals, had been travelling up and down for years. Almost every well defined spur in the country that led to the grass line had those mysterious tracks. Various theories were promulgated. It was the moa. It was wild sheep or goats, that had by some means strayed over the range, or it was some animal unknown to science, perhaps the typo [goblin or devil] or the mysterious beaver. No one at first suspected it was the Kakapo, although any of the Bruce bay Maories could have told them. The tracks were made by that bird travell[ing] up to the high grass country. The rounded dust holes, here and there on the spurs, might have told them it was a bird of no great size and one who had occasionally to shake fleas out of his feathers. [*The 'dust holes' made by kakapo are used for booming and display.*]

Before the advent of the white man with dogs, almost the only way the Maories had of catching the kakapo was on those tracks, sitting down along side of one in the night time. The birds could be heard, coming along snarling and squealing as is their wont. When the Maorie knew that a bird was close, he suddenly flashed a light with a torch, the bird stopped and glared in amazement and so was easily caught. At other times they could be caught in the moonlight, when on the low scrub, by simply shaking the tree or bush till they tumbled to the ground, something like shaking down apples. I have seen as many as half a dozen Kakapos knocked off one tutu bush this way.

Although so formidable looking, the Kakapo appears to have little idea as to how to defend itself against dogs, ferrets or men. If a dog puts its nose, or you put your fingers into the claws or beak, you will both know it, and be more carefull in future. If the bird only knew its powers, it wouldn't fall such an easy prey [to] stoats and ferrets. One grasp of his powerful claws would crush either of those animals, but he has no idea of attack or defence.

That they can fight to the death among themselves I once had a good illustration, having brought into camp five live kakapos, intending to send them to town. When in the bag carrying, they were quiet enough. So they were, when tumbled into a bush cage, but when it got fairly dark war commenced, and for hours it was pandemonian with their cries, yells and oaths. On overhauling the cage next morning, only one was alive. The rest were scalped and almost featherless, the survivor was marching triumphantly over the slain, but he had not escaped scathless. He had lost one eye and part of his scalp, and looked a most disreptuable object. It is probably they fought so desperately, because they couldn't get away; no doubt each blamed the other for getting them in the lock up. I have both seen and heard kakapos fighting in the wilds. They make noise enough and leave feathers behind, but I never found a dead one or even one much injured.

To know what it was like to be in a good kakapo country before the advent of the ferret and stoat, one had to go to the flats of the Landsbro, or the Thomas range. The birds used to be in dozens round the camp, screeching and yelling like a lot of demons, and at times it was impossable to sleep for the noise. The dog had to be tied up or matters would have been worse. It would have been killing and fetching all night long, but alass this is a thing of the past, when last up the Landsbro there wasn't a bird to be found unless by going high up on the spurs.

Dogs are very fond of kakapo hunting, not alone for the fun, but because they are good eating. Few dogs will eat a weka, a kea, or a kiwi, but I never saw one that refused a kakapo. Although such a large bird, there is not so very much eating on them. The head, legs and crop making up most of the bird. The quantity of food they can stow away into their cropes is wonderfull. Just when returning home at daylight, they are swelled out with provisions. This they chew at leisure, spitting it out when masticated, whether this could be called chewing the cud, I leave to others to decide.

There are said to be two varities of kakapos. The mountain variety, which is larger and lighter in colour, and the low country variety which is smaller and has more green its plumage. This I dont believe, and am certain they are the same bird. The larger, which are probably the older ones, keep to the high grass on the hills, leaving the younger ones who are smaller and darker in plumage to the low country where the feed is softer. There must be some change in the anatomy of a bird to make it a different species. If one turkey is black and another white, who would dream of calling them different species. Even a change of habits does not alter a species – the kea, for instance, is a case in point. Does the fact that in Otago, the bird having turned from vegetarian to a carnivori, make it a different from the Westland bird who still adheres to the food of his ancestors, roots, berries, beetles and with an occasional blow out on a dead animal? The East Coast Weka is far larger and lighter coloured than the West Coast variety. Does that make them a different species?

There is far too much deviding and subdeviding now a days in classifying bird and animal life, and the reson is, some people are so eager to get their name in print as the discoverer of something new, that if those beings found a cock-a-bulla with its tail bit off, they would put it down as a new fish and murder the Latin language and their own name in fixing that fish's position in the world of waters.

There is no doubt that at present the Kakapo is a ground owl [*in fact a parrot*], and strictly vegetarian in habits. Whether it will get demoralised and become a flying carniveron, remains yet to be seen. Whether it is a bird in a transition state, developing into a flying owl, or whether he will degenerate into a kind of feathered mole remains also to be seen, that is if he survives long enough in the country to undergo a change, which is not very likely. He is, I doubt, doomed to extinction long before the Kiwi and roa are a thing of the past.

He is certainly a strange bird. His tail is always dirty and draggled, and not of the slightest use to him. It is very seldom a complete tail can be got, there are always some feathers half broken off. This looks either that he once could fly, but intends to do so no longer, as it is of no further use, or that he is getting his tail gradually ready for flying when his breast bone expand a little more.

The kakapo has certainly some powers of flight, but it is only a sailing from one tree to another, always alighting lower than where it started, and often miscalculates the distance and tumbles down ignomiously like a bird that had been shot. What distance they can fly or sail I can't say, the furthest I ever saw one go was accross an open creek bed a distance of over a chain, but he landed very much lower than where it started.

The bird is afflicted with one complaint, probably caused by his vegetarian diet, at least I never saw it in any other: the complaint is tape worm, at least it looks like the same beast I have seen in bottles in quak Doctors windows. The worm is to be found in both the crop and the stomach. They are generally small, but in one instance I got one nearly six feet long. A bird that has tape-worm can at once be known, it is a skeleton. In its healthy state, the bird is mostly always fat, the fattar it is, the less chance there is of eating one with any of those objectionable insects in them.

Kakapos are very good eating, whether old or young, but the old ones are too tough to roast, so the best way is to boil them over a slow fire for four or five hours, or cooking them in a Maorie oven which is by far the quickest and best plan. To know if a bird is young and fit to roast, pluck a tuft of feathers out of the neck with a sudden jerk. If the skin comes away, then roast away before the fire. When very fat, the bird gives almost as much oil as a weka, it is of a clear light straw colour and may be good as a medicine, quak or otherwise. At any rate, the oil is usefull for frying or making cakes and shortbread.

Bush Birds
The Pigeon
[New Zealand (wood) pigeon, kereru, *Hemiphaga novaeseelandiae*]

The New Zealand pigeon, except for its superlative stupidity, is very like a home cushat [*another name for the wood pigeon in Britain*], only slightly larger and lighter coloured and travells like the Ka ka all over the country, according to the feed. Unlike the home pigeon, the New Zealand varity does not rob cornfields, but strictly adheres to the food of his ancestor: leaves and berries. Its life seems to be a continual struggle for existance. When certain berries are plentifull, it gets very fat in a few weeks, then when that food fails, although it eats leaves by the bushel, they become skeletons; so on all the year round.

As for shooting them, it is pot hunting pure and undefiled. Sit under a tree and blaze away, they seldom fly for any great distance. Often when half a dozen are on a tree, they can be shot down one after another. When stuffed and roasted or made into a pie, they are said to be a feast for kings. Well that may be. When I dine with a king, his highness can have my share of pie. I like them well enough for soup, but roasted they are in my opinion dry and tasteless, and in stews or pies they are my abomination. This may be preduce [prejudice], perhaps it is, but let anyone live for months on nothing but pigeons, and they may have the same opinion.

I dont know of any more aggravating position for an awkward man to be placed in than to have the carving a pie of this confounded bird – perhaps to a critical dinner party. Why will not some benefactor of his species, some hoary old philosopher, come forward in aid of suffering humanity, and invent some other way to cook this bird instead of the usual style, pie, or stew, where everything is so covered up with gravey, broken potatoes, pie crust and other unknown ingredient, that fellow doesn't know which is the breast and which the back. Whatever way he tries to cut, the knife is sure to strike against a castiron merrythought [wishbone], or an india rubber breast bone, and often when you have harpooned a bird, it flies off the fork into some bodies lap or over the table cloth, carrying of course a pint or so of gravey along with it.

I understand a pigeons anatomy perfectly, till it gets into a pie. Then the nature of the bones and their position appears to undergo some mysterious change; they seem to acquire in that state, armour plated breast bone, a dozen merrythoughts, and some unknown substance that feels under the knife like watchspring.

There are only two ways to act when in such a predicament: either hack away at random, oblivious to the scowls of the landlady whos table cloth is suffering, or put a whole or a half bird on each plate till the dish is finished, then sit down happy.

The first plan shows your awkwardness to people who are enjoying your discomforture; the other, besides having an air of libarality about it, transfers the carving to your neighbours.

In ancient days the Maories captured the pigeon by spearing, using a long thin rod with a barb on the end, which they drove into the birds breast. This plan is easy, and successful only when the birds are on the low scrub, which no doubt they were much oftner in those days than they are now. It is a wonder that the Maories never invented the bow and arrow to shoot with. Bow and arrow certainly requires much practice, but a crossbow does not, and one can be made in almost any bush in half an hour. Lance wood for a bow, and almost any other wood for stock and dart, and flax for a string. I never used any wood but lance wood, and unfortunately it soon loses its spring, but no doubt there are plenty of other trees in the bush, which, if seasoned properly, would make good bows. I never had occaison to make a cross bow, but once, so never payed any attention to trees that might be suitable for bows.

The New Zealand pigeon builds its nest like any other wood pigeon. A few bundles of sticks thrown together anyway, in which they lay the usual white eggs. The nest at first is so thin that the eggs are often seen through it. The bird generally builds in such inaceable [inaccessible] places, that their nests are seldom seen, and many thought at one time that they migrated to some other country to breed. The Maories have a saying that the man who sees a pigeons nest will die. Perhaps this is a saying with some foundation of truth. Where the bird builds generally, is on the gei gei [kiekie] and scrub on the edge of the high sea bluffs, and it is dangerous often trying to reach them, so a native or two may have gone over a cliff looking at a pigeons nest.

The New Zealand Thrush
[Piopio, *Turnagra capensis*]

This is not the bird that sings its 'love song to the morn' but a sort of parody on the Mavis. It has no song and its cry is only a harsh twitter, a note the bird is evidently ashamed of, as it seldom uses it.

When camped in the bush, they will come round like Wekas or robins, but with none of those bird's funny and impudent ways. Sometimes a dozen thrushes will be round a tent eating off your plate, or even out of your hand, and if the camp is shifted, they will follow it to the next place if the distance is not too far.

They are a good deal larger than the home thrush. The same nearly in plumage, and are a clumsey stupid sort of being, nothing comical about them, or interesting in any way, except perhaps in their tameness. They take food out of a man's hand with an indifference to his presence, as if he was merely a stuffed effegy of some sort, or a kind of walking tree, that grew crumbs and bits of butter. They have one virtue, that ought reccommend them to the peace society, they never seem to quarrel among themselves, or with any other birds.

The piopio is generally accepted as being extinct. It was last recorded in 1902, but there are later, unconfirmed reports from various localities, including Fiordland.

The New Zealand Crow

[Kokako, *Callaeas cinerea*]

Here is an account of this bird, extracted from a scientific work, which I will insert to see how it looks with its jawbraking Latin.

'The Glaucopis, a genius of birds belonging to the Consisrostral tribe of the order passeres and family Corvidae; it is also know by the name of Callacas. The typical species is Glaucopis Cinerea, the New Zealand Crow, called by the natives Ka-ka-po [Kokako]. This bird is of a dark green plumage, coarse black legs and strong beak, its habits are those of the crow.'

Who ever wrote this discription of the Glaucopis Cinerea, as it appears to be called, evidently never saw one, or he must have had wonderfully contorted powers of discription.

Here is my discription, and as I write they are about the camp in dozens. A very grey black plumage, with the exception of a jet black marking at the root of the beak. The bill is strong and a powerfull cutter down of potatoe, stocks, peas etc. At the side of the jaws, are two bright red wattles, hanging down like those of a domestic fowl, only much smaller. In some birds those wattles are blue. A long thin tail, and long ungainly black legs that appear to be week in the knees when running along the ground. The feet and to the knee make an impression on the sand, the claws forming the usual government brand, the broad arrow, but as the leg from claws to knee also press on the sand, it leaves a mark like a large bird with a very long spur. The crows flight, when it does fly – which is very seldom, is a short one and very awkward. Altogether in appearance and habits, it no more resembles a crow, than it does a turtle dove.

They are strictly bush birds, seldom on the ground. They prefer to run about the limbs and trunks of the low scrub, they never actually walk, but run with a strolling gait that is very funny.

They are a harmless playfull sort of bird, easy to tame and can be caught either with a snare, or by applying salt to their tails.

I have just remarked that the crow is harmless, which is not exactly the case. If they get into a garden, where young peas, cabbages and potatoes ar shooting up, the crows goes in for a little fun, or mischief soem people would call it – he doesn't eat anything apparently, but cuts the young plants close to the ground, and lays them carefully down.

The cry of the crow is indiscribably mournfull. The wail of the wind through a leafless forest is cheerfull compared to it. Perhaps the whistling of the wind through the neck of an empty whiskey bottle is the nearest approach to it, and is sadly suggestive of departed spirits.

Few people are aware that the Crow is a song bird, as it is only in the depths of the forrest they can be heard to perfection. Their notes are very few, but are the sweetest and most mellow toned I ever heard a bird produce. When singing, they cast their eyes upwards like a street musician expecting coppers from a fourth story window, and pour forth three or four notes, softer and sweeter than an aeolian harp or a well toned clarionet.

It would be well if some bird fancier, as an experiment, try to train and give more variety of note to this bird, retaining at the same time the original sweetness of tone. If successfull, they would soon become popular as cage birds. Then the canary, gold finch, bull finch and other chattering songsters might go and make pies of themselves.

The South Island kokako has not been seen since the 1960s and may be extinct.

The Tui or Parson Bird
[*Prosthemadera novaeseelandiae*]

Here is another extract, evidently by the same individual who described the crow. The name of the bird is a crusher, however, and ought to atone for any imperfection in discription.

'Prosthemedra Cincinati, is a native of New Zealand, and possessis remarkable powers of imitation; there is no note of any bird but what it exactly imitates. When confined in a cage, it learns with the greatest ease and correctness to speak long words or sentences, bark like a dog, mew like a cat and imitate any sound which is repeated two or three times. It is hence called the New Zealand Mocking bird, and as its plumage is a glossy black, it is known by the name of the Parson bird; it is about the size of a thrush and is delicious eating.'

This is the last extract I will give, trusting to my own powers of observation in future. Any one can understand what it is like, if it resembles a thrush, a starling, or a robin, than if I gave it even such a splended name as Prosthemedra Cincinati.

To say this bird is called the parson bird, simply because it is black, would apply just as well to the crow, raven, or rook. If the writer of the article had ever seen a tui, he would have known why it got such a clerical name as parson bird. It was so called, because it has a tuft of snow white on each side of its throat, giving it the appearance of wearing a white chocker [choker], and the bird is not black but a dark green or grey. The head, neck and breast are gray with white mottled feathers, gradually shading off to the darker parts of the body. It is certainly a beautifull plumaged bird, and the closer it is examined, the better it looks. The bird that most nearly resembles it in appearance is the home starling, and its habits are alike in some respects. It has the same inquisitive way of inserting its beak into small holes, and trying to make them larger if possable. It can look along a marrow bone or down the neck of a bottle nearly as comically as a jackdaw, but unlike them it is not mischievous when tamed about a house.

As for there being called the mocking bird, I never heard such a name applied to them. I see them all round me every day, have tamed them, and seen other people do the same, and never once heard the tui imitate anything. In captivity I believe a few have been taught to say a word or two. The same may be said of the black bird. In rare instances some of them have been taught a few words but no one would call it an imitative bird. [*In fact tui will imitate all sorts of sounds.*]

It is seldom the tui will live long in captivity. They are either short lived birds, or they soon mope themselves to death if caged up. But if tamed, and allowed to fly in and out of a house, they thrive well enough, and develope a singular jealousy of any bird or beast that comes inside, attacking even dogs and cats with undaunted courage. Their motions on the wing are so rapid and they dash themselves with such force upon the intruder, that even a bird catching tom cat finds outside more comfortable, and he goes out rubbing his eyes with the back of his paw. They understand bluff, and that the first blow is half the battle, so when he has to fight, tui always begins the combat. Hawks – especially the large one – have a terror of them and well they might. The first tui who sees the enemy attacks it at once, screaming all the time, which musters the clans from every bush and tree who pour to war with evident delight. The hawk does not attempt to retaliate, but puts on steam and gets out of the country as fast as possable. Although courageous against enemies, the tui seem to agree very well among themselves, seldom quarrelling except during the courting season when they sometimes have a scuffle. I suppose even pigeons have a row now and again.

The Tui is one of the best known song birds, as they are numerous and always performing especially on a wet day. In my opinion, their song is more amusing they beautifull. Their note is something between a snort and a snore, with that aggravating sort of phew with which a snorer terminates his nasal melody. When singing the bird ruffles his feathers, and looks like an invalid. It hitches up it shoulders, I mean wings, till they are on a level with his head and the whole attitude, white chocker included, reminds one of a pulpit thumping parson; see picture of John Knox preaching before Mary Queen of Scots.

If a solitary tui's song is peculiar, they are almost as good at a chorus as the bell birds, although it is a good deal of what is called a Dutch chorus; every one singing on his own hook.

To wind up, they are splendid eating when fat especially in a pie. But it wouldn't be safe to invite a policeman or a member of the Acclimatization

Society to dinner when you have such a pie, as the bird is protected for all time, a very unnecessary precaution as the tui can take very good care of himself. He has the mountain tops, and the far south to fall back on where he will never be disturbed. [*The tui, which lives naturally in the bush, is one native bird that has adapted quite well to human civilisation, and may be found even in cities.*]

The Saddle back
[Saddleback, *Philesturnus carunculatus*]

This bird was never very plentifull on the Coast at any time, and was generally local, only to be seen in certain places. Now it is one of those which have almost dissappeared, and are only to be found near the grass line, and in the wilder parts of the far South, where there are no inhabitants. They appear to detest anything like settled civilization. They will come round a tent, but not for long, and they avoid a hut or a house. At least I never saw a saddle back near either of them.

The saddle back is in shape, something like a tui, and the male bird is black in plumage, with a small wattle at the root of the beak like the crow. Accross the back, is a marking in shape and colour like a new riding saddle, giving the bird a strange appearance and it equally strange name. The femal has no saddle and its plumage is a dirty green shading to black. [*In fact the female does have a 'saddle' in its plumage; it is the immature bird that is a drab olive-brown.*] They have no song only a skirrling, harsh twitter like the thrush, when they do come near a camp which is seldom. They dont tame like most other birds, looking on man with a contemptuous indifference. I never even got them to take butter, an article most New Zealand birds except the pigeon and some insectiverous birds would commit a burglary to get at.

I have been told by many people, some of them deep in science, that this is a mistake. The bird with the saddle, and the one without, are not male and female, but two birds of a different species. If this is the case, then they are in a transition state, and crossing the breed and must finally develope into a new bird. But I am simply stating a fact, when I say I have seen the saddled one and the other attending to the same nest and young ones.

The Bell Bird
[Bellbird, korimako, makomako, *Anthornis melanura*]

This in my opinion is the king of chorus singers. Those birds first attracted Capt. Cooks attention and he – or somebody else for him – gives a very correct discription of their wonderfull fairy like song, sounding in the early morning like the tinkling of hundreds of well tuned silver bells. As a solo, their ding dong is monotonus, but when the tune is taken up by hundreds, from hill and vale, the effect is magnificent. What improves it the birds are not seen being hide in the dense foliage of the forrest. To hear it is a pleasure soon to be a thing of the past, or at least only to be heard in the very wildest districts below Jacksons Bay. The bird became silent, long before he dissappeared; he always knocked off a few years after the digger and settler appeared in a district. Then the cats finished off the now songless bird or drove them into the wilds. They were not a timid bird, and appeared to be able to take care of themselves, better than many birds that are still flourishing. Perhaps the birds are the spirits of the now departed faries, and fly in disgust from unpoetical steam engines, shoddy clothes, and patent medicines. If such is the case, they are indeed doomed; for where can they now go to? No land is left unvisited. Even on those rocky island near the Antartic circle a boats crew landing finds traces of salmon and sardine tins, Perry Davis painkiller, and Holloways ointment pots. It is sad to think on such a subject.

The bell bird is something like a green linnet, only its bill is long and slender, the bill of a honeysucker, or an investigator of rotton logs. The head is very flat on the top, giving the bird a very low intellectual appearance. As mentioned before, it is not a shy bird and will live well enough in a cage – till the cat gets it. In the bush, although they come close enough, they dont come inside a camp like the robin and other birds, showing the same contemptuous indifference to man's presence that distinguishes the thrush. They go dodging about among the tree branches, looking into holes with an aimless broken hearted expression, like a being who had lost something valuable, and had very little hopes of finding it. Perhaps they are looking for the graves of their ancestors to give them a last farewell. [*In fact the bellbird has adapted reasonably well to the incursions of humans and their civilisation, and is often to be heard and seen in the bush and in gardens with suitable plants.*]

The Fantail

[Piwakawaka, *Rhipidura fuliginosa*]

There are two or more varities of this pretty little bird, with its long tail and monkey face. Whether the black and white and the black one are male and female or different species, I am not sure. I can see no difference except in plumage.

They are about the size of a wren, and have a tail three inches long, which they can spread out at pleasure like a fan. They are entirely insectiverous feeding on sandflies, mosquitoes and other insects hunting always on the wing, using their tail not only as a rudder, but apparently as a sort of natural broom arresting arresting the flight of the insects and sweeping them towards it.

There skill in catching sandflies is wonderfull. They will sweep round a man, pick a fly off his nose, light for an instant on his hat, whirl round capturing flies by the dozen and in a few minutes not one will be seen. The fantail would be invaluable in Westland if a fellow could only tame one and carry it about with him. They would soon have the tent cleared of objectionable blood suckers, but alas they wont tame, clearing out whenever their hunting is done and to pastures new.

When two are fighting, they are so deeply interested in the combat, that I have caught the pair grappling together and even when in my hand the two would glare defiance at each other. When caught they must be very carefully handled, as the whole of the tail feathers come out at the slightest touch.

The fantail was a very common bird at one time in the New Zealand bush, now they are scarce, still a few are to be seen all over the country. They have a sort of twittering song; at least it does duty for a song in their estimation. [*The fantail is another bird that has adapted to living in towns as well as in the bush.*]

The New Zealand Robin
[South Island robin, Toutouwai, *Petroica australis*]

At one time I would have required the assistance of all the Mueses, and Bacchus to boot, to sing the praises of this well known bird, but an adventure I once had with a couple of them in this country, and they are the same frauds as at home – considerably modified my opinions about those birds.

It makes me wild when I think that as a child I have even wept at the tale of the babes in the wood and centered my sympathies on the noble cockrobins who covered them with leaves. Poetry and legend have combined in howling panegeries on this bullying, ill tempered, greedy little cannibal. To hear a lot of ladies talking thus when they see a robin 'Oh! the dear little innocent thing. Oh! look at the confiding expression in its dear little eyes etc.etc.etc.' makes me wild.

A lot of robins burying the babes with leaves is totally against their nature. The first thing they would have done would have been to fight like savages for the chance of picking out the cherubs' eyes. Why, two robins cant come within ten yards of each other without a fight. Then again, that other piece of nonsense about the bird singing its song of love to its mate who is sitting on the nest, soothing her weary labours with its cheerfull note. Song of love be hanged, that song is the wretche's manner of swearing at the other cock robins. I know by the expression of their countenance, that is what they are doing. If we only knew the language of birds like King Solomon, we would find its song of love was a flood of Billingsgate that would disgrace a bullock driver.

Even if it was as poets say, wouldn't it be a more practical mode of showing their love if they carried worms to her, instead of cheep, cheep, chitter, chittering on a branch all day, only making fools of themselves, as no one is taken in by the imposture.

But to my tale: one day when reposing alongside of a bush track my attention was attracted by a couple of Robins who were playfully hopping about, jumping on my head or standing on my breast, innocently looking in my face with that earnest gaze so peculiar to them. Here I thought is a noble confidence reposed in man, perhaps an innocent desire to worship what to its innocent mind appears a superior being dropped from the azure skies. Where I thought, getting heroic, is the villian who would injure confiding innocence; where the being who could write anything but praise of this noble songster? No doubt I thought those two birds will go home to their young and tell about a noble looking being who fed them on crumbs.

While going on in this strain, a donkey passed along with that sleepy contemplative look that only a donkey with nothing to do, or a horse towed behind a bullock dray can put on. Hopping after it was two robins, and humiliating to relate, my two left me, a lord of creation, to fight with the other two, for the honour of following that long eared quadrupid. It may be sad, but alass it is true, the robin only follows man about the bush, because he turns up grubs and worms with his two hoofs, and they would like him all the better if he had four.

When the robin is looking so ernestly at you showing every now and again a tuft of white feathers at the root of his beak, the wretch is only thinking how he can gauge [gouge] your eyes out. I know that is the meaning of the look, the white tuft shows when they are fighting other robins. And throw a dead pigeon down before them and the same tuft appears as they start to get out the bird's eyes; the first place they always make for.

I know it would be far better if we could think otherwise, believe or make believe in the pretty legends of our youth, that have cast a halo of protection round the robin and a few other birds. The story of the redbreast plucking the thorn from the brow of the dying Christ was not written in vain. It has saved generations of robins from the shanghai of the small boy.

To speak of the expression of a bird's eye is not nonsense, as most people would imagine. As said before, birds and animals have their likes and dislikes, and to an observer it is the eyes that show what they are thinking about. Take the eye of a living hawk and a living pigeon, one shows pure cruelty and savagedom, the other quiet harmless stupidity. How innocent a sheep looks, yet watch the eyes of two rams engaged in battle, they flash and glare with hate in every glance. That some birds, like many dogs, have a sense of humour I am certain. A Jack daw looking down a marrow bone is funny. The bird may not feel so, the expression may have some anxiety in it, the bone might be empty, but no one can deny the Weka a sense of humour who has once seen its backward glance, when disappearing in the bush with an ivory handled pocket knife, or a long cherished meerschaum.

To return to the robin: with the exception that it has a white breast, instead of a red one, and is slightly larger, if I recollect, the New Zealand robin is the counterpart of the Home country species with all its tamness, impudence and villiany. Any hut in the bush, that does not keep a cat, is sure to have one as a permanent residenter, and who is ready at any moment to assert his rights against all other robins. As the one who first comes derives a sort of moral force in right of possession, he generally manages to keep his place, celebrating with a song of triumph every successfull encounter. Although like human beings, when he gets licked, he doesn't go about the country mentioning the fact.

The song of the robin is something like that of the cage canary, quite as varied and prolonged, and in my opinion softer toned. They sing at all seasons, even in winter when most birds are silent, and I consider it the first of the solo singers in the country till the crow is educated. They will however never be a cage bird, as he soon mop[e]s to death in captivity. He was born free and scorns slavery, even in a gilt cage and no trouble about his food.

Tom Tits

[South Island tomtit, ngiru-ngiru, *Petroica macrocephala*]

There are evidently several varities of tom tits [or] wood peckers as some people call them, but I will only mention them, as the birds are not of much interest. They are tame like the robin, and will often build their nest in the thatch of a house or even inside with no fear whatever of the residents. I watch a pair feeding their young, and they had hard work from daylight to dark of a long summers day without a moments rest. They apparently didn't go far for food, as no sooner had one bird feed the young and flew away, then the other flew in with a fresh supply. The young ones were always on the gape and their stowage capacity must have been enormous.

In many districts where the other birds have almost if not entirely vanished, the tom tit alone remains, but they are few compared to what they once were.

One varity makes it nest in a hole in a tree, and feeds more on grubs and small worms, poking its beak into every crack and crany where insects are likely to be. The other varity live on seeds and berries but worms are not re-fused. Tame as the tom tits are, they have none of the impudence of the robin and don't eat everything handy.

Wrens

[South Island rifleman, titipounamu, *Acanthisitta chloris*,
South Island bush wren, *Xenicus longipes*,
Rock wren, *Xenicus gilviventris*]

There are three varities of this tailess bird, somewhat alike in appearance, but differing in size, from that of a tomtit to one very little larger than a humming bird. [*The bush wren was last recorded in 1972 and may be extinct.*] They are all as a rule mountain birds and true troglodites, but sometimes they visit the low country. But it is seldom they come to the low country nowadays. Their place of saf[e]ty is in the high back ranges among the rocks at the grass line.

The largest wren is a funny bird to watch, hopping about a camp. He is continually on the move, wings and legs going all the time. If he ever sleeps except hopping, I dont know, never having seen one quiet except on its nest. Like so many other small birds, they are either getting distroyed even in the ranges – or are leaving the country. Wild cats must kill great numbers of them and cats are to be found even up close to the snow line.

Dr Robert A. Falla, then Director of the Dominion Museum in Wellington, provided John Pascoe in 1953 with a brief comment on the worth of Douglas's monograph on birds:

In spite of some limitations Douglas gives a fuller and more reliable account of the habits of New Zealand birds than any other writer of the period 1850–1900 except perhaps T. H. Potts, author of *Out in the Open* (Christchurch, 1882). The main limitation, a sturdy distrust of scientific dictum or indeed of anyone else's opinion, is also an advantage in that it renders his testimony independent. Even when his views are mistaken, as in his rejection of Maori reports of Notornis in the high passes, his own opinion is never didactic and always rea-soned. The shrewdness of his observations arises from genuine sympathy for all wild life, and this gives freshness and value to his records. As a contribution to the natural history of rare and vanishing birds some of the accounts, notably that of the kakapo, are of real value. Others are slight, and often a mere vehicle for some flight of humour or philosophy. But all are readable, and in the true tradition of natural history as a liberal study.

The most remarkable result of this sturdy independence and intelligent observation is that Douglas expresses opinions on conservation that are more in line with what modern research is indicating than were many of the theories current in his time. Thus his doubts about serious depletion being caused by natural predators, and his caution about the black swan as a usurper of feeding-grounds, indicate views well ahead of contemporary thought on such matters. His contribution to conservation philosophy and to a knowledge of what today are called ecological factors, is definitely significant.

TWENTY-THREE

'Soliloquy Letter', 1902–03

The 'Soliloquy Letter' of 27 December 1902 and October 1903 is found in pencil draft in the Waiatoto–Copland notebook. Although the second part indicates it may have been a draft of a letter to relations in Scotland, John Pascoe named it the 'Soliloquy Letter' because it reads as though Douglas was musing to himself, even unburdening himself, in a mood of both retrospection and some disillusionment. This writing is not the whole truth of Charlie Douglas, or his world, but it is very revealing of the older man and thus most significant.

27 Decr 1902

This ought to be one of the eventfull epochs of in my life, as this day forty years I was sailing into Port Chalmers on the road to fortune. I didnt know myself in those days, and it is my only regret that I came to a small country like New Zealand. I ought to have gone to a continent where there was unlimited scope for exploring & roaming about, but alass I didn't find out my mistake till too late. Making money I never could do or ever felt any inclination that way. If I made any discovery, other people got the credit for it. I never could be bothered bargaining & haggling over terms with anyone. So constitutionally & from what some call a perverse inclination I have been doomed to be a solatary, & as some people say a failure.

Lying in a camp on a wet day I often think what is this impulse which drives me & many others out into the wilds. had I remained at home or even settled down in the Colonies, I might now be a respectable father of a family, passing every day the same lamp post & at the exact time. I don't think I would ever have become an elder in the Kirk, but I might have been a comfortably situated old foggy [fogey], a tooth in a wheel of a Mercantile Machine, with just sufficient thinking powers to gabble on the topics of the day, but with my reasoning powers dormant. Or I might years ago have passed through a lunatic asylum to my coffin, with 'well out of the road' as my only funeral oration. But life in the Old Country was not for me. The impulse which drove the best and bravest of Rome & Spain to face death and danger in Asia Africa & America impells the Britain [Briton] to do likewise, and plant his flag all over the World, indifferent as to whether the danger faced was among prowling savages, fever smitten jungles or Arctic snows. All was the same to him the impulse was their, and he had to go the result being we have grabbed all the best places on the earth.

When he does emigrate, the average Anglo Saxon generally settles down and becomes what the world calls a usefull, patriotic &c cityzen, and when he dies his most flattering requiem would be he left a lot of money.

The impulse drove me out into the World, but the desire to settle down must have been omitted. As here I am, after forty years, mostly crouched under a piece of calico or a sheet of bark a homeless almost friendless vagabond, with a past which has little to show – the general public at least – of work done, and a dreary future. Still I have never regretted the life I have been leading and can see that even if I and hundreds of others fail in life and perhaps die miserably, the impulse which impells some people to search for knowledge in the un-known is for the benefit of the world, and cheaply bought at any price. Fools say that knowledge can only be acquired from books & men – cribbing as it were, other people thought – and call me a fool & even worse for wasting my life in mountain solitudes, simply because I don't open up mines of gold & silver. I have now been wandering about the uninhabited parts of New Zealand for over five & thirty years always finding something in nature new to me & the world. Whether I'll ever give what I have found to the world, or leave it for somebody to publish after I am dead, I neither know nor do I care. I have found many secrets of nature & glimmerings of truths unknown to others, which if they don't benefit me in this world, will in the next when it is to be hoped darkness will be light.

The word vagabond is used as a term of reproach, but give it its real mean-ing. Wander [wanderer?], and who is it that has really made the Colonies, or at least opened out the countries for people who could never have done it them-selves? Every emigrant has the before mentioned impulse more or less, but it is the vagabond who put in the energy. Take the first settlers in Otago, it was to be a sort of Free church paridise on earth. No one but of that Kirk was to be allowed in the holy ground. Emigrants had to get a certificate from their par-son in the old country that they were God fearing regular attenders at church. Canterbury was the same, only Church of England, and what was the result? The two provinces hated each other like rival sects of Christians. An Irishman couldn't get work, neither could other people if they didnt attend church. The settlers kept near where the ships ate drunk fed themselves. A special hero now and again penetrated a few miles into the country making his will first.

The place no doubt might have gone ahead, but it would have taken years. But the home government refused to allow any special Kirk colonies in the country & the vagabond made his appearance. His first advent was as a pioneer from Victoria & New South Wales looking for sheep country & in a year or two nearly the whole of Otago province from the sea to the main range was taken up, & the country became better know. A few years more and a still more energetic vagabond in the person of the digger landed in the country. He brought money with him and soon dug more out. Fortunately the digger was not a saving being, he dug wealth out of the country & recklessly spent it & soon this vagabonds influence was felt in every province in New Zealand.

The Australian colonies may now be considered as fairly settled, and the necessity for the vagabond no longer exists, so the few old cripples who represent the last of them can retreat into the poorhouse, or an asylum & no one will care twopence, or ever give them the least credit for what they have done for the country. The native born colonial, as a rule, has little of the roaming instinct. He work just as hard probably as imported emigrants but he has no idea of working on a future chance. He must have his wages every Saturday night. If forrest have to be sold to pay interest on debts or mines have to be opened the Colonial does not work them himself, but puts them into the hands of Cockney & American Syndicates or Hamburg Jews. He calls this bringing money into the country, but never thinks what those beings take out. The much abused digger scattered his money in the country. The Syndicate man takes it out. Most of the machinery used comes through Syndicate hands although the Colonial could make a great part of it himself. All the country gets in return for its resources are the wages for the men working as ordinary labourers. The wealth goes direct home to shareholds who never saw the country or ever intended to. The Colonies, espicially New Zealand, are in feverish haste to work out all their future resources; resources that ought to be kept for future generations. And before long they will have to import coal & other minerals, timber & many other articles, at high prices, if the country is ever to be a manufacturing one, and that is the only hope New Zealand ever will have in the future of being other than a petty appendage to the Australian Continent.

Forty years is considered a long period in a mans life to look backward on, but somehow it does not appear so to me (the early days I spent in the country appear to me like yesterday.) I have been writing when the humour seized me some account of my travells, and have finished a complete discription of Westland without having had to consult notes, maps, books or anybody. My memory retains almost every incident worth remembering ever since I landed in the country. But it is strange that for the last five or six years, memory has completely failed me in small things, which is very awkward at times. I may be introduced to a man or woman, & if I meet them half an hour afterwards I dont know who they are, & have often to ask or manuever round to find out their names. The same with other things. Once or twice I have even put my spectacles on my nose, to look for them on the floor, where I thought they were. This I suppose is what they call the beginning of the end. I know I am failing physically & have had to give up hill climbing. But my head I hope is I hope right yet & for a few more years to come, & it is not likely I'll die from the head downwards like Dean Swift.

The reason for this is not hard to seek. By constantly living in the uninhabited parts of New Zealand, I dont see the changes going on in other countries. I haven't seen a field of wheat or turnips since I left Scotland, and I have not been in a town larger than Hokitika for nearly forty years. I am perfectly aware of the changes going on all over the world, but I have not seen them. The only thing that now and again pulls me up is to see a fellow whom I have carried about when young, sitting with all the airs of a paterfamilias, with a grandchild on his knees. It makes a fellow think now & again, but for all that, wild as my life has been, I have always kept myself posted up in the Worlds affairs, except for politics, and always had plenty books to read, or something to keep my brain from getting stagnant.

October 1903

The older a man gets the less he is inclined to write, and unless he is forced to do it & keep his hand in, the time comes when he can't write at all. At least this is what I am finding out. Writing Government reports about the country has been the ruin of me. Through them I am beginning to hate the very sight of pens and ink. To write concerning what I take an interest in is easy, but when a fellow has to repeat the same thing over & over again it is weary some. In New Zealand there is a sameness in the scenery, notwithstanding all our blowing about the Britain of the South, to which it doesn't bear the slightest resemblance except being an Island. One valley is very much like another, so with everything else, lakes, Mountains, trees, plains & spurs; if you see one you can have a very good idea what all the others are.

At first I expanded in discriptions of the magnificent scenery, mineral & timber resources. All was new to the Public & comparatively new to me, but after a while things became stale & I got to writing less & less, till now I can scarcely write on any subject. Enthusiasm is dead in me, and interest in most things has ceased to inspire. So you can make some allowance for my poor corresponding. I may take a fit of industry & start some day but I doubt it.

Another thing which makes me hate writing, is the manner in which discriptions of the country have to be written – the writer is not supposed to tell lies – Oh No. But proper Government reports, like mining prospectus, are or ought to be genius in the art of concealing the truth. Many of my reports have either been suppressed or so torn to pieces that I often can't recognise my own work. All through being too independent to write just to please people. I generally say what I think, not others wish to think.

Photographing has been another nuisance. At first it was all right. I banged away at everything, but soon I got nearly ruined taking portraits that never pleased. It was in vain to tell people that I didn't carry rapid plates & couldn't catch there favourite racer showing its paces. Cows would keep their tails steady in a photo of a homestead. If a group of children didnt all show full cabinet size, there was a growl & I was set down as an impostor. The last straw however was when a settler brought two prize porkers & demanded portraits. This finished me & after that I refused to take anything but scenery. An evil fate followed me also in scenery. As I cant carry chemicals about the ranges, all plates had to be sent to Hokitika to be developed & printed. Not doing this myself made my exposures almost entirely guess work. This I could have survived as most of them were tolerable, but, unless the scenes pleased, the plate was chucked away as no good. I started photographing, not for the benefit of Tourist guide books or to fill up young ladies album, but to get scenes for topographical purposes. Scenes showing the shapes of spurs & valleys, the lines of glacier ledges & such like. They would be usefull to me and others who are mapping out a new country. But no, I was told such views were no good, and didn't show the splendid mountain scenery of New Zealand, which is far superior to that of Switzerland or any other land &c. The cry now all over the land is bring in Tourists. They leave money & are easily gulled. Switzerland pays her expenses loafing on Tourists, why should we not do likewise? So my work is objected to unless this object is kept in view.

New Zealanders in their eagerness to crack up their mountain scenery as the most wonderfull in this Planet or any other, nearly put their foot in it. Once a chart of this Island was made out by the Government Geologist. It was a birds eye view in plaster, showing all the mountains & vallies, according to scale. It was to go to Paris or Chicago or some other exhibition & showed the country as it really is – almost all rugged mountain. Some one however remarked that if that was like the country, the people at Home would naturally ask where are the immense areas of rich agricultural land you blow about & on the strength of which you are the record borrower of the World? That chart was suppressed.

In writing a letter home, I don't know what interests you. I would send Newspapers but from a letter I once got, you don't seem to care about them. In fact you abused them and I daresay I would do the same, if you sent me out the Lanarkshire Gayzett, Fifeshire News & such like. Yet our newspapers are like them – merely local, and will be so for years to come. Our real newspaper literature is from home; the best London Edinburgh & Glasgow papers & magazines. The country isn't old enough, or populated enough, to be able to run in opposition to high class illustrated, comic, or other large town papers. So we have to be satisfied with the regular telegrams to keep us going till the mail arrives and I think this is an advantage, & at least I find it so. The jumble of telegrams coming every day, confuse a fellow. Now at least there is time to think over and be ready for what is coming. Telegrams are no doubt usefull in business, but they are demoralising to the human race. Only a scrap of news is given, say in the morning; in the evening it is flatly contradicted. items in commerce, politics, fashions, deaths are all mixed together. In fact I never read them now, but wait. I never shone in a Home telegram but once, and it was a tolerable speciemen. Here it is as far as I recollect.

'The Tzar of Russia has had a slight attack of influenza.

'Mr Charles Douglas has been awarded the Peak prize [Gill Memorial] for explorations in the Southern Alps.

'Huggins the Derby murderer has been hanged.

'Price of Consols 3%' –

Then look at the general use of abrieviations & wholesale murder of the English Language, the result of people trying to save sixpence on a telegram.

I get the Scottsman newspaper very regularly, and it is in great demand here, though singularly enough I believe yours is the only copy that comes to the Coast direct, most people borrowing it if they can. It is about the only paper I read right through, leaving out Politics births and marriages. I see the Scottsmen are just as local in their patriotism as the various Colonies are. They get their bristles up at the slightest slur on the land of mountain & flood. Patriotism may be a very good thing, if not carried too far when it developes a narrowness of mind & injustice to other countries. The death columns in the Scottsman I still read, but now seldom see the name of anyone I once knew. Forty years makes a great gap in ones acquaintances & I suppose if I went home, there wouldnt be half a dozen people who would recollect me. It is the same out here. Friendships I have never made, and my acquaintances have been few, and of them scarcely any are left. Most of them are drowned, disappeared or met with some other violent death.

I suppose there are now very few of the old hands left in the bank who would remember me, but I sometimes see an account of a death in the papers. I got hold of an Oliver & Boyds Almanack down here & saw a good few names I knew, but the volume was ten years old, so there must be changes since then.

In the last Scottsman I saw about the late John Gowan Accountant, C.B. of S., what has become of Anderson? Mitchell is no doubt dead. He was old Mitchell when I was there. The Gowan mentioned is no doubt the twin brother of Robert, who was a teller when I last heard of him. They were at school with me & had long yellow hair & they used to say at Dysart or where ever they came from, they were called the Angel Twins. Were they the Original of the Heavenly Twins in a book I once? Tom M'Crie, by the same book, is still in Kirkwall [Orkney Islands]. Sholto wrote to me about something he want me to catch, as Tom has gone in for science but although Sholto writes very distinctly, I couldn't make out what the word was intended for.

If I knew what it was and could get it, I would do so with pleasure but in general I am rather scarry collecting for Science. These Proffessors appear to think they are honouring an outsider, by requesting them to collect for them. They never consider the trouble and expense I would incur, collected in a country in Westland, where everything would have to be carried on my back or on somebody elses. One Proffessor, a Norwaygean, wrote to Dunedin to another Proffessor, to get me to collect invisable crustaceans that frequent the high mountain Lakes. With my usual baggage, I would have to carry besides, a Jar of Sp't [spirit] of Wine, a copper drag net, and a few dozen glass stoppered bottles. I got out of it by explaining that I had rheumatics, as I had at the time.

Another Proffessor, botanical this time, requested me to collect speciemens of wood, a good sized block required, two lb weight each of all the different seed of different plants trees & flowers. Besides I would have to carry into the wilds, two big pressing boards & unlimited blotting paper, all at my own expense. Had I got what he wanted, I would have had to spend the remainder of my existance in carrying them out to a Sea port. They would have weighed a good many tons. None of them even hinted at payment. The Crustacean certainly slightly hinted that my name might be mentioned, but Botanical never even offered so much. Besides these two, I have requests of bird skins, fish, crystals, shells and numbers of other things, as the Auctioneers would say, too numerous to mention. I am free enough in giving information or curios to those I think really care for them, but a fellow must draw a line sometimes. It was a lucky idea of Tom M'Cries to take to a hobby, whether it is collecting beetles, butterflies or going in for botany. Anyone with brains would go mad in such an out of the way place as the Shetlands, unless he took to something outside the dull routine of a bank. Still it is wonderfull how people get along in out of the way places, even without a hobby.

As the Lord tempers the wind to the shorn lamb, so people in desert places can be comfortable and happy. We in Westland consider ourselves, if not the center of civilization, at least not far off it. We all know the opinion the Minis-

ter of the Combries had about his abode, and I recollect when the Act came
into force that all cheques required a penny stamp. The bank agent at Kirkwall
wrote to say that such an act might suit distant islands – meaning no doubt
Britain & Ireland, but would never do for the Shetlands. Still I think without a
hobby, a man mind in such places would soon get stunted.

As to what I myself am doing, it is the same old work. I have been out now
for nearly twelve months, and will be a few more before I am done. It is now
thirty five years since I started this exploration business. For the last fifteen I
have been at it regularly. Before that I was generally about half my time only. I
started first in the Okarito District, and here I am finishing up in the same
place. Then my work is done for ever, having no more in Westland to do and
being now unfit to go to any other country. I ought to have given up the work
ten years ago, when I found my nerve going & my physical strength failing, but
I wanted to finish the work as there was no one to take it up after me. Except
some half dozen who take an interest in mapping rough unknown country. I
don't get credit for doing anything. The reverse if the truth was known. I am
abused & sneered at because I have not found payable mines. Whether they
exist or not doesn't matter. I ought to have found them. If some one tries to
float a Company, to work some immense block of valuable timber, he says he
knows about, I am abused for trying to keep capital out of the country, if I say
there are only about thirty or forty acres which could be worked out in a few
months. The same way with mines. I have certainly found some which will be
worked to pay when labour is cheaper & the country opened out more, but that
wont be in my time or theirs. These & many other discoveries I keep to myself.
Let others find them if they like. Was it Carlyle who said that most men were
fools, which may be true, but by far the bigest fools are those who, knowing
nothing about the country, allow their money to be invested in Westland by
Syndicate frauds, & the country is right enough in its way, and wealth will be
dug out of it some day, but let people wait for a generation or two.

What is going to be done with my maps reports & discriptions of everything in Westland except the inhabitants, I dont know yet, but now that I am
nearly finished I intend to soon know. The maps at least belong by rights to the
Survey, and if they publish them as they are, I have no objection. They can stick
my name on, and leave me out altogether for all I care. But as long as I am alive,
I'll take care no body else get hold of them, and tares them to pieces to suite
their ideas, not of what is, but what they think should be. In such a case I'll put
my foot down and send them home to the Geographical or Geological Societies. I know they would jump at the offer if they only knew the work I have
done. What I am going to do now that my employment on the Survey will soon
cease, I neither know nor care. My work done, I will soon lose all interest in

life. It is too late to commence anything new. Even if I were mentally or physically capable which I am not. How I have stood the ware & tare of the life so long, is a puzzel to myself and everybody else. An how I have escaped drowning, braking my neck, or mysteriously dissappearing is a still greater puzzel. I have always been fertile in rescource & never lost my head in danger, and no doubt I started life with a castiron constitution, which may account for my being alive at present.

I dont know whether I am becoming missanthropic, but I cant write or do anything if there are any people about. If I start to write, even if no one is in, I never know at what moment some blatherskite may come. So I never can get steam up. People here are too sociable for me. If I am by myself, some fool thinks I must feel lonely, come in & spins away about bullocks, sheep horse or the latest football match. I have almost given up reading, not that I can't get books but I never get peace to read them. I think my next move will be either to a small uninhabited island, or put a hut up in the most inaccessible part of the country & lay in a stock of books & papers. I believe I could write something worth reading, if I could only be sure of twelve or even six months of quietness, undisturbed by football or horsey maniacs. I would at last be able to brush up my grammar & spelling if nothing else.

An Appreciation

TWENTY-FOUR

Charlie Douglas the Man

Age and the climate of Westland added innumerable wrinkles to the sensitive face of Charlie Douglas, and his own inclinations added a beard and long hair, both seldom trimmed. 'What on Earth is up with the Mosquitos,' he wrote in the Waiatoto; 'Is it because they have caught me in the bush for the first time with short hair?' His head would usually be covered with a wide-brimmed hat and his clothes would be rough as a bushman's usually are, which gave rise to a legend that if he got a new suit he would roll in the mud in it. Colin Macfarlane recalled that in the late 1870s Douglas used periodically to receive from his relatives in Scotland a box of clothes and provisions which he would give away to anyone who needed them. Possessions would have been a hindrance to a rover who had nowhere to leave them, and giving came easily to him.

In the field the exploring bushman dressed in a blanket while he dried out after a storm. On expeditions such as the Waiatoto, Douglas would spend a day drying his only change and note that he would not live long if ever he had to wear a stovepipe hat and kid gloves. He felt more at home in a thin ragged calico shirt and drawers, with boots he regularly wore out on his feet. He could laugh at his disreputable appearance, as he did in a 1908 letter to Harper: 'I always look like an old clothes man in a bush photo.' In town he wore a tie, but never in the wilds.

His dogs often filled a need for companionship, and they allowed him to express a fondness for animals. Old-timers talked of Douglas as 'wet, ragged and hungry after many weeks . . . his only company his faithful dog'. Topsey, Betsey Jane, another of the same name, and others could gather birds, help with route finding, provide fellowship for wet or lonely days, and never be critical.

A pipe was as inseparable a companion as a dog. Douglas was a heavy smoker. In letters he referred to his need for tobacco, and to his affection for an old pipe. As long as there were birds to eat and tobacco to smoke he could manage on short rations of tea, sugar and flour. Although some photographs show Douglas smoking a long churchwarden, his usual pipe was a short one. In the mid-1890s he smoked 'niggerhead', a tobacco of two dozen thin sticks to the pound. It was said that when Douglas ran out of tobacco, he was physically affected, and found tutu leaves a substitute if used sparingly.

The only accounts available in detail showing how Douglas spent money are from 1896 and 1903. An analysis of the August 1896 account reveals that it must have been for the survey party in the Whitcombe valley and region. Owing to the West Coast ironmonger and merchant, Carl. J. E. Linnemann, was: £2 19s 6d for tools such as axe, half-axe, hatchet, trimmers, scythe stone, files, nails, clothes lines, pick, hammer, gold-dish and spokeshave; £2 0s 8d for calico, sheeting, twine and sailor's needles; 2s 6d for a magnifying-glass; 6s for freight, and so on to a total of £13 15s 0d.

Harper has commented: 'We paid for our own tools such as axes etc. except the compasses, chain, survey calico, aneroid etc.' and added, 'When he and I were working together we got 8/- a day – raised to 10/- "wet or fine" – for 6 days a week. If we worked as we did on Sundays (if fine) I do not remember getting paid anything extra – My recollection is £3 a week – wet or fine.' This was about the average wage at the time, though the work was much more difficult than ordinary occupations. The 1903 accounts in a pencil notebook show that William Gunn received 8/- a day as wages, and Douglas 10/- a day, computed at the number of days actually worked each month. For example, the number of days paid were: January, 27; February, 24; March, 26; and April, 26. There were not many days off, even with the West Coast weather.

The personal items in the 1896 account for Douglas were: dog chain and collar, tin whistle, cards, clock, comb, pills, ink, blankets, bootlaces, shirts, towel, handkerchiefs, braces, moleskin trousers, three wooden pipes, etc. A look at the accounts from 4 May to 24 August 1903 reveals amounts spent by Douglas: tobacco – £7 at 6s 6d a lb; 'lollies' – £1 2s; butter – £1. Standard provisions then were oatmeal, milk, rice, tinned tongues and beef, bacon, onions, potatoes, tinned peas and beans, cheese, sugar, salt, pepper, cocoa, jam, pickles, sago, tea, apples, flour and soap. 'Painkiller' was the favourite medical supply.

These lists are but glimpses of his domestic economy. The main point is that his needs were simple ones, and indeed there were no luxuries for men working hard on the Survey. Apart from the need to economise, the loads to be carried also had to be limited. Perhaps Douglas's earlier expeditions would have showed even less variety, for then bird life would have been more abundant.

Ambitions by commercial standards did not exist for Douglas. When Mueller and Roberts urged him to take on regularly paid work, his ears were deaf to them. He was content with the modest pay of the survey. 'I never had any Ambition worth speaking about,' he wrote to Harper in 1895. And again the next year: 'I never hungered after money the article is really of very little use to me.' But this freedom from ambition did not carry freedom from want, and there must have been times when he could have done with a more substantial income.

His theme that the vagabond or wanderer was essential to the success of a frontier society was well developed between the 'Waiatoto' manuscript of 1891 and the first part of the 'Soliloquy Letter' in 1902. He did not regret his life, though he could be bitter about some of its aspects. It had been rich in discoveries if empty of material gains. 'Making money I could never do or ever felt any inclination that way' was the attitude of many a loner. It was a sufficient, if fortuitous, reward to have used his brains as well as his physical energy in finding out something about the secrets of nature in South Westland.

Philosophy, wild life, natural beauty, minerals and discovery were Douglas's main interests in mountain travel, but an introspective man like Douglas needed creative work. Not for him the extrovert exuberance and release of physical vigour that is often so completely satisfying for a mountaineer away on an annual holiday. Douglas needed to think as well as to journey through and over the mountains. The writing of his diaries and reports gave him pleasure, though in his old age he felt stale and unproductive. It was in his writing that he expressed views and feelings which would otherwise have been suppressed.

His sketching too, though amateurish, was another creative joy. Lacking a home, and worldly wealth, he sent sketches to repay the kindnesses of various friends: Mueller, Roberts, the Macfarlanes, Harper, Wilson, Marks the storekeeper and survey staff. Primarily sketches by Charlie Douglas were valuable for topographical reasons. He had the surveyor's instinct for showing peaks and passes, undistracted by pictorial considerations. He was limited by scant materials and by having to carry what he needed, as well as by the climate and the sandflies. He owed much to the generosity of Roberts in sending drawing materials. He found it hard sometimes to see colour properly, and in the Waiatoto he wrote, 'I would like to see a good Water colour drawer at work, were it only for a few minutes.'

His sketches sent to Scotland are lost, but in New Zealand there are good collections that show the many natural features of Westland that Douglas sketched with his limited and monotonous technique, but with some period charm. From the collections available it is clear that he duplicated some drawings many times, probably to give to different people. Douglas's sketches are not art but they are human and interesting records of documentary value.

Another sideline with Douglas later in life was photography. This began as an object of cynicism. In the 'Cascade' manuscript he wrote with some glee: 'the Solitude of the Martyrs [gorge] will be profaned by the Photographic fiend and his box of Vile chemicals'. In the 'Waiatoto' record Douglas observed:

I'll allow the box & chemicals to have a high moral character if allowed–
but the manipulator can demoralize it if he likes, & make an otherwise
honest box travell the downward path, in company with the Horsedealer
the Promoter of Duffer Cos [companies] & other descendants of Annais.

And in the 'Copland' manuscript he referred to 'the ubiquitous photographer
with his unpoetical box'. Yet only four months later, on 29 September 1892, he
wrote to Roberts: 'How did the photos turn out?' Still in 1892 he was moved
by the view of Mount Evans from Cave Camp and wrote in the 'Whit-combe'
manuscript:

we took a few Photo's of this place, avalanches on the move &c. but they
were not a success. The Camera one of those lensless toys takes in a distant scene with the same optical results as looking through the wrong end
of a telescope.

It took time to learn to take good photographs, and Douglas was given assistance as he began to change his views. On 23 August 1893 Roberts asked Harper
for details of the best alpine camera, as he wanted one for Douglas. It was the
photographic efforts of his new mate Harper that fully convinced Douglas and
gave him an appreciation of good photography. He commented frequently to
Harper on this subject, as on 10 July 1894 when he was 'well pleased' with
Harper's photographs. A year later he wrote that he preferred Harper's shots
to professional portraits.[1] His own efforts he found interesting but at times
exasperating: 'There are so many bolts & screws about the Camera'.[2] Thus he
preferred the simpler camera that Harper gave him to the more complex one
given by the Royal Geographical Society as the Gill Memorial.

Douglas persevered with his photography. On 14 October 1897 Roberts
reported to Harper that when Douglas was up the Whitcombe he happened on
'one or two fairly good pictures out of dozens of abortions and now he has gone
south with a packload of plates'. Douglas asked Roberts on 30 January 1898, to
explain to his wife that the photographs were for topographical not 'Artistic'
purposes, and referred to a new camera to replace the half-plate one that 'makes
me groan to carry it'. Harper recalled that one photo by Douglas that was a
confused blur turned out to be Betsey Jane's rear end out of focus, and that the
'big half-plate weighed about 20lbs.' in its leather case. How many mountaineers would today consider carrying 9 kilograms of camera gear plus glass plates,
in addition to food and climbing equipment for a long trip?

The statement in the 'Soliloquy Letter' of 1903 – 'Photographing has been
another nuisance' – must reflect a time of brief disillusionment with life in
general. Even as late as 1908 he was still persisting in his hobby, and he wrote
to Harper on 14 January that at last he had got a good photograph of Lake
Kaniere. Photography was never one of his skills, but in attempting it he found

yet another reason for enjoying mountain travel. Unfortunately no reproducible prints by Douglas have been preserved.

In examining the life of a man, there is a temptation for his biographer to invest him with the glamour of all the virtues, which is as wrong as the opposite tendency to debunk him by attributing to him all the vices. The nearest approach to the truth is to refer to both virtues and vices, and the paler hues between such arbitrary moralising. Thus the reader can empathise with the subject of the biography as a human being, sometimes close to goodness, sometimes showing undesirable traits, steering his course as uncertainly as any person, whether of oblivion or of destiny. Douglas was no exception. References to his achievements and sorrows would not be complete without a consideration of his failings.

To understand the difficulties of exploring it helps to know the health that equips a man to meet them. In his younger days Douglas must have typified the vigorous Pakeha pioneer. His lithe physique would have enabled him to stand up to all the hard work, and the irregular or poor meals which marked his life. These demands would inevitably have impaired his capacities in time. By the age of fifty, advancing years and his exacting lifestyle were leaving a mark, but very few active people, including mountaineers, can claim that their speed and endurance is the same in middle age as it was in their prime, if indeed they even persevere in strenuous activity into and beyond middle age.

On 5 July 1890, when he had many years of exploring and struggle left to him, Douglas wrote to Roberts: 'I can't carry on this life much longer', and referred to a 'hard but still glorious existance'. Next year, in the 'Waiatoto' manuscript, he complained about 'that confounded old rupture', which no doubt made feats such as carrying two swags exhausting. He needed spectacles for sketching, and found that any cheap pair that suited Duncan Macfarlane's eyes would do for him. He observed: 'The older a fellow gets, the more things he finds he can't do without.'[3] A number of references to his rheumatism and to its effect on his work have been made. In 1896 he asked for a syringe for his deafness, but noted that such a state was a blessing when listening to boring yarns.[4] He was not chronically deaf, however, because friends such as Harper remember him as a good talker and listener, if a reserved one. Of the strokes that affected him in his last years, it can only be observed that such afflictions finish the careers of many men less energetic than Douglas.

Even in his prime Douglas was taciturn, and a certain dourness could be explained by the fact that he was often on his own, and by the routine monotonies of Westland travel. In the 'Waiatoto' manuscript he wrote: '. . . have got awfully stiff and lazy lying cramped up in a Tent that I feel the truth of the old saying. The less you have to do, the less you do.' His misanthropy about some of the inhabitants of South Westland could be intensified by his rheumatic pains, and what he described as 'the seamy side of human nature'[5] would seem all the seamier when he was ill. In the same way, his joyous appreciation of rough country could be tempered by the occasional rebellion against his own ideals. In the 'Whitcombe' manuscript he wrote: 'I confess I would sooner look on a field of wheat or turnips, than the finest glacier in the World. The first two I haven't gazed on for over thirty years; glaciers & mountain peaks are always before my eyes, & familiarity breeds contempt.' But such comments are rare and it seems he willingly chose both the isolation of life on the West Coast, and to be primarily a loner there.

This led, perhaps, to the development of some suspicion of others, expressed most commonly as a concern that his discoveries would be abused, either stolen or not acknowledged. By the 1890s Douglas was becoming tinged with bitterness that the amateur geologist was likely to be ignored by the professional, and Roberts' testimonial of 1908 suggested that this happened with Douglas's work generally. At one time Douglas was worried that Sir James Hector would use his power to deprive him of an explorer's job: 'Sir Hector . . . would talk of the Insolence of an amateur meddling with Geology & put his Veto on it', and there were other forebodings in the same undated letter to Roberts. His dislike of scientists may have stemmed from his early contacts with Haast, but years later Douglas could still be very sarcastic about them. In the 'Cascade' manuscript, he praised nature for foreseeing that 'the World would be overrun with a two-legged beast, wearing green spectacles and carrying a hammer and bag', and elsewhere he wrote:

> . . . some people are so eager to get their name in print as the discoverer of something new, that if those beings found a cock-a-bulla with its tail bit off, they would put it down as a new fish and murder the Latin language and their own name in fixing that fish's position in the world of waters.[6]

This showed a very human paradox in Charlie Douglas's nature. While he was scornful of amateur so-called explorers, he himself was sensitive about being considered an amateur in geology and science generally. Geology was important to Douglas. He remembered the terms used by Julius Haast on their 1868 expedition, and over twenty years later he had his own copy of *The Handbook of New Zealand Mines* (1887). However, in reporting on surface geology Douglas paid 'little attention to mere strings of jawbreaking names'. He was interested in why a rock 'is there, why hills take different forms in one district & not keep uniform, and why rivers run in certain direction'.[7] He acknowledged his own early limitations, writing in the 'Geology' manuscript: 'I was very green in those days in a knowledge of metals and minerals.' Later geologists recognised

Douglas's intense interest in geology, which was shared by many of his time. But he was never more than a 'good and thorough prospector' and a keen amateur geologist. His lack of training and direction from others more knowledgeable than himself remained a severe handicap that he never overcame.[8]

Douglas derided self-styled explorers who did little that was useful or ignored the work of others before them. He disdained the habits of boastful globetrotters and casual visitors, and refused to imitate their vulgarity in giving exaggerated heights and listing strings of glacier names. Douglas liked to use Maori names if they could be spelt, and he approved of descriptive names, such as the Roaring Billy tributary of the Haast, named by early diggers. He also noted: 'It requires insperation to put a name on a natural feature which will last'.[9]

When he came to the waterfalls dropping from Stargazer and Moonraker to the Therma Glacier of the Waiatoto, he 'measured their height roughly with chained base line and clinometer'. But in the 'Islets, Towns and Glaciers' manuscript he declined to give a height: 'No one will credit it, so some future explorer can have a try, he may be believed at least if he happens to be nobody less than a JP or the chairman of a school board'. He refused to name all the minor glaciers he had seen, 'but they are all down in field or sketch book, so Globe trotters can put names on if they like, but don't imagine they are the first [who] discovered them'. He noted of the Arawata glaciers: 'As no great man has visited them, they remain unknow outside my maps.'

Douglas was very impatient of tourists, at least in his writings. In the 'Copland' manuscript he expressed the view, 'It isn't by trotting out of comfortable Hotel & back the same day that Nature's real wonders can be seen', forgetting that not everyone lived in his timeless way. In the 'Whitcombe' manuscript he asked: 'Is the Tourist, as a class simply a collection of fools who believe what they are told . . . get carted through the world at so much per day, simply to say they have been & seen such & such a place?' He focused particularly on women tourists and their supposed demands when he wrote in the 'Balfour River' manuscript: 'The public won't walk now-a-day – chiefly through that modern creation – the female globe trotter, so nothing but expensive grade horse tracks at the very least, will do.' The irony was that, for all his dislike of tourists, Douglas, more than most, through his exploration opened up for them the scenic glories of South Westland, and his maps were the basis of their future trips.

There was a similar aversion to alpine climbers. In 1885 he wrote that saddles from the Turnbull River would only be used by 'an Alpine Explorer or other Lunatic'. As recreational alpine climbing developed in the next ten years, the surveyors sometimes found their maps were used by mountaineers without acknowledgement. Lunacy was thus coupled with piracy when the amateur mountain explorer suggested he was first on the spot. And when such 'travellers' (a pejorative term) boasted in books or articles about their activities, their vainglory angered the survey men. Not only was their work not recognised, but the new mountaineers also seemed to ascend peaks and cross passes just so they could say they had been there.

Douglas had much to write on the subject. On 17 February 1892 he noted to Roberts: 'Some Ministers son or nephew who will explore the country through a Telescope & come back with as many accounts of his hairbreadth escapes as that Blather Geo Park.' This referred to George Park's trips in the late 1880s and early 1890s into the Callery River. Douglas could also take the offensive for his friends as well as for himself. His comments on FitzGerald's proclamations of discovery have been noted elsewhere. He was indignant when he found that Malcolm Ross had, in 1897, taken the credit for original work in the Copland, ignoring Harper's east-to-west crossing of the pass in 1895. Douglas expressed his distaste for the climbers and the New Zealand Alpine Club of his period in no uncertain terms.

> Those Alpine explorers who have crossed the range or visited the head of the Kellery [Callery] have left no record of their adventures except photos which describe nothing in particular, and heartrending accounts of their sufferings and dangers. This remark applies to most of the Alpine club explorers, on the Kellery or anywhere else, their geographical work has seldom been of much value.[10]

In his 'Passes' manuscript Douglas referred to 'that gang of amateurs called the New Zealand Alpine Club they have done nothing and explored nothing that wasn't known long before'. Elsewhere, in the 'Cook River' manuscript, he made a remark about 'some crack brained idiot who wishes to make what he calls a record, & who's ambition is to be a small hero in a lecture hall, drawing room, or even pot house'. Roberts expressed similar opinions as well,[11] and indeed this attitude was not uncommon on the West Coast, then and in later years. Alpine feats were not ones about which to boast, and pretentiousness in any form was to be condemned.

Yet Douglas was rather unjust and ungenerous in many of these comments. People like Park, FitzGerald and Ross may have seemed boastful, but their achievements were worth recording, and through books and newspaper articles they publicised mountain areas more widely than the reports of the Survey Department. The Callery, where Park ventured three times, was country as difficult as any Douglas ventured into. Ross did make the first west-to-east crossing of the Copland Pass, and he had just before, in an extraordinary trip with Tom Fyfe, made a first crossing of Lendenfeld Saddle from the Tasman

Glacier to the Whataroa River. The new young climbers had a different attitude because their mountaineering was recreational and part time, but they also explored. A later age can see that they were brave souls kindred to Douglas, but seeking different mountain adventure – his primary exploration could never be repeated. And after all, it was only by writing articles, giving lectures, publishing books and telling people about their mountaineering that members of the Alpine Club, and others, could inform fellow New Zealanders of the mountain glories and adventures that awaited future tourists and climbers.

The subject of women in the life of Douglas is a short one. He was innately shy, even timorous of women, and of strangers. He could be jocular about women in occasional comments, such as this from the 'Birds' manuscript: 'Almost the first kiwi caught on the Coast was purchased by an enterprising publican, who found it attracted more custom to his house than half a dozen auburn haired barmaids.' There was also the cynical Douglas version of love in the 'Waiatoto' manuscript: 'Miss Brown chewing the corner of her apron was sitting coyly on the bank, while the untruthful Macadam pitched awfull Cuffers.' James Cowan claimed to have met Douglas and implied that in the 1860s he was keen on a night out with the Alhambra song-and-dance girls in Hokitika,[12] but this can only be regarded as conjecture.

The most consistent attitude towards women in a frontier or pioneer community was respect, and in this Douglas was no exception to other men. In 'Waiatoto' he wrote, 'Some one says there are only fifty good stories in the World & thirty-nine of them can't be narrated to Women.' Some of the pioneer and survey wives in Hokitika and South Westland undoubtedly warmed to Douglas because of his regard for their husbands. And Douglas could enjoy the company of women. The examples of Mrs Catherine Roberts and Mrs Marion Harper have been given. Mrs Mildred Westland, later Lady Westland, visited Hokitika and further south in 1894. She impressed Roberts with her vivacity and charm and he wrote: 'Even old Douglas was captivated and no wonder.'[13] Harper remembered that it took some time for the ice to be broken, but that Douglas enjoyed Mrs Westland's company and talked till late over the fire. Douglas placed women on a pedestal, as did many of his contemporaries. If they tolerated his eccentricities, he could become at ease with them, but he was always respectful.

Of Maori, Douglas had a low opinion, but the few he met in South Westland were but shadows of their former selves and ancestors, and, like many other Pakeha of the time, he never knew their real hospitality, courage, physique or intelligence. Their state in the latter part of the nineteenth century was the result not just of the Pakeha invasion of people, material goods and diseases, but also of the attacks on Poutini Ngai Tahu by other Maori tribal groups in the

1820s and 1830s. In his 'Swamps' manuscript Douglas noted, 'Now a Maorie is scarcer than a whiteman" and elsewhere he wrote: 'The present Maories on the Coast are no more the original owners of the soil than I am. They appear to be a scratch crew.'[14] Douglas was likely to use a phrase such as 'vile aboriginal' or 'the old cannibal', as in the 'Birds' manuscript, until it became almost a cliché. He also accused Maori of being careless with the greenstone they prized.[15] But, in a manner that was unheard of by his contemporaries, he gave them credit for conserving wildlife.[16]

In writing to friends Douglas was sometimes blistering in his comments on South Westlanders with whom he was at odds, probably because they expected him to produce evidence of valuable reefs, for which they themselves could not be bothered to search. There were also basic differences of lifestyle and expectation. Although some of his friends were settlers, Douglas seemed unable to understand the migrant settlers' need for security and their desire to better themselves. Douglas had no such ambitions. He made things easier for those who came after him, and then despised them for not roughing it as the first settlers and diggers had done.

But for the early pioneers in remote country Douglas had nothing but admiration – men such as Andy Williamson whose names were perpetuated on maps of the Arawata, and 'Maori Bill', whom he revered. The latter was an Irish deserter from the New Zealand Wars who had made a hide-out in the Cascade valley, clothed himself in kiwi skins, and only came out for stores and tobacco. According to the 'Swamps' manuscript, 'the immortal wild man Maorie bill . . . actually planted a patch of strawberries, the only piece of work he was ever know to do'.[17] Douglas never met William O'Leary, known as Arawata Bill,[18] though he referred to his transalpine crossing from the Dart in the 'Passes' manuscript.

The Survey Department has been criticised by A. P. Harper for its lack of generosity and public recognition, but it is only fair to note the departmental policy of not publicising individual explorers and surveyors. And though Douglas was a very likeable, even loveable man, in an institutional situation he might not have been easy to handle. Civil servants drew wrath from Douglas, who disliked 'that thirst for Paper Collar occupations which unfortunately distinguishes the rising Colonial',[19] but they may have been just as scathing of him. Douglas found that 'reports are as a rule dry work to write & worse to read', and for this reason, he continued: 'I consider I am quite at liberty to relieve my feelings now & again.'[20] So he wrote his reports as he wished, in language that was often pungent, and with inconsistent spelling and punctuation. His notes were 'scattered over note books scraps of paper & backs of letters'[21], which did not always survive, and some of his reports he did from memory.[22]

Whatever Douglas's problems with some aspects of his employment, his friends from the Survey Department, such as Mueller, Roberts and Wilson, were loyal to him throughout his career and they did what they could to help him. According to Colin Macfarlane, when Douglas's health left him unfitted for continuous work in the field and he was too proud to take pay for inactivity, Roberts solved the problem by having him write up his reports in Hokitika. Work on his reports, and on the geological maps, became standby occupations from the mid-1890s, especially in the winter months.

Indeed, the quality and consistency of Douglas's friendships is remarkable. The surveyors stuck to him with all the tolerance and affection implicit in solid friendship. Harper recalled that some of the South Westland folk who were close to Douglas included Harry Friend, Ned Gibbs and Fred Blanchard, all of Okarito, and Joe Collyer, the glorious classical scholar/storekeeper of Okuru who could talk in Latin and Greek. There were also the Macfarlanes, the Harrises and the Wards. Alec Graham added to the list his wife's uncle, Arthur Woodham, who was with Douglas as companion and camp cook. He collected specimens when Douglas was too ill to fossick for them himself, and later helped look after him in Hokitika. In October 1903 Douglas wrote in the 'Soliloquy Letter', 'friendships I have never made', but this must have been merely a mood of temporary disillusionment and not a final judgement. His self-analysis was generally accurate enough, but sometimes too cynical. With recognised self-pity he could refer to himself as 'wandering about a homeless orphan' in the 'Cascade' manuscript, but in fact he made lasting friendships.

Like many men of his time, Douglas did have binges of drinking alcohol, especially after he returned from the mountainous wilds. But there was wide tolerance for such behaviour and this escape of the lonely man in a pioneer period was typical and needs no moralising. Some of the legends of Douglas on a spree are entertaining but apocryphal. There is no evidence that in drinking Douglas did harm to anyone except himself, and he was not offensive in his behaviour. His contemporaries such as Harper noted that when on a 'bender' he 'drank quietly and generally kept to his room in a pub till it was over'. G. T. Murray, Douglas's companion on the North Olivine Range in 1886, recollected that when Douglas was in liquor, he had great schemes for the reformation of the world.[23] But Douglas was aware of his weakness and that it was a handicap. It was to his credit that he did not inflict it on any community where he stayed, and possibly his willingness to spend such long periods away from civilisation was a way to avoid a greater problem with alcohol.

Nothing in his papers showed that Douglas was religious in the conventional church-going sense of the word, though in the 'Soliloquy Letter' he referred to the next world, 'when it is to be hoped darkness will be light'. It is likely that he nursed, unexpressed, a mysticism or sense of providence common to loners seeking solace in remote country and in hazardous conditions.

Douglas was not any more interested in politics, as a few comments show. On 17 February 1892 he made a reference to the future Premier when he wrote to Roberts: 'Richard John [Seddon] great as he imagines himself to be, when an election is near, has to crawl & cring to every ignorat shirtless vagabond who happens to have a vote.' The climax to a story about weka was that a farmer ruined by their intelligence might as well 'turn burglar or politician', and in reading his newspapers from Britain he skipped political articles.[24]

But Douglas did think and read deeply, and he used his past education. Harper recorded a Douglas remark about the *Review of Reviews* 'providing food for the mind and light for the pipe'.[25] His inclination for placing classical names on his maps was stimulated by both his education and his reading. He was glad to share Harper's copies of Homer, Cook's *Voyages*, and Milton. He always had plenty of books to read and left them scattered among his friends along the coast. Field Book 493 of 1881 gave a list of a hundred books, either those he wanted to read or had read. The titles included works on British history, classics including the *Pleiad*, Virgil and Plato, a biography of Napoleon, and Boswell's *Johnson*. There was travel literature. There were novels by Fielding, Thackeray, Rabelais and Victor Hugo, humour in *Punch* albums, and poetry by Milton, Byron, Dryden and Pope. In his reading Douglas was a citizen of the world.

Although Douglas was never an owner of Westland soil, his moral stake in spiritual ownership of the back country was undoubted. He knew he belonged to the West Coast. He had an antiquarian interest in its early history and told stories about it. His privations and efforts over many years had extended the frontiers of New Zealand knowledge. This gave him the right to express opinions as dogmatic as any patriarch or mortgagee of broad and cultivated lands. Douglas could be in turn as possessive, whimsical, dispassionate and emotional as any other creative writer or thinker.

He could also be factual and realistic in his writing. The 'Geology' manuscript included the following objective comment on West Coast harbours: 'the Grey, Hokitika and the Buller are only make shifts, notwithstanding West coast brag. A coal port to be any good must be a place where the largest battle ship or ocean liner can call and fill up in any weather.' He could comment intelligently on the spendthrift exploitation of depletable resources such as forests, coal, gold and overstocked land.[26] Yet he at times he was fantastical, as when he described a glacier ice-cave in the 'Cook River' manuscript: 'its walls were ornamented with glittering ice pinnacles, ledges & cornices, giving to the whole a X'mass pantomime appearance . . . we wouldn't have been surprised if a fairy in gauze had made her appearance, or a voice had shouted out "How are we all tomorrow".'

Douglas not only applied his intelligence to what he observed, but he was genuinely and consistently interested in the natural world of the West Coast and he developed theories of conservation unusual for his time. He could even be whimsical about the sandflies and mosquitoes: 'the Philosophical mind can derive instruction & amusement from even them', though 'a mosquito is said to carry about with him to aid in torturing humanity, a scythe, brush, auger and pump'.[27] Douglas wrote about the fish in the rivers, and one expert noted that 'there is much good observation, a canny approach to hearsay tales and a few wise speculations', though his notes were of 'general interest rather than scientific value'.[28]

Douglas might be annoyed by sandflies and mosquitoes, but he feared only the weta, especially those of Open Bay Islands off the Okuru River mouth. He wrote that there

> The Typos [as he called them] are swarming all over and appear to burrow in the stalks of the gei gei [kie kie], on the mainland this repulsive insect is rather bashfull, only showing if flooded, burnt, or dug out of their holes, but on the island they show an affection for mans society that is extremely disagreeable. Sit down for a smoke, and they are out of their holes and climbing up your person. At night when you have covered yourself up in blankets, you can feel the playfull creatures running races, and dancing hornpipes all over you.[29]

As was natural with a bushman, Douglas studied the trees and other plants of the bush and knew them well. In 1954, Jack Holloway of the New Zealand Forest Service, then officer in charge of the South Island's native forests, was 'greatly impressed' by what he read of Douglas's observations on forestry, and by his attitude to the bush:

> Douglas was certainly an extraordinarily acute observer. The pity is that he did not start off with a trained scientific background. If he had we would have been many decades in advance of our present knowledge of the forests. Many of his items of information . . . we did not discover again until a few years ago . . .
> Douglas, to my mind . . . was a 'natural' as a forest ecologist, born 100 years before his time. The whole approach is that of a well-trained ecologist of the most modern and practical school . . .[30]

Another forester, Geoffrey Chavasse, then of Hokitika, saw the value of Douglas's recorded observations in assessing the changes that had occurred in forests since the advent of the Pakeha and introduced animals.[31]

But it was the wildlife that was Douglas's real love, and some of his most vivid writing was about the birds he encountered. His account of kaka in the Mikonui (pages 166–67) is a classic, and he often personified the birds, giving them human feelings and other attributes. In the 'Whitcombe' manuscript he wrote: 'The Caw Caws all the way up appear to have been to school & learned that a gun carried by a long legged biped is a thing to be avoided.' In the same year, 1892, he showed his awareness of the impact of people on the bird life when he wrote:

> The Weka prowled round the Tent, annexing anything portable, & the Kiwi made night hedious with its piercing shreik, the Blue Duck crossed over to whistle a welcome. The Caw Caw swore & the Kea skirled, Pigeons, Tuis, Saddle backs & Thrushes hopped about unmolested. The chorus of the Bell bird was heard in the dawning & all were tame & inquisitive, but now all this is altered. The Digger with his Dogs, Cats, rats, Ferrets and Guns have nearly exterminated the Birds in the lower reaches of the southern rivers . . . But the Flats of the Copeland put a fellow in mind of old days; it was full of birds all tame & inquisitive as of old.[32]

Douglas did eat birds, often caught by his dog, but with his profound love for wildlife he never killed wantonly, only to survive, and as the years passed he became more and more concerned about the disappearance of many of the birds he had known. He declined to give the location of a heronry, as he did not want it plundered by scientists seeking specimens, and he became more and more suspicious of hunters:

> if people travelling the wilds would only shoot what birds they actually want, & not go blazing away . . . the murderous instinct is still strong in man. The law wont allow us to gratify it on each other, so we relieve our thirst for blood by slaughtering dumb animals.[33]

When he saw grey ducks playing prams with their young he wondered 'if any human being would shoot them while so imployed'. Elsewhere in his 'Birds' manuscript he wrote: 'I have lived for weeks on dry bread, rather than kill birds knowing they had young.' Douglas was tough, but he was a gentle soul, at ease with the forest, rivers and wildlife of the Westland he did so much to explore and record.

TWENTY-FIVE

Charlie Douglas the Explorer

Charlie Douglas spent nearly forty years in active exploration and surveying on the West Coast, work that extended from the shore to the mountains. For much of the time he was employed by the Survey Department, but there was a very basic difference between Douglas's expectations and those of the department. The latter, especially officials away from the West Coast, expected him to find routes and saddles that were useful, and valuable metals that could be exploited. Although Douglas was always looking for passes, prospecting and studying the geology of the country he traversed, he did not really care if what he found was purposeful or profitable. He explored because he was curious and he enjoyed the process of discovery in the region he adopted as his home.

Douglas should be recognised for the breadth of his observations and discoveries. His reports and other writings show that his interest in the West Coast was all-inclusive. He sought to develop as complete a view as possible of the areas he explored and surveyed. The Survey Department may have wished primarily for maps and the discovery of valued minerals and useful passes, but Douglas went much further. At his best he observed and recorded something of every facet of the natural world. In doing so he noted changes Pakeha were bringing, especially in the form of predators and alterations to the landscape. He also observed other people with a cynical and amused eye.

There was, however, much more to Douglas than just journeying, observing and recording. In the process he thought deeply. Douglas developed his own ideas of evolution, of geology and glaciation, of flora and fauna, in his attempts to understand the terrain and life of the West Coast. He philosophised on the human world as he saw it. He also showed an awareness of what was being lost through settlement, and even through his own efforts – the unknown wilderness was disappearing. In 1900 he wrote:

> Let us keep a few spots in Westland, uncontaminated by the ordinary tourist, the picnicker and the photographic fiend, some almost impassable place where what is inside can be left to the imagination . . . keep them for those who care to risk there necks and enjoy scenery in a state of nature.[1]

By the end of the nineteenth century Douglas was a conservationist, aware of what was being irremediably lost and hoping some of the natural world he loved would be preserved.

The country he ranged over was both extensive and difficult. Douglas examined part or all of nearly every West Coast river, from Hokitika south to Martins Bay and the Hollyford River. This was a distance of some 200 miles (300 kilometres) in a direct line, but much, much further on the ground and on foot. At times Douglas reached over 30 miles (50 kilometres) from the coastline, but by much longer, more tortuous routes up rivers and glaciers and over ranges. This area was filled with fearsome terrain that few humans would face. Both the mountains and the valleys were disjointed and abrupt, the weather was erratic and at times downright dangerous, and the bush was often near to impenetrable.

A reviewer of A. P. Harper's *Pioneer Work in the Alps of New Zealand* (1896) recognised Charlie Douglas as the hero of that book, because there was so much of Douglas in Harper's account of his own exploratory work. Some of Douglas's solo efforts of exploration were heroic in their scope and stamina. Yet Douglas himself might have protested that he was just doing what he enjoyed, with only his hard work deserving recognition. He had no great surveying skills or scientific knowledge to support his work and opinions, but he examined and recorded the topography and geology of South Westland. He also observed and noted the flora and fauna he came across, and his splendid enthusiasm for mapping was clear in his letters to his friends and in the maps and diagrams he produced. So much was achieved in very difficult circumstances that it can be concluded his was an heroic existence.

It was very much his own work, this steadfast and adventurous exploration of the wilds of South Westland. Much of the time he depended on himself alone because he was without companions. The government and the Survey Department did not really wish to put much money into the close examination of this unknown and isolated corner of New Zealand. The result was that much of Douglas's progress was restricted because it was unsupported, though Mueller and Roberts did their best. Douglas was often not as well equipped as he needed to be: his clothing was poor, his boots kept falling to pieces, he often lacked useful survey instruments or a barometric aneroid that would have helped him predict the weather.

The greatest problem was probably the slow pace of Douglas's exploration, which made his efforts vulnerable to West Coast weather. His solo trips often took months because he had to carry camps and food on his back. There were limits to the capacity of a rolled-up swag. As it was, he carried heavy loads, but still the experience of hunger was familiar to him. How much more time could Charlie Douglas have spent in the headwaters of West Coast rivers if he had

had the support of other men and horses to pack his gear in the lower reaches of those rivers? Douglas wrote: 'I can combine the Swagging abilities of a Mule, the stowage capacity of the Pelican with the digestive powers of an Ostrich so can go into places where few dare venture through fear of starvation,'[2] but his explorations would have been more thorough if he had had greater assistance. Yet for at least twenty years he enjoyed working solo, and his strength and willingness to endure made him someone out of the ordinary.

The official records of the Survey Department contained two significant summaries of Charlie Douglas's work on the West Coast, one in 1895 and the other for his retirement in 1908. The first commendation appeared over the name of David Barron, the Chief Surveyor of Westland, but it probably came from the pen of G. J. Roberts.

> Mr. Douglas is a born explorer, and has . . . undergone extreme privation in carrying out his duties. He is a man considerably beyond the average. His attainments as a botanist and geologist would have placed him in a much better position were it not for his retiring habits. For twenty years he has led the life of an enthusiastic explorer, and is undoubtedly the first bushman on the coast. He has frequently gone for months, without cutting a track, or the assistance of a comrade, up the untrodden densely-timbered inland valleys of Westland, traversing the rivers and streams, scaling peaks, determining geological features, patiently tracing mineral belts, making sketches of the scenery, and afterwards sending up plain good maps, replete with information of the greatest interest and importance. He is most painstaking in his work, and his reconnaissance surveys, when afterwards checked by the positions of peaks determined by the Westland triangulation, have proved to be remarkably accurate. He conducted the pioneer surveys of the Main South Road from Mahitahi to Haast Rivers . . . The topographical and geological survey of the wild inland country from the Kokatahi to Lake McKerrow, the exploration of the coalfields of Paranga and Bullock Creek, the mineral belts of Mount Argentine, and the copper-lodes of the Matakitaki Range are all due to his indomitable perseverance.[3]

This was high praise from officialdom for someone who had made his own life doing something he was passionate about. Thirteen years later, for Douglas's retirement, Roberts was even more complimentary.

> On the 30th June next Mr. Explorer Douglas retires from the service on a well-deserved pension. For upwards of forty years he has led the arduous life of exploiting this wild and rugged country, and has furnished large numbers of valuable reports and plans, replete with expert information on topography, timbers, geology, &c., besides furnishing reliable notes of the country for settlement purposes. He also for many years conducted explorations for nearly all the main roads in our southern country—a well-read and educated man, a keen observer, of great originality of thought, and

most honourable and conscientious in the performance of all his duties. A man of wide repute, yet modest to a fault, of winning, unassuming manner, he never advertised himself, but was ever willing to impart his knowledge, with the result that many publications regarding Westland contain much of Mr. Douglas's wheat amongst the chaff of their egotistical compilers. He is respected and honoured throughout the district, and has nobly earned a high and enduring position on our official roll. We part with our faithful comrade with great reluctance, and wish him a long and happy season of rest in the quiet of his well-earned retirement.[4]

Other surveyors could understand the importance of someone like Douglas, who came early in the process of Pakeha settlement on the West Coast, and stayed, to contribute what he could through discovery, whether it was for the Survey Department or out of his own interest. He was a key person on the frontier of Pakeha knowledge, a wanderer who, unlike most other men, continued his roaming for most of his life. For him there was no easy living, but in the midst of all his difficulties he recorded what he found and observed, to inform both his own age and subsequent generations.

His expeditions over forty years gave Douglas unique experiences of months spent in the ranges and of adventures in glaciated valleys and sometimes above the level of perpetual snow. His sense of humour enabled him to cope with difficulties and disappointments. His restless curiosity and courage drove him on, and his tenacity of purpose sustained his efforts. He stood out also for his absorption in the unknowns of Westland, and for his survival in some of the harshest country in New Zealand. His was a singular life and achievement and his name is deservedly marked on a pass, a glacier, a river and a fine peak.

But at the same time Douglas was part of a raw colonial society. He was an immigrant to New Zealand who found an almost anonymous niche for himself. His very humanity, his combination of strengths and weaknesses, makes it possible to admire him and understand him. He was a pioneer not just in his search for new country, but also in his thirst for knowledge.

Douglas belongs among the ranks of those whose names are remembered in the story of New Zealand exploration. That he was diarist, philosopher, bushman, geologist, climber, artist, naturalist and surveyor is but to state his diverse talents. His achievement lay in the breadth of his accomplishments, in the extent and durability of his explorations, and in his thoroughness of observation, recording and thinking. Most of all, in his life and works he has revealed to others his humanness, his success in spite of failure and weakness, because of the relentless nature of his curiosity.

Charles Edward Douglas was a great explorer and remains an imperishable part of our frontier tradition.

Appendices

ONE

Charlie Douglas's Stories

Charlie Douglas liked stories. He listened to the tales of others, including the outlandish ones of Bill Hindley, and enjoyed telling stories himself, but very few of his own have been recorded. His companions noted the fact that he told stories, but there is little information about the stories themselves. All that is known about Douglas suggests that they would have shown an ironic view of people. The fragments that remain indicate Douglas's stories were often about 'treasure', perhaps part of his dream.

In his field book of 1881 Douglas wrote the stories 'The Puller of the Longbow', (also known as 'The Billy of Gold'), using the pseudonym Ak Smith, and 'King Penguin', though he crossed both out and only a fragment of the second remains. Len Boot transcribed both for John Pascoe.

The Puller of the Longbow
Ak Smith

Scene a bush Shanty among the ranges. A number of Diggers sitting Drinking and talking enter a Semi respectable individual no swag seedy Tweed suit & dirty paper collar.

After calling for a pint of beer and smiling benignantly on the company the stranger commences. 'Good evening gentlemen, glad to see you enjoying yourselves. The Work we have to perform as Pioneers of Civilisation requires occasionally the moderate use of stimulating beverages. I myself have just come from a most exhausting and perilous exploration of the surrounding ranges.'

'Do you know them ranges?' says some one. 'Every Inch of them Gentlemen, every inch of them and if you will be kind enough to give your attention I will relate a most extraordinary discovery I made among them some time ago.

'I had come over from the Cardrona on a prospecting tour and one day I happened to be sitting on a very steep razorback with a Billy in my hand. While Admiring the magnificent scenery, the billy unfortunately dropped and went Tink Tinkle down into a gully some five hundred feet below.

'Now Gentlemen I need not remind you that Billys are scarce & valuable in the ranges, at least the money to purchase them at that time was scarce with me, so I descended into the gully for my billy. On reaching the bottom I found – Gentlemen you will scarcely credit it – but I found the bottom of that gully actually paved with Gold.

'Will I have another Pint, certainly gentlemen, I will have much pleasure in drinking with you. Landlord, English Ale if you please.

'Gentlemen when my eyes rested on the bottom of that Gully I was petrified. Yes Gentlemen actually Petrified and for some moments I was unable to comprehend the importance of my stupendous discovery. Gradually collecting myself I sat down on a boulder, did I say a boulder gentlemen. No gentlemen I sat down on a mass of pure Gold and gentlemen I am sure you will appreciate my emotion when I tell you that I sat on that Block of Gold and wept.

'But gentlemen I soon recovered myself and proceeded to collect specimens, but those which attracted my eyes with their beauty and symmetry, with which I filled the Billy and commenced to climb up the ridge. And Oh, Gentlemen that ascent was fearful, what with the weight of the gold, the steepness of the face and the excitement I was labouring under I thought I would never reach the top, but I attained it at last and Gentlemen just as I was at the last step the bottom of the Billy unfortunately fell out and the Gold fell again to the bottom of the Gully. As the shades of Evening were closing in and as I saw that assistance would be required in removing the Deposit – '

A pause.

A Voice 'have another Pint Mate.'

'Gentlemen I accept your kind offer with pleasure.

'H-m Gentlemen as I was saying I required assistance so I built a small cairn on the top of the ridge and placing on it the bottomless billy I left for Cardrona to acquaint my mates. As might be expected they were strongly excited and before many days we had collected all the empty flour bags and all the spare pack horses in the District and proceeded to our destination.

'But Gentlemen I am sorry to state that I have never been able to find the Gully from that day to this.'

King Penguin

. . . in the district. It couldn't be a woman either from the same cause. No profanity came from the depths so it couldn't be a man.

A Dog perhaps but then a dog would whimper when it saw me.

A spirit maybe – but then why did it not come out or yell up what it wanted. For a moment I thought it might be Ruth in her orthodox position but dismissed the thought at once. she would be entirely out of place in Westland unless five hundred miles under the surface.

Every Bushman carries a piece of candle and flax was handy so I lowered a light slowly down and saw an unfortunate King Penguin that had fallen in, and if I live a thousand years I'll never forget the piteous emploring look of that wretched hypocritical bird. Leaving the lighted candle dangling about a foot off the water I got another line with a noose on the end and after some manouevuring got it over the birds neck. He gave a yell on finding himself coming to the surface. Perhaps it was delight, perhaps he thought his head was coming away. I wish it had for when taking the noose of its neck – that ungrateful bird bite me and before I could take vengeance had escaped into the scrub.

There is evidence of other Douglas stories. Mentioned briefly in the 'South of Jacksons Bay' manuscript is 'The Frenchman's Cave', a Douglas story that Frank Herveldt briefly related in 1955 to Len Boot in Hokitika.

The Frenchman's Cave

In the dusk Douglas stumbled across the cave when looking for shelter in a storm, and found two lots of kegs. One set of kegs clinked when he moved them; the other sloshed. Douglas opened the one that clinked, and out poured a golden stream of coins. He tried to sleep but was haunted by the ghost of the Frenchman. Later he left with some of the gold, but could get no peace, so camped in the rain. He threw the gold away. When telling this story he said his mistake was to open the wrong set of kegs first. And he said that he never returned to the cave which was covered by a slip.

This tale seems to have been one of the glorious leg-pulls perpetuated by Douglas to his friends. It is possible that sometimes the kegs in the story were gumboots full of nuggets. Alice McKenzie of Martins Bay told two versions of such a story in her book Pioneers of Martins Bay *(1952).*

John Pascoe also had another reference to this story from a different source, which suggests this must have been one of Douglas's favourite tales.

G. T. Murray, reminiscing to Frank Simmons in Auckland on 14 August 1935, referred to a similar story that he heard about 1886. Douglas 'had a tale of his visit to the Frenchman's Den he was fond of relating but would never explain the reason for his statement that even if the cave was full of gold he would not return there. Quite what was his experience there is not known.'

Perhaps the answer lay in the ghost, and in Charlie Douglas's sense of humour!

James Cowan claimed in Tales of the Maori Bush *(1934) that he knew Charlie Douglas. He met the old explorer, but some of Cowan's 'facts' must be regarded with suspicion. However, he did relate a story that was probably out of Douglas's repertoire. He tells of a group of Maori attempting to pole a canoe up the river under the Franz Josef Glacier to reach the eastern side of the Southern Alps, where, they believed, the gold originated. Their journey was ignominiously unsuccessful, and Douglas, who had no very high opinion of Maori, may have enjoyed poking fun at them in stories such as this.*

TWO

FitzGerald and the Copland Pass

Edward FitzGerald, a young English climber, arrived in New Zealand late in 1894 with his guide Mattias Zurbriggen to attempt New Zealand's highest peaks. New Zealanders Tom Fyfe, George Graham and Jack Clark climbed Mt Cook on Christmas Day 1894, before FitzGerald reached the mountains, but he and Zurbriggen ascended Mts Tasman, Silberhorn, Sefton, Haidinger and Sealy. Clark was with them on all but Sefton. Zurbriggen later climbed Mt Cook, reaching the summit alone.

FitzGerald was admired and praised for these successes. However, his manner, his assumptions of superiority and expectations of service did not endear him to New Zealand climbers. His disparaging treatment of Jack Clark was soon known, and A. P. Harper did not appreciate the way Fitzgerald dismissed the mountaineering abilities of all New Zealanders, including himself.

The longer-term controversy involving Douglas originated in FitzGerald's claims of discovery. On 24 February 1895 he and Zurbriggen crossed the Main Divide from the Hooker valley to the Copland River, and then spent days struggling through the bush to Scott's at Karangarua. Where they crossed was named Fitzgerald Pass. At about 7,000 feet, it was very close to what became the standard route over Copland Pass.

FitzGerald returned to England in 1895 to pose not only as a great mountain conqueror, but also as the first to cross the Southern Alps and the discoverer of an easy pass across the Main Divide adjacent to the Hermitage. His claims of discovery and exploration annoyed New Zealand mountaineers intensely because they knew how much guidance he had been given and how little he had done that was original. In particular, the part played by surveyors such as Douglas was ignored or dismissed.

Thomas N. Brodrick had surveyed the Hooker Glacier on the eastern side, and Douglas had explored up the Copland in 1892. He was asked to look for a route, free of snow much of the year, which would be suitable for mules, horses and tourists – a narrow road rather than a track or route. Certainly Douglas was not looking for an alpine pass, though that was what FitzGerald found.

The Englishman failed to mention the assistance he received. On the crossing he had with him a map of the Copland prepared by Douglas after his 1892 trip. Later he gave this map to Harper. FitzGerald wrote that the idea for the crossing came from views of the Main Divide during the climb of Mt Sefton, but the notion was current well before that. There had been discussion at the Hermitage about the route, and FitzGerald had seen a photograph of the area taken from The Footstool by Fyfe.

In 1895 and 1896 FitzGerald's articles and book inflamed the situation because of their claims, exaggerations and inaccuracies. FitzGerald overstated the assessments and difficulties of Douglas in 1892, presumably to make his own achievements appear all the greater. He also exaggerated the ease with which a bridle path could be built over FitzGerald Pass, and mistakenly assumed, perhaps out of ignorance, that it would be snow-free for much of the year because there was little snow in late February, at the end of the summer melt. Furthermore, the map of the Southern Alps in FitzGerald's book was copied from one put out by the Survey Department but not properly acknowledged.

A. P. Harper and George Mannering of the New Zealand Alpine Club tried to correct the impression FitzGerald left in English Alpine Club circles. Harper, who had led FitzGerald and Zurbriggen back to the Hermitage via Graham Saddle, was particularly offended. He well knew the work of explorers and surveyors, and he was also a stickler for accuracy. His book *Pioneer Work in the Alps of New Zealand*, published late in 1896, clarified some issues but not all. There was a lengthy correspondence and discussion in the *Alpine Journal* 1896–99, much of it centred on what the Southern Alps were. Alpine Club heavyweights like Martin Conway and Douglas Freshfield, knowing little of New Zealand, considered the colonials were too sensitive and favoured FitzGerald. However, other Alpine Club members, such as Cecil Slingsby, who did exploratory climbing in Norway and knew FitzGerald was 'a rotter', privately supported Harper. The controversy in the *Alpine Journal* fizzled out before the end of the century in a mass of ignorance, apology and colonial inferiority complex.[1]

Douglas was most unimpressed by FitzGerald's claims. On 5 October 1896 he wrote to Harper: 'Let me know if you have survived Fitzgerald's book . . . He evidently is the real discoverer of N.Zealand, not Tasman as so long supposed.' FitzGerald's lack of recognition for the survey work of men like Roberts, Douglas and Harper was infuriating to the New Zealanders, and probably accounts for some of the bitterness expressed by Douglas towards alpinists and globetrotters from overseas.

G. J. Roberts also commented on FitzGerald's 'discovery' in 1898. He wrote the text for a guidebook, *Southern Alps & West Coast Tour*, in the series *New Zealand Tours and Excursions*. One small section, pages 42–43, was devoted to the issue of FitzGerald. It was apparently written by the editor, F. W. Flanagan, the Chief Draughtsman in the Department of Lands and Survey, but in fact it must have come from Roberts.

In 1880 the trig. surveyor made a topographical study of the Divide, &c., from station J.M., and especially noted a double depression at head of the Copland Valley; it was heavily coated with snow. Afterwards Mr. C. E. Douglas explored this valley, and obtained a clear view (near at hand) of this dip; but it was so high, and the eastern face had been reported as so rough, that the idea of further exploring it for a viable route was abandoned until, finding that the passes southward were too circuitous and expensive, it was resolved to survey it right across; and Mr. Harper – in the absence of Mr. Douglas, who was ill – was actually on his way up when Mr. Fitzgerald came over. The year before this, photographs of the locality taken from the Footstool, which is immediately above this pass and close to it, had been received from Mr. Fyfe. Some years ago Mr. Huddlestone, formerly of the Hermitage, wrote to the Westland Land Office for information and a map of the western slope abreast of the Hermitage, stating that he meant to bring a party over. The same surveyor prepared a map, which was sent to Mr. Huddlestone, with the proviso that it was to be hung up at the Hermitage for the benefit of the public. This, we are told, was not done. Along with the map was also sent a description of such country as had been actually reached, and Mr. Huddlestone was especially told that, if his party came over, the exploited territory would be named after them, and their names were requested for that purpose. Further, that the district would be left unnamed until it was actually traversed. Mr. Huddlestone never got over, but in due time Mr. Fitzgerald did so, and the pass was named after him. He had Mr. Douglas's map of the Copland with him, and with it could not possibly miss his way. Afterwards a topographical map was prepared and forwarded to Mr. Fitzgerald, the information on which he has appropriated without acknowledgement to the Survey Department. So far as is known, Mr. Fitzgerald has not advanced topographical knowledge concerning the Southern Alps, although posing as an explorer who has determined and mapped peaks, &c., which were actually worked out and recorded on the map by Mr. G. J. Roberts, who has spent several years of hard work, outside his usual duties, in what is to him a labour of love. – EDITOR

THREE

The Story of the Douglas Manuscripts and Sketches

by John Pascoe

For John Pascoe, the work on Charlie Douglas and the Douglas manuscripts was a labour of love. Pascoe was intrigued by unknown country himself, and by the explorations and writings of Douglas. He devoted time on and off for many years to researching and collecting Douglas material. Then, in the years 1953 to 1955, working on Mr Explorer Douglas *became Pascoe's main occupation, outside his family and his work for the New Zealand War Histories.*

This story of the Douglas manuscripts, sketches and the creation of Pascoe's book, reveals a process only too common in New Zealand history, of neglect, destruction, chance and research leading to rediscovery. That so much material was gathered is a tribute to Pascoe's energy and dedication.

The story of the survival of part of the Douglas papers is characteristic of our islands. Destruction, neglect, chance and good fortune all have their parts. Fire has ravaged our pioneer literary sources no less than our bush; enterprise or foresight has sometimes saved both. Forgive the personal note in these pages but the publication of Douglas papers is for me the culmination of the interest of twenty-four years in an active period of my life

In 1932 I was a young mountaineer of only three seasons' experience, but even then I had some sense of historical purpose and had grieved to learn that the Douglas manuscripts did not exist. Arthur P. Harper, friend and companion of Douglas, had in his book *Pioneer Work in the Alps of New Zealand* (1896) written: 'Had I time to look over his diaries and reports I could, with help, produce a very thorough and valuable record of this southern country – but I am not a man of leisure, and the diaries are in the safe of a Government Department' and had followed this in the *New Zealand Alpine Journal* of 1925 with: 'All this is lost, because Charlie's diaries cannot be found. He must have destroyed them before he had the stroke that paralysed him some years later. He had them when I saw him in 1908, and said that I could have them to use after his death – but they have gone.'

As a law clerk I was to learn of the survival of many of the papers. A client of the Christchurch firm for which I worked was Alexander Aitken, an old West Coaster. I used to yarn to him occasionally. He knew of my enthusiasm for mountains and for travel in Westland. One morning he said to me: 'Well, young fellow, I had a good time last night. I was reading about every pass in the Southern Alps.' My ears pricked up. 'Yes,' he persisted, 'it's a fact. I was with old Charlie Douglas.' I gaped and said I thought that his manuscripts were destroyed. And so, before his death, Alexander Aitken, peace to him, lent me a manuscript of the Douglas report on the passes (1899). I gave myself leave from swotting one weekend, copied the report longhand, and promised not to use it for publication. I was told that William Wilson of Hokitika held the bulk of the manuscripts, and that he had published some of the reports in serial form in the *Hokitika Guardian* newspaper. I helped J. W. Mitchell, then editor of the *Canterbury Mountaineer*, get authority to publish some topographical reports by Douglas on the Wanganui and adjacent rivers, in that journal of 1936 and 1937. Mr Harper has since told me that this publication was the first he knew that some reports still existed.

By 1937 I had left law clerking to work on historical research for the New Zealand Government Centennial publications, of which I became the Illustrations Editor. I was directly under E. H. McCormick, a brilliant and unselfish scholar, and J. W. Heenan (later Sir Joseph), Under-Secretary of the Department of Internal Affairs, another stimulating man of great vigour and character. On 10 May 1938 I read in the newspaper of the death of William Wilson, and immediately gave Heenan a long memorandum, as he was an old West Coaster and would appreciate the issues involved.

I explained that the Douglas papers might be in danger of becoming scattered, that G. J. Roberts had taken them over when Douglas died,[2] and that on the death of Roberts, Wilson had added them to manuscripts he already held as a friend of Douglas. Heenan signed a letter I drafted from him to D. J. Evans, a close friend of Wilson's, urging him to enquire whether the Douglas papers were safe and whether they could be copied for the Alexander Turnbull Library in Wellington, the central repository of many valuable manuscripts of New Zealand and Pacific history. Three days later Evans promised his support. On 23 May I was at the Hocken Library in Dunedin and received instructions to go to Hokitika to meet the widow of William Wilson.

Before May had ended I had spent some days in Hokitika and made a detailed list of the forty-three items of Douglas manuscripts, sketches and letters held in the Wilson estate. [*Dr Ebenezer Teichelmann, of Hokitika, also supported the preservation of the Douglas papers.*] Mrs Wilson agreed to give the whole mass of material to the Turnbull Library to be known as 'The William Wilson (Hokitika) collection – Charles Douglas exploration material' subject to conditions of which the following were essential: Item 43 (Birds) to be copied and the original returned to her; personal letters Douglas to Roberts not to be quoted (a ban since removed); and W. G. McClymont and myself approved as joint editors. I also made a list of Douglas sketches in the museum at Hokitika, of Douglas maps and field books in the office of the Lands and Survey Department at Hokitika, and arranged to borrow from Dr Teichelmann his Douglas reports on the Waiatoto and Copland for copying.

As the pressure of Centennial publication work made it impossible to start editing the Douglas papers, I contented myself in noting, and where possible acquiring for the Turnbull Library, further material. For some years I continued this work of corresponding about Douglas problems, not the least of which were topographical puzzles still to be solved by young mountaineers climbing in his country. I collected photographs of Douglas and relevant valleys, and on some of my transalpine trips to the Perth, Whitcombe and Arawata valleys I gained a necessary first-hand knowledge of some of the difficulties he had met so many years before.

By 1953 I had seen some of my own books through the press but had scrupulously kept Douglas manuscripts intact. The bar laid on others not to use his papers, I observed myself. By the time I was clear to tackle the Douglas work, I was fully engaged by day as Illustrations Editor for the New Zealand War Histories. My researches and writing on Douglas and all editing would have to be strictly a spare-time job, which called for and obtained full sympathy from my wife, who would have to forgo some of my company and leisure. As in all my writing projects, she gave me encouragement and understanding.

By this time McClymont had undertaken to write the campaign volume of the 2nd NZEF in Greece in the Second World War, which gave him no hope of collaborating with me as originally planned. But he promised to help, particularly with information of the Scottish origins, and generously placed all his notes at my disposal. By April 1953 I used most of my spare time on the Douglas project, and wrote to many people reputed to have relevant material, but mostly these clues were unprofitable. In August the Librarian of the Turnbull Library agreed to have the manuscripts copied into typescript suitable for publication, which was ably done in Australia by Miss Kate Ross, later Mrs Kotunovic, a former member of the library staff. This saved me a formidable chore but entailed the careful checking of manuscript with typescript (as the typing progressed) which was nearly a year's work. I sent a copy of the birds report to Dr R. A. Falla of the Dominion Museum for correct scientific annotation.

In November I located the Waiatoto-Copland manuscript, which after Dr Teichelmann's death in 1938 had disappeared. After some negotiation I was able to add it to the Turnbull Library records through the kindness of Dr Hugh Webb of Christchurch. I found the copy imperfect and had to make many corrections in the pre-war typescript, and also to type important pages that had never been copied. I interviewed survivors of the Douglas era and checked their reminiscences against contemporary papers. Mrs. Wilson gave me permission to publish the Douglas–Roberts letters. She died shortly afterwards.

In 1954 the work progressed. I saw the Geological Survey staff about the reports on geology. In March Arthur P. Harper offered help in all ways possible. In his second book, *Memories of Mountains and Men* (1946), he had explained that Douglas had wanted him to edit the papers.[3] For Harper, a contemporary of Douglas, to weigh in with assistance to a younger man was generosity of the most invaluable kind. He lent me his files of letters in the original from Roberts and Douglas to himself, and photographs for copying, as well as his own essential recollections from a virile memory.

With such additional primary source material I could hope to expand my introduction into a long biographical study. I listed Douglas reports as published in Parliamentary Papers [*AJHR*], and found that the latter had sometimes distorted the former, probably without permission from Douglas. The reports by Douglas were usually edited by Roberts, as I knew from their respective handwriting, but the Parliamentary Papers could no longer be regarded as primary sources because some unseen hand in head office of the Lands and Survey Department had so tampered with originals that instructions were altered and omissions made. The destruction by fire of the department head office records in 1952 removed further traces of the alterations.

In May I wrote letters to the *Hokitika Guardian* and the *New Zealand Listener* which appealed for further manuscripts and information. The response was good and families such as the Gunns were very helpful. Miss M. V. Mueller of Auckland lent her father's letters and sketches for copying and we exchanged details of research of mutual interest. By this time it was clear that I would have more material to publish than there would be room for in a book of moderate size. The purely technical reports did not need immediate publication but could be handled later by geologists and foresters in their own special journals as they wished. Included in the unusable material were flashes of Douglas introspection, humour, perception and cynicism that should be quoted, so I made a cross-referenced index of all the Douglas papers for my future use when writing my introduction and biographical chapters. Thus equipped I planned a book, two-thirds of which would be edited Douglas reports, selections and letters, and one-third my biographical study.

When McClymont gave me a family tree of Douglas back to 1706 and some clues from Edinburgh I could follow up myself, I wrote to the Commercial

Bank of Scotland, the Librarian of the Royal High School in Edinburgh (strangely enough, Alexander Aitken, namesake of the client who in 1932 had started me on my researches), the Registrar General of Scotland, and the Keeper of the Records of Scotland. All these letters brought back vital details. Steady correspondence with New Zealand helpers such as Peter Graham, the Gunns, and McClymont gave further good results and further calls on Arthur P. Harper and Colin Macfarlane were rewarding. L. W. [Len] Boot gathered data from the field books in Hokitika, assistance of the most valuable kind. By the spring of 1954 I wrote my first draft of my third of the book, and in November was able to have copies read by Boot, Harper, McClymont, Miss Margaret Broadhead of the Turnbull Library, my wife and Mrs Nancy Taylor (a fellow researcher in exploration). All these wrote critical comments which stimulated me to correct mistakes and to revise further where necessary.

Although I had never met Charlie Douglas, I hoped that he would have approved of my diligence on his behalf. Above all I strove to avoid romanticising him. I aimed to let his life and career emerge with all its achievements, its bewilderments and its sorrows into the wider scope of New Zealand history. That my labour was of love must be obvious; love of tolerance, respect, sympathy and with a feeling for the great ranges and gorges where Douglas and his fellow explorers had lived their days of inner struggle and physical endurance.

In February 1955 I rewrote the whole of my first draft in the light of the comments of my critics. To revise and to polish, to correct and to weigh evidence with all the objectivity of which one is capable, is one of the most fascinating experiences for a writer groping for biographical perspective. I cannot claim to have written the last word about Charlie Douglas, but I do hope to have laid a reasonable foundation for my successors in the field of exploration of South Westland.

In May 1955 Arthur P. Harper died. He was followed in October by Colin Macfarlane. Thus ended the last links with Douglas. In December I made a three weeks' transalpine crossing from Lake Ohau to Karangarua. As my friends and I carried heavy packs over the Landsborough and Twain [Douglas] ranges we often talked of the pioneers Mueller, Douglas and Harper. In following their trails I found a renewal of faith that one day this book would be published and thus open for New Zealanders the pages of a fine explorer.

Between completion of the manuscript and acceptance for publication, there were delays and disappointments for John Pascoe. These were finally resolved by support from the New Zealand Literary Fund and the positive attitude of A. H. & A. W. Reed, who published the book in 1957. Such were the sales that it was reprinted in 1957 and again twelve years later.

FOUR

Douglas Resources

The text, notes to each chapter, and Appendix 3 make it clear how much John Pascoe was indebted to other people and a variety of resources for information about Charlie Douglas, his period and his region. The same is true for this edition. Holdings of most of the existing Douglas manuscripts and sketches are listed here. Further relevant material available in print is also detailed below.

Manuscripts and Sketches

Alexander Turnbull Library, Wellington
The majority of the existing Douglas material is held in the Manuscript section of the Alexander Turnbull Library.

John Pascoe organised forty-six items he collected as 'The William Wilson (Hokitika) Collection' in the Turnbull Library. Now these are part of the sixty-nine items in the Charles Edward Douglas MS Papers (0090). Most of the items are Douglas manuscripts, but included in these papers is other material, such as relevant letters of his time and all Pascoe's correspondence about Douglas.

The Manuscript section also holds the John Dobree Pascoe Papers (75–241), and the first two boxes include Douglas material, such as photographs, typed manuscripts and Pascoe's drafts.

Elsewhere in the Turnbull Library are maps, photographs and a large collection of Douglas's sketches in albums and notebooks.

Land Information New Zealand, Hokitika
The Hokitika Office of Land Information New Zealand (LINZ) holds twenty-one topographical and geological maps drawn by Douglas, numbered between SO 3967 and SO 4039. It also has forty-one field books, numbered between 415 and 747, written by Douglas while out surveying and exploring.

West Coast Historical Museum, Hokitika
This regional museum holds several items of Douglas material, notably a diary recording exploration trips in the 1890s. It includes also an account of a steamer

trip on the coast in 1877 and other smaller notes. There are photocopies of a geology notebook and various field notes. The other significant item is an album of twenty sketches, formerly held by the Westland District Library (Hokitika Public Library).

National Archives, Christchurch

The Christchurch Regional Office of National Archives holds nine maps and plans drawn by Douglas, five of them signed by him. CH505, folder 1, items 1–9, Lands and Survey, Hokitika District Office.

The Hocken Library, Dunedin

The Hocken Library holds two volumes containing 120 Douglas sketches, formerly the property of David Barron, Chief Surveyor of Westland 1895–96, donated to the library by his daughter Vida.

There is also a scrapbook of thirty-three Douglas sketches in the New Zealand Alpine Club Archives in the Hocken Library. This was purchased and given to the Auckland section NZAC by G. T. Murray. Formerly it had belonged to H. A. Gordon of the Mines Department.

Further Reading

Appendices to the Journal of the House of Representatives (AJHR), 1875–1908, variously H.–1, C.–1A, C.–3, C.–1.

Barnett, S., 'Charlie Douglas: West Coast Explorer Extraordinaire', *New Zealand Wilderness*, December 1999, pp. 6–8.

Douglas, C. E., 'Report on the Waitaha Valley', *Canterbury Mountaineer*, No. 5, 1936, pp. 31–37.

Douglas, C. E., 'Report on the Gordon River', ibid., pp. 38–42.

Douglas, C. E., 'The Wanganui River', *Canterbury Mountaineer*, No. 6, 1937, pp. 37–54.

Grzelewski, D., 'Travels With "Mr Explorer" Douglas, *New Zealand Geographic* No. 32, October-December 1996 pp. 22–45.

Harper, A. P., *Pioneer Work in the Alps of New Zealand*, T. Fisher Unwin, London, 1896.

Harper, A. P., 'C. E. Douglas, Explorer', *New Zealand Alpine Journal*, 1925 [pub. 1926], pp. 248–53.

Harper, A. P., *Memories of Mountains and Men*, Simpson & Williams, Christchurch 1946.

McClymont, W. G., *The Exploration of New Zealand*, Department of Internal

Affairs, Wellington, 1940 pp. 174–80; 2nd edn, Oxford UP, London 1959.

McKenzie, A., *Pioneers of Martins Bay*, 1947, 2nd edn Whitcombe & Tombs, Christchurch 1952.

McKerrow, B., 'Charlie Douglas: his final years', *New Zealand Alpine Journal*, 1995, pp. 99–100.

Mueller, M. V., *My Dear Bannie*, The Pegasus Press, Christchurch, 1958, pp. 213–21.

[Pascoe, J. D.], 'Charles Douglas, Mountain Explorer', *Navigators and Explorers Making New Zealand Pictorial Surveys of a Century*, Vol. 1, No. 3, Department of Internal Affairs, Wellington, 1939, pp. 26–27.

Pascoe, J. D., 'More of Mr Explorer Douglas', *New Zealand Listener*, 24 January 1964.

Roberts, G. J., *Southern Alps & West Coast Tour: Westland*, F. W. Flanagan (ed.), *New Zealand Tours & Excursions*, Government Printer, Wellington 1898.

NOTES

Chapter 2

1. 'Soliloquy Letter', December, 1902.
2. Colin Macfarlane, Wellington, 1954.
3. R. Pinney, *Early Otago Runs*, Auckland, 1981.
4. W. H. Scotter, *Run, Estate and Farm*, Dunedin, 1948, pp. 18–19.
5. 'Fishes' manuscript.
6. 'Birds' and 'Copland' manuscripts.

Chapter 3

1. P. Madgwick, *Aotea: A History of the South Westland Maori*, Hokitika, 1992, pp. 11–27; H. Evison, *The Long Dispute*, Christchurch, 1997, p. 20. For Maori links between the West Coast and other parts of the South Island, see B. Brailsford, *Greenstone Trails*, Wellington, 1984.
2. Madgwick, pp. 27–31.
3. T. Brunner, *The Great Journey* (ed. J. Pascoe), Christchurch, 1952, pp. 64–66.
4. P. May, 'Exploration and Purchase' in R. A. Kay (ed.), *Westland's Golden Century 1860–1960*, Greymouth, 1960, p. 17.
5. *New Zealand Alpine Journal* 1921, pp. 75–81; Brailsford, *Greenstone Trails*, pp. 121, 155–57; Evison, p. 266.
6. R. C. Reid, *Rambles on the Golden Coast*, London, 1886, p. 21; Madgwick, pp. 79–88; Evison, p. 268.
7. Robert P. Bain, 'The West Coast Expedition', *Lyttelton Times*, 24 March 1864.
8. N. Taylor (ed.), *Early Travellers in New Zealand*, Oxford, 1959, pp. 387–419.
9. P. R. May, *The West Coast Gold Rushes*, Christchurch, 1962, pp. 98–101,520–27.
10. 'South of Jacksons Bay' manuscript.
11. Ibid.
12. 'Islets, Town and Glaciers' manuscript.
13. Ibid.
14. Ibid.
15. 'South of Jacksons Bay' manuscript.
16. *The Press*, 14 September 1939: T. L. Raife,

'Historic Hokitika', citing a correspondent of November 1865.
17. 'Fishes' manuscript.
18. A. P. Harper, *Memories of Mountains and Men*, Christchurch, 1946, p. 86.
19. Ibid., p. 114.
20. Douglas letters to Harper, 10 May & 8 July 1895.
21. M. V. Mueller (ed.), *My Dear Bannie*, Christchurch, 1958.
22. M. V. Mueller to John Pascoe, 4 June 1954.

Chapter 4

1. *Journal of the Royal Geographical Society*, Vol. XXXVII, 1867, p. 328.
2. H. F. von Haast, *The Life and Times of Sir Julius von Haast*, Wellington, 1948, pp. 528–33, 555.
3. Letter G. J. Roberts to A. P. Harper, 23 August 1893.
4. 'Passes' manuscript.
5. W. H. S. Roberts, *Place Names and Early History of Otago and Southland*, Invercargill, 1913, p. 111.
6. Ibid.; W. G. McClymont, *The Exploration of New Zealand*, Wellington, 1940, pp. 140–41.
7. N. Baker (ed.), *A Surveyor in New Zealand*, Auckland, 1932, pp. 48–49; P. R. May, *The West Coast Gold Rushes*, 2nd edn., 1967, pp. 522–25.
8. 'Passes' and 'Geology' manuscripts.
9. *Province of Westland: Journal of Proceedings of the Provincial Council*, Session 1 (24 February –14 March 1874), Department Reports, p. 29.
10. Ibid., pp. 9, 15, 21, 29, 51.
11. *New Zealand Government Gazette*, Province of Westland, 1874, Vol. I, No.42, Schedule II, p. 170.
12. *West Coast Times*, 8 December 1874.
13. Family history information, including newspaper accounts, from Tom Ward of

Eastbourne, April 1999. John Pascoe was misled by Colin Macfarlane on many details about the original Tom Ward.

14. J. Acheson, 'Mr Surveyor Roberts', *NZAJ*, 1973, pp. 104–11.
15. *AJHR*, 1875, H.–1, p. 18.
16. *AJHR*, 1877, H.–1, pp. 8–11.
17. 'Passes' and 'Islets, Towns and Glaciers' manuscripts.
18. *AJHR*, 1878 H.–17, p. 2.
19. *AJHR*, 1879 H.–19, p. 19.
20. *AJHR*, 1881 C.–4, ii–iii.
21. In 1955 L. W. (Len) Boot provided a summary of field books held in the Hokitika office of the Lands and Survey Department, giving some idea of the nature and scope of Douglas's work in the 1880s.
22. Frank Howe to Mildred Mueller at Waihi. She then sent the story to Pascoe. 13 December 1954.
23. 'Passes' manuscript.
24. 'Passes' and 'Islets, Towns and Glaciers' manuscripts.
25. Field Book 415.
26. *AJHR*, 1885, C.–1A, pp. 25–27 & map; Field Book 497.
27. For an alternative view, that Douglas made a first and solo ascent in 1884, see *NZAJ*, 1948, p. 207.
28. John Pascoe made such a visit in late 1952.
29. 'Islets, Towns and Glaciers' manuscript.
30. *Canterbury Mountaineer'* No. 22, 1953, pp.8–16. John Pascoe was a member of this party 1952–53.
31. Simmons passed the material to W. G. McClymont. See also Field Books 454, 498
32. Alf Dale to Len Boot, Woodstock, 1955.
33. *AJHR*, 1887, C.–2, pp. 12–13 & map; 'Passes' manuscript.
34. 'Balfour River' manuscript.
35. 'Cook River' manuscript.
36. Field Book 499.
37. Harper, *Memories*, p. 44.

Chapter 5

1. *AJHR*, 1890, C.–3, pp. 96–97.
2. Douglas wrote 'Eggling', as appeared on some early electoral rolls, but 'Eggeling' is the preferred spelling.
3. 'Waiatoto' manuscript; Field Book 586; P. Temple, *New Zealand Explorers*, Christchurch, 1985, pp. 154–59.
4. G. McCallum, *Tararua*, 1950, pp. 82–83, confirmed as most likely by others and aerial mapping. Yet doubt remained for John Pascoe and others, and it is just possible that Douglas saw a Divide route to the Wilkin.
5. 'Wanganui' and 'Waiatoto' manuscripts; Field Book 523.
6. 'Copland' manuscript; Field Book 531; *AJHR*, 1893, C.–1, pp. 39, 42–47.
7. Alf Dale to Len Boot, Woodstock, 1955. The discovery of the springs must have been after Harper's *Pioneer Work* was written, since that book, published in 1896, does not mention it.
8. 'Mikonui River' and 'Waitaha River' manuscripts
9. Field Books 593, 587.
10. *Pioneer Work in the Alps of New Zealand*, London, 1896, and *Memories*, 1946.
11. *Pioneer Work*, pp. 73–76.
12. Field Book 561; *Pioneer Work*, pp. 93–94.
13. *Pioneer Work*, p. 138.
14. G. J. Roberts, *Southern Alps & West Coast Tour: Westland: New Zealand Tours & Excursions*, ed. F. W. Flanagan, Wellington, 1898, p. 41,
15. *Pioneer Work*, pp. 178–269.
16. E. FitzGerald, *Climbs in the New Zealand Alps*, London, 1896, pp. 227–318; *Pioneer Work*, pp. 270–95.
17. *AJHR*, 1895, C.–1, p. 34, Harper's Report, pp. 105–10.
18. Douglas to Harper, 25 April 1895.
19. Douglas to Harper, 5 October 1896.
20. *AJHR*, 1896, C.–1, pp. 110–11.
21. Alf Dale to Len Boot, Woodstock, 1955; *AJHR*, 1896, C.–1, p. 79; Field Book 586.
22. Field Books 650, 660,
23. D. Welsh, Librarian, Royal Geographical Society, to John Pascoe, 1 June 1954.
24. Alf Dale; Field Book 639; *AJHR*, 1898, C.–1, p. 38, with Douglas's Fox Glacier Report, pp. 18–19.

25. Field Book 649; 'Islets, Towns and Glaciers' manuscript.
26. *AJHR*, 1899, C.–1, p. 41.
27. *AJHR*, 1900, C.–1, p. 40; Field Book 649.
28. Carl Pfeifer to John Pascoe, March 1954.
29. Alex Gunn, James Bettison and Henry Vickers ('Harry the Whale') reached the Havelock Divide from the Perth – letter Gunn to Roberts, 7 April 1892.
30. *AJHR*, 1901, C.–1, p. 44; 'Wanganui River' manuscript.
31. John Bartrum to John Pascoe, 18 August 1938.
32. Field Books 587, 660.
33. *AJHR*, 1902, C.–1, p. 53; Field Book 494B.
34. 'Waiatoto–Copland' manuscript (contains 1903 Okarito work).
35. *AJHR*, 1903, C.–1, p. 81; Field Book 494A.
36. *AJHR*, 1907, C.–1, p. 15; Cowan, *Official Record . . .*, Wellington, 1910, p. 218.
37. Mildred Mueller to John Pascoe, 23 May 1954.

Chapter 6

1. Jim Gunn to John Pascoe, 11 June 1954.
2. P. Graham, *Peter Graham Mountain Guide*, Wellington, 1965, p. 57.
3. Frank Gunn to John Pascoe, 18 May 1954.
4. Harper, *Memories*, p. 93; See Introduction.
5. Suggested dates range from early 1908 to early 1909.
6. Harper, *NZAJ*, 1925, p. 251; Harper, 'C. E. Douglas "Diaries"', 11 October 1949, Hocken; Peter Graham to John Pascoe, 1954.
7. See Introduction. Harper always believed Douglas died soon after his second stroke and retirement, and there is little evidence that West Coasters 'protected' Douglas from Harper, or needed to.
8. *AJHR*, 1908, C.–1A, p. 18; see Chapter 25.
9. Bob McKerrow, 'Charlie Douglas: his final years', *NZAJ*, 1995, pp. 99–100.
10. McKerrow, pp. 99–100, shows this clearly.
11. Ward family members to John Pascoe,

1954–55.
12. Christened 'Thomas Falconer' but known as 'Robert Falconer Ward'.
13. McKerrow, p. 100.
14. McKerrow, p. 100.

Chapter 24

1. Douglas to Harper, 8 July 1895.
2. Douglas to Harper, 10 May 1895.
3. 'Waiatoto' manuscript.
4. Douglas to Roberts, 1 October 1896.
5. Douglas to Harper, 5 October 1896.
6. 'Birds' manuscript.
7. 'Geology' manuscript.
8. H. J. Harrington & G. W. Grindley (Geological Survey Office) to John Pascoe, 18 & 20 November 1954.
9. 'Islets, Towns and Glaciers' manuscript.
10. 'Islets, Towns and Glaciers' manuscript.
11. Roberts to Harper, 28 July 1897, 31 March 1898.
12. Cowan, *Tales of the Maori Bush*, p. 263.
13. Roberts to Harper, 25 February 1894.
14. 'Islets, Towns and Glaciers' manuscript.
15. 'Geology' manuscript.
16. 'Wanganui River' manuscript.
17. See also A. McKenzie, *Pioneers of Martins Bay*, 1947, Christchurch 1952, pp. 33–36.
18. I. Dougherty, *Arawata Bill*, Auckland, 1996.
19. Douglas to Roberts, undated.
20. 'Whitcombe' manuscript.
21. 'Waiatoto' manuscript.
22. 'Islets, Towns and Glaciers' manuscript.
23. Murray to Frank Simmons, Auckland, 14 August 1935.
24. Soliloquy Letter, October 1903.
25. Harper, *Memories*, p. 91.
26. Douglas to Roberts, 5 July 1890; 'Whitcombe' manuscript; 'Soliloquy Letter' 1902.
27. 'South of Jacksons Bay' and 'Fishes' manuscripts.
28. D. F. Hobbs, Senior Fisheries Officer, Marine Department, Wellington, to John Pascoe, 2 February 1955.
29. 'Islets, Towns and Glaciers' manuscript.
30. Holloway to John Pascoe, 13 & 24 August 1954.
31. Chavasse to John Pascoe, 1954.

32. 'Copland' manuscript.
33. 'Whitcombe' manuscript.

Chapter 25

1. 'Wanganui River' manuscript.
2. 'South of Jacksons Bay' manuscript.
3. *AJHR*, 1895, C.–1, p. 34.
4. *AJHR*, 1908, C.–1A, p. 18.

Appendix 3

1. *The Contemporary Review*, August 1895; *Alpine Journal* XVII, 1894–95, pp. 469–75, XVIII, 1896–97, pp. 38–43, 69–84, 190–92, 202–5, 333–48, 482, XIX, 1898–99, p. 158. See also: *AJHR*, 1896, C-1, xii; A. P. Harper, *Pioneer Work in the Alps of New Zealand*, London, 1896, pp. 324–27; J. Adamson and A. P. Harper PP, NZAC Archives, Hocken Library; R. Clark, *The Victorian Mountaineers*, London, 1953, pp. 217–18, 222; G. Langton, 'Only Virgin Peaks: the imperial challenge of Edward FitzGerald', *NZAJ*, 1995, pp. 93–95.

2. Pascoe was incorrect here, since Roberts died before Douglas. In the late 1930s Pascoe assumed, with Harper, that Douglas died soon after his second stroke. According to Pascoe's letters, he did not discover when Douglas actually died until mid-1954. Roberts possibly took over Douglas's papers after his second stroke, especially if some had been burnt, but the legal ownership of Douglas's private papers, involving Harper, Roberts and Wilson, remained uncertain after Douglas's death.

3. p. 89. There is considerable doubt about whether Douglas wanted Harper to edit his papers. Probably he made no decision. Harper may have wanted to edit Douglas's papers, and there may have been some vague agreement between Harper, Roberts and Douglas (before his second stroke) that the papers should be published, but it is unlikely there was any firm decision. Harper is equally definite about the matter in his typed note 'C. E. Douglas "Diaries"' (11 October 1949), in the A. P. Harper PP, NZAC Archives, Hocken Library, though he is confused about the provenance of the Douglas papers. He also relates there an incident (concerning ownership of Harper's photographs taken on survey expeditions) that may have turned Roberts, quite unreasonably, against Harper about 1909–10. The whole later story of Harper being disliked on the West Coast may stem from this, though his personality doubtless contributed. What should not be forgotten is the clear regard Douglas and Harper had for each other for many years, until they lost contact after 1908.

INDEX